THE CABINET OFFICE 1916–2016

The Cabinet Office 1916–2016

The Birth of Modern Government

ANTHONY SELDON
WITH JONATHAN MEAKIN

Biteback Publishing

First published in Great Britain in 2016 by
Biteback Publishing Ltd
Westminster Tower
3 Albert Embankment
London SE1 7SP

ISBN 978-1-78590-173-7

10 9 8 7 6 5 4 3 2 1

A CIP catalogue record for this book is available from the British Library.

Set in Garamond by Adrian McLaughlin

Printed and bound in Great Britain by
CPI Group (UK) Ltd, Croydon CR0 4YY

CONTENTS

To CHRIS MARTIN (1973–2015),
distinguished Principal Private Secretary to the Prime Minister,
who epitomised the values of the Civil Service at its best.

Profits from this book are going to the Chris Martin Foundation.

Preface and Acknowledgements

I HAVE BEEN FASCINATED by the Cabinet Office and Civil Service mandarins ever since I wrote my first book, *Churchill's Indian Summer: The Conservative Government, 1951–1955*, nearly thirty-five years ago, for which I interviewed large numbers of officials, and learnt first-hand from those who had worked with them about the formidable Edward Bridges and Norman Brook. Learning more about the eleven Cabinet Secretaries has made writing this book a delight and a pleasure.

The circumstances of writing over 120,000 words over the summer and autumn of 2016 in under ten weeks were not the easiest. I started writing on the Via Sacra walk from Switzerland to the English Channel along the Western Front in July, returned to find my university is in full swing over the summer, Britain in Brexit, and more importantly have had family illness as a daily concern.

My thanks thus are, far more than usually, profound, though the errors of fact and judgement are entirely my own. First, I would like to thank Jonathan Meakin, my associate author and senior researcher on the book, who has worked for me for seven years and on eight books. He has been a formidable presence. Next came the researchers – Beth Oppenheim, Clementine Bunting, Mark Davies, Jennifer Doyle, Ruari Hutchinson, Khurram Jowiya, Sapan Maini-Thompson and Valentina Milanova – all highly able, hard-working and good company. I would like to thank a previous co-author, the intellectually brilliant Daniel Collings, for his research in the archives in the United States, and for interviewing Henry Kissinger for the book. All worked tirelessly to ensure that this book was written to an extremely challenging timetable. Without their efforts, this book would not have happened.

I would like to thank the Cabinet Office for their support. My thanks above all to Sue Gray, Robert Honey, Roger Smethurst, Richard Heaton and Alex Thomas, who have been wonderfully helpful and supportive from the first day of the book to the last.

I am particularly grateful for the assistance given by Professor Stuart R. Ball, Professor Jeremy Black, Professor Eugenio F. Biagini, Dr Peter Paul Catterall, Professor David Dilks, Professor Andrew Roberts, Dr Roland Quinault, D. R. Thorpe and Professor Philip Williamson, who all helped with historical information, thereby strengthening the book enormously. My greatest thanks go to my doctoral supervisor and lifelong academic mentor, John Barnes, as well as to Sir David Butler, to Professor Vernon Bogdanor, Professor Dennis Kavanagh and Professor G. W. Jones, four of the leading lights of British contemporary history who have guided me since I became an undergraduate, and to my colleague in contemporary history of over thirty years, the greatest Whitehall scholar of them all, Professor Lord (Peter) Hennessy.

Many hours have been spent in research institutes and archives for this book. I would like to single out Mark Dunton at the National Archives for special thanks; without his efforts this book would not have happened. Thanks also to Stephen Twigge and Neil Cobbett at the National Archives. At the Royal Archives, I am particularly grateful for the assistance of Oliver Urquhart Irvine, Lynnette Beech and Julie Crocker. Additionally, my thanks also to Ceri Humphries at the Churchill Archives Centre at Churchill College, Cambridge. Thanks also to the archivists of the Presidential Library system in the United States and Mary Curry of the National Security Archive at George Washington University.

Thanks to Angela Reed, Peter Mallinson, Robin Dyer and Tim Bunting from Wellington College for continuing to support and inspire me. Thanks to Virginia Preston and Michael Kandiah at the Institute for Contemporary History at King's College London. Further thanks are due to Colin Harris and Michael Hughes of Oxford University's Bodleian Library. Thanks to Katie Guest at Wolverhampton Grammar School for finding out about Norman Brook's schooldays. Especial thanks go to Mark Bridges and Lord (George) Bridges for their information about their grandfather, Edward Bridges.

I would like to offer my special thanks to all the many officials I have interviewed over the years whose words and experiences have shaped the text, none more so than Chris Martin, the brilliant Principal Private Secretary to the Prime Minister until his death aged forty-two in November 2015. My thanks specifically to former officials including Chris Brearley, Bruce Mann, John Chilcot, Philip Rycroft, Paul Britton and Diana Goldsworthy, who agreed to be interviewed for this book.

This book is based on well over 3,000 interviews I have conducted on the subjects covered here for a host of books, articles and projects, from Sir John Colville in March 1977 to Lord Donoughue and Joe Haines with this book in proofs in October 2016. I thank them all.

I would like to thank two retired diplomats, Christopher Everett and Sir Anthony Goodenough, for proofreading the manuscript. Thank you also to Mark Fox for reading the book, and above all to the great historian David Dilks, for reading the book and making suggestions, and whose knowledge of the first four Cabinet Secretaries is unsurpassed.

At the University of Buckingham, I would like to thank my staff and students, Council, Senate and Executive, for their support and encouragement, and especially the Chancellor, Lady Keswick, Chair of Council, Professor Ken Siddle, and Deputy Vice-Chancellor, Professor Alistair Alcock. In my office, I would also like to thank Purnima Anhal, Colleen Carter, Jenny Carter and Sarah Rush for their unflagging support.

At Biteback Publishing, I would like to thank Iain Dale, James Stephens, Olivia Beattie and Victoria Godden for their hard work (especially considering the book's narrow timetable). Thanks also to Namkwan Cho who designed the front cover. They have been a very impressive publisher.

Above all, thanks go to the cast of Cabinet Secretaries: Lord Armstrong of Ilminster, Lord Butler of Brockwell, Lord Wilson of Dinton, Lord Turnbull, Lord O'Donnell and Sir Jeremy Heywood, who have been so supportive of this project throughout. Their contribution went further than simple help; the examples that they set of crisis management and cool counsel in demanding circumstances helped to inspire me through this book's more difficult periods.

Finally, I would like to thank my wife Joanna and my children, Jessica, Susannah and Adam. I am very proud all three now work in public service, two of them in the Civil Service.

ANTHONY SELDON,
October 2016, University of Buckingham

FOREWORD

by Jeremy Heywood

I'M NOT SURE whether it was the intention, but Anthony Seldon has created in this volume a manual, a set text, on being the Cabinet Secretary.

When I mentioned the idea, one of my predecessors said how much he wished that there had been something like this when he first got the job. The book is not just a great gallop through the past 100 years of British administrative history; it succinctly captures the evolving relationship between civil servants and ministers and the nature of collective responsibility.

I am currently privileged to hold the unique position of Cabinet Secretary, and I am lucky to have a number of my distinguished predecessors to turn to for wisdom, reassurance and support. There are situations and challenges that only they have experienced. This book will help everyone else to gain an insight into the role. I hope, too, that it helps people inside and outside the Civil Service to understand our role, and that of the Cabinet Office more generally, in the administration of the country.

The Cabinet Secretary, to me, is someone who helps make things happen. We support the Prime Minister and Cabinet in delivering their manifesto, we make sure their decisions are turned into action by the Civil Service, and we ensure that the Civil Service itself retains the capability and professional experience needed to serve not just the government of the day, but future governments, without fear or favour.

From Maurice Hankey tearing around from meeting to meeting at the Versailles negotiations after the First World War, to Norman Brook at his desk contemplating the fallout from the Suez Crisis, to Gus O'Donnell midwifing the coalition in 2010, the Cabinet Secretary has had a unique dual responsibility. They are at the Prime Minister's shoulder to provide support and advice based on the best evidence, while working to make the administration run smoothly and properly so that the public experiences the outcomes the politicians intended.

The Cabinet Secretary's role is sometimes a lonely one. But my predecessors and I have always been able to count on the support of the wider Cabinet Office – some of the country's greatest minds and most talented and committed administrators, working quietly to bring Whitehall together and help improve the lives of people across the United Kingdom and beyond.

In recent times, the Cabinet Secretary has also usually been the Head of the Civil Service. That brings the privilege of working with, leading and inspiring hundreds of thousands of civil servants to deliver the elected government's objectives.

As the world changes, the Cabinet Office changes with it. From the Central Policy Review Staff to the Delivery Unit to the Implementation Unit and the National Security Council, our structure has developed over the years to provide the best advice to the Prime Minister and the Cabinet. Cutting-edge innovation, like the Behavioural Insights Team and the Government Digital Service, started in the Cabinet Office, and their benefits are felt around the UK and the world. I hope that as big data becomes more readily available and understood, we can become ever more certain that what we do has a real, positive impact.

Given the nature of historic records, this book is largely what Thomas Carlyle would call a 'Great Men' history, meaning it is told from the perspective of the few people at the top of the organisation. I'm afraid that with the – significant – exception of two Prime Ministers, they are all white and male. The Cabinet Office and the rest of the Civil Service has, over the past 100 years, reflected other large organisations and the prevailing culture of society as a whole, and most of our senior staff in that time have been white and male.

We are working hard to change that. My vision for the next century is of men and women of all races and backgrounds, of all faiths and none, whatever their abilities, overcoming the challenges before them as part of a digital, diverse, brilliant Civil Service.

JEREMY HEYWOOD
October 2016

Introduction: The Argument

And so while the great ones depart to their dinner,
The secretary stays, growing thinner and thinner,
Racking his brains to recall and report
What he thinks that they'll think that they ought to have thought

(ANONYMOUS)

T HE CABINET OFFICE, set up in December 1916 with the name the 'Cabinet Secretariat', has been at the very heart of the British government and state for the past 100 years. Modern British government can be dated back to its founding. Yet while Britain's other great Whitehall departments – the Treasury, the Foreign and Commonwealth Office, the Ministry of Defence, as well as No. 10 – are well known to all, the operation and even the existence of the Cabinet Office remains shrouded in mystery. This is partly because, unlike other government departments, it has few dealings with the general public. But its importance to the history of the country means its work and leadership of the Civil Service deserves to be much more widely known.

When it was established in December 1916 in the midst of the First World War, many expected it not to survive after it ended, still less to acquire the central role it did. Almost all government decisions of enduring importance in the last 100 years have been overseen by the Cabinet Office. It has been run since 1916 by just eleven Cabinet Secretaries: these very different men (there have been no women) have all been influential, working alongside the nineteen Prime Ministers who have served during those years, from the thirty-sixth Prime Minister, David Lloyd George, to the fifty-fourth, Theresa May.

The book advances the following core propositions:

- The country has benefited greatly over the 100 years from a substantially impartial, non-partisan and highly skilled senior Home Civil Service, overseen for much of that time by the Cabinet Secretary. The Cabinet Office has been far from infallible, but for the greatest part has sought to serve governments of all complexions loyally, while providing a crucial check to PMs who sought to ride roughshod over convention and Cabinet at large. In 2010, the word 'Home' was dropped, and the position became known as Head of the Civil Service. Because civil servants rarely write memoirs or publish diaries, and rarely talk to the press, the role and significance of the Civil Service has been insufficiently understood and has been marginalised in the public eye, and in the history books written about Britain during the last 100 years. A central argument of my first book, *Churchill's Indian Summer*, published in 1981, was that the role of officials, especially those in the Cabinet Office, needed to be taken far more seriously by historians. Little has changed in the thirty-five years since. Civil servants, unlike ministers, have often found it as hard to defend as to assert themselves when attacked. An aim of this book is to elevate public perception of the role of the Cabinet Office, and to widen understanding of the pivotal contribution it has made to facilitating and supporting governments of the day since 1916.
- Modern British government can be traced back to the creation of the Cabinet Secretariat in 1916. The size and breadth of government expanded greatly in the First World War, and rather than shrinking back to its 1914 size after it was over, it continued to expand, with new departments principally in the economic and social policy spheres, e.g. labour, health and transport. It needed the Cabinet Office to act as the glue binding together these often very diverse Whitehall departments in a massively expanded postwar government.
- Prime Ministers have been at their most effective when they have worked *with* the Cabinet Office and with the Cabinet Secretary in particular,

and within the conventions of Cabinet government, including collective responsibility, rather than trying to operate their own presidential, top-down systems. Lloyd George and Churchill thus worked closely with the Cabinet Office in both world wars, while two of Britain's most successful peacetime Prime Ministers, Clement Attlee and Margaret Thatcher (contrary to popular perception), worked very successfully with officials and mostly within the norms of Cabinet government. The Cabinet Office has played a particularly vital role in supporting administrations that have been troubled, principally because of parliamentary arithmetic, including Lloyd George's coalition (1916–22), Ramsay MacDonald's Labour government (1929–31), Churchill's peacetime Conservative government (1951–55), Harold Wilson's second government (1974–76), Major's Conservative government (1990–97) and David Cameron's coalition government (2010–15), which faced a fresh set of challenges. The history in the pages that follow shows again and again that without the Cabinet Office's steadying and expert hand, Prime Ministers would have found their tasks far harder.

- The eleven Cabinet Secretaries have all made distinctive and different contributions. Maurice Hankey (1916–38) moulded the Cabinet Secretariat and ensured its survival; Edward Bridges (1938–46) led the Cabinet Office with eminence throughout the Second World War, working in harmony with his military counterpart, Hastings Ismay, without a trace of jealousy or difficulty, creating the modern Cabinet Office and committee system in the process; Norman Brook (1947–62) adapted and developed the system to meet the requirements of recovery after the war, the expansion of the welfare state, the decline of British world power and two floundering Prime Ministers, Churchill in particular and Anthony Eden; Burke Trend (1963–73) maintained the highest ethical standards of the Civil Service at a time of unparalleled questioning of convention from Harold Wilson and some of his Cabinet ministers, and new challenges from trade unions, from Irish terrorism and economic turbulence; John Hunt (1973–79) led the Cabinet Office strongly through three difficult premierships; Robert Armstrong (1979–87) brought back together the roles of Cabinet Secretary and Head of the Home Civil Service (HCS), encouraged Margaret Thatcher to accept and observe the correct norms and procedures of Cabinet government, while also guiding her towards accommodation with the Irish government in Dublin over Northern Ireland; Robin Butler (1988–98) guided a declining Thatcher through her last two years, supported a beleaguered John Major at war with his party, and inducted Tony Blair; Richard Wilson (1998–2002) worked hard to preserve the system of Cabinet government during a difficult period and provided strong leadership to the Civil Service; Andrew Turnbull (2002–05) similarly battled to maintain Cabinet government while helping to modernise the Civil Service; Gus O'Donnell (2005–11) ensured a smooth transition from Blair to Brown, guided the Brown premiership, and oversaw Britain's first peacetime coalition government since the interwar years; and finally Jeremy Heywood (2012–present) helped steer the coalition government through a series of crises to its conclusion in 2015, oversaw two referendums, and accelerated the modernisation programme of the Civil Service initiated by his predecessors.

- The job of Cabinet Secretary has an unresolved ambiguity between its responsibilities to the Prime Minister, and to Cabinet as a whole. The job has always been called *Cabinet* Secretary, and all have been very conscious of their responsibilities to Cabinet ministers as a whole, but this has inevitably led to periodic tensions with the Prime Minister of the day, especially with those who see themselves as presidential rather than *primus inter pares.*

- Their advisory role to the PM is another ambiguity: Hankey made great play of retaining the title Cabinet 'Secretariat', and asserting, alongside Lloyd George, that its role was merely taking minutes and executing secretarial roles. But when does being asked for advice by the Prime Minister on the conduct of Cabinet business and appointments stray into offering *policy* advice? When does responding to requests for advice and anticipating problems ahead spill over into *volunteering* policy advice? To having and promoting *their own* views? No Cabinet Secretary was more brazen about doing the last than the only one to have his diaries published, Maurice Hankey.

- Another ambivalence over the 100 years is whether the position of Cabinet Secretary should be combined with the headship of the HCS. For the first thirty years of the creation, the big Whitehall beasts were the

Permanent Under-Secretaries at the Treasury, Foreign Office and Home Office, and to a lesser extent those at the Admiralty and War Office. But long before Bridges's retirement from the Civil Service in 1956, it had become clear that the big Whitehall beast was Norman Brook, who took over the joint title as Head of the HCS when Bridges finally departed aged sixty-three. Split away again in 1963 on Brook's retirement, the separated arrangement rarely worked satisfactorily, and there was general applause when Robert Armstrong took it back in two bites, in 1981 and 1983. The Cabinet Secretary job remained double-hatted with the headship of the HCS thereafter, with a brief reversion to separation in 2012–14. The benefits of combining both jobs in one person is that the *official* Head of the HCS is in daily contact with the *political* head of the executive, i.e. the Prime Minister. The disadvantage is that the job is exceedingly challenging for just one person to manage, while doing justice to both roles, a position eased since 2014 by the creation of a new senior post to help the management job.

- The functions of the Cabinet Office have come and gone over the 100 years, at the whim principally of the Prime Minister of the day, but also circumstances and changes in thinking about the role of government.[1] The core activities that have remained in the Cabinet Office throughout are the secretarial functions to Cabinet and its committees, intelligence, advice on propriety and ethics, the machinery of government, the honours system and the historical section. Areas that have come and gone include science, statistics, civil contingencies, oversight of the Commonwealth, a strategic planning capacity, crisis management (through the Cabinet Office Briefing Room or COBR) and a plethora of agencies and units. The Cabinet Office was heavily involved in Britain's relations with the European Union from the outset, coordinating the government's position across all departments; it will now have an important role to play in Britain's exit from that organisation.

- The job of the Cabinet Secretary has clear antecedents in the chief advisers to monarchs dating back to the medieval era. Their jobs, which had a variety of titles, were in essence to be the senior adviser to the monarch, to help coordinate their government, keep the realm safe, protect its records and accounts of its history, and ensure that the realm was not undermined internally. Monarchs from 1530 ruled from Whitehall Palace; Cabinet Secretaries operated from offices on the site of Whitehall Palace.

- During the last 100 years, there have been eighteen Permanent Under-Secretaries of the Treasury, eighteen at the Home Office, twenty-five at the Foreign Office, but only eleven Cabinet Secretaries, who have served twice as long on average. They have become more valuable to the Prime Minister than any other senior official, in part because their field and expertise cross *all* departments. Cabinet Secretaries have maintained high ethical standards during their period of office, and none has been a source of embarrassment after their retirement.

- The Cabinet Secretary embodies the wisdom on how to make the machine deliver for the Prime Minister and government who arrive with a set of policies they want to be executed. When the partnership works well, the Cabinet Secretary is like the left-hand side of the brain, i.e. emphasising the logical, analytical and objective dimensions, while the Prime Minister provides the right-hand side strengths of being intuitive, politically aware and subjective. When both the PM and Cabinet Secretary work together in harmony, optimal results flow. The Cabinet Secretary wants the Prime Minister to manage the politics: in return, the Prime Minister wants extreme competence in day-to-day handling of business, and expert anticipation of future problems.

- The survival of the Cabinet Office was not a foregone conclusion. It had to stake out its territory against the great departments, principally the Foreign Office and Treasury. The latter has constantly tried to tame the Cabinet Office, and to insist on its own appointees as Cabinet Secretaries, as well as the Principal Private Secretaries (PPS) to the Prime Minister, and has been mostly successful in achieving this. The Treasury equally has come under attack from Prime Ministers, notably in the 1960s and 1980s, and the PMs have often allied themselves with the Cabinet Office against it. The Cabinet Office, from its earliest days, established its pre-eminence over the Service Departments, from the 1950s over the Foreign Office, and since the 1980s over the Treasury.

- Proximity is power. To be physically close to the leader is vital. During the Second World War, and since 1963, the Cabinet Office has been adjacent to the home and workspace of the Prime Minister. Proximity helps explain why the headship of the HCS task often sits better with the Cabinet Secretary than with a more physically remote head, who cannot have regular contact with the Prime Minister.

- Cabinet Secretaries have been at risk of losing their objectivity because of the acute demands of the Prime Ministers. Maintaining objectivity and appropriate distance from the Prime Minister has been often a challenge, especially when they seek to make the Cabinet Secretary 'part of the family'. Norman Brook arguably became too close to Churchill, Eden and Macmillan; Burke Trend was arguably too austere and detached from Wilson and Heath. Bridges accomplished the perfect balance.

- Personal chemistry trumps any job descriptions. The relationship between the Prime Minister and the Cabinet Secretary varies subtly with the personalities of the two people concerned, even when there are no changes in the functional relationship.

- The precise significance of each Cabinet Secretary has ultimately been a mystery. For all the millions of pages of documents in the archives, and personal testimonies, ultimately it is impossible to discern with exactitude their influence.

- Cabinet Secretaries have come from a narrow social band: they were all male, all white, all from England, and all middle-class. All but two (Turnbull and O'Donnell) attended British public schools, and all but two (Hankey and O'Donnell) went to university at Oxford or Cambridge as undergraduates.

- Parliament has been much copied across the world, but so too has the Cabinet Office. It is unusual in retaining, despite many challenges, its objectivity from the political masters that come and go from No. 10 and across Whitehall.

ANTHONY SELDON
October 2016

H. H. Asquith, Prime Minister 1908–16, photographed c.1913.
He was the last Prime Minister to serve before the
Cabinet Office's foundation in 1916.

CHAPTER 1

CABINET GOVERNMENT BEFORE 1916

T HE CABINET OFFICE was established in December 1916. But it would be quite wrong to believe that Cabinet government and even Cabinet Committees had not existed from long before. Before we discuss why the revolution in government came about in 1916, we need to consider thus the Cabinet system that existed before, and its emergence in the early modern period onwards.

THE EMERGENCE OF CABINET

The Cabinet emerged in the fourteenth century out of the Privy Council, which for several centuries was the most important body in the country under the monarch.[1] The fall of James II (1685–88), ousted by William III (1689–1702) and Mary II (1689–94), began a process which led to the emergence of the First Lord of the Treasury, who would ultimately become known as the Prime Minister.

The year 1689, the first full year of William III's reign, is pivotal to our understanding of the emergence of modern government. During it, he introduced a host of innovations that were to profoundly shape the country.[2] Parliament was consolidated as a permanent feature of the constitution, meeting annually, and voting on the finances the monarchy would need for government. To avoid the monarchy subverting Parliament, the Triennial

1

Act of 1694 decreed elections had to be held for the House of Commons at least every three years (changed to every seven years in 1716, and every five years in 1911). Debates ensued on the proper balance of power between Parliament and the King's government, in the form of the Cabinet Council, and whether ministers were primarily answerable to the monarch or to Parliament.

The word 'cabinet' derives from the French word *cabinet*, which can be defined as a 'small inner room serving as an accessory to a larger room'.[3] By the mid-seventeenth century, the word had acquired a political sense, as the 'private room where advisers meet'. Even as early as the 1630s, during the reign of Charles I (1625–49), the term 'Cabinet Council' had been in common usage. By 1694, the word 'Cabinet' could be found in the writings of the Earl of Warrington, when he refers to the King's advisers as the 'Cabinet', using it as a shorthand for the 'Cabinet Council': 'the King does hereby forbid all those but those of the Cabinet either to come near him, or give him any Advice'.[4]

The work of government in the late seventeenth century was restricted largely to three activities: security, based on the army and the navy; raising and spending finances; and directing trade. Most of the very limited welfare provision including education was provided by local agencies and the church.

The Acts of Union in 1707 ended the Scottish government in Edinburgh, merging the Scottish and English Parliaments, and was far more extensive than the Union of Crowns of 1603, when James succeeded Elizabeth I. The Declaratory Act of 1719 meanwhile established the superiority of English legislation over that passed by the Irish Parliament in Dublin. By the early eighteenth century, the territorial mass of Great Britain had thus become largely consolidated. These years also saw the foundation in 1694 of the Bank of England and Parliament's guarantee of the national debt, allowing the British state to borrow at a lower rate of interest than any European counterpart.

The pre-eminent figure of the day, Robert Walpole, is rightly seen as Britain's first Prime Minister, though the term was not common for more than a century. Serving from 1721 to 1742, he remains Britain's longest-serving Prime Minister, in the post for twenty-one years, a total unlikely to be overtaken. He moved into 10 Downing Street only in 1735, as the First Lord's official residence, though many of his successors found it uncongenial to their tastes, preferring to live and work from their own grander houses. Walpole, like many of his successors, was no great fan of Cabinet, believing that 'no good ever came of it'. He only began convening it regularly from 1739, when his powers were waning after the outbreak of war with Spain. Three years later, he was succeeded by second Prime Minister, Lord Wilmington (1742–43), then by Henry Pelham (1743–54). It is significant that all four of the great eighteenth-century Prime Ministers (Walpole, Pelham, North and Pitt the Younger) sat in the House of Commons. All four indicatively were also First Lords of the Treasury, as were most Prime Ministers of the eighteenth century.

The key figure in the Cabinet Council early on was not the First Lord, but the monarch. It was the King, not the First Lord, who appointed the ministers. Even as late as 1755, Lord Hardwicke, the Lord Chancellor, reminded the House of Lords that the King was not obliged by the constitution to seek consent of Parliament for any treaty he made – unless he required money. What the monarch did need was to get his business through Parliament and to have them vote him money. That entailed working with the Cabinet Council and choosing its members carefully. Working with the two parties of the day, the Whigs and the Tories, weak though they still were in structure, was also necessary if the monarch was to be assured of parliamentary majorities.

The ascendancy of the Hanoverian dynasty initially under George I (1714–27) began the process of distancing the monarch from the political running of the country. The monarchy had already abandoned the ruined Whitehall Palace, choosing not to rebuild it after the last fire during the 1690s, and had moved to the more distant, but far more luxurious, Kensington Palace. The old Palace at Whitehall, situated along the site of the current road Whitehall, might have been falling down and disease-ridden, given its proximity to the Thames, but it was at least close to Westminster. The move to Kensington Palace put physical distance between the monarch and the government. George I's uncertain command of English further distanced him from his government. George I and George II (1727–60) liked to spend summers in their beloved Hanover, entailing long periods away from London. George I fell out with his son, and George II with his son, so when they were abroad, they were reluctant to trust them to rule in their absence. This forced the monarchs to rely more on their ministers. With transport so slow and communications so unpredictable, especially sailing from the Hook to Harwich against the prevailing westerly winds, it threw more responsibility on ministers to govern in the monarch's absence. When not away George II liked to preside over Cabinet Council himself. But his absences lost him much ground.

George III (1760–1820) was much more sedentary, not holidaying on the Continent, nor travelling further north than Worcester, nor west than Plymouth (as Jeremy Black reminds us). He was much more hands-on than many believed, though, and until his eyesight began to fail in his forty-fifth year in 1805, he wrote voluminously to his ministers. His increasing mental deterioration from 1810 was, however, to play a further part in transferring power from the monarch to the politicians, with the Cabinet Council gradually superseded by the First Lord's Cabinet. Not without reason did the German Chancellor, Angela Merkel, jest with Prime Minister David Cameron (2010–16) that it was the Germans who were responsible for the emergence of his job.

The development of the Cabinet was thus a prolonged and messy affair, as was the nascent position of Prime Minister. Eighteenth-century First Ministers were anxious to avoid using the term 'Prime Minister' as it could be seen as an insult. Unlike those countries with codified written constitutions, notably the United States, the British political system was characterised by historical accident, opportunism and the always-uncertain impact of personality. So too was the recording of discussions by Cabinet. Accounts of Cabinet meetings in the eighteenth century were sent to the King, though they were of very uneven quality. When George I and George II were in Hanover, they wanted reports of what was being discussed in London, imposing a certain routine and rhythm.

Some of the more complete eighteenth-century Cabinet minutes in the National Archives' collection of State Papers relate to the aftermath of the Jacobite uprising of 1745, the last time the position of a British government was seriously threatened by a domestic rebellion. On 17 April 1746, the day after the Jacobite army was crushed by government forces on Culloden Moor, Cabinet met. Eleven ministers were in attendance, including First

Lord of the Treasury Henry Pelham (1743–54), and his brother, Secretary of State for the Southern Department the Duke of Newcastle (later First Lord of the Treasury 1754–56, 1757–62). The topic was the punishment of the defeated rebels. The minutes record that '[t]he Lords are of the opinion, that a Bill of absolute Attainder should be proposed against the principal persons who are [in] Rebellion against His Majesty'.[5] An act of attainder allowed the government to find guilty groups of persons, in this instance the defeated Jacobites, and punish them accordingly.

In the months after the Jacobite rising, Cabinet met to consider whether captured Jacobites should face the noose or a reprieve. On 24 November 1746, Cabinet met at Whitehall. The minutes recall that 'Mr Sharpe [the Treasury Solicitor] laid before his Lordships a State of the Evidence that appeared against the Rebel Prisoners, now under sentence of Death in the new Gaol at Southwark: and several petitions … in behalf of the said prisoners were read'. The minutes listed those 'Persons [who] should be reprieved, in order for their being transported for life', including seventeen-year-old Charles Gordon and sixteen-year-old James Gordon. Another, Frederick MacCulloch, was 'a young man who was barbarously wounded by the Rebels in endeavouring to prevent the murder of one of His Majesty's subjects'. For others, there would be no clemency: 'the following persons should be left to the law: John Wedderburn, Alexander Leith, James Bradshaw, James Lindsay, Andrew Wood, Thomas Watson'.[6]

The following March, Cabinet met to consider the case of the elderly Lord Lovat, who had shifted allegiance many times in his long life and had aided Charles Stuart's uprising in its dying days. He had already been stripped of his title. Cabinet was uncompromising: 'The Late Lord Lovat's petition to the King and his letter to the Duke of Newcastle were laid before the Lords and their Lordships do not see any reason for them to presume to recommend him to his Majesty's mercy … Mr Sharpe to order the sheriffs to show the Head of a Traitor.'[7] Lovat would be the last man executed by beheading in Britain.

The Duke of Newcastle was more meticulous than many in writing a record of Cabinet meetings, though often ministers made their own notes for their personal use. Shortly after the accession of George III in 1760, the task of sending accounts of meetings to the King was given to a Secretary of

State, a job taken at different times by figures including Lord Conway and Lord Stormont. The latter recorded how, in the 1780s, he 'regularly took to the King a minute of every meeting of Cabinet'. Historians hoping for a meticulous and full report of the proceedings of Cabinet will be disappointed to discover that the records are far more capricious, often reading as responses to requests from George III for the insights of certain ministers.[8]

By the late eighteenth century, Cabinet was becoming more established, a process accelerated by conflict. During the Seven Years' War (1756–63), decisions were taken by a forerunner of the twentieth-century 'War Cabinet', a group of ministers, including the Duke of Newcastle, William Pitt the Elder and Lord Hardwicke, referred to as a 'conciliabulum'.[9] Cohesion was helped further by the holding of regular dinners, which can be dated back to Lord Grenville (eighth Prime Minister, 1763–65) during the 1760s, who invited Secretaries of State to his London home in the evening to conduct Cabinet business over dinner and a glass of wine. At one such dinner in 1820, the 'Cato Street' conspirators plotted the assassination of the whole Cabinet, foiled because their conversations had been penetrated by the authorities and the planned dinner was a ruse to gather the plotters for their arrest.[10]

The American War of Independence (1775–83) saw Cabinet's position at the head of the King's government become even more consolidated. A minute of a meeting held at the London home of the Earl of Sandwich on 21 January 1775 recorded the decision that those present

> [a]greed that an address be proposed to the two Houses of Parliament to declare that if the Colonies shall make sufficient and permanent provision for the support of the civil government and administration of justice, and for the defence and protection of the said Colonies, and in time of war contribute extraordinary supplies, in a reasonable proportion to what is raised by Great Britain, we will in that case desist from the exercise of the power of taxation ... and in the meanwhile to entreat his Majesty to take the most effectual methods to enforce due obedience to the laws and authority of the supreme legislature of Great Britain.[11]

The British government's position therefore would be unyielding: the rebellious American colonists would have to accept a settlement, or they would have one imposed on them by military means. The policy would not change until 1781, when military reserves forced the government to accept American independence.

A War Cabinet was constituted to preside over the war, chaired by the First Lord, with the three Secretaries of State in attendance, as well as the Lord Chancellor, the Lord President of the Council, and, from 1778, the Commander-in-Chief. Normally, six to eight attended, though in times of particular crisis, decisions were taken by a smaller group. Meetings were generally held weekly after Cabinet dinners, with decisions recorded and forwarded to the palace for the King's approval. The war also accelerated the doctrine of 'collective responsibility', with ministers being collectively bound by decisions taken in Cabinet. In a key speech to the House of Lords on 23 April 1779, Lord Sandwich told peers that 'every expedition in regard to its destination, object, force and number of ships, is planned by the Cabinet, and is the result of the collective wisdom of all His Majesty's Confidential Ministers'.[12]

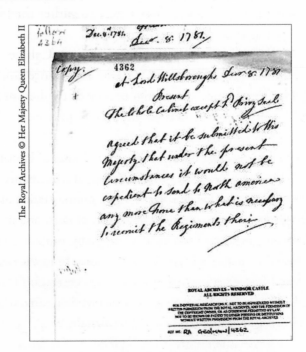

Cabinet Minute from 8 December 1781

Cabinet minutes from these years survive unevenly in the Royal Archives, with minutes usually recording military discussion, and sometimes appointments. One particularly consequential minute dates from 8 December 1781, recording a meeting of 'the whole Cabinet except the Privy Seals': '[It was] agreed that it be submitted to His Majesty, that under the present circumstances it would not be expedient to send to North America any more home [forces] than what is necessary to recruit the Regiments there.'[13] The British government was conceding the war to the American rebels. Other minutes were less portentous: at Lord Sandwich's on 30 August 1781, the Cabinet (minus Lord North), 'agreed that it be submitted to his Majesty to approve of the election of John Staples Esq made by the East India Company'.[14]

Since earlier in the eighteenth century, it had become clear that Cabinet needed a chairman to convene meetings and preside, and it equally suited the monarch to have one such figure in charge, not the least to record a regular account for when he was away or ill. Government was also becoming larger and more complex during the century, especially as foreign involvement grew, and its navy, which was far more technically difficult to run than the army, became the world's biggest. By the 1770s, the principal ministers were: the First Lord of the Treasury (or Prime Minister); the Secretaries of State for the Northern and Southern Departments, who shared domestic affairs but divided foreign policy between the northern and southern areas (the Southern Secretary of State was senior); and a third Secretary of State, the First Lord of the Admiralty, who initially looked after Scotland but from 1768 oversaw the burgeoning colonies. In 1782, the Southern and Northern Departments became the Foreign Office and Home Office. A third secretary reappeared in 1794 to oversee the War Department (i.e. the army), and subsequently a fourth (colonies) and a fifth (India) Secretary of State were established. Government was becoming a complex affair.

The doctrine of collective responsibility was strengthened further when Pitt the Younger (1783–1801 and 1804–06) was in office, with the practice becoming generally accepted that all ministers were bound to support decisions taken by the Cabinet as a whole. The doctrine was to prove vital in ensuring effective government during the long wars with Revolutionary and then Napoleonic France from 1793 until 1815.

The Eclipse of the Monarchy: The Nineteenth Century

Britain was at war, bar two short breaks, for twenty-two years from 1793. Simultaneously, the government was faced by the war with America in 1812, the Irish rebellion of 1798, unrest in India, adverse economic factors, and riots at home shortly after the Napoleonic Wars in 1819.

Accounts of Cabinet were still sent to the Palace at this time. Following the assassination of Prime Minister Spencer Perceval (1809–12) on 11 May, Lord Chancellor Eldon thus wrote to the Prince Regent to inform him about a Cabinet meeting two days later. He wrote that the Cabinet 'would feel it to be their duty, if called upon by the Prince Regent, to carry on the administration of the Government under any member of the present Cabinet, whom his Royal Highness might think proper to select as the Head of it'.[15] The Prince Regent attempted to form an alternative administration before giving up, and eventually appointed Lord Liverpool (1812–27), Secretary for War and the Colonies in the preceding government, to be Prime Minister.

The future George IV (1820–30) proved an ineffective regent, and much of the burden of leadership fell on Liverpool, who steered Britain well through these dangerous years which were to prove so formative in the development of Cabinet government. Clever use of patronage by Liverpool helped build a loyal coalition around him, and to perpetuate electoral success for the Tories. After a long period of stasis, these years saw the modernising of the country, with income tax, the Ordnance Survey and the introduction of the National Census from 1801.

The death of George IV in 1830, the 1832 Reform Act, and the subsequent emergence of recognisably modern political parties, all furthered the power of the First Lord at the expense of the monarch. To historian Robert Blake, the 1830s were pivotal: the decade was marked by 'the change from the concept of government as the King's government to that of ... party government'.[16] The continued distancing of the monarch from Cabinet meant that the recording of its deliberations became all the more important if monarchs were to remain in regular touch with their ministers and the nation's affairs. By the second half of the nineteenth century, Walter Bagehot would argue that 'real power is not in the Sovereign, it is in the Prime Minister and the Cabinet'.[17]

9

Cabinet minutes sent to the monarch from the late eighteenth and early nineteenth centuries can be seen in the Royal Archives, but are highly erratic. The minutes appear at moments of crisis, such as when the Marquis Wellesley (Wellington's brother) and George Canning refused to join Liverpool's government, when a minute was sent to the Prince Regent: 'no beneficial result is likely to arise to your Royal Highnesses' devices ... to bring about a union'.[18] Minutes seem to have fallen into abeyance for long periods. But then William IV died in 1837. Lord Melbourne (Prime Minister 1834 and 1835–41) was famously besotted with the young Queen Victoria (1837–1901), and saw it as his mission to coach her for the role she would play in national life in the years to come. His handwritten letters would set the precedent for the rest of the century, as Prime Ministers wrote personally to the monarch about procedure in Cabinet, and institutional memory of formal Cabinet minutes disappeared. Subsequent Prime Ministers continued with this practice, and it would be another eighty years before the recording of Cabinet discussions was formalised. Historian R. K. Mosley is one of many historians flabbergasted by what happened: 'Even [Charles Dickens's] Pickwick Club kept its records, but not so the British government. This must surely be one of the most remarkable non-happenings since the invention of pen and ink.'[19]

Government in Victorian Britain muddled through, with the Crimean War (1854–56) a major period of hostilities, when decisive government action was urgently required and bureaucratic efficiency was at a premium. The mood of these years was set by Gladstone's seminal Budget of 1853, announcing a phased extension of income tax, introduced by Pitt the Younger, a slashing of import tariffs, and a clear determination to keep the British government as small as possible, compatible with the defence of the realm.[20] Government spending as a percentage of GDP remained below 15 per cent from 1830–1900. Seven years after Gladstone's Budget, it fell to a low of 8.5 per cent.[21]

The doctrine of Cabinet 'collective responsibility' did, however, become consolidated during the Victorian era. Lord Palmerston (1855–58 and 1859–65) thus defended the colonial policies of his ministry by arguing that, once ministers joined the government, they were collectively responsible for that government's decisions.[22] In 1864, Palmerston would write to future Prime

Minister William Gladstone (1868–74, 1880–85, February–July 1886, 1892–94) that a minister 'divests himself of that perfect Freedom of individual action which belongs to a private and independent Member of Parliament' upon joining the government.[23] Collective responsibility enabled Palmerston to fend off criticism from the Queen because, in the words of historian D. S. Brown, 'it was useful to be able to point to collective decision making', albeit 'Palmerston was not overly fond of ministerial interference, especially once a general course or principle had been agreed upon'.[24]

Expansion in the role and ambition of government in the nineteenth century led to attempts to professionalise the government service, notably following the Northcote-Trevelyan Report in 1854, which introduced promotion on the basis of ability throughout the Civil Service. But there was no disguising the lackadaisical, amateurish nature of Britain's leadership at the top level. Cabinets continued to meet throughout the Victorian era into the twentieth century, with meetings largely unrecorded, and ministers themselves responsible for recording action on decisions reached. The most consistent record during these years remained the Prime Minister's letters to the monarch, informing them of what had been discussed.

The letters reveal much about the men who wrote them. Disraeli's letters to Victoria tended to be excitable, colourful and closely argued, recording one of his greatest triumphs. In November 1875, he wrote to Victoria about the Suez Canal in Egypt. The Khedive's shares had been placed on the market, and Disraeli knew that if the British government were the buyer, it would give Britain a controlling interest. On 8 November, he wrote to Victoria, telling her that the Khedive was planning to sell, but warning that '[t]here is a French Company in negotiation with his Highness…' Then he wrote: 'It's an affair of millions; about four at least', and went on to justify the decision by writing: 'It is vital to your Majesty's authority [and] power at this critical moment that the Canal should belong to England.' Cabinet, he wrote, 'was unanimous in their decision'.[25] A few days later, an ecstatic Disraeli wrote back to Victoria: 'It is quite settled: You have it Madam.'[26]

By contrast, the letters of the dour Lord Salisbury (1895–1902) to the aged Victoria were far less flamboyant, his manner was austere and business-like. In the run-up to the Boer War in September 1899, he wrote a typical letter:

At Cabinet today the messages from Natal were considered urging that troops should be sent to protect the Natal frontier and colony against attack on the part of the Boers, of which there were many signs and which might suddenly come to pass. It was therefore decided to send a thousand men from India, and four Battalions with some artillery and cavalry from England: orders for the expedition to be given without delay. There was a very long discussion on various military questions – which had to be decided.[27]

Within a few weeks, he wrote to Victoria '...the Boers are obstinate', and that '[i]t was thought necessary that the Reserves should be called out as it appeared probable that a considerable force might be required. But for that purpose it will be necessary under the Statute that Parliament should meet.'[28]

As historian Andrew Roberts says, 'Salisbury took Cabinet seriously. Meeting once a week, in No. 10 or the Foreign Office, there were only five or six ministers present, and he believed his power of argument would prevail. He wrote religiously to Victoria once a week when he informed her about politics more generally and foreign affairs. He believed deeply in Cabinet government and in proper constitutional form.'[29] He even made a virtue of the amateurish government. As his niece and biographer Lady Gwendolen Cecil recorded, Cabinet was a legally unrecognised body that sprung from spontaneous gatherings of political friends and colleagues: the values of the public-school gentleman held sway. 'The first rule of Cabinet conduct', Salisbury believed, 'was that no member should ever "Hansardise" another, – ever compare his present contribution to the common fund of counsel with a privately expressed opinion. Any record kept of the discussions must gravely restrict this invaluable liberty.'[30] Gentlemen (they were all men), who had often been to the same schools (principally Eton and Harrow), believed they did not need, or want, the intrusion of 'managerialism' dictating how to organise their meetings and decision-making.

Cabinet in 1900 met fairly regularly as my survey of Cabinet from 1900 to 2000 shows, though occasionally missing a week, and it took a long recess between 3 August and 17 November. Papers were provided for Cabinet to make decisions, and in that year, of ninety-two such documents, thirty-one concerned the Boer War, twenty-four defence issues and twenty-four foreign affairs or empire.[31] During the Boer War (1899–1902) it was considered important that Cabinet be kept well informed: communications from military commanders telegraphed to the Secretary of War would be presented to Cabinet as soon as possible. It seems clear that the Cabinet was the supreme decision-making body at the beginning of the last century, with frequent discussions and decisions made collectively. Official documents often feature phrases like 'we ought to' and 'we should consider'.

When the Conservatives returned to power in 1895, Salisbury had established a 'Defence Committee', to help coordinate military arrangements, under the Lord President. Such sub-Cabinet Committees had a long history, often being convened over defence matters from early in the eighteenth century. In 1900, the Defence Committee appears to have been the only such Cabinet Committee. It is difficult to say with certainty what its jurisdiction was, because, just like Cabinet, it was an amateurish affair, with no regular agenda nor minutes. It did sometimes, however, make decisions, for example ordering the raising of twelve new army battalions in January.[32]

Cracks, however, had begun to appear in the system long before Salisbury's premiership ended in 1902. A significant issue was the strain it placed on the Prime Minister to oversee the execution of Cabinet decisions, on top of all his other work. Robert Peel (1834–35 and 1841–46) complained back in 1845 that he believed it was impossible for the Prime Minister to do his job properly:

> to read all that he ought to read, including the whole foreign correspondence; to keep up the constant communication with the Queen, and the Prince; to see all whom he ought to see; to superintend the grant of honours and the disposal of civil and ecclesiastical patronage; to write with his own hand to every person of note who chooses to write to him; to be prepared for every debate ... and also sit in the House of Commons eight hours a day for 118 days.[33]

Some Prime Ministers coped with the workload better than others. William Gladstone would, in the words of historian H. C. G. Matthew, run an 'embryonic "Cabinet Office"' during his first term. He enlisted Private Secretaries to answer his 'letters about deputations, invitations to speak, begging letters and the like', thereby freeing him up to answer more important letters. He was also careful to keep thorough records of his time in power, reflecting 'not only his awareness of the importance of records for the smooth running of business, but also his awareness of his role as an historical phenomenon'.[34]

Confusion was inevitably commonplace. In 1882, a Private Secretary wrote to a Cabinet minister to complain 'about yesterday's Cabinet proceedings': 'They cannot agree about what occurred. There must have been some decision, as Bright's resignation shows. My chief has told me to ask you what the devil was decided, for he be damned if he knows. Will you ask Mr. G. [Gladstone] in more conventional and less pungent terms?'[35]

Twenty years later, social reformer Beatrice Webb complained in her diary about a similar problem:

'Impossible to find out after a Cabinet meeting', Morant tells us, 'what has actually been the decision. Salisbury does not seem to know or care, and the various Ministers, who do care, give me contradictory versions. So I gather that Cabinet meetings have become more than informal – they are chaotic – breaking up into little groups, talking to each other without any one to formulate or register the collective opinion...'[36]

In September 1900, Lord George Hamilton wrote to Lord Curzon, substantially confirming Webb's picture. Cabinet, Hamilton wrote is 'a most effete organisation. This is mainly the Chief's fault. He won't press for a decision, he does not keep people to the point, and all sorts of irrelevant trivialities are discussed *ad nauseam* to the exclusion of affairs of real importance.'[37]

War, as we have seen so often, was to be the catalyst for change, in the form of the South African War of 1899–1902. The difficulty that the mighty British military had in defeating the Boer guerrillas proved a sobering experience. Reappraisals of public health, education, the military and the very processes of British government were inevitable.

THE COMMITTEE OF IMPERIAL DEFENCE

Shortly after the end of the South African War, a Committee of Imperial Defence (CID) was established by Prime Minister A. J. Balfour (1902–05).

Proposed by an advisory committee to investigate the Boer War under Lord Elgin, the CID was the first investigative commission of its kind, with members travelling to South Africa to take evidence. Its stated objective was to 'collect and co-ordinate ... information bearing on the wide problem of Imperial Defence ... [and] to make possible a continuity of method'.[38] The CID, with a proper Secretariat from 1904, replaced the preceding Cabinet Committee on Defence. Initially, its work was handicapped by intense rivalry between the army and the navy, but its effectiveness began to improve after the Liberals came to power in December 1905: one of its reports in 1909 led to the establishment of MI5 and MI6. The CID helped the government, in the critical years leading up to the First World War, to focus attention on the threat posed by Germany in the North Sea, and Russia on the North West Frontier of India. In the summer of 1914, before the outbreak of war on 4 August, the CID produced an eleven-chapter 'War Book' setting out the administrative steps that would have to be taken in the event of a major war. Responsibility for coordinating the national response in the event of war was indeed to be one of the core functions of the Cabinet Office throughout its first 100 years.

This is the moment that the pivotal figure in the evolution of the Cabinet Office makes his entrance. Maurice Hankey, who became the first and longest-serving Cabinet Secretary, had attended Rugby School, before entering the Royal Marine Artillery. His early career was successful but not stellar, as he climbed through the ranks. But his prodigious gifts at mastering and marshalling diverse information, and ensuring it was acted upon, began to mark him out. He joined the CID as its Naval Assistant Secretary in 1908, and was appointed Secretary (i.e. the Chief) in 1912 with a clear vision of his own. Hankey later said: 'My own idea was that the Committee of Imperial Defence should be reorganised and tuned up to the pitch of actual war and should take over the control.'[39]

The CID under Hankey sought to become a coherent military planning agency for government. But, for all its endeavour, when war broke out in 1914, there was still no agreed plan for the expansion of the army or its armaments, or to keep the economy fully running. The CID, moreover, was underpowered in its scraps against the mighty War Office and Admiralty, which showed little enthusiasm for adapting themselves to accommodate the new body.

THE FIRST WORLD WAR: 1914–16

It would be the First World War that swept away this system of government. The war was to prove the catalyst that transformed Britain's inexpert central government into a highly professionalised one.

Accounts of the Cabinet meetings that took Britain into war can be found in the letters sent to George V (1910–36) by either Prime Minister Asquith (1908–16) or the Leader of the House of Lords, Lord Crewe, during the summer of 1914. Some letters were sent by other ministers: Churchill, for example, sent letters to the King when he was Home Secretary (1910–11).[40] Lord Crewe sent this review of a critical Cabinet meeting to George V on 2 August 1914:

> Sir Edward Grey gave an account of his conversation with Monsieur Cambon [the French Ambassador] ... adding a further statement of the reasons which at the present juncture make it impossible for Your Majesty's Government to send our military force out of the country, without pledging themselves either way in the future.
>
> The precise form of the statement to be made in Parliament tomorrow was not fully discussed, as Your Majesty's Ministers will meet again tomorrow morning. It was argued, however, that the communication in regards intentions on the employment of the German fleet should be made to Germany beforehand ... As regards Belgium, it was agreed ... that ... a substantial violation of the neutrality of that country would place us in a situation contemplated as possible by our government in 1870, when interference with Belgium independence was held to compel us to take action...[41]

The following day, Crewe wrote to the King to say that 'Sir E. Grey communicated to his colleagues the telegram from Brussels to the Belgian minister here which summarises the German ultimatum'. He added that 'Mr Asquith regrets to say that four of his colleagues – Lord Morley, Sir J Simon, Lord Beauchamp and John Burns – have tendered their resignation'.[42] Despite these resignations, two of which were later recanted, Britain went to war with Germany the following day.

The outbreak of the First World War proved a far greater shock to British government than the outbreak of the Second, largely because the latter war could draw on the experience of the First. In 1914, Britain had not been involved in a major war, with the exceptions of the Crimea and Boer Wars, since 1815, and had no inkling of the demands that the first total war in history would make upon it. Nor did it have any idea of how the economy would react to the massive requirements of fighting this kind of war. As government spending as a percentage of GDP more than tripled from just 16 per cent in 1910 to 55 per cent by 1917, the Civil Service swelled to its largest size in history.[43] Entirely new government departments were created, including the Ministries of Munitions, Pensions, and National Service, while other departments increased in size by a factor of ten, including the War Office, Admiralty and Foreign Office.[44]

The advent of instantaneous communications, with telegraph cables encircling the world, meant that decisions could become centralised, with commanders in the field and diplomats in foreign capitals able to refer much more back to London for instructions rather than being left largely to their own devices, as had been the case for Wellington a century before. The sheer scale, too, of Britain finding itself at war simultaneously with three major powers – Germany, Austria-Hungary and the Ottoman Empire – presented novel challenges.

Within three months of the outbreak of hostilities, Asquith had established a War Cabinet. Initial planning, such as it was, had not bargained on the war being so prolonged. Hankey was asked to provide a record of Cabinet meetings to help galvanise action, albeit by shorthand, apparently for secrecy.

As the military and politicians planned a series of offensives to wrest control from the other side along the 450-mile line from Switzerland to the English Channel, it became clear that the apparatus of government in Whitehall was inadequate for the task. The War Council met too infrequently and was not served by any kind of bureaucracy, heightening the opportunities for turf wars between Whitehall departments. For a critical period between March and May 1915, which included the Battle of Neuve Chapelle, the War Council did not meet at all.[45]

'The root difficulty in the early conduct of the War on our part', Asquith later wrote, 'was how to combine rapid and effective executive action in the various theatres with the maintenance of Cabinet responsibility and control.'[46] He identified the problem, but his personal credo was partly responsible: he strongly resisted the illiberal measures that total war demanded. His 'business-as-usual' approach to the war envisaged a continuation of the structures and mindsets of Edwardian and Victorian Britain. His strategy was indeed similar to the one that had defeated Napoleon a century before: the overwhelming use of naval power, financial support for allies, the crippling of the German economy by blockade and the seizing of German colonies, with the army remaining on a voluntary basis and of moderate size.[47] But much had changed in the 100 years separating both wars.

Asquith's attention wandered, not least due to his romantic attraction to Venetia Stanley, a friend of his daughter Violet, to whom he wrote heartfelt letters, even during Cabinet meetings. Sometimes he wrote to her three times a day, seeking her advice on military strategy and on dealing with difficult colleagues. As a result, the letters provide one of the best records for historians of what was happening in Cabinet. Two days after the outbreak of war in 1914, he wrote to her, in terms surprising for the ultimate custodian of government secrecy:

> We had our usual Cabinet this morning, and decided with much less demur than I had expected to sanction the despatch of an Expeditionary Force of four divisions. We also discussed a number of smaller schemes for taking German ports & wireless stations in E&W Africa & the China Seas were discussed with some gusto: indeed I had to remark that we looked more like a gang of Elizabethan buccaneers than a meek collection of black-coated Liberal Ministers.[48]

Six months later, he was divulging details of discussions on Gallipoli:

> Our War Council lasted nearly two and a half hours. Winston was in some ways at his worst – having quite a presentable case. He was noisy, rhetorical, tactless, & temperless … [Kitchener] I think on the whole rightly, insisted on keeping the 29th Division at home, free to go either to the Dardanelles or to France, until we know … where the necessity is greatest …[49]

The relationship between Asquith and Stanley had been broken off when she married minister Edwin Montagu in April 1915. Unfortunately for historians, Asquith and Stanley's epistolary relationship was discontinued at this point, ending the insights into the Cabinet meetings.

The inadequacy of Asquith's style of leadership became all the more apparent when, in May 1915, a coalition government formed with the Conservatives: Lord Curzon became Lord Privy Seal and Andrew Bonar Law, the Leader of the Conservative Opposition, became Secretary of State for the Colonies. Now there were many more big beasts wanting to air their views, with a corresponding challenge to effective decision-taking. As Churchill wrote before the coalition:

> [A]ll the important matters connected with the war had been dealt with … by four or five ministers … At least a dozen powerful, capable, distinguished personalities who were in a position to assert themselves had now to be consulted … At least five or six different opinions prevailed on every great topic, and every operative decision was obtained only by prolonged, discursive and exhausting discussion … Meanwhile the destroying war strode remorselessly on its course.[50]

Lord Curzon, who as Viceroy had run India firmly ten years before, was particularly contemptuous:

> Meetings of the Cabinet were most irregular; sometimes only once, seldom more than twice, a week. There was no agenda, there was no order of business. Any minister requiring to bring up a matter either of departmental or of public importance had to seek the permission of the Prime Minister to do so … No record whatever was kept of our proceedings … The Cabinet often had the very haziest notion as to what its decisions were.[51]

The year 1915 saw a number of failed British military offensives, including the Battles of Aubers Ridge in May and Loos in October. Cabinet ministers agitated for far stronger resolve by government, including the creation of a conscript army. On 16 October 1915, Hankey, after a lunch with Asquith, recorded in his diary: 'It appears that Lloyd George is out to break the government on conscription if he can. Much talk about conscription and PM agreed that a dictatorship was the only legally satisfactory form of government in time of war.'[52] Hankey himself was convinced that change had to come, concerned as he was about

> the scrambles of Ministers to get their pet subjects discussed at chaotic Cabinet meetings ... the endless rambling discussions with no one to give a decision ... the exasperating waste of time while the affairs of a department were discussed by people who knew little of the matter and had received no memorandum on the subject ... the humiliating and dangerous doubts of what the decision was, or whether there had been a decision at all.[53]

Events in the east highlighted even more cruelly the clumsiness and inadequacy of the Cabinet structure and approach. Long before Christmas 1914, it was clear in Whitehall that the war would not be over that year, and that a breakthrough on the Western Front would be difficult to achieve – though it did not stop a series of offensives being planned. Hankey, whose writings seldom missed an opportunity for drama, takes up the story of an all-day War Council in January 1915:

> The blinds had been drawn to shut out the winter evening. The air was heavy and the table presented that rather dishevelled appearance that results from a long session ... At this point events took a dramatic turn, for Churchill suddenly revealed his well-kept secret of a naval attack on the Dardanelles! The idea caught on at once. The whole atmosphere changed. Fatigue was forgotten. The War Council turned eagerly from the dreary prospect of a 'slogging match' on the Western Front to brighter prospects, as they seemed, in the Mediterranean.[54]

Thus was hatched the Gallipoli Campaign of April 1915 to January 1916, a British Commonwealth attack against the Ottoman Empire to capture Constantinople and provide a sea route through to the Russian allies.

But, as with a number of other British wars, too many to mention, insufficient thought was given to planning after the initial attacks. Was it to be primarily a naval or an army operation? Churchill, with all the vim of an experienced First Sea Lord, favoured the former, while Secretary of State for War, Lord Kitchener, supported the latter. Churchill won this clash of personalities, but his attempt to run the Dardanelles Straits with obsolete naval vessels incurred heavy losses.[55] On 19 March, Hankey wrote to Asquith imploring him to appoint a 'naval and military technical committee to plan our attack on the Dardanelles so as to avoid a repetition of naval fiasco, which is largely due to inadequate staff preparation'.[56] Historian Tim Travers says of the major meeting on 6 April between Churchill, Kitchener and Hankey, with no one obviously in charge, that decision-making on 'the simpler colonial warfare of the past' was clearly inadequate for 'the professional needs of modern warfare'.[57]

The landings on 25 April, which involved British, Australian, New Zealand and Indian forces, along with a token French contingent, proved to be a disaster. Hankey considered it 'like an American cinema show', i.e. heavily advertised beforehand, dooming the operation even before it began.[58] In June, a 'Dardanelles Committee' was created to try to bring coordination to the campaign, and two months later Hankey travelled to the Dardanelles to see the stalemate for himself. Soon he was advising the operation be terminated. In November 1915, Asquith replaced the Dardanelles Committee with a 'War Committee' including Churchill, Arthur Balfour, Lloyd George, Andrew Bonar Law and the Chancellor, Reginald McKenna. But it proved no more efficient or effective than its predecessors. In the view of Hankey, 'in spite of the brilliancy of its members [it] was a coalition of parties that never really coalesced'.[59] Lack of top-level coordination in Whitehall provided a deeper problem. When, on 22 November 1915, the War Committee advised the evacuation of Gallipoli, Cabinet refused to endorse the decision for almost a month, with Asquith insisting Cabinet was the supreme decision-making body. As a result, the Gallipoli peninsula was not evacuated until 9 January 1916.[60]

The previous month, December 1915, saw the British and French commanders gather in Chantilly, France, to hammer out Allied strategy for 1916, in the light of the failure at Gallipoli. Major offensives were planned for the Eastern and Western Fronts to regain the initiative. The British and French were to engage in a devastating joint attack where their armies met on the River Somme in Picardy to bring about victory and the collapse of Germany.

A week after final plans had been agreed in February 1916, the Germans attacked at Verdun, reducing considerably the French commitment. The Battle of the Somme, which lasted from 1 July to 18 November 1916, was to be the eventual undoing of Asquith and the whole ad hoc system of government at the centre. The planners had failed to anticipate German resilience, and their digging dugouts deep into the chalk, safe from the Allied bombardment designed to flatten all opposition. As a result, German soldiers proved able to ferociously resist the clumsy British advance, inflicting enormous casualties. Hankey himself suffered personal tragedy in the battle. He had already suffered the loss of one brother: Hugh Hankey had been killed at the Battle of Paardeberg during the Boer War. On 16 October 1916, his brother Donald, to whom he was particularly close, died on the Somme. He was dictating in Whitehall when the phone rang. On putting down the receiver, he said: 'Donald's gone', before asking his secretary: 'Where was I?' As his biographer Stephen Roskill suggests, this stiff-upper-lip response, which shocked those around him, was perhaps his way of coping.[61]

Asquith's position became increasingly untenable. By mid-July it became clear that the high hopes of the military commanders for the offensive, notably Commander-in-Chief General Douglas Haig, had proved wildly ambitious. Casualties mounted, with no breakthrough taking place. Asquith's morale had been badly damaged after the death of his beloved and brilliant son Raymond at the Somme Offensive on 15 September. On 17 September, the news was conveyed by telephone to Margot Asquith. She told her husband in No. 10, who 'put his hands over his face and we walked into an empty room and sat down in silence'. He lamented: 'Whatever pride I had in the past and whatever hope I had for the future – by much the largest part I had of both was invested in him. Now all that is gone.' Margot noted that now it was 'only a question of time when we shall have to leave Downing Street'.[62]

Lloyd George, who had worked so closely with Asquith as Chancellor during the pre-war Liberal government, became increasingly exasperated, and in the end triggered the final crisis by threatening to resign if crucial decisions were not delegated to a three-man committee which he chaired. Eventually, divisions in the Liberal Party undermined Asquith's parliamentary support and on 5 December 1916, he resigned, with Lloyd George his inevitable successor.

[This Document is the Property of His Britannic Majesty's Government.]

1

Printed for the use of the Cabinet. December 1916.

SECRET.

D. Clarkes File.

53

[To be returned to the Secretary, 2, Whitehall Gardens, S.W.]

WAR CABINET, 1.

Minutes of a Meeting of the War Cabinet, held at the War Office on Saturday, December 9, 1916, at 11·30 A.M.

Present :

The PRIME MINISTER (in the Chair.)

The Right Hon. A. BONAR LAW, M.P.	The Right Hon. the EARL CURZON OF KEDLESTON, K.G., G.C.S.I., G.C.I.E.
The VISCOUNT MILNER, G.C.B., G.C.M.G.	The Right Hon. A. HENDERSON, M.P.

In attendance :

The Right Hon. SIR E. CARSON, K.C., M.P., First Lord of the Admiralty.	Admiral SIR J. R. JELLICOE, G.C.B., O.M., G.C.V.O., First Sea Lord.
The LORD HARDINGE OF PENSHURST, G.C.B., G.C.M.G., G.M.S.I., G.M.I.E., Permanent Under Secretary of State, Foreign Office.	General Sir W. R. ROBERTSON, K.C.B., K.C.V.O., D.S.O., Chief of the Imperial General Staff.

Lieutenant-Colonel SIR M. P. A. HANKEY, K.C.B., *Secretary.*

Lieutenant-Colonel W. DALLY JONES, *Assistant Secretary.*

Offices of the War Cabinet.

1. The War Cabinet decided that their offices should for the present be at Montagu House, which up to now has been occupied by the Shipping Control Committee, and was about to be transferred to the Ministry of Munitions. The Secretary was instructed to place himself in communication with the Office of Works with a view to the immediate transfer of these or other convenient offices to the War Cabinet at the earliest possible date.

Secretariat.

2. The War Cabinet discussed the advisability of strengthening the Secretariat of the former War Committee by the addition of a civil side. The question was adjourned for further consideration.

Greece.

3. The War Cabinet discussed a telegram, dated the 6th December, 1916, received by His Majesty the King from the King of Greece, and approved, with slight alterations, and subject to the concurrence of Mr. Balfour (who was unable to attend the meeting), a draft reply submitted by the Permanent Under-Secretary of State for Foreign Affairs. Copies of the telegram from the King of Greece and the reply are attached. (Appendix I.)

[1365—1]

B

Page I of First Cabinet Minutes

David Lloyd George (centre), Prime Minister 1916–22, photographed here during the First World War on a visit to France. He was the first Prime Minister to experience the Cabinet Office.

CHAPTER 2

The Creation of the Cabinet Office: The Cabinet Secretariat and the First World War, 1916–18

MAURICE HANKEY, like all Cabinet Secretaries, had a steely eye for power, and how and when to exercise personal influence. Rarely was it seen more blatantly than in March 1916, when a delegation of British policy makers, including Lloyd George, then Minister for Munitions, was in Paris for conversations with senior French politicians at the Foreign Ministry at the Quai d'Orsay. Lloyd George and Hankey broke away at one point for a long walk together through the streets of Paris to ruminate on the conduct of the war. Hankey saw it as an opportunity to air his vision for improving the organisation of government at the centre. As Lloyd George wrote:

> I can recall that as we passed the Vendome Column, Sir Maurice paused and said: 'You ought to insist on a small War Committee being set up for the day to day conduct of the war, with full power. It must be independent of the Cabinet. It must keep in close touch with the PM, but the PM as Head of the Government could not manage that. He has a very heavy job in looking after the Cabinet and attending to Parliamentary and Home Affairs. He is a bit tired, too, after all he has gone through in

the last two and a half years. The Chairman of the proposed Committee must be a man of unimpaired energy and great driving power.'[1]

Hankey's masterly playing on Lloyd George's vanity and desire for ultimate power, and his subtle disparaging of Asquith, was deftly done.

THE SETTING UP OF THE WAR SECRETARIAT, DECEMBER 1916

Asquith resigned on 5 December 1916 and Lloyd George became Prime Minister, though not, as was the custom, till the next day, after he had been invited by George V at Buckingham Palace. He became head of a new coalition government, with Conservative leader Bonar Law as Chancellor. That evening, at about 10 p.m., Lloyd George summoned Hankey to his room at the War Office:

> He informed me that he was the new prime minister, though he didn't much like it, and we had a long talk about the personnel of the new Govt., the procedure of the new War Ctee., and the future of the war. He and Bonar Law, who was there part of the time, consulted me on many points, and I thought they were going to offer me a place! Ll. G. asked me to write a memo giving my views.[2]

Hankey was the only Cabinet Secretary to become a minister, albeit much later: his comment reveals the weight of his advice. Lloyd George had spent many exasperated months planning for this exact eventuality. He could thus speedily form a War Cabinet with supreme authority, composed initially of five members, including Bonar Law, Curzon, Labour leader Arthur Henderson and the Conservative, Lord Milner, the latter two as 'ministers without portfolio'. Later, others would join, including South African leader General Jan Smuts, Labour politician George Barnes and the Conservative Austen Chamberlain.

At last, after twenty-eight months of fighting since August 1914, Britain had an all-powerful body to direct the war. Lloyd George had absorbed another lesson from Hankey about the need for effective bureaucracy. As he later wrote, in terms that are still relevant to the work of the Cabinet Office 100 years later:

> Another departure from Cabinet traditions which I had decided to initiate was the setting up of a Cabinet Secretariat … I came to the conclusion that it was desirable to have a secretary present who would make a short precis of the discussions on all important issues and take a full record of all decisions. Where these decisions affected one of the departments, a copy of the minute was immediately sent to the minister concerned. I thought it was of primary importance that a written intimation of the character and terms of the decision of the Cabinet should be sent formally to the department, not merely as a reminder to the minister, but in order that the officials who advised him and carried out his orders should be fully informed. I also thought it not only desirable but imperative, having regard to the number of decisions in the past which had not been carried out, to charge the Secretary with the duty of keeping in touch with further developments and of reporting to me from time to time what action had been taken in the various departments concerned on those Cabinet Orders. I subsequently found that these enquiries addressed from the Cabinet Office, and the reports which had to be made in response, were very helpful in keeping the departments alert and well up to the mark. Where the Secretary reported failure or delay in carrying out decisions, I sent for the minister, and where unexpected difficulties had arisen, steps were taken to remove them.[3]

At last, Lloyd George had his dream job. So too did Hankey. 'Lloyd George gave me *carte blanche*' to set up the Cabinet Secretariat and staff it, wrote Hankey. He had already spied a suite of houses in Whitehall Gardens, to the east of Whitehall, close to the River Thames. The Office of Works were, at pace, instructed to knock doors and openings through the walls to create a unified office:

> How my staff managed to carry on in those [early] days is still a mystery. Working three or four in a room, one would be dictating, trying to make

his voice heard above the din of hammering and sawing; another conducting a business interview on some high matter of State; a third trying
to compile a Memorandum. They were a loyal and enthusiastic team or
they never could have done it.[4]

Hankey divided his new office into two sections: Military, which he oversaw
himself, and Civilian, overseen by G. M. Young (who later wrote the authorised biography of Stanley Baldwin), who was soon replaced by Welshman
and diarist, the remarkable Thomas 'T. J.' Jones. Hankey proceeded to
bring together what he called a 'nucleus of unbiased men, unhampered by
departmental prejudices, whose sole standpoint was that of winning the
war'.[5] Hankey set to work at once, and on the morning of 12 December
saw Thomas Jones, who stated his intentions to associate with top people,
and not be burdened by menial tasks:

> I saw Sir Maurice Hankey and talked over the sort of work I might do. L.G.
> had spoken to him. I explained I didn't want to touch office machinery
> but rather to act as a fluid person moving amongst people who mattered
> and keeping the PM on the right path as far as possible. He quite under-
> stood. He is to see L. G. again. His place is at 2 Whitehall Gardens and
> they will overflow on both sides into 1 and 3 I think.[6]

Hankey had a keen eye for talent and recruited a strong team, including Leo
Amery, more noted for his ability and creativity, whose Cabinet posts culminated in his becoming Secretary of State for India, and William Ormsby-Gore,
who would become Colonial Secretary, and father to the celebrated British
Ambassador to the US when J. F. Kennedy was President (1961–63).

The first meeting of the War Cabinet was convened at the War Office,
not in the Cabinet Room at No. 10, on Saturday 9 December at 11.30 am.
The five ministers were in attendance, along with Edward Carson, First Lord
of Admiralty, and Admiral John Jellicoe, First Sea Lord. Hankey attended
every meeting of the War Cabinet, with an assistant secretary to help with
notes, except when matters were highly secret, when he recorded matters
alone. On the evening of 9 December, he recorded in his diary that 'it was
"off with the old love and on with the new"'.[7]

Lloyd George was the first Prime Minister in British history to have risen from reasonably modest origins, and to have been educated in a church school, unlike his privately educated colleagues around the Cabinet table. He was at the height of his powers, restless for urgency and change to win the war, and to ensure a better deal for the British people after it. To achieve it all, he considered he needed more operational firepower at his elbows in No. 10, in addition to the Cabinet Secretariat. And so a temporary hut made an appearance in the No. 10 garden, becoming the headquarters for Lloyd George's personal secretariat, widely known as the 'Garden Suburb'. What he had created was an embryonic 'Prime Minister's Department', an ambition in the mind of some Prime Ministers, and an idea which came and went over the next 100 years, but never became a reality.

Lloyd George's new development was greeted with much suspicion in Whitehall, particularly by Hankey, especially when it developed into a source of independent intelligence for Lloyd George on the work of government departments, and initiated policy in the areas he directed, while beginning to fashion some of his speeches. Among the staff flooding into the dilated Downing Street was his mistress Frances Stevenson, who shared the building with Lloyd George's wife, Margaret.[8] According to A. J. P. Taylor, 'he was the first Prime Minister since Walpole to leave office flagrantly richer than he entered it, the first since the Duke of Grafton to live openly with his mistress'.[9] He had become infatuated with her shortly after he employed her to become his daughter Megan's governess in 1911. Two years later, she agreed to become his personal secretary, and mistress. She remained close to him throughout the war and after, marrying him two years after Margaret died in 1941. Within eighteen months of their marriage, he too died in 1945.

Hankey worked all hours to entrench the Cabinet Secretariat into the Whitehall architecture, and define it against the Garden Suburb. Historian Kenneth O. Morgan believes that by at least mid-1917 Hankey had succeeded in this task.[10] He delineated four main roles for it: to record the proceedings of the War Cabinet; to transmit the decisions of the War Cabinet on the same day to those departments required to bring them into effect; to prepare agenda papers in advance, ensuring that the appropriate ministers and other figures, including military, attended; finally, to attend to the correspondence connected with the work of the War Cabinet.[11] He painstakingly laid out the rules and procedures of his baby:

> Questions may be referred to decision by the War Cabinet by the prime minister, or by members of the War Cabinet, or by any member of the government or by any government department. The normal procedure for raising any question should be a communication to the secretary, accompanied, when practicable, by a short memorandum containing the summary of the points on which a decision is required.
>
> Before reaching their final conclusions on any subject the War Cabinet will, as a general rule, consult the ministers at the head of the department concerned, who will lay out before them all the evidence, written or oral, relevant and necessary to a decision.
>
> After each meeting the secretary will circulate the copies of the draft minutes to members for their remarks. He will also circulate to ministers summoned for particular subjects, drafts of the minutes on those subjects for their remarks. When their remarks have been received, the secretary will submit a final draft of the minutes for the approval of the prime minister. After the prime minister has initialled the minutes of the War Cabinet, the conclusions formulated therein will become operative decisions to be carried out by the responsible departments. The prime minister can delegate his powers in this respect in case of absence or the claims of other urgent business.
>
> As soon as the prime minister's initials have been received, the decisions of the War Cabinet will be communicated by the secretary to the political and civil heads of the departments concerned, who will be responsible for giving effect to them.[12]

HANKEY 'ON MANOEUVRES'

Hankey was a military man to his fingertips, so it is no surprise that one of his early personal accomplishments as Cabinet Secretary was helping to devise the system of convoys in response to the German policy of unrestricted submarine warfare, unleashed on 1 February 1917. That month, 400,000 tons of shipping was lost and a further 500,000 went down in March. The German Navy was working on the belief that if the losses continued at these levels for a further six months, the British war effort would collapse. Never one to underestimate his own role in history, Hankey recorded in his diary:

> Had a brain wave on the subject of anti-submarine warfare, so ran down to Walton Heath [Lloyd George's home in Surrey][13] in the afternoon to formulate my ideas with Ll. George, who was very interested. I sat up late completing a long Memo on the subject. My Memo was an argument for convoys, but contained a great number of suggestions.[14]

Hankey reasoned that the policy of convoys had proved effective during the Napoleonic Wars, and could work equally well in the new century. In the vastness of the Atlantic Ocean, a convoy would appear little bigger than a single ship, and it would allow the Merchant Navy to be protected by guns from Royal Navy vessels. The Admiralty was unimpressed, however, and on 21 February, First Sea Lord Jellicoe summoned ten senior naval figures to meet Hankey at the Admiralty, where he learnt of their firm opposition. Hankey persisted in his lobbying, and on 23 April, Lloyd George confronted Jellicoe in Cabinet over it. A week later the convoy system became the Admiralty's official policy.[15]

The policy proved a success: whereas 600,000 tons of shipping had been lost in April 1917, the figure dropped markedly after convoys were adopted, and the threats from U-Boats, which had appeared overwhelming earlier in the year, faded.

The supply of food and shipbuilding was another area where Hankey and the Cabinet Secretariat's impact was felt. On 29 March 1917, he wrote a memo to Lloyd George which opened: 'Unless we are to lose this war, I submit the following measures should be taken in regards to the food and shipping problems…' Hankey, when suggesting the Minister of Munitions release shipping to allow wheat to be brought from Canada and the United States, came across more like a highly activist minister than a civil servant. So too when he recommended that ports be organised 'for night as well as day work. This would greatly increase the rate at which ships are turned round and set free tonnage.' To increase the supply of ships, he urged 'great numbers of men' be diverted from munitions 'to be used in shipbuilding yards'. He concluded: 'I submit that the shipping peril is so great that we run a great risk of losing the war unless the most drastic measures of this kind are adopted, and that nothing should be allowed to stand in the way.'[16]

Hankey was adept at playing the press, as well as politicians. As historian Andrew Roberts has said, 'if you wanted anything done in Whitehall you'd have to get Hankey, or Lord Esher [a key bridge to the French], on side'.[17] On 19 March 1918, just two days before the Germans launched their major Spring Offensive, a laudatory article about the Cabinet Secretariat appeared in *The Times*. One can readily discern Hankey's voice in the article. No Cabinet Secretary after him would be so brazen in lobbying the media: indeed, most, for good reasons, steered a wide berth.

We learn from the article that, from its inception in December 1916 'until the end of December 1917', 300 meetings of the War Cabinet were held, indicating 'the great change which has taken place in the work of the Cabinet', and that '248 [experts] other than members of the War Cabinet … and the Secretariat have attended its meetings'.

DIFFICULTIES IN 1917

Progress in the war on land remained mired in the mud, regardless of the change of leadership in London. One commander who had emerged energised from the Battle of Verdun in 1916 was Frenchman Robert Nivelle, who was promoted as commander of the French Army in December. When British politicians saw him in mid-January 1917, he fired those present with his ambitious plans for an offensive on the Chemin des Dames to the north of Paris, though Haig himself was cautious. Lloyd George was unconvinced by Haig, and agreed for Nivelle to be placed in overall command of Western Front operations for his great offensive, known as the Second Battle of the Aisne.

British forces attacked near Arras in April, with the French attack terminating in May, having secured only some minor tactical gains and a loss of some 187,000 French casualties. Nivelle's failure to meet his ambitious targets resulted in his being replaced as French commander later in May by

Philippe Pétain. Hankey had failed to prevent Lloyd George backing Nivelle over Haig, and he again failed to prevent arguably the most ill-judged military decision of the war – the Third Battle of Ypres, about which Haig again had reservations, and which only received agreement from Cabinet on 25 July. Attacks began on 31 July 1917 and lasted until November. The battle is known generally by the name of the village on the slopes above Ypres where the battle finally petered out: Passchendaele. It failed to achieve any significant breakthrough: estimates of British casualties vary, though the official war history placed it at a quarter of a million. The ground taken was recaptured by the Germans four months later in the March 1918 offensive. Among the many criticisms of the Third Battle of Ypres were the delayed timing of the battle's commencement, the choice of water-logged Flanders as the battlefield, continuing the fighting when it became clear that a break-through was impossible, and not delaying the entire battle until troops from the United States, which entered the war in 1917, arrived in Europe.

For all these travails, Hankey considered Lloyd George a significant improvement on Asquith. Hankey was apt to believe that his grasp of both bureaucratic and strategic affairs was superior to that of the Prime Minister, and was not bashful in recording Lloyd George's reliance upon him, as regularly recorded throughout his diary, as at Easter 1917: 'On the evening of Good Friday 29th March, LG went to St Anne's Church, Soho to hear Bach's passion music. He would hardly let me out of his sight, and I spent the whole evening smoking and chatting. He is very anxious but more sanguine than I.'[18]

The closeness of Hankey's relationship to Lloyd George can be seen again in a critical breakfast conversation on Monday 15 October 1917, in which Hankey paints a picture of himself as being more forceful than Lloyd George in arguments over future British offensives, while also deferring to the Prime Minister's judgement. Hankey had come down decisively on the generals' side, who argued that pressure had to be maintained on Germany with fresh offensives in 1918, because of the damage it would do to German morale and their ability to continue fighting. Lloyd George had become very concerned by the escalating number of British casualties: 'A man took twenty-one years to make, and human life was very precious,' he observed to Hankey. Scared by the Somme and Passchendaele, he urged delaying an offensive until the United States had fully mobilised and was present in France, even if not till 1919. He wanted the British Army to emerge from the war 'in every respect as good as the army of the United States, and possibly a revived Russian army, so this country will be the greatest military power in the world'.

Hankey was regularly exasperated that Lloyd George's command of good government was not as sure as his own. In March 1917, just three months into the new regime, he confided to his diary:

> The War Cabinet has met every day this week, but is not working satisfactorily. They never discuss their Agenda at all – in fact they have not done so properly for a fortnight … Consequently, all the work is dreadfully congested … Another difficulty is that Lloyd George will not initial the conclusions (without which they do not become operative), and will not give me a reasonably free hand to act without them, so that all the business of the War Cabinet goes into arrears, and the Departments, tired of waiting for their decisions, get discontented.[19]

Two weeks later, he complained on 1 April:

> War Cabinet at 11:30 a.m. very jumpy and ratty; positively indignant that I had arranged a War Cabinet, although he had given me no instructions to the contrary! After getting rid of his colleagues in a very cavalier manner, he held an important conference on the method of transporting troops from USA.[20]

Hankey sounded off to his diary six weeks later in a still more exasperated vein:

> Our PM has invented a new and most tiresome method of doing business. He puts the War Cabinet at noon and has a private meeting of his own with Lord Milner and CIGS [Chief of the Imperial General Staff, Sir William Robertson] at 11 a.m., when I have to attend and am expected to keep a record. He really is a trial. Just as I have got the War Cabinet system in good working order so as to relieve myself of overwork,

he overburdens me again. For this means an hour extra in the morning and an hour in the afternoon dictating, a really terrible inroad on my limited time for office business. Luckily he is sure to tire of it soon, but anyhow he ought not to rely so entirely on me.[21]

Barely a Cabinet Secretary down the decades did not feel similar exasperation with the capricious organisational practices of their Prime Ministers. Cabinet Secretaries indeed, excelling in 'left-brain' logical skills, were bound to be irritated by their 'right-brain' political masters.

Hankey was at the height of his powers in 1918. Lloyd George, too, had become a far more commanding and experienced war leader than just the year before: together, they achieved a qualitatively better grip over the machine and war strategy. But it was the Cabinet Secretary who could often see further strategically than the Prime Minister, and who understood the Whitehall machine better, in part because he could spend long hours mastering the detail, and because the military was his area of expertise.

On 19 June 1918, Lord Curzon gave a celebrated defence of the Cabinet Secretariat from critics, including Viscount Midleton, in a speech to the House of Lords. Curzon dismissed reports of chaos in government as a 'caricature', and spoke of the pre-1916 Cabinet as an 'irretrievably broken down' system.[22] He saluted the achievements of the government, and asked the Lords how a disordered organisation could ever have achieved such things.[23] He finished by summarising the measures that he believed would become permanent:

> the preparation of an agenda in order that we may know in advance what we are going to discuss is an inevitable and essential feature of business-like procedure in any assembly in the world ... I doubt whether it will be possible to dispense with the assistance of a secretary in future ... I think that a record and minutes of the proceedings will have to be kept; and, lastly, I hope for a very considerable development of the system of devolution and decentralisation of Government work which I have described ... my own opinion is that when the war is over and the history of this time is written, it may be found that we have left a not inconsiderable mark upon the constitutional development of this country.[24]

Curzon looked ahead to the retention of the War Secretariat into peacetime, a controversial idea. But first, the war had to be won. The initiative was seized in early 1918 not by the Allies but by the Germans, who launched a series of ferocious attacks along the Western Front between March and June 1918, known as the 'Spring Offensive' or *Kaiserschlach* ('Kaiser's battle'). It was a last, desperate attempt to win the war and to break the deadlock on the Western Front before the US Army arrived in full force, using reinforcements from the Eastern Front freed up following the Bolshevik Revolution of late 1917. The German plan was to divide the British from the French forces and trap them by the coast. Initial successes in March saw the Western Front pushed back significantly. Hankey was anxious, writing on 22 and 23 March that 'the situation was menacing' and 'we could not but fear a debacle'.[25] Lloyd George, however, remained 'buoyant', galvanised by the urgency of the situation. The Allied armies, though, did not break, and by late April the main threat had passed. Over the following few weeks, 220,000 men were funnelled across the Channel, with two divisions joining from Palestine and one from Italy. The Prime Minister urged President Wilson to provide an additional 300,000 American soldiers.[26]

The German attacks culminated in the Marne offensive on 15 July, which finally came to a halt on 6 August. The British Empire and French forces, with American support, launched a counter attack, the 'Hundred Days Offensive', from 8 August to 11 November. By early November, the German Army was exhausted and an armistice was not far off. On the morning of Monday 11 November, Cabinet assembled at Downing Street at 9.45 a.m. The minutes reveal that the Prime Minister spoke first. He 'announced that he had received a message from France stating that the armistice had been signed at 5 a.m. that morning, November 11, 1918, and that hostilities were to cease six hours later'. Cabinet agreed to take several steps, including an immediate announcement through the Press Bureau, and that the news should be celebrated by the 'firing of maroons, playing of bands, blowing of bugles, and ringing of Church bells throughout the Kingdom'.[27] With some 900,000 dead after four and a quarter years, the most deadly war in British history was at an end.

Hankey convened a celebratory party for his officials in the Cabinet Secretariat on 19 November, an event that had had to be delayed because he had been ill earlier. By the end of the war, he had acquired seventy-seven staff, with all the senior positions held by men: its forty-two women, almost all unmarried, held the secretarial and subordinate positions. He invested great trouble in writing his speech, which he recorded for posterity. He told his assembled staff about the highlights of their work together, including the convoy system, and their building up the office in the midst of war in very little time. The staff came in for high praise, not least for 'the late hours and the Sunday work. Very often I have asked you to sacrifice your leisure without almost a word of warning. I know that very often means inconvenience in your domestic arrangements.' He concluded: 'We can all feel that we have done our bit towards winning the war.' Already alert to the future, he told them how 'I think we can feel that we have built a tradition here which will live in history. We have created a system of government, which, though made specially for the war, I think cannot be without its effect on the permanent constitutional history of the country.'[28]

Colonel Dally Jones, a senior official, gave the speech in reply, which, carefully annotated by the speaker, can be found in the National Archives. It gives its own insight into Hankey and the way he worked:

> We have watched the extraordinary way in which you have applied yourself to any task which was set before you and which you have stuck to until you have seen that task accomplished. We have admired your immediate grasp of the situation, and your intelligent anticipation of events, and we have been inspired by your unflagging energy ... We do not deny it – [laughter] – but I can say this, that never, at any time, have we given you anything but the most ungrudging and willing co-operation – [Hear, Hear].[29]

Praise came too, much later, from A. J. Sylvester, Hankey's Private Secretary at the CID, who moved with him to the Cabinet Secretariat, and became Private Secretary to Lloyd George until his death in 1945. He wrote to Hankey's biographer Stephen Roskill in 1968, praising Hankey's

> machine-like efficiency and integrity. He had a most amazing memory, never spared himself and did not spare others. In his work he was ruthless,

had very little consideration; little if any humour, and little or no senti-
mentalism in his nature ... He was very abstemious, hated the limelight,
avoided most kinds of social engagements and distractions.

Edward Spears, the liaison officer between British and French forces in the
First World War (and indeed the Second), wrote of Hankey:

> I think it was Mr Asquith who described him as the cement that bound
> all Cabinets together, and it was true. Attending every meeting, where
> he took down everything in long-hand, prepared minutes and dealt with
> every conceivable matter with the industry of a continental housemaid,
> he was never ruffled, never out of temper, only a little in a hurry some-
> times, rushing off with a roll of the upper body, torso well forward, using
> his elbows as if he were pushing his way through a wood. His voice was
> musical, his sentences balanced. He has probably never said a foolish
> thing in his life, betrayed a secret, made a tactless remark or spoken out
> of turn. I have often thought that in the next world he will certainly be
> selected to help St Peter in his arduous duties. He will put difficult ques-
> tions so as to cause the minimum of embarrassment, and always he will
> be writing, in long-hand, in an enormous book.[30]

Such praise sets the bar high for Hankey's successors. Hankey was even
granted £25,000 from public funds in gratitude for his work during the
war, but when the war ended, there would be existential challenges to the
Cabinet Office and to Hankey's standing. He had, moreover, only had a
tenth of his time as Cabinet Secretary. His remaining twenty years would
prove far from straightforward. The Treasury and the Foreign Office were
the two great departments that viewed Hankey and his Secretariat with
suspicion, as did the Admiralty and War Office, and looked forward to
its submersion after the war. But Hankey had no intention of letting the
Cabinet Secretariat be disbanded once it was over. First up, it had to last at
least as long as the peace settlements at the conclusion of the war. Hankey
deftly achieved a more central role for the Cabinet Secretariat in the treaty
discussions that might have naturally gravitated to the Foreign Office.
Hankey had experienced his difficulties with the Prime Minister, but he

was unequivocal in his praise of Lloyd George as 'the man who won the war'.[31] Lloyd George, who held the fate of the Cabinet Secretariat in his hands, was equally complimentary about Hankey's conduct of the Paris Peace Conference at Versailles:

> The work of the conference would never have been accomplished at all had it not been for the accuracy, rapidity and extraordinary efficiency with which the Minutes and Decisions of the Council of Four [President Wilson, Lloyd George, French Prime Minister Clemenceau, and Italian Prime Minister Orlando] were recorded and circulated … You know what I think of your share in this Conference. Your work has been beyond the praise of words.[32]

But once the peace conferences were over, what would be the continued need for the Cabinet Secretariat?

MAURICE HANKEY, PHOTOGRAPHED IN 1917
BY WALTER STONEMAN

CHAPTER 3

Maurice Hankey and the Interwar Years, 1918–39

T HE CABINET SECRETARIAT played a vital part in helping to win the First World War, but it had also made enemies in White-hall. For several years, its continuation was far from assured. Many of the great Whitehall departments had been in existence for several generations, including the Treasury, Foreign Office and Home Office. Government had functioned perfectly well for all those years, it was said, without this new device that had the Prime Minister's constant ear. Why would it be needed in peacetime? The Treasury in particular was wary of its domestic influence, as was the Foreign Office of its role in foreign policy. Cabinet ministers of all parties disliked the way that it had effectively given the Prime Minister his own department, and argued that it breached longstanding traditions of collective responsibility, while Hankey's own role and hunger for influence inevitably incited more personal jealousy.

Hankey was quick to identify the dangers. He calculated that his own position, and the continuation of the Cabinet Secretariat in peacetime, would be dependent on Lloyd George's remaining in power. This realisation did not mean that his constant drip-drip of criticism of Lloyd George dwindled in his diary: only a month after war ended, Hankey wrote that he was trying to 'absorb too much into his hands. He seems to have a sort of lust for power: ignores his colleagues or tolerates them in an almost disdainful way.'[1] The general election on Saturday 14 December 1918 would decide Hankey's fate. The first for eight years, the first to be held on a single day, and the first in which women (over thirty) could vote, it might have killed off the Cabinet Secretariat had the result not been a landslide victory for Lloyd George's coalition government. Many Liberals and all of Bonar Law's Conservatives received a coupon letter indicating their endorsement by the government, differentiating them from Asquith's Liberals and Labour who did not support the government, hence the name 'the Coupon Election'. The coalition won 473 seats, of which the Conservatives, with 332 seats, were the largest single party, a fact that was to cause constant difficulties for Lloyd George.

Hankey's relationship with Lloyd George was far from straightforward. Jealousy of Lloyd George's relationship with his Deputy, Thomas ('T. J.') Jones, was part of the problem. Jones was much more of a Lib/Lab radical than the conservative-minded Hankey, and Lloyd George was clearly more at home with Jones, and in tune with his ideas too, as on Ireland. Lloyd George's idiosyncratic working methods unsettled the orderly Hankey. Lloyd George liked to work through his 'Committee of Ministers' rather than full Cabinet, which led him to worry whether its ad hoc decisions counted as Cabinet decisions involving collective responsibility or not. Lloyd George's style foreshadowed later Cabinet Secretary headaches in another way, too; his continuation of the 'Garden Suburb' under Philip Kerr, his Private Secretary, provided a rival source of advice to the Cabinet Secretariat, which Kerr showed tact and skill in handling. (Kerr had been Lloyd George's Private Secretary since 1916. As Lord Lothian, he went on to be British Ambassador in Washington from 1939 until his death in 1940.)

Hankey immediately set to work to firm up the Cabinet Secretariat by securing an understanding from the new Cabinet that it would remain a regularised part of a civilian government. Cabinet had other matters on its mind, but in November 1919, it approved a modus operandi drawn up by him:

Instructions to the Secretary of the Cabinet:
The Secretary will attend Meetings of the Cabinet to keep a record of the Cabinet proceedings. These will be confined to conclusions similar to

those circulated recently in connection with the War Cabinet discussions. In addition, a single copy of a fuller note will be kept by the Secretary in cases where the Cabinet explicitly desires it.

The Secretary is to circulate complete copies of the draft conclusions and final conclusions to the King, the Prime Minister and the Leader of the House of Lords. As soon as possible after each meeting he is to send copies of the draft Minutes for their remarks to the Ministers at the head of Departments which are particularly concerned in them whether for action or otherwise.

The Secretary is responsible for ensuring that copies of the final Conclusions of the Cabinet are forwarded to Ministers, whether Members of the Cabinet or not, whose Departments are affected by them. The Ministers are themselves responsible for communicating the conclusions to the Departments as necessary. Any member of the Cabinet has the right of access at any time to the Cabinet Minutes.

The Cabinet Secretariat will supply Secretaries for Cabinet Committees and such Conferences as the Prime Minister may from time to time summon for the discussion of questions referenced by the Cabinet or dealing with matters which could more conveniently be discussed in this manner than in the Cabinet itself. The records of Cabinet Committees and Conferences shall as a rule be kept on the same principles as are laid down for Cabinet Records.

Subject to any special instructions the Prime Minister or Chairman of the Committee may give in individual cases, the Secretary will circulate the minutes of the Cabinet Committee and Conferences to all Members of the Cabinet.

Subject to any instructions he may receive from the Prime Minister in regard to any particular Paper, the Secretary will circulate to all Members of the Cabinet all Memoranda and other docs prepared for the use of the Cabinet. Subject to reference to the Prime Minister in doubtful cases, the Secretary will use his discretion in circulating Cabinet Papers to Ministers outside the Cabinet and to the Permanent Secretaries* of Departments affected.

*In the case of the fighting Departments, the Chief of Staff may be substituted for the Permanent Secretary.[2]

By 1919–20 the Cabinet system had settled into a postwar rhythm. Cabinet met eighty-two times in 1920, usually in No. 10 and occasionally in the South Kensington home of Conservative leader, Andrew Bonar Law. Meetings tended to be chaired by Lloyd George, unless he was absent, in which case they were chaired by Bonar Law, as was the case for every meeting from 12 April to 19 May. Occasionally, meetings were held in the evening, but otherwise were held at 11.30 or noon.[3]

The circumstances of peacetime coalition gave Cabinet a different hue; Lloyd George had to keep his Conservative colleagues informed to ensure their cooperation. On occasion, it overruled Lloyd George, for example preventing him from granting recognition to the Soviet Union. Conservative grandees did not have it all their own way either: Cabinet decided against Lord Curzon's argument that the British try to retain possession of Constantinople, instead deciding that it should be returned to Turkey in the Treaty of Sèvres. The episode confirms that Cabinet was still *the* major decision-making body in Whitehall.[4]

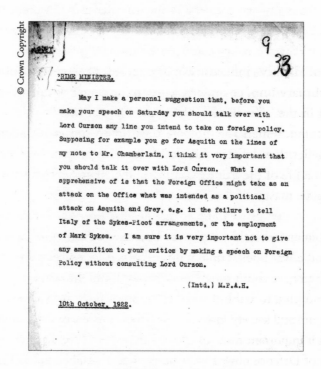

Note to Lloyd George from Hankey

A significant difference from pre-war government, however, was the growth of Cabinet Committees. In 1900, there had been only one: the Defence Committee. By 1920, several standing committees had come into being, including the Home Affairs Committee. These committees tended to take small or uncontroversial decisions on behalf of the government, freeing up time in full Cabinet. For some Cabinet ministers, however, the Cabinet Committees were in danger of being too powerful, with Austen Chamberlain describing the Home Affairs Committee as 'almost a Cabinet within a Cabinet!'[5] Furthermore, ad hoc committees, such as the committee for policy towards Ireland, were created to focus on specific topics.[6] The Cabinet Committee system would grow further in the twenty years that followed, with a Foreign Policy Committee, established by Austen Chamberlain's half-brother Neville. But the twentieth-century system of Cabinet government and committees run by the Cabinet Office had been largely sketched out by 1921.

HANKEY'S WIDE REACH, 1919–22

The extent of Hankey's influence can be seen in a memo he wrote to Thomas Jones in February 1919, envisaging a central role for the Cabinet Secretary as outlined in the 'War Book', which already planned for the next world war. The memo, remarkable not the least for its musical analogy, reveals Hankey's belief that defence, his great area of expertise, would always be central to the life of the Prime Minister. Hence his desire for the Cabinet Secretary to be master of the War Book.

> … My opinion is that the time has now come when we ought to get a move on about the War Book. I do not make this suggestion because I think we are going to have another war. God forbid! But unless the Departments have something to work to they will not go into their records properly. The musical society must always have a concert in sight. Moreover, I think it is important from another point of view. I feel sure that the real Minister of Defence must always be the Prime Minister of the day, and that it is very important that the Prime Minister should keep under his

own hand, and in his own Office, the co-ordination of defence matters. I doubt if we have yet come to the time when we ought to re-establish the Committee of Imperial Defence. It seems to me that while the Peace Conference is sitting no real progress can be made in the great questions of defence policy, and if the League of Nations becomes a reality, it will have a paramount influence on these questions. Nevertheless, I think we ought to keep the idea of the CID alive, and I have always felt that the Department that has the War Book has the key of the whole defence organisation in its hands.[7]

Hankey's continuing importance in peacetime can be observed in a long paper, 'Towards a National Policy', he sent Lloyd George in July 1919. Its rationale, he explained, was that he had prepared periodic overviews during the war, and that the 'very heavy problem of reconstruction that now confronts the government' demanded similar treatment. The document reveals Hankey moving far beyond the position of a civil servant into direct policy advice. The rationale for him doing this in the war, when he had exercised greater influence than many ministers or senior service chiefs, was that party politics was in abeyance. Hankey was moving beyond deference: rather than presenting a range of options for the Prime Minister to decide between, he was offering his own views. The document opened by outlining the severe problems that postwar Britain faced, railing against the 'profligate waste of effort which the War proved to exist in so many branches of our national life', and recommending the rapid adoption of 'mechanical methods … in agriculture, industry, coal production, transportation or dock labour'. He recommended 'every effort [must be] made to improve the physique of the nation, to bring up healthy children and to educate them, thus avoiding expenditure on the maintenance of inefficients [sic] and weaklings'.

Hankey was sceptical whether the new League of Nations could be relied upon to achieve its objective of securing peace in the postwar world. Italy was a worry, which 'seem[ed] to be playing a waiting game' while the 'principal threat to the peace of Europe' lay in the 'exploitation by Germany of the resources of Russia'. Further afield, he foresaw Japan as a potential danger, if not an immediate one.[8] War with the United States he considered a possibility, concluding, though, that it would be impossible to prevail against them, and thus 'war is almost unthinkable', despite some significant differences of opinion, including the US's 'antagonism to the British Empire' and disagreements on settling the 'Irish question'. The continued supremacy of the British Navy, under increasing challenge, was a major worry for him. He wrote, with unintentional double entendre: '[O]ur fleet should not be allowed to sink below the level of the United States' fleet.'[9]

Hankey's high-profile and utterly seminl role at the Paris Peace talks at Versailles on the future of Germany caused some upset in Whitehall, as did his closeness to Lloyd George. His role in the Austrian peace treaty at Saint-Germain in 1919, and at San Remo in April 1920, where the League of Nations mandate for Palestine was assigned to Britain, similarly ruffled feathers. The extent of Hankey's personal involvement in the talks can be seen in this letter to Helen Bakewell, his wife, from Paris in April 1919, with its pro-Italian (he was close to his Italian opposite number) and anti-US and anti-League of Nation sentiments:

> ... It has been a shocking week ... The pressure on a secretary, working single-handed, of two meetings a day, is simply incredible ... President Wilson, with his wretched, hypothetical Fourteen Points, has already alienated the Italians, and is now about to alienate the Japs. I don't mind his alienating them from the League of Nations, but I do mind his driving a wedge between them and us...[10]

Hankey's expertise on naval matters was responsible for his posting to Washington DC for three months, from November 1921 to February 1922, to support Balfour's British negotiating team during discussions over the Washington Naval Treaty. The conference was attended by the British Empire, the USA, Japan, France, Italy and China, and aimed to limit naval armaments.[11] Shortly after arriving, Hankey set about embedding his bureaucratic system, in the offshoot set up in the US, proffering advice to the 'inexperienced' secretariat, commenting in a letter to his wife: 'I want to help them. When they are more efficient I shall drop this [tactic].'[12] He found time to tell Lloyd George about a meeting with ex-President Woodrow Wilson, a morose figure, who had been afflicted by a stroke, and who was scornful that his countrymen had rejected his dream:

... I think you may be interested that I saw Mr Woodrow Wilson yesterday ... I was rather shocked at his appearance, which somehow reminded me of a waxwork. Obviously he is paralysed on one side ... [Though] [h]is mind was active and his memory fresh. He is extraordinarily bitter against his opponents, and said he was ashamed of his fellow-countrymen for throwing over the League. I ... begged him to take the long view and to believe that he had laid the foundations on which some great scheme for world peace would be built; but he reverted almost at once to his bitter scorn for his opponents.[13]

While in Washington, Hankey was plagued by insecurities about his relationship with his Prime Minister. He was wont to believe that Lloyd George had only sent him to Washington because he preferred to work with 'T. J.' Jones, preferring to have a companionable Welsh speaker on hand while he negotiated the Irish peace treaty.[14] The delicate negotiations with the Irish were being conducted in parallel at the end of 1921. 'As secretary to the British delegation in the negotiations between October and December 1921, [Jones] could converse with Lloyd George in Welsh both to maintain secrecy and to impress Sinn Féin. He also acted as a vital go-between between Lloyd George and the Irish leaders,' wrote historian Rodney Lowe.[15] Throughout, Jones, mindful of his subordinate position to Hankey, took pains to send him messages in Washington to keep him abreast of progress on the talks. They culminated in the Anglo-Irish Treaty signed in No. 10 in December 1921, creating an Irish Free State within the British Empire, with Ulster remaining in the United Kingdom.[16]

Hankey was not sanguine about the prospects of peace: 'The Irish, like the poor, are always with us,' he wrote.[17] Irish affairs were about to become central to Hankey's life. On 22 June 1922, the former Chief of the Imperial General Staff Henry Wilson (1918–22) was gunned down by two members of the IRA outside the soldier's home in London. 'No one can tell what the political effect will be,' wrote Hankey to his wife. 'It might mean a stampede of Unionists against the Coalition, but personally I am convinced it will not, unless followed by other murders. It is a great thing that the assassins were captured, and a great credit to the courage of the police who [were] unarmed...'[18]

That same month, Irish rebels, opposed to the peace treaty because they saw it as betrayal of the idea of an Irish republic (the treaty left Ireland within the British Empire), seized the Four Courts building in Dublin. Lloyd George believed that those who had organised Wilson's assassination were hiding among the rebels, and was frustrated by what he saw as the new Irish government's lethargy in tracking them down. Near the end of June, an order to attack the Four Courts was sent from Lloyd George and Churchill (Secretary for the Colonies, 1921–22) to British soldiers still stationed in Dublin. The British commander prevaricated – a wise move given that the jurisdiction was now that of the Irish Free State, and British intervention might have escalated the Irish Civil War. Within days, the Irish Army itself crushed the rising. When Lloyd George's government collapsed four months later, Churchill's secretary phoned Hankey to ask him to burn the draft proclamation intended to be issued to the British troops. Hankey resisted and handed it over to the Secretary of the Ireland Committee.[19]

CABINET OFFICE UNDER ATTACK, 1919–22

The Foreign Office was stirring. Under their noses, the Cabinet Secretariat had established itself as the provider of core staff and advice for the postwar international conferences. Worse, as an official document put it, it had become 'the channel of communication between the British Government and the League of Nations'.[20] Foreign Secretary Lord Curzon (1919–24), a friend of the War Secretariat in the war, was becoming aggravated, as were his senior diplomats. They feared Lloyd George was usurping the role of the Foreign Secretary, with the Cabinet Office becoming his diplomatic corps. Hankey, fully aware of the sensitivities involved, and the dangers it presented him, tried on several occasions to make Lloyd George aware of them too. In October 1922, he wrote to him: '[B]efore you make your speech on Saturday you should talk over with Lord Curzon any line you intend to take on foreign policy … I am sure it is very important not to give any ammunition to your critics by making a speech on foreign policy without consulting Lord Curzon.'[21]

His intervention was insufficient to prevent Curzon that same month from drafting yet another protest, a letter of complaint to Lloyd George: 'There has grown up a system under which there are in reality two Foreign Offices: the one for which I am for the time being responsible, and the other at No. 10.'[22] Other Foreign Secretaries over the following 100 years would recognise his sentiment. Before the letter could be sent, however, Lloyd George had fallen from power.

Hankey and the Cabinet Secretariat had a weightier critic in the form of the Treasury. For its first four years in existence from 1916, the Cabinet Secretariat had in fact been a sub-department of the Treasury. In 1920, however, Hankey, with Lloyd George's backing, had managed to secure its status as a department in its own right, breaking it away from the Treasury, a move of great symbolic importance. Earlier that year, the Treasury had been arguing for 'restoring the normal practice under which the financial aspects of questions of policy involving expenditure are discussed with the Treasury by the Departments concerned before being brought before the Cabinet'.[23] Chancellor of the Exchequer Austen Chamberlain (1919–21), a Conservative like Curzon, was one of those most agitated. He had earlier served as Chancellor for two years under Balfour (1903–05) and had strong views on the commanding role of the Treasury. In July 1920, a terse letter was received in the Cabinet Office stating 'Mr Chamberlain's view is that, if Treasury control is to be effectively exercised in the manner laid down by the Cabinet, the Treasury should have an opportunity of expressing its views before and not after the circulation of a paper.'[24] Chamberlain had Hankey in his sights. In November, he wrote to complain that his minutes 'are not complete and hardly do justice to what I consider the serious elements in the situation' that he was trying to convey. He added: 'Under the circumstances I should have preferred that my views should have been expressed as nearly as possible in my own language.'[25]

The Cabinet Secretariat was under attack from many sides, not least as a way of Conservative ministers undermining Lloyd George, whose creature the Cabinet Secretariat so definitely was. It was not only Conservatives who were hostile: a principal critic was Asquith, no less, who abhorred the 'big government' approach that the Cabinet Secretariat exemplified. In a speech in the Commons in June 1922, the former Prime Minister said:

I am perfectly certain, if I may venture to say so – for I have not had experience of the new system – that Mr Gladstone and Lord Beaconsfield [i.e. Disraeli] would have shuddered in their graves at the thought of an outsider being present [at Cabinet] – and taking notes of what was going on. They would have considered it a breach of the fundamental practice of the Constitution.[26]

It was left to Austen Chamberlain to provide a defence, arguing that critics have

a misconception of what the duties of the Cabinet Secretariat are. Its duties are to receive from ministers or departments notification of questions on which Cabinet decisions are required; to see that the papers which the Cabinet has to have before it, before it takes those decisions, are properly presented; to record so much of the discussions as from time to time they may be directed to record; to take note of the decisions, and to communicate them to those who have to execute them. But they are not themselves authorized to take the initiative in any matter of legislation, or in any matter of executive action.[27]

Chamberlain was of course defending a very limited notion of the Secretariat's work. The problem was precisely that Hankey was going way beyond mere secretarial and administrative duties, and was taking the initiative in abundance.

The Times now joined the attacks. It launched a vehement onslaught in an article entitled 'The Secretariat', arguing: 'The truth, as all Downing Street knows, is that the country has a peace time Government conducted in accordance with the arbitrary principles accepted as an emergency measure at the crisis of the war … The all-important Secretariat remains with its powers unimpaired.' It continued that '[t]he Secretariat is in fact a new department of the Prime Minister, strengthening the central power and derogating from the old constitutional principle of the collective responsibility of the Cabinet'. The Secretariat, it said, had become 'the devoted slave of Downing Street'. The body had 'clearly upset the balance of the Constitution and given the Cabinet a sense of irresponsibility which it had not enjoyed for a century'.[28] This was very serious stuff.

A debate in the House of Commons in mid-June 1922 gave critics and friends the opportunity to air their views. *The Times* returned to their attack: 'Of all the many constitutional changes which were made during the war and carried on into peace-time, none is more insidious and unjustifiable than the Cabinet Secretariat … The Cabinet got on quite well for two centuries without a staff to perform "secretarial duties."' Pitt the Elder, it argued 'did not need a Cabinet Secretariat to found a Colonial Empire, or Pitt [the Younger] to withstand Napoleon, Disraeli needed no such thing to negotiate at the Congress of Berlin, nor Gladstone to guide the country through his four periods as Prime Minister'.[29] Lord Northcliffe, the owner of the *Daily Mail* and the *Daily Mirror*, was behind the opposition to the Cabinet Secretariat. The *Mail* argued that 'Sir Maurice Hankey's share in the direction of the country has been distinctly unconstitutional'.[30] The strength of the attacks struck home, even if they were directed as much at Lloyd George's bloated staff in No. 10, notably the 'Garden Suburb', and weakened an already vulnerable Prime Minister.

Lloyd George was under fire on many fronts: for the trade agreement with the Soviet Union in March 1921, which struck many as appeasing the Bolsheviks; for the granting of independence to southern Ireland; for the economic downturn from 1921; and for corruption over the selling of honours. Divisions with the Conservatives during the Chanak Crisis with Turkey in September 1922 provided a catalyst for a dramatic development: Chamberlain summoned a meeting of Conservative MPs at the Carlton Club in London's St James's Street, where the majority of those present voted to fight the forthcoming general election as an independent party, not as a coalition one. On 19 October 1922, Lloyd George resigned. The coalition was over. Suddenly, Hankey's position looked very precarious.[31]

Bonar Law and the Survival of the Cabinet Office, 1922–24

Two days after Lloyd George's resignation and the succession of Andrew Bonar Law (1922–23), Hankey arrived in the Cabinet Secretariat on Saturday morning, 21 October. He was horrified by what he saw:

When I arrived in the office I found that the usual batch of Foreign Office telegrams had not arrived. This looked ominous, as I had read in the newspaper that Lord Curzon had been seeing Bonar Law, and it rather looked as though this was a sign that the insistent and much repeated newspaper stories were true and that they had decided to scrap the Cabinet Secretariat.[32]

Hankey decided to act quickly. He asked his secretary to ring the Foreign Office (officials worked on Saturday mornings then) and to speak to Eyre Crowe, the Permanent Secretary. Crowe was unapologetic in his reply that he had given instructions that the distribution of Foreign Office telegrams to the Cabinet Secretariat would cease. Hankey saw no alternative but to walk over to the Foreign Office himself, where he set about trying to win Crowe over. He told him that the Cabinet Secretariat in the future would no longer be involved with international conferences, and blamed Lloyd George and Foreign Secretary Balfour for insisting that he participate in them, which his biographer Stephen Roskill observes was a 'half-truth'.[33] He nevertheless left the Foreign Office believing he had reached an understanding with Crowe.

At noon, Hankey went to 24 Onslow Gardens in South Kensington, where the new Prime Minister Bonar Law was residing. 'I feel as though I were going from a doctor's waiting room to his consulting room to know my fate,' he confided to the others in the Prime Minister's anteroom. When Hankey eventually saw Bonar Law, he looked 'flushed ... he had not slept' and brushed aside Hankey's offer of congratulations.[34]

Then he asked me point blank if I was prepared to serve him as loyally as I had served Lloyd George. I replied that, if he wanted me, I would serve him as loyally as I had served Asquith and Lloyd George and that the latter was quite prepared that I should do so.[35]

T. J. Jones recorded the sorry scene in his diary for Saturday 21 October: 'No work at the office. All concerned with its fate in view of the persistent attacks upon it in the press and the confounding of it with the "Garden Suburb".'[36]

Bonar Law was suitably impressed by Hankey's expressions of loyalty: 'That is the answer I had expected ... and you can help me at once because your experience in these matters is unique.'[37] Bonar Law knew full well that no other figure in Whitehall had the grasp across the Prime Minister's territory, a job that had expanded considerably in scope from its pre-war role. Whitehall had several experienced and commanding Permanent Secretaries, notably Warren Fisher at the Treasury, John Anderson at the Home Office and Eyre Crowe at the Foreign Office. But these senior mandarins saw themselves as primarily leaders of their own departments: they lacked cross-Whitehall knowledge or savvy.

Bonar Law asked Hankey's advice on the ministerial jobs he needed to fill before Parliament was dismissed on the following Wednesday, and for Hankey's thoughts on economies to reduce Cabinet Secretariat costs, a criticism that particularly concerned him. Hankey could barely conceal his delight: 'I said that I would work out plans for this, if he would decide the broad lines, and I could suggest the lines to him in three minutes.'[38] Hankey had already mentally estimated how to halve the cost of the Cabinet Secretariat from £37,000 per annum to £15–16,000 a year. Upon hearing this response, Bonar Law declared that the Secretariat could continue to operate. 'I think I have saved the ship by chucking much ballast overboard,' Hankey wrote the following day.[39]

Hankey, however, had not reckoned on the formidable Warren Fisher, who combined being Permanent Secretary of the Treasury with headship of the HCS (1919–39). On Wednesday 25 October, he and Fisher met on Bonar Law's doorstep. To Bonar Law's discomfort, Fisher laid into Hankey: 'I had understood that the Cabinet Office was to revert to its previous status under the War Cabinet system, when it appeared on the general vote of the Treasury in precisely the same manner as the Committee of Imperial Defence.' Fisher was plain, the Cabinet Office must revert to being a branch of the Treasury.[40] As for Hankey personally, Fisher did not want him to leave the scene entirely, but thought he should become one of several 'Controllers' at the Treasury, i.e. one of his subordinate officials. An embarrassed Bonar Law, preoccupied with other pressing matters that Saturday morning, left it to his senior staff to thrash out an agreement, promising to 'make some announcement on the subject' in a speech the following day, when he was to speak in Glasgow, in preparation for the general election due on 15 November.[41] Hankey left the meeting somewhat reassured. But more powerful forces were operating on the new Prime Minister than were apparent to Hankey. As Jones wrote in his diary, Bonar Law's Glasgow speech 'pronounced the doom of the Secretariat'. Jones himself was surprised. Hankey had not, it seemed to him, accurately communicated the conversations he had been having. Jones records the Prime Minister's words in Scotland:

NO CABINET SECRETARIAT. BUT A RECORD OF DECISIONS TO BE KEPT ... We have decided to bring the Cabinet Secretariat in its present form to an end (cheers). That does not mean that everything connected with it has got to go ... We must have an agenda at our meetings, and we must have a definite record of decisions ... But there is no need of the big body which was necessary during the war and immediately after it, but which can come to an end now. I am convinced the work can be done ... far more economically by having the Cabinet secretary ... treated as part of the Treasury.[42]

Fisher had carried the day, as well he might as the senior official in Whitehall bent on Treasury denomination, and with considerable mandarin, ministerial and press support on his side. Central to Fisher's argument was that His Majesty's Treasury was not like finance ministries in other countries. Rather, in its position uniquely under the Prime Minister, as First Lord of the Treasury, it is 'the central and co-ordinating organ of government. As such it is the natural body to provide for the secretarial needs of the Cabinet.'[43] Hankey and Fisher met once more that weekend, but again reached no agreement: 'We each held our ground tenaciously for a very long time.'[44]

Hankey was desolated about Bonar Law's public promise to bring the Cabinet Secretariat 'in its present form to an end', and his exalting of the Treasury as 'the central Department of Government'.[45] He had been outmanoeuvred by the Whitehall old guard who had got to the new Prime Minister and alerted him to the dangers of the highly irregular peacetime modus operandi of Lloyd George at No. 10. Hankey confided to his friend and ally Balfour on 26 October that he would resign as Cabinet Secretary rather than accept Fisher's plan to absorb the Cabinet Secretariat into the Treasury and curb his powers.[46]

Friday 27 October was a bleak day for Hankey. He gathered his staff together and read out a copy of Bonar Law's speech. He concluded by thanking them for all their support over the years. As he wrote, 'during the morning I found all my colleagues very depressed, and much incensed against Bonar Law'.[47] Hankey went to see the Prime Minister on 29 October to present his letter of resignation. Bonar Law realised he had pushed Hankey too far and began to backtrack when confronted with losing him. Did Hankey use his stated resignation as a ploy? He certainly believed that his grasp of the Whitehall machine might prove too great for Bonar Law to risk losing it. The Prime Minister held Hankey's letter in his hand for what seemed a long time. 'He read it, asked a few questions' and then said he was being too sensitive. To Hankey's delight, he proceeded to make a number of suggestions to try to unblock the impasse. He would make a statement in Parliament refuting the accusations that the Cabinet Office had encroached on foreign policy, that it was overstaffed and extravagant in operation, and that it had been lobbying the press. Most sweet to Hankey's ears of all, though, was the promise that the Secretariat would not be 'swallowed by' the Treasury, and that Hankey would continue to be in command of his own team.[48] Hankey could barely believe what he was hearing. 'The Treasury began by trying to swallow us from the head. The mouthful was too big,' he recorded wryly. But, he continued, with some prescience, that 'now they will try and swallow us from the tail'.[49]

The crisis was not over. While Hankey was content with the Cabinet Secretariat coming back within the jurisdiction of the Treasury, where he believed he would be able to control it, the Foreign Office was not. On 8 November, Curzon launched an open attack, railing against the 'too powerful and too numerous Cabinet Secretariat'. Hankey was livid at the injustice of the words, as he saw it, and by the lack of warning. He stormed over to the Foreign Office the next day for a terse meeting that left the Foreign Secretary, in Hankey's own words, 'frightfully upset'. Hankey was pleased to receive a letter of apology from Curzon.[50] Even allowing for a degree of self-aggrandising in Hankey's account, for a Cabinet Secretary to take on and emerge victorious from a head to head with a Foreign Secretary, particularly one who had been Viceroy of India, marks a significant coming of age of the still-new job.

Within days, Hankey was proving himself indispensable to the new Prime Minister. Proximity was vital as ever, as was Hankey's silky ability to insinuate himself into the trust of Prime Ministers. Within no time, Bonar Law was asking Hankey to amend a 'shocking [*sic*] bad draft' of military instructions prepared by the Earl of Cavan, Wilson's successor as Chief of Imperial General Staff, for a military crisis. At the end of November, Bonar Law was asking Hankey, rather than the Foreign Office, for assistance with a conference on war reparations due to take place at No. 10. This was the occasion on which Italian leader Benito Mussolini visited, and the only time that any of the interwar dictators entered No. 10: neither Hitler nor Franco did. Hankey's spirits had recovered astonishingly quickly. Overjoyed that the status quo in Whitehall had been restored, he recorded gleefully: 'I attend all meetings of the Cabinet and keep the Minutes exactly as before.'[51]

Despite some continuing talk of 'Cabinet Committees' and 'Conferences of Ministers' being unconstitutional, the crisis had passed, and Hankey was able to write: 'My relations with Bonar Law are almost the same as my relations were with Lloyd George.' He added that 'force of circumstances has forced the new Government to adopt this method of transacting its business'.[52] In May 1923, Bonar Law was ordered by doctors to go abroad for rest; for the previous few weeks he had barely been able to speak in the Commons because of the pain in his throat. Beaverbrook went to see his old friend at the Hôtel de Crillon in Paris, where Bonar Law's doctor, who had travelled over to see him, had diagnosed cancer of the throat. The two men decided not to tell Bonar Law the grave nature of his affliction, but advised him that it would be best to retire from politics immediately. He was succeeded on 23 May by Chancellor of the Exchequer Stanley Baldwin. Bonar Law's departure was bad news for Hankey, though it took him a long time to realise it. Baldwin was to dominate the interwar years, yet he had other close allies, and Hankey never bonded with him as he had with Lloyd George and Bonar Law.

The final moment in the story of the postwar survival of the Cabinet Secretariat came with Britain's first Labour government in January 1924. This came because the Conservatives had fought the December 1923 election on tariff reform and had lost eighty-six seats, leaving Baldwin, after a vote of no confidence, no longer able to stay in power because, when combined, Labour and the Liberals, who both supported free trade, outnumbered him. As Labour had thirty-three seats more than the Liberals, though fewer than the Conservatives, they formed the subsequent government. Widespread apprehension gripped the nation about what a socialist government might do, and how they might sweep away the traditional bastions of the British state. Hankey had no personal cause for alarm. Incoming Prime Minister Ramsay MacDonald (January–November 1924, 1929–35) made it clear from the outset that he did not wish for change in the operation of Cabinet. Minutes of his first meeting, held at No. 10 on Wednesday 23 January 1924, show evergreen Hankey very much in evidence. MacDonald opened the meeting by asking his ministers 'to make every effort to secure punctuality in regard to Meetings of the Cabinet'. After this, the Cabinet agreed to 'adopt the principle of a Cabinet Secretary', and that the Secretariat should continue in the same way that it had under Lloyd George, Bonar Law and Baldwin.[53]

Ever the deft courtier, Hankey had taken stock of the needs and insecurities of the incoming Prime Minister, including his material requirements. MacDonald, from a humble background in Lossiemouth, Scotland, lacked the means of earlier Prime Ministers to provision Downing Street domestically, dispatching his daughter Ishbel to the post-Christmas sales in Oxford Street to acquire cutlery and crockery. Hankey spied an opportunity. He invited MacDonald, who had no plans for dinner on his first evening as Prime Minister, to join him at the United Services Club for champagne 'to celebrate the occasion'.[54]

A moment of tension between MacDonald and the Cabinet Secretariat occurred in the summer of 1924 due to the so-called Campbell case. This concerned an article in the 25 July edition of the Communist *Workers' Weekly* newspaper calling on British soldiers to resist any orders to go to war or suppress their 'fellow workers', and instead fight against the 'exploiters and capitalists'. The Attorney General, Patrick Hastings, announced his intention to prosecute the editor of the publication, John Campbell, under the 1795 Incitement to Mutiny Act. Such a course of action was against the wishes of many Labour backbenchers, leading to a quickly convened Cabinet meeting on 6 August in the Prime Minister's Office in the House of Commons and a decision to drop the charges. After these shambolic proceedings, Parliament passed a vote of no confidence against MacDonald leading to his asking George V to dissolve Parliament and trigger a general election.[55]

The exact events of the Cabinet meeting of 6 August were disputed. MacDonald himself later told the House of Commons that he left the matter to 'the discretion of the law officers', but the very fact of a Cabinet meeting seemed to suggest otherwise.[56] Thomas Jones, who had stood in for Hankey at the 6 August meeting, wrote that 'a shiver went down my spine' when he heard MacDonald's words and Hankey himself wrote that MacDonald's statement was 'a bloody lie'.[57]

MacDonald himself challenged the conclusions to the Cabinet minutes. The minutes stated that the Attorney General took responsibility for his previous steps, and that the case could be dropped 'if Cabinet so desired', and that Cabinet agreed that 'in the particular case under review the course indicated by the Attorney-General should be adopted'.[58] Hankey wrote a covering letter making the Prime Minister's concerns clear.[59] The Labour government was defeated in the November election, and MacDonald resigned. Hankey was away on a mission to his beloved Italy when the government fell, and was wrong-footed by the news. Jones took minutes and recalled its final hours:

The Labour Government met at 10:30. Hankey had not returned from Venice, so I took it. There was pretty widespread expectation outside that the Cabinet might decide to resign at this Meeting, and I believe that was the intention of the Prime Minister. There was a slight difficulty owing to the King being at Sandringham, but we knew that the King would readily come up to town if required, and there was no reason why the PM should not go down and resign at Sandringham. All the members were present except Webb and Wheatley, who were detained in their constituencies, and Jowett (Office of Works) who had been defeated. I entered the Cabinet Room a few minutes before 10:30, and a minute or two later the Prime Minister came in. There was no demonstration of any kind. He was dressed in a dark suit, with a dark tie, looked pale and serious, and entered as if not certain what his reception was going to be.

One gathered a general impression of everyone trying to maintain a cheerful countenance and determined to say nothing unpleasant about anybody or anything.[60]

THE CONSERVATIVE GOVERNMENT, 1924–29

Hankey and the Cabinet Office, as it was increasingly being called, emerged with its position strengthened from the short-lived first Labour government. It had now proved its ability to serve loyally, in impartial Civil Service tradition, a Liberal-led coalition under Lloyd George, a Conservative government under Bonar Law, and a Labour government under MacDonald. By the end of 1924, the Conservatives were back in power under Baldwin.

The General Strike of May 1926 was to prove the most difficult episode the Conservative government confronted over its five years in power. Hankey's voice was one of calm moderation, in stark contrast to Chancellor of the Exchequer Churchill, who favoured a much more hardline policy against those on strike. Hankey's minutes of Cabinet from 5 May 1926 record that instructions had been given for horseracing to be stopped, though '[t]here was a general agreement that cricket should not be'.[61] Two days later, Cabinet met again to set out the exact measures required to combat the strike. Hankey's minutes recount

regular troops should only be used in the last resort, and should, as far as possible, be kept away from the disturbed areas until the moment for their use had arrived ... That the first line on whom fell the responsibility for providing protection was the regular Police and that the Home Secretary should have authority to augment them by recruiting Special Constables on the present lines up to the largest scale deemed practicable and necessary.

The Secretary for War would have the authority to issue instructions for military officers to use '"tear" gas in any case where a situation became so serious as to involve the alternative between that course and the use of firearms'.[62]

Hankey had gained the confidence of three Prime Ministers, but how would he succeed with Baldwin over the five years from 1924–29? Baldwin certainly found the Cabinet Office indispensable, and valued its work bringing order and cohesion to the dispatch of government business. He valued Hankey's judgement, and his command of the detail, but they did not become close personally. Hankey struggled to establish a close personal relationship with him. Personality played a part: the personal chemistry between Baldwin and Thomas Jones was simply much stronger. Politics, too, mattered. Hankey was no more sympathetic to the trade unions than he was to Labour. Jones, in contrast, was a conciliator, which chimed far better with Baldwin's own instincts. Union issues dominated the government's work, and Baldwin became intensely reliant upon the advice of Horace Wilson, Permanent Secretary at the Ministry of Labour.

Baldwin kept his opinions of others closely guarded, so we will never know what he truly thought of Hankey. It is a matter of record, though, that Thomas Jones became Baldwin's ally and periodic speechwriter, supplanting much of the confidential adviser role that Hankey had sought, to his chagrin.[63] After Jones's retirement in 1930, he became the first Secretary of the Pilgrim Trust, of which Baldwin was the chairman.[64]

Denied the *consiglieri* role he so enjoyed, working as the closet adviser to the Prime Minister, Hankey sought to busy himself in other areas, entrenching the position of Cabinet Office whenever he could. In May 1923, he became Clerk to the Privy Council, which he enjoyed, and which was a major position at the time: he continued in office until July 1938, and was the only Cabinet Secretary to serve as Clerk. The 1920s saw the Dominion governments in Australia and Canada send officials to London to learn about the Cabinet Office, and assist them in creating their own.[65] From Canada, Prime Minister Mackenzie King dispatched Burgon Bickersteth in 1927, while Australian Prime Minister Stanley Bruce sent Richard Casey. Hankey started a trend. Dominion and Commonwealth affairs would continue as a core preoccupation of subsequent Cabinet Secretaries, even after the Commonwealth Secretariat was set up in 1965.

The vetting of retired ministers' autobiographies was another long-standing aspect of the Cabinet Secretary's role that would emerge during the interwar years, as part of their responsibility for propriety and ethics.

Hankey thus had to read over the memoirs of his first boss, Lloyd George, during the 1930s to ensure that nothing was published that might damage the state,[66] the first time the Cabinet Secretary had been active in this arena. Lloyd George had been active in politics after he fell from power in 1922, and may possibly have joined the National Government in 1931 if he had been well. There were fears that his need for money might lead to indiscretion in his memoirs: his war memoirs were published in six volumes from 1933, the year Hitler came to power. His subsequent pro-Hitler comments after their meeting in Germany in 1936 were an embarrassment: 'Germany does not want war. Hitler does not want war. He is a most remarkable personality, one of the greatest I have ever met in the whole of my life, and I have met some very great men.'[67] Hankey helped Lloyd George gain access to secret government papers, but also vetted what he wrote, sending chapters to the relevant Whitehall departments to be checked. He deleted passages he viewed as damaging, but did not succeed in achieving balance and preventing the memoirs being self-aggrandising.[68]

The Historical Section was another area that took Hankey's time. Its creation predated the Cabinet Secretariat, though not the CID, set up in 1915 to oversee the writing of the history of the war. Historian Andrew Green describes the purpose of this novel addition to Cabinet Office work as threefold: to provide a popular and authoritative account for the general reader; for professional reference and general education; and to provide, in Hankey's sardonic words, 'an antidote to the usual unofficial histories which besides being generally inaccurate, habitually attribute all naval and military failures to the ineptitude of the government'.[69]

The interwar years saw the bulk of volumes of the *Official History of the First World War* published. Overseen by the Cabinet Office, the activity had Hankey's full support, though, as is the tendency with official histories, what seemed like a good idea at genesis can look less happy when the costs and disruption escalate. Hankey's response, when told of their poor sales, was that 'the histories need no defence. They were essentially educational',[70] and that the Office of the Official Histories worked thriftily; the French and German official history offices both employed about 130 people – by contrast, the British operation consisted of one editor, five administrative staff and eight writers.[71] Focusing on the Western Front and subsidiary operations, the bulk of the British volumes were published between 1920 and 1948.

The 1931 Financial Crisis

Following the election of the second Labour government on 30 May 1929, Hankey lost no time in getting back on terms with MacDonald. His appointment diary from the week beginning Monday 3 June showed no less than six meetings with the new Prime Minister during Labour's first full week in power.[72] His diary is peppered with criticisms of MacDonald and his government for a lack of clarity in their objectives, and for its handling of the economy. But he did his best to serve the Cabinet and Prime Minister during the two difficult years. The collapse of the Labour government in August 1931 provided a fresh crisis for Hankey. He was on holiday in La Grave in Dauphine in the French Alps when it occurred. He rushed home, but not before the critical decisions had already been taken, and a National Government was established. Nevertheless, as he recorded in characteristic style, 'everyone from the King and the Prime Minister downwards seemed very glad to see me'. Indeed, more than glad: '[W]hen I saw the King, to coach him before the swearing-in Council, he said: "Thank God you are back."'[73]

Hankey was summoned to No. 10 that evening. One of his first tasks was to draft a manifesto for the three party leaders who had agreed to form the National Government: MacDonald, Baldwin and Herbert Samuel for the Liberal Party.

> Each gave me a written contribution. It was to be ready for their consideration at 8:30 [one hour later]. It was an awkward thing to draft. It was impossible to say, as they wanted to say, that the intention of the new Cabinet was 'so and so' … For the new Cabinet was not formed, much less sworn, and technically the old Ministers were in office until the new ones were sworn. However, I did it and got it vetted by Graham-Harrison (Parliamentary Counsel, whom I dragged away from his dinner) before submitting it. They modified, but approved my draft, which was issued that night.[74]

Hankey's original draft of the agreement survives:

> The specific object for which the new government is being formed, is to deal with the national emergency that now exists. It will not be a Coalition Government in the usual accepted sense of the term, but a Government of co-operation for this one purpose. When that purpose is achieved the political parties will resume their respective positions.[75]

The National Government chose to trigger a general election for October 1931. The Conservatives won back many seats, consolidating their hold over the National Government. This was also to be the first election that Hankey voted in since the war, and he had done so at the insistence of the King. He had told George V before election day that 'I have rather made a point of not voting … I like to keep a very detached point of view.' The King was having none of this, and told Hankey that 'this time it is different [and] I want the National Government to get every vote possible'. Hankey asked: 'Is that a command, Sire?', to which the King said: 'Yes, you really ought to vote.' The military man had his orders, and replied: 'Very well, Sire.'[76]

The National Government would remain in existence until 1939, initially with MacDonald, a decreasingly effective leader, then with Stanley Baldwin as Prime Minister from 1935 and Neville Chamberlain from 1937.

DWINDLING INFLUENCE: THE 1930S

These years were not without difficulty for Hankey, including mounting fatigue after twenty years at the top without a break. In 1934, he would pay a visit to the Dominions, South Africa, Australia, New Zealand and Canada, and although ostensibly on extended holiday, he discussed defence planning with the Dominion leaders. The most sensitive mission was to South Africa, where Historian John Naylor comments that Hankey 'carried out official conversations which normally would have been assigned a minister'.[77] Hankey wrote a disingenuous message to Herbert Stanley, the British High Commissioner:

Although I am most reluctant to do any official business in South Africa, I can see that from the point of view of the politicians there are some merits in taking advantage of my visit at the present time. To begin with, I am a person entirely without responsibility; I can commit no-one; I can only explore; and if I go too far I can even be repudiated. I have been accustomed to work in this odd kind of position for a great many years, both in international and inter-Imperial business, and have sometimes, I think, made a useful contribution to the settlement of tiresome questions.[78]

The Afrikaner press learnt of Hankey's visit and saw through claims that it was innocuous. *Die Volksblad* ran an article on 10 August 1934 entitled: 'What is afoot?', accusing the South African government of attempting 'to deny the military significance' of Hankey's trip, while *Die Burger* published a cartoon showing Hankey meeting the Defence Minister, who is locking the door with 'an exaggerated gesture of secrecy'.[79] The nature of Hankey's visit provoked questions in the House of Commons, too, with MacDonald's insistence that Hankey's three-month trip had 'no political significance' considerably stretching the truth.[80] Nevertheless, the fact that Hankey was allowed to be away for so long on a visit not of prime domestic importance shows that he was becoming a more marginal figure.

The Abdication Crisis, 1936

The most dramatic event of Hankey's final years in power was the Abdication Crisis at the end of 1936. The crisis proved arduous for Hankey, in his role as Clerk to the Privy Council and in its domination of Cabinet discussions.[81] The crisis had occupied Hankey's attention all year. In a diary entry from 20 January 1936, he recounts a conversation with Queen Mary, the future Edward VIII's mother, in which she expressed her concerns 'as to whether the Prince had fully realised his responsibilities, and how far he would have to alter his manner of living'. Hankey replied he 'had gathered that the Prime Minister had had some serious talks about the future with the Prince, and had impressed on him the magnitude of this task'.[82]

Hankey was present at the elderly King George V's last Privy Council meeting on 20 January, the day he died, which took place in the royal bedchamber at 12.15pm. He writes poignantly of the King's appearance: he was 'sitting up in the middle of the room in … an armchair with an attachment … across the front on which rested the Warrant', 'dressed in a bright flowered dressing gown'. This juxtaposition of the stately and the domestic instilled in the proceedings a sense of pathos. Hankey recounts: 'I for my part [was] under the stress of an emotion greater than I can remember, and with tears in my eyes.' The King struggled to 'get a proper hold of the pen' to sign the order paper but eventually managed to make 'two distinctive marks', leaving 'one and all convinced that he knew what he was doing'. After the signing of the warrant, the Council left the King's bedchamber, assembling downstairs, with Hankey responsible for drafting the minutes under dictation from Lord Chancellor Hailsham and Home Secretary John Simon.[83] The King died just before midnight.

Cabinet met almost a year later on the late afternoon of 2 December. The addendum to their discussion was deemed so secret that it was placed in an envelope 'to be opened personally by the Secretary to the Cabinet or Deputy Secretary' in thirty years, and it was then made public in the 1980s. The addendum records that

> the Prime Minister said that he was to see the King at 6:00 p.m. that evening, at His Majesty's request. All he wanted to be in a position to say was that the Cabinet did not consider that legislation in respect of a marriage under which Mrs Simpson would not become Queen was practicable.

At the end of the minute, it notes that the Cabinet agreed that

> the Prime Minister should be authorised to tell the King their view that in view of the result of the Prime Minister's inquiries as to the state of Opinion in the House of Commons and in the Dominions, it would be useless to proceed with any legislation designed to enable him to marry Mrs Simpson without her becoming Queen.[84]

On 6 December, Cabinet met at 10 a.m. The minutes record that '[t]he Prime Minister said that the present Meeting was one of the greatest importance. On the previous evening he had seen the King ... he was prepared to sign the abdication, which would enable the necessary legislation to be got through the House of Commons.' Baldwin outlined his intended speech to the House, which said that this was not a constitutional struggle between King and his ministers, but rather

> a struggle in the human heart, a struggle in which he himself was trying to find a solution. He would then propose to tell the story ... how the King had always insisted on his intention to marry Mrs Simpson and had said that in order to carry this out he would go. On this he had never wavered for an instant.[85]

With his government and the Dominions set against any marriage between him and Wallis Simpson, Edward knew that such a marriage would trigger a huge constitutional crisis. He chose to abdicate on 10 December.

Hankey's pivotal role in setting up the Joint Intelligence Committee in 1936 shows how vital he could still be. His understanding of intelligence was without parallel. He warded off plans, too, for a Channel Tunnel, a personal obsession.

HANKEY AND THE COMING OF WAR, 1936–38

Hankey's star, though, was on the wane, as was Baldwin's energy. A tired man, Hankey had a complete breakdown in the summer of 1936: one reason Dilks believes he was such an energetic presence in the latter part of the year over the abdication was because he had spent four months away from the fray.[86] Baldwin listened to him closely on defence matters but on economic matters he wanted help from elsewhere, so he brought in Horace Wilson, who had been Chief Industrial Adviser since 1930, as his special adviser from 1935. This was particularly key as unemployment was a major concern for the Prime Minister. Baldwin liked to listen to his Permanent Secretaries too, with whom he would have regular meetings: Fisher at the Treasury and Vansittart at the Foreign Office were his two closest. The departure in 1930 of T. J. Jones from the Cabinet Office had not led to a closer relationship with Hankey; 'the personal chemistry never developed', said Baldwin biographer John Barnes.[87] Hankey had, until 1934–35, seen Japan as much more of a potential threat than Germany, and even his expertise on defence was bypassed in his final months. Hankey greeted the change of Prime Minister in May 1937 from Baldwin to Chamberlain with some relief. But Chamberlain had little time for Hankey as a close adviser, and embraced Horace Wilson in an even more central role in No. 10, while speaking to the Foreign Secretary or to Vansittart's successor from 1938, Alexander Cadogan, if he wanted foreign policy advice. Chamberlain was very much more his own man: his biographer Dilks argues that Chamberlain 'had much more grip on policy and fact than Baldwin; and to an extent, therefore, was more self reliant'.[88]

Chamberlain had clashed with Hankey in a formative experience while sitting on the Defence Requirements Committee (DRC) as early as 1934. As a naval man, Hankey saw Japan, with its powerful navy, as a threat to the Empire, while Chamberlain worried more about Germany and its emerging air force. Further, according to Dilks, 'on more than one occasion Chamberlain objected to the minutes drafted by Hankey ... there was at least a difference of emphasis'.[89]

In February 1938, estimates were circulated of projected British and German first-line air strength for that autumn. The German figure was 1,755 aircraft with 810 heavy and medium bombers, and the British 1,736 with 990 heavy and medium bombers; Britain had 420 fighters while the Germans had only 324. It is likely, Roskill suspects, that the German Under-Secretary for Air, General Milch, circulated deliberately low figures so as to encourage complacency in Britain. Further, these statistics falsely assumed that the British expansion programme, Scheme F, was going to plan. It was not. Against this background of British laxity, Milch disclosed Germany did indeed have greater production capacity.[90] The government, meanwhile, refused emergency measures to bolster production. It was Hankey who wrote to Thomas Inskip, Minister for Coordination of Defence, to voice concerns about 'the Germans ... further increasing their first-line strength'.[91] Inskip, with the help of Hankey, devised 'Scheme K', which emphasised fighters, providing for 1,360 bombers and 532 fighters by summer 1938, and proving a crucial strand of the war effort.[92]

Hankey never trusted Churchill – they disagreed vehemently in 1919 over the war in Russia, on which Churchill was an enthusiast – and entered a heated dispute with him about the figures for the Luftwaffe's strength. Churchill provided alternative figures to those of the Air Staff, whose figures Hankey was inclined to believe. He wrote to Hankey concerned about this disparity in numbers, but Hankey declined, somewhat superciliously, to address Churchill's concerns 'without Ministerial authority'. Churchill responded sharply: 'I certainly did not expect to receive from you a lengthy lecture when I went out of my way to give you, in strict confidence, information in the public interest ... you may be sure I shall not trouble you again in such matters.' Hankey had grown weary and intolerant towards Churchill's constant, pressurising reminders of his 'great responsibility'.[93] As it transpired, Churchill's figures were exaggerated and, by the end of 1938, the Western Allies and Luftwaffe's bomber strength was on a par.

Hankey's last Cabinet was on 26 July 1938. At the end of the meeting, Chamberlain paid him a handsome tribute. 'He could fairly be called the creator of the modern Cabinet,' Chamberlain said, and that 'the members of the present Cabinet were the last of a great body of statesmen who had passed through his hands, with all of whom he had been on intimate terms, and who had all given him the fullest confidence'. He continued to say that Hankey had been sounded out on different occasions about joining the government but, however tempting, 'he had preferred to work in comparative obscurity'. Chamberlain said that Hankey had 'seemed to them all to be a part of the Cabinet Room, and without him it would be a different place. He had gained the respect and affection of every one of them, and they would miss him very greatly.' After being presented with the gift of a clock 'of modest dimensions', Hankey responded that he was so unused to speaking in the Cabinet Room 'that he hardly knew the sound of his own voice there'.[94]

Hankey reminisced about working for seven Prime Ministers, 'fourteen or fifteen' governments, and taking the minutes of 'more than 1,100 Meetings of the Cabinet proper, or over 1,700 if the War Cabinet were included'. He described himself a little oddly as 'something of a robot', though added: 'Robots had their feelings, their criticisms and their admirations.' He said he was delighted to end on the one word which the Prime Minister had used to sum up his feelings: 'affection'.[95]

On his retirement, the offices of the Cabinet and Committee of Imperial Defence were amalgamated on 1 August 1938, under the unwieldy title 'Offices of the Cabinet, Committee of Imperial Defence, Economic Advisory Council and Minister for Co-ordination of Defence'. Hankey's successor, Edward Bridges, was to be described as 'Permanent Secretary and Secretary of the Cabinet'.[96]

Cabinet in 1939 was fundamentally the same body that it was in 1920. That year, there were forty-nine meetings of Cabinet, until the rude interruption of the Second World War in September necessitated the creation of a War Cabinet. Ordinary meetings of the peacetime Cabinet took place at No. 10 on Wednesdays, at 11 a.m. The size of Cabinet fluctuated between twenty to twenty-three, and was not significantly different to the regular twenty that it had been in 1920.[97] One difference was that agendas were now attached to the previous Cabinet's minutes, a consequence of the growth of bureaucratisation during the interwar years. Nevertheless, aspects of the pre-1916 regime endured; the records omit details of budget entirely – 'In view of the great importance of secrecy, the details in accordance with precedent are not recorded in the Cabinet minutes.'[98] The Cabinet Committee system had continued to grow during the interwar years. The Home Affairs Committee was the pre-eminent body, overseeing domestic policy as well as legislation. The 1920s and 1930s had spawned dozens of Cabinet Committees, some meeting frequently, others only once or twice in order to make a decision or oversee the passage of legislation.[99]

Hankey was busy during the remaining years of his life. Chamberlain turned to him for advice on appointments to the War Cabinet in September 1939, going further and appointing him Minister Without Portfolio in October, and a member of the War Cabinet. Chamberlain particularly valued Hankey's unrivalled familiarity with industrialists and scientific matters.[100] Thus he became the only Cabinet Secretary to go on to become a minister, though Churchill took him out of the War Cabinet in May 1940, marginalising Hankey as the war progressed. He nevertheless played a seminal role leading investigations into MI5 and MI6, and into universities, producing a far-seeing report. His opposition to war crimes trials for both Japanese and German leaders after the Second World War aroused concern. In a series of letters to *The Times* and in a book published in 1950,

Politics, Trials and Errors, he argued that war criminals should be released and their crimes forgiven, and failure to do so would only lead to bitterness, as it had done after the First World War.[101] He had been ennobled in 1939 as Lord Hankey, as were subsequent Cabinet Secretaries, but he was the only one to have his recollections published posthumously (1970–74), in the form of books of biography based on contemporary documents and his diaries by fellow naval historian Stephen Roskill. To Christopher Andrew, 'Better perhaps than any other modern British statesmen, Hankey fits the definition of genius as an infinite capacity for taking pains.' Or, as Neville Chamberlain said of him in 1937: 'In this country we have long regarderd Sir Maurice Hankey not as an official but as an institution indispensable to the British state.'[102] He died in January 1963 in the middle of the long, cold harsh winter.

Hankey was the most controversial of all the eleven Cabinet Secretaries, and the closest to breaching the invisible line separating the unelected official and the minister. He once admitted to writing minutes ahead of meetings in his notebook on the train on the way up from Oxted, in Surrey, because he knew what ministers would say, and boasted in his diaries of the freedom that drafting minutes offered the writer. Despite that, the Campbell case was the only main occasion when a Prime Minister challenged his minutes. Not surprisingly, the ever-proper Edward Bridges moved swiftly, as we shall see, to turn back the excesses of Hankey's empire, and caused Hankey further upset by preventing the publication of his diaries for many years, regarding it as a wholly improper action by a Cabinet Secretary.[103]

Edward Bridges, photographed in August 1940
by Walter Stoneman

CHAPTER 4

EDWARD BRIDGES AND THE
SECOND WORLD WAR, 1938–45

I N JULY 1938, aged sixty-one, Maurice Hankey was in his twenty-
second year as Cabinet Secretary when he was eventually persuaded to
stand down. Indeed, he and Robert Armstrong are the only Cabinet
Secretaries to have gone beyond the official retirement age of sixty. Warren
Fisher, Permanent Secretary of the Treasury (1919–39), had no hesitation in
recommending that Edward Bridges succeed him.[1] Despite his remarkable
longevity, Hankey, as we have seen, was not flawless as Cabinet Secretary.
He may have been the creator of the office and definer of the role, but he
was too ready with his own opinions, and too often mistaken in those
he advanced, distancing two Prime Ministers, Baldwin and Chamberlain,
in the process. Bridges, whose qualities defined the role of Cabinet Secretary at its best, was always correct in observing the constitutional position
of a civil servant. He allowed the Prime Minister and ministers to take
decisions on the best advice, but it was always their decision.

On 1 August 1938, Bridges officially took up appointment as Cabinet
Secretary, adorned with the formal title of Secretary to the Cabinet and
Permanent Secretary of the Combined Offices of the Cabinet, Committee
of Imperial Defence, Economic Advisory Council, and Minister for the
Co-ordination of Defence.[2] Bridges had impressed Fisher at the Treasury,
proving his mettle at the highest level, while reassuring Fisher that,
unlike Hankey, he would not try to make the Cabinet Office a bastion of

independent power. Under Bridges, the Cabinet Office secured its central place and its importance was enshrined permanently in British government, ensuring it would remain at the heart of Whitehall ever after. But who was this unassuming man who was following in Hankey's colossal footsteps?

EDWARD BRIDGES

Bridges was born in 1892 to Mary 'Monica' Waterhouse and Robert Bridges: their only son among two daughters. His mother was the daughter of Alfred Waterhouse, the distinguished Victorian architect, while his father had given up a career in medicine to write poetry, becoming Poet Laureate in 1913, in succession bar one to Wordsworth and Tennyson. In 1905, the family moved to Boars Hill, overlooking Oxford, and Bridges was raised in a house regularly populated by literary visitors, including W. B. Yeats. This upbringing had a profound impact on the young Bridges. A sensitive and artistic child, one of his hobbies was to collect and study the floor plans of all the English, and many of the Continental, Gothic cathedrals. He was unhappy at prep school, but went on in 1906 to Eton, where he thrived, especially under the tutelage of History teacher C. H. K. Marten, later the Provost of Eton, from whom he said he learnt more than any other teacher at school or university. To Marten he ascribes his ability to learn 'how to get inside a subject, how to order his thoughts and how to set them out in a convincing way'.[3] He went up to Magdalen College, Oxford in 1911 to read Greats, achieving a First in July 1914, and after the war was awarded an All Souls Fellowship in 1920, testifying to his intellectual calibre.

The First World War broke out on his twenty-second birthday, 4 August 1914, and the following month he joined the 4th Battalion, Oxfordshire and Buckinghamshire Light Infantry, the only Cabinet Secretary to see service in the First World War. Many soldiers carried with them into a battle a copy of his father's bestselling philosophy and poetry anthology, with dedication to George V, *The Spirit of Man*, published in 1916. The war undoubtedly had a huge influence on Edward: '[H]e lost virtually all his friends, which gave him a wariness of close friendship,' said his grandson, Mark Bridges, who believes that 'the loss of so many of his contemporaries in the war [created] a very private man'.[4] Another grandson, the government minister George Bridges, has written about his service in the First World War, based on the regimental war diaries that Bridges was responsible for during his time on the front line: '[W]hat is striking about [the diaries] is not merely the detail but the handwriting,' George Bridges writes:

> The writing is in a steady, tight script. There are few crossings out, the style is crisp, the grammar much better than mine. Every place, every name and every battalion is recorded in capitals. It is as if he wrote it in bed, [surrounded] by pillows and blankets, sipping hot milk, not crouching in a trench, knee deep in muck, shells shrieking over his head.[5]

He writes of his grandfather: '[L]ike many who survived the trenches, he apparently never spoke about the War. History now speaks for him through these densely written pages.'[6]

At the Battle of the Somme, which opened just a few weeks short of his twenty-fourth birthday, Bridges honed the skills of writing accurate records under the most intense pressure. On 18 July, the Ox and Bucks was ordered to attack on the Somme at 1.30 a.m., between Ovillers and Pozières. The first advance 'struck a trench not expected according to the map', then they 'were met by rifle fire from the left and enfilade machine gun fire from the right ... the enemy then opened fire with a heavy barrage of 15cm [shells], chiefly shrapnel, all along the trench, causing considerable casualties which, owing [to] the shallowness of the trench, made re-organising very difficult'.[7]

Bridges's gallantry resulted in him being awarded the Military Cross in January 1917, but he was severely wounded two months later. He was not passed fit for home service until March 1918, and not fit for active service until October 1918, just two weeks before the war ended. The prolonged absence from hostilities may have saved his life.

While waiting for the shattered bones in his arm to mend, the Treasury, who had heard of his academic prowess at Oxford, wrote to see if he would like temporary work. He so impressed his new bosses there that, in April 1918, the Chancellor of the Exchequer himself, Bonar Law (1916–19), urged the War Office to allow him to stay longer.[8] Bridges became so intrigued by the work at the Treasury that he decided to enter the Civil Service after the war was over, eschewing the opportunity of a career as an Oxford academic. Even before the results of the Civil Service 'reconstruction' competition for new entrants was known, the Treasury brought him back in, joining formally as an Assistant Principal in 1919. He rose swiftly through the ranks, becoming Secretary to a series of Royal Commissions and departmental inquiries, none more important for his future career than the Tomlin Commission into the Civil Service (1929–31), which gave him an understanding of the entire work of Whitehall.[9]

In 1922, he married Katherine 'Kitty' Farrer, who, not insignificantly, was the sister of his main surviving friend from the war, Old Etonian Cecil Farrer. Bridges's happy married life and children became thereafter the focus of his world and source of emotional stability.

Despite being such a private man, Bridges could also be warm and affectionate. Robert Armstrong, the later Cabinet Secretary (1979–87), came across Bridges early in his career in the 1950s:

> He was a lovely man. A no-nonsense man – very direct. He was rather short-sighted: if he liked you when he met you, he would hit you, a good natured blow to the chest or clap on the arm. If he didn't like you, he was very polite! He added greatly to the fun of the place.

Armstrong remembers one episode that captured much about Bridges:

> I was the Chancellor's [Private Secretary] and somebody wrote to him demanding a higher honour than the one that had been proposed … The rule was you don't yourself ask for honours, so I composed a rather chilly reply, but thought I had better clear it because I was still young. So I sent it across to Edward Bridges's private office, and a note came back from Bridges himself: 'Mr Armstrong, your reply will do as well as anything to this importunate customer. My advice for you is to put it in the refrigerator for a fortnight, and then despatch without defrosting.' You couldn't help loving that.[10]

Jock Colville, Private Secretary to Churchill during the war and from 1951 to 1955, believed that Bridges 'possessed an infectious sense of humour and became one of the most powerful men in the land without ever losing either his humility or his sense of the ludicrous'.[11]

Bridges demanded the very highest of moral and professional standards from himself, and from all others in the Civil Service. He was 'a man who lived a life to high Christian standards and ethics', recalled Mark Bridges.[12] He was scrupulous about correct form, discretion, impartiality and service. He saw much in common, as one might expect of an academic *manqué*, between the academic life and that of the civil servant:

> [I]n both you have to cultivate the capacity to analyse complicated situa-
> tions, and to set out the results clearly and accurately. You cannot do that
> unless you have an inner determination to find out the right answer at
> all costs ... In both academic life and in the Civil Service, you need this
> combination of intellectual integrity (horrid phrase) with the ardour of
> the chase ... It is the pride of the Civil Service that it is non-political, and
> that it can serve Governments of all parties with equal loyalty and obtain
> their confidence. This confidence is perhaps more easily obtained by civil
> servants whose general attitude is slightly detached and withdrawn.[13]

Bridges ran a different operation from that of Hankey, whose military background and experience were so different to his own. With the prospect of war in Europe looming, moreover, and with Hankey's departure, Chamberlain (1937–40) decided to split the Cabinet Office against his advice in August 1938, into civil and military sides (the CID).[14] He delegated the latter to General Hastings ('Pug') Ismay, who had worked in the CID in the 1920s and earlier 1930s, and was a thoroughbred, Sandhurst-trained military man. When Churchill became Prime Minister in May 1940, he further asked Ismay to be his Staff Officer and Chief Military adviser, becoming the principal link between him and the Chiefs of Staff. Churchill was much closer to Ismay, whose company he found more convivial, than to the more ascetic Bridges. Colville summed up the relationship between Bridges and Ismay thus:

> [T]hey galloped side by side, in perfectly matching harmony, without
> a whisper of jealousy, antagonism or indeed disagreement ... Perhaps
> ... Ismay was nearer to being indispensable to Churchill than any other

man, but Sir Edward Bridges followed close behind. What Ismay was in the military sphere, Bridges was in the civil.[15]

Bridges's colleague and friend, John Winnifrith, wrote: '[H]e and Ismay were one of the fixed points in what was otherwise a constantly changing world. They could have used their power to be obstructive, instead they oiled the wheels.'[16] Bridges's methodical mind worked differently from Ismay's. Precision in language, unsurprisingly given whose son he was, was one of his hallmarks. Another of his hallmarks was ensuring all the relevant facts had been assembled, and the right people consulted, before decisions were taken: 'His cardinal rule was that his function was to see that [ministers] took the initiative in putting forward their problems for decision, and provided all the facts, figures and arguments needed for informed decisions. It was not his job to take over this role,' wrote Winnifrith, highlighting a stark difference in approach to Hankey. Winnifrith's insights into Bridges, which formed his biographical memoir for the Royal Society, were informed by the two years he spent with him from 1942 at the War Cabinet Office. Winnifrith himself went on to become Permanent Secretary at the Ministry of Agriculture in 1957.[17]

BRIDGES'S FIRST YEAR, 1938–39

Bridges purports not to have foreseen his appointment, at the age of forty-six: '[N]obody was ever more surprised than I was when I was appointed Secretary to the Cabinet. I never had the faintest idea that I could be considered for the post.'[18] Taking over from Hankey and earning the loyalty of the Cabinet Office team was never going to be easy for him, having never been a member of the Cabinet Office staff. As historian Richard Chapman noted, most of the Cabinet Office staff had been recruited by his predecessor and owed their loyalty primarily to him. Any major change was bound to be regarded with suspicion, especially for a Treasury import much younger than many of the old guard. Bridges, indeed, was the first Cabinet Secretary schooled in the Treasury and modern Civil Service norms of conduct, and from the outset thought very differently about the job to Hankey.

Bridges soon won over the office, testifying to his extraordinary skill and capacity for building trust.[19] In Bridges's first few weeks in September 1938, Chamberlain wrote to Hitler asking for a personal meeting in an attempt to avert a war. Two days later, he flew to Germany to meet him at his residence at Berchtesgaden. On 29 September, Chamberlain flew back to Germany for a meeting with Hitler in Munich, this time along with Italian leader Benito Mussolini and French leader Édouard Daladier. The 'Munich Agreement' that emerged from their deliberations was finalised at 1.30 a.m. on Friday 30 September. That day, after little sleep, Chamberlain went back to Hitler and asked him to sign an agreement between Britain and Germany. He famously flew back to Britain later that day to deliver his 'Peace in Our Time' speech, echoing the words of Disraeli returning from the Congress of Berlin in 1878.

That same evening, Cabinet met at No. 10 at 7.30 p.m. Bridges recorded John Simon, Chancellor of the Exchequer, saying that he would like to express, 'on behalf of the whole Cabinet, their profound admiration for the unparalleled efforts the PM had made and for the success that he had achieved'.[20] Bridges perhaps felt he was present at a major moment in history as he recorded Chamberlain's response: '[H]e appreciated that the journey he had undertaken might easily have failed to achieve satisfactory results. As things had turned out, he felt he could now safely regard the crisis as ended.' Chamberlain proceeded to give an account of the discussions of 29 September, continuing 'throughout the night until after 1 a.m. on Friday morning'. Not all ministers shared Simon's enthusiasm. First Lord of the Admiralty Alfred Duff Cooper said: 'He was afraid that we might get into the position in which we were drawn into making further concessions to Herr Hitler.' Bridges noted: '[T]he PM said he thought that matters arising out of the First Lord's statement should be discussed between him and the First Lord.'[21] Duff Cooper resigned immediately afterwards. No Cabinet Secretary ever had a more dramatic first two months.

The Munich Crisis, and Hitler's subsequent annexation of Czechoslovakia in March 1939, were to have a profound impact. With a renewed sense of urgency, ministers and civil servants accelerated Britain's war planning. Horace Wilson, who had succeeded Warren Fisher as Permanent Secretary at the Treasury and Head of the HCS earlier in 1939, was strongly pro-appeasement. He had been sent by Chamberlain to Hitler in September 1938 during the 'Sudetenland Crisis' to tell him Britain would go to war if he invaded Czechoslovakia. He was a major power in the Chamberlain court, so was a natural figure for Bridges to lobby about new arrangements at the centre of government in the event of war. Bridges had clearly mapped it out in his mind, writing to Wilson on 5 November to say that there were:

> two fundamental considerations to bear in mind. The first is that in a big war there must be a body which meets every day, or twice a day if need be, and which can give immediate and authoritative decisions. From these two conclusions flow: (a) that the body must be small in numbers, so as to shorten discussion: (b) that it ought to be mainly composed of ministers who are not engaged in day-to-day administration of departments vitally concerned in the war effort.
>
> The second point is to reconcile the direction of the war by a body of six ministers, or super-ministers, with the doctrine of Cabinet responsibility. The War Cabinet system solves the problem quite simply by cutting the Gordian Knot. If this system is adopted, members of the government outside the War Cabinet in effect cease to be Cabinet ministers, since they can have no collective responsibility for the government's war policy. The position can, of course, be eased a little by setting up the Home Affairs Committee.[22]

Bridges was anxious to draw on the lessons from the First World War, where the conventional wisdom was that great harm had been done by the division between the military and the civilian commands overseeing the war. 'To take an example from the last war,' he wrote, 'the evacuation of the Dardanelles was referred by Mr Asquith's War Committee to the full Cabinet. This led to a most unfortunate delay, and a delay of this kind is precisely what must be avoided at all costs in war.'[23] Bridges saw for himself from his earliest days in office how the key decisions over British policy to Germany were being taken by a small group around Chamberlain, and he believed that only such a tight group, properly constituted, could take the decisions needed for the prosecution of the war.[24]

Even before war broke out on 3 September 1939, Bridges was galvanising the Cabinet Office. On the outbreak, it consisted of six senior civilian staff, ten staff under Ismay on the military side in the CID, three in the Economic Advisory Council and seven in the Historical Section, making twenty-six altogether, with a further 180 'subordinate staff', totalling 206.[25] Not everything was ripe for change though. Bridges insisted on maintaining Hankey's rigorous standards in the preparation of the paperwork, and in the military-style routines of Cabinet Office life: 'To collect all the Cabinet minutes together we had to stand in a line, and they were all laid out on a big table right through the room [in Richmond Terrace], and you'd pick one up after another and stitch them all together at the end,' recalled Margaret Walker.[26] A supervisor stood over the secretaries to ensure that they minimised their mistakes in typing up the notes: '[T]hey had to be ever so carefully checked. And if you made more than six mistakes in a stencil, you were told off.'[27]

CABINET OFFICE UNDER THE 'PHONEY WAR', SEPTEMBER 1939 – MAY 1940

During the long, hot summer months of 1939, war increasingly looked inevitable. The expectation was of a massive aerial bombardment of London from the Luftwaffe the moment war was declared. As Ian Jacob, another key figure in the wartime Cabinet Office, who worked on the military side, recorded: 'Just before the actual outbreak of war – it must have been the last day of August – the Chiefs of Staff were asked to advise the government on the best time of day for issuing an ultimatum for the Germans, it being assumed that within six hours of the ultimatum, there would be a heavy air attack on London.'[28] Long discussions ensued about whether it would be less perilous to have civilians just arrived at work, or having just arrived at home.

The moment war was declared, the CID and its secretariat were absorbed back into the Cabinet Office. In line with Bridges's views, the number of ministers was reduced by Chamberlain from twenty-one to nine. Hankey was very much still in evidence, and advised Chamberlain on the structure of the Cabinet: this could not have been easy for Bridges, still less when

Hankey became one of the non-party political appointees to join the War Cabinet as Minister Without Portfolio. But he bore it stoically. Stationery from Richmond Terrace was promptly changed to read 'Offices of the War Cabinet' rather than just 'Office of the Cabinet' as it had a month earlier. Bridges was in his element. His confidence had grown immeasurably in his first year, bolstered by the support of Horace Wilson.

On 5 September, two days after war broke out, Bridges sent around a confidential note about changes to the Cabinet Office in the light of war. 'Meetings of the War Cabinet', it said, 'will be held daily at 11.30 a.m. in either 10 Downing Street or in the Central War Room, beneath the Government Offices at Great George Street [i.e. the current Treasury building].' Bridges was very clear about who was to attend:

[I]n accordance with the practice established in the last war, arrangements will be made through the War Cabinet Secretariat, in the light of the matters under discussion, for the attendance of meetings at the War Cabinet of ministers not in the War Cabinet, and of the Chiefs of Staff and officials as may be required.[29]

Bridges was equally explicit about the form that the minutes would take:

[E]xcept by the orders of the Prime Minister, who may otherwise direct, the War Cabinet Minutes will not contain a detailed record of the discussion. The record in respect of each item will be limited to the conclusion of the War Cabinet, together with a brief explanatory summary. Any corrections of draft minutes ... should reach the Agenda Branch by no later than 1:00 p.m. on the next day ... Immediately thereafter the minutes will be sent to be printed in final form.

The three most senior staff in the War Cabinet Secretariat during these early months were, as the documents clarify, Bridges himself, as Secretary of the War Cabinet, R. B. Howorth, as 'Deputy Secretary (Civil)', and H. L. Ismay, as 'Deputy Secretary (Military)'.[30] Howorth retired in March 1942, to be succeeded by Norman Brook until Brook was appointed Permanent Secretary to the new Ministry of Reconstruction in December 1943. Brook, an anti-appeaser, had been uplifted by Churchill in the Phoney War period – 'here was a man who could be trusted to prosecute [war] with vigorous determination'.[31] Brook was to prove a massive figure at the Cabinet Office and, when he left, the Deputy job was subsequently split between two Under Secretaries. In February 1945, Bridges was appointed Permanent Secretary to the Treasury after the retirement of Richard Hopkins (1942–45). Brook rejoined the Cabinet Office in February 1945, sharing the Cabinet Secretary job for a while with Bridges after he left for the Treasury, and taking on the job on his own in January 1947.

Bridges eyed the arrival of Churchill somewhat warily: '[W]hen Churchill joined the War Cabinet in September 1939, I was virtually a stranger to him. Nor did I have much to do with him … when he was First Lord of the Admiralty.'[32] Their relationship had not got off to a good start, with Bridges suspecting Churchill was one of those 'ultras' who 'still retained some doubts as to the constitutional propriety of the very existence of the Cabinet Secretariat'. Early on, Churchill strode over to Bridges at the end of a Cabinet meeting, proffering the advice that the minutes that he was writing were far too full and detailed. 'To all intents and purposes', Churchill told him, he was 'running a magazine. The minutes should be far shorter.'[33]

Bridges's handwritten Cabinet notebooks sadly do not survive. Official regulations were totally clear that sensitive paperwork was to be destroyed, and that those who kept any documents could be sacked and even prosecuted under the 1911 Official Secrets Act. The ever-meticulous Bridges is known to have largely destroyed his own papers.[34] Effective governance was the beneficiary; but history, most definitely, was the loser.

In these first nine months of war, the Cabinet Office's working assumptions were that government structures and the conduct of war would largely resemble the First World War, and that France would continue to be the main British ally. In 1939–40, the French Army stood at five million, consisting of 117 divisions, compared to the meagre thirteen British divisions sent to France. The French had more tanks and artillery than the Germans, and combined with a modest British force, they constituted a formidable presence in northern France, where it was assumed that the Germans would attack. By the end of September, a small Cabinet Office staff had been established in Paris to assist with liaison, a constant preoccupation in the earlier war. By late April 1940, Bridges was becoming agitated by the state of the French preparedness for war and lethargic liaison with Britain: '[B]roadly speaking', he wrote, 'the position is that on the military side, the French War Cabinet is not functioning.'[35] On 9 May, one of the liaison officers wrote to a senior British official in Paris that he would be busy 'for the next few days', but would 'love to have dinner' at some point. There would be a long wait. The following day, the German Army invaded France, Belgium and Holland.

CHURCHILL BECOMES PRIME MINISTER, MAY 1940

Bridges must have had mixed feelings on a personal level about the arrival of Churchill in No. 10. Churchill, nearly twenty years his senior, had been his boss at the Treasury when Chancellor (1924–29). The new Prime Minister sized up Bridges. His war record and obvious dedication and competence were all to his credit. But, as Winnifrith wrote, he 'could never forget that Bridges had served Mr Chamberlain', though he added: 'he did not regard him as a man of Munich'.[36] For many middle-ground officials and politicians, Churchill remained a dangerous adventurer who might lead Britain into grave peril or a foolish campaign, as he had done in the Dardanelles. Bridges had gained the respect and trust of Chamberlain over the previous twenty months, and while he did not go as far as officials like Private Secretary Jock Colville, who drank a champagne toast to the 'King Over the Water' on the night of 10 May, he was still sad to see his old master go. So it was with some trepidation that Bridges went across to see Churchill at Admiralty House on the morning of 11 May 1940, the day after he became Prime Minister. As he sat in the waiting room, he wondered: '[W]ould congratulations be in place when one considered the desperate situation that the country faced?' When the summons at last came, Bridges offered the measured words: '"May I wish you every possible good fortune." Churchill gave one of the little grunts that one got to know so well, and after a long look said, "Hum. Every good fortune! I like that! These other people have all been congratulating me. Every good fortune!"'[37]

Bridges possessed the essential trait of every great civil servant, the ability to serve different political masters without trace of obsequiousness. He described the trick himself thus:

> [Y]ou had to make Churchill feel that you were on his side, that you sympathised with his general views, and that any criticism you made was genuinely intended to be helpful. Once convinced of this, he would listen to what you had to say, and you became, so to speak, a licensed critic.[38]

Bridges had absorbed much subtlety from his parental home, which came into good service when learning how to play the mercurial new Prime Minister.

Churchill immediately imparted much-needed urgency and drive into the whole Whitehall system. 'There was a remarkable intensification of national effort in every field,' wrote Ismay:

> All the considerations affecting any problem – political and economic as well as military – could now be brought into focus more readily, and thanks to Mr Churchill's personal exercise of the wide powers given to him by the War Cabinet, and to his astounding drive, firm decisions could be reached and translated into action far more quickly.[39]

Bridges was in receipt of constant directives from his new boss, known colloquially in the office as 'prayers', as they often began: 'pray, let me have your views', or 'pray, explain'. Churchill would want everything written down on a single page of foolscap paper, creating great challenges for Bridges and his team who had to précis often complex arguments: 'It's far harder to compress your thoughts into that compass, than to write a novel,' Bridges once complained to Winnifrith.[40] One device Ismay adopted was to attach voluminous appendices containing the details: one such document finished with Appendix 'T'.[41] Over time, Bridges and Churchill drew closer, even if they never lost a certain professional distance: '[I]n these war years, there were no regular office hours,' wrote Bridges:

> Nor indeed was there any frontier between the Prime Minister's office and quarters in the new Public Offices overlooking Birdcage Walk in which

he and Mrs Churchill lived for much of the war. We might find ourselves working with Churchill in his study or in his bedroom, or be called in to take some urgent orders while he was having a meal with his family. Before long he had us all feeling that we had in some sense become honorary members of his family.[42]

Bridges was struck by how 'within a few days of his becoming Prime Minister, the whole machinery of government was working at a pace[,] and with an intensity of purpose, quite unlike anything which had gone before'.[43] Or, as Brook put it: '[E]verything he wanted had to be done at once: all demands, however exacting and unreasonable[,] had to be met … the work was heavy, and the pace was hot.'[44] Churchill's personal messages reverberated like clanging machinery throughout Whitehall, stamping his personal authority on government: '[L]et it be very clearly understood that all directions emanating from me are made in writing,' Churchill wrote, 'and that I do not accept any responsibility for matters relating to national defence on which I am alleged to have given decisions unless they are recorded in writing.'[45]

Bridges's job became harder as the war ground on. Churchill became tired and his working patterns more erratic, inspiring discontent and anger among Chiefs of Staff and ministers. 'The Prime Minister's favourite times for meetings got later as the war went on,' wrote Jacob. 'They started about 10:30 in the evening. One didn't finish the meeting until about midnight. Then of course one had to dictate the minutes and see them typed, so I didn't get to bed until about 2 or 2:30.'[46] Complaints by Bridges's fellow Cabinet Secretaries and their staff about having to write up minutes late into the night have been a leitmotif throughout the years.

Churchill immediately cut Chamberlain's small War Cabinet down to just five. Besides Churchill, it included Chamberlain as Lord President (he turned down Churchill's invitation to return as Chancellor of the Exchequer) and Halifax as Foreign Secretary, the only figure with a departmental responsibility and not one of Churchill's natural allies. Nor were the two Labour figures, Clement Attlee as Lord Privy Seal and Arthur Greenwood as Minister Without Portfolio. But Churchill was determined to have a broad-based government, and he accepted he was not strong enough to purge Chamberlain supporters. Nor was he able to tempt a frail Lloyd George back into the government, a move resisted by Chamberlain. Additional senior ministers who attended the War Cabinet were Kingsley Wood, Chancellor (Conservative); Ernest Bevin, Minister of Labour (Labour); and Max Beaverbrook, the newspaper proprietor and friend of Churchill, as Minister of Aircraft Production. When Chamberlain died of cancer in November 1940, Churchill handed the Lord Presidency and heavy burden of domestic coordination to the former civil servant John Anderson (Permanent Secretary at the Home Office, before entering Parliament as an Independent MP in 1938). Anthony Eden replaced Halifax in December 1940 when the latter became British Ambassador in Washington. The Liberal leader and Air Minister, Archibald Sinclair, was also a regular attendee of the War Cabinet.

Bridges was kept busy. The War Cabinet was to meet 919 times between 10 May 1940 and 18 May 1945, averaging three and a half meetings a week. It met 193 times in the remaining seven and a half months of 1940, with 138 meetings in 1941, 174 in 1942, 176 in 1943 and also 1944, and sixty-two meetings until the war ended in 1945. That meant a lot of agendas to prepare and minutes to write. In contrast, Lloyd George's War Cabinet met 615 times during the First World War, including twenty-three times from 9 to 31 December 1916, 285 in 1917, 205 in 1918 and 102 until 14 August 1919.[47] No. 10 and the Cabinet War Rooms remained the usual venues, but the Cabinet was also to meet at a disused Underground station in Westminster, the rotunda in Horseferry Road, at Church House, and at the GPO Research Station at Dollis Hill.[48]

In February 1942, Churchill reported to the House of Commons on how the War Cabinet was working, in particular in relation to the crucial and sensitive oversight of the Dominions:

> The members of the War Cabinet are collectively and individually responsible for the whole policy of the country, and they are the ones who are alone held accountable for the conduct of the war. However, they have also particular spheres of superintendence. The Leader of Labour Party, as head of the second largest party in the National Government, acts as Deputy Prime Minister in all things, and in addition will discharge the duties of Dominions Secretary, thus meeting, without an addition to our

numbers, the request pressed upon us from so many quarters that our relations with the Dominions ... shall be in the hands of a member of the War Cabinet.[49]

Churchill's style of chairing was not always applauded. Labour minister Ellen Wilkinson, an occasional attendee, contrasted it unfavourably to Attlee's style:

When Mr Attlee is presiding over the Cabinet in the absence of the Prime Minister the Cabinet meets on time, goes systematically through its agenda, makes the necessary decisions, and goes home after three or four hours' work. When Mr Churchill presides we never reach the agenda and we decide nothing.

She was not wholly negative, however, conceding: 'We go home to bed at midnight, conscious of having been present at a historic occasion.'[50] Criticisms of Churchill's chairing came from other quarters, including, in late 1944, from those well-disposed to him. 'For the next fortnight the Cabinet were exasperated by Churchill's concentration on the sole issue [Greece],' recorded Colville, who rapidly became a staunch Churchill admirer. Edward Bridges and Sir Alexander Cadogan (PUS, the Foreign Office) said that 'no business could be done at the Cabinet table, and item after item had to be postponed because the Prime Minister was only prepared to discuss the Greek theme'.[51] Similar irritations had been expressed at Lloyd George's conduct of the War Cabinet twenty-five years before. Both men remained defiantly impervious. Bridges, whose frustrations unlike Hankey's were not recorded for posterity, however, gave a more rounded tribute of Churchill:

At times of crisis, when big issues had to be settled promptly, Churchill was always superb and most business-like. The essential points and arguments would be quickly brought to the surface. They would be searchingly discussed and decisions taken. But when the matters on the agenda were less important or pressing, Churchill's love of argument, and his enjoyment in following up some point raised in the discussion which interested him, could lead to a far longer meeting than was necessary.[52]

Significant Cabinet Meetings

A flavour of the 919 War Cabinets can be gained through exploring a few. Bridges's first months with Churchill were every bit as dramatic as his early Cabinets with Chamberlain. Few Cabinets could have ever rivalled in intensity the desperate series of meetings in late May 1940, against a background of Belgium and the Netherlands conquered, France crumbling, and Hitler's forces at the doorstep.

A decisive meeting took place in the House of Commons 'Committee Room 8' on 28 May 1940. One can only speculate how Bridges felt about being present at such an occasion, and what his personal views might have been. As it was Bridges, and not Hankey, we will never know. Halifax, the Foreign Secretary, urged the government to accept the French government's offer to make a 'direct approach ... to Italy by France and this country', to sue for peace with Hitler's Germany. Churchill's response was that 'it was clear that the French purpose was to see Signor Mussolini acting as an intermediary between ourselves and Herr Hitler'. He was adamant that France could terminate hostilities against the Germans if they wanted to, but there would be no deal between Britain and Germany. 'If we once got to the table, we should find that the terms offered us touched our independence and integrity. When, at this point, we got up to leave the conference table, we should find that all the forces of resolution which were now at our disposal would have vanished.'[53]

Churchill continued:

Signor Mussolini, if he came in as mediator, would take his whack out of us. It was impossible to imagine that Herr Hitler would be so foolish as to let us continue our rearmament. In effect, his terms would put us completely at his mercy. We should get no worse terms if we went on fighting, even if we were beaten, [than those] open to us now.

Halifax persisted that 'he still did not see what there was in the French suggestion of trying out the possibilities of mediation which the Prime Minister felt was so wrong'. The Lord President, the most influential minister in Cabinet after Churchill, interjected: 'It was clear to the world that we were in a tight corner; while we had said openly that we would fight to preserve our independence, we were ready to consider decent terms if such were offered to us.' Churchill absorbed his words, before responding that 'the nations which went down fighting rose again, but those which surrendered tamely were finished'.[54]

The meeting was suspended at 6.30 p.m., while Churchill went off to address ministers not in the War Cabinet. He rallied them with one of his most stirring speeches, asking them not to relent: 'If this long island story of ours is to end at last, let it end only when each one of us lies choking in his own blood upon the ground.' The reception was thunderous, with ministers applauding and banging their hands on the desks. Churchill knew that this support from wider government ministers would strengthen his hand considerably in Cabinet.[55]

War Cabinet reassembled at 7 p.m. with Alexander Cadogan joining them from the Foreign Office. Churchill told Cabinet that in the interval he had been talking to ministers about the latest news from the battlefront. Bridges's minutes record him saying:

> They had not expressed alarm at the position of France, but had expressed the greatest satisfaction when he told them that there was no chance of our giving up the struggle. He did not remember having ever before heard a gathering of persons occupying the higher places in political life express themselves so emphatically.

If France went down, Britain must fight on alone, he said, resisting suggestions of an appeal to the United States. 'If we made a bold stand against Germany, that would command their admiration and respect,' he told the Cabinet, 'but a grovelling appeal, if made now, would have the worst possible effect.'[56] Churchill had outmanoeuvred critics by appealing to government ministers more widely. Soon Chamberlain offered support to Churchill's position, and with Attlee and Greenwood already in favour of continuing the war, Churchill had a clear majority in the War Cabinet.

The mighty French Army had collapsed rapidly before the German military machine, and Churchill's attention turned to the French fleet, desperate it should not fall into German hands. By mid-June, France was pressing for peace with Germany. Before France surrendered, Churchill commanded the British fleet to surround the port of Oran in Algeria, and ordered their captains to convince the French to defect to the British. If they would not, then they were to ensure the French fleet was rendered inoperable.

The Cabinet met at 11.30 a.m. on 3 July and was informed 'that HMS *Foxhound* had arrived off Oran early that morning, but Captain Holland had reported that the French Admiral had refused to see him. A letter had therefore been handed in, setting out the terms offered': that the French Navy should sail to Britain, or to the neutral USA, or they should scuttle their ships within the next six hours. The War Cabinet decided a message should be sent to Admiral Somerville: 'If you consider that the French fleet are preparing to leave harbour, inform them that if they move you must open fire.'[57] The French refused to respond positively. Churchill ordered the British fleet to attack, resulting in the loss of nearly 1,300 French servicemen and the sinking of three battleships. Chief Whip David Margesson worked with Chamberlain to bring Conservatives MPs on side, so when Churchill went to the House of Commons the next day, he received a unanimous standing ovation from MPs, his first since becoming Prime Minister.

A week later, War Cabinet discussion moved on to another core concern of the Cabinet Office: the wellbeing of the civilian population in the event of a German invasion. Ministers debated a draft leaflet, prepared by the Ministry of Information, which opened: 'If this island is invaded by sea or air, everyone who is not under orders must stay where he or she is. This is not simply advice: it is an order from the Government, and you must obey it just as soldiers obey their orders. Your order is: Stay put.'

The worry was that, as in France, the Netherlands and Belgium, crowds of refugees would block the roads, making it almost impossible for the army to defend the territory. 'Stay put. It's easy to say. When the time comes it may be hard to do. But you have got to do it; and in doing it you will be fighting Britain's battle as bravely as a soldier.'[58]

Bridges minuted most of the key Cabinets himself during Churchill's five years. Another of the most fraught was on 10 June 1942, when Cabinet debated their response to the massacre at the Czechoslovakian village of Lidice, on the orders of Hitler and Himmler, as a reprisal for the assassination of the high-ranking SS officer Reinhard Heydrich. Over 173 men in the village aged over fifteen were murdered, while the women and children were deported to concentration camps. Churchill spoke to Czechoslovakian

DRAFT LEAFLET ON INVASION.

STAY PUT.

Issued by the Ministry of Information
in co-operation with the War Office and
the Ministry of Home Security.

If this island is invaded by sea or air everyone who is not under orders must stay where he or she is. This is not simply advice: it is an order from the Government, and you must obey it just as soldiers obey their orders. Your order is "Stay Put", but remember that this does not apply until invasion comes.

WHY MUST I STAY PUT?

Because in France, Holland and Belgium, the Germans were helped by the people who took flight before them. Great crowds of refugees blocked all roads. The soldiers who could have defended them could not get at the enemy. The enemy used the refugees as a human shield. These refugees were got out on to the roads by rumour and false orders. Do not be caught out in this way. Do not take any notice of any story telling what the enemy has done or where he is. Do not take orders except from the Military, the Police, the Home Guard (L.D.V.) and the A.R.P. authorities or wardens.

WHAT WILL HAPPEN TO ME IF I DON'T STAY PUT?

You will stand a very good chance of being killed. The enemy may machine-gun you from the air in order to increase panic, or you may run into enemy forces which have landed behind you. An official German message was intercepted in Belgium which ran:

"Watch for civilian refugees on the roads. Harass them as much as possible".

Our soldiers will be hurrying to drive back the invader and will not be able to stop and help you. On the contrary, they will have to turn you off the roads so that they can get at the enemy. You will not have reached safety and you will have done just what the enemy wanted you to do.

HOW SHALL I PREPARE TO STAY PUT?

Make ready your air-raid shelter; if you have no shelter prepare one. Advice can be obtained from your local Air Raid Warden or in "Your Home as an Air-raid Shelter", the Government booklet which tells you how to prepare a shelter in your house strong enough to protect you against stray shots and falling metal. If you can have a trench ready in your garden or field, so much the better, especially if you live where there is likely to be danger from shell-fire.

HOW CAN I HELP?

Civilians who try to join in the fight will only get in the way. To beat off an enemy attack is the job of the military forces, which include the Home Guard. If you have no other wartime task join the Home Guard at once. For those who cannot join there are many ways in which the Military and Home Guard may need your help in their preparations. Find out what you can do to help in any local defence work that is going on, and be ready to turn your hand to anything if asked by the Military or Home Guard to do so.

If you are responsible for the safety of a factory or some other important building, get in touch with the nearest military authority. You will then be told how your defence should fit in with the military organisation and plans.

WHAT SHALL I DO IF THE INVADER COMES MY WAY?

If fighting by organised forces is going on in your district and you have no special duties elsewhere, go to your shelter and stay there till the battle is past. Do not attempt to join in the fight. Behave as if an air-raid were going on. The enemy will seldom turn aside to attack separate houses.

But if small parties are going about threatening persons and property in an area not under enemy control and come your way, you have the right of every man and woman to do what you can to protect yourself, your family and your home.

STAY PUT.

It's easy to say. When the time comes it may be hard to do. But you have got to do it; and in doing it you will be fighting Britain's battle as bravely as a soldier.

Page Leaflet related to Invasion Preparations 1940

Section from Cabinet Notebook

Prime Minister Edvard Beneš about the possibility of a counter-attack by the RAF, with the suggestion of wiping out German villages on the basis of '3 for 1'. Bridges's minute records in precise detail the opinions of the Cabinet and various ministers. Archibald Sinclair, the Secretary of State for Air, 'disliked it', arguing that such a course was a diversion from military objectives, and claiming it was 'risking aircraft and crews'. Herbert Morrison said the Cabinet should consider 'reprisals on English villages, where [there is] no shelter ... Public [would] say "why did you draw this down on us?"' One minister argued that the 'German responds to brute force & nothing else'. John Anderson, the Lord President, then said the '[d]anger is that it costs us something & them nothing'. Ultimately Churchill said: 'I submit (unwillingly) to the view of Cabinet against.'[59]

CABINET COMMITTEES AND LIFE IN THE CABINET OFFICE DURING THE WAR

'There are far too many Committees of one kind and another which ministers have to attend and do not yield sufficient results,' wrote Churchill testily to Bridges on 24 May 1940.[60] Prime Ministers often write in a similar vein at the outset of their premiership. Bridges's memo at the start of the war had envisaged a wholesale review of the entire Cabinet Committee structure, with the elimination of some committees, the creation of others, and rationalisation under the War Cabinet.[61] Churchill's ambivalence to Cabinet Committees increased during the course of the war, despite their helping ensure the smooth running of his government. At their apex was the Lord President's Committee (under Attlee after Anderson became Chancellor in September 1943), the principal domestic policy organ of the War Cabinet. It was responsible for 'coordinating on the social and economic aspects of the war happen[ing] on the home front',[62] while the Defence Committee, the Chiefs of Staff Committee and the Joint Planning and Intelligence Staff were the principal committees on the military side.

The War Cabinet Office in total 'provided a secretariat for 400 War Cabinet Committees and sub-committees, which held an aggregate of over 8,000 meetings'.[63] They oversaw every aspect of the war, some of the principal committees being Home Defence, Food Production, Civil Defence,

North American Supply, Reconstruction, and Post-War. Some waned as the war continued: Defence (Operations) met fifty-two times in 1940, but only ten times in 1944, and never again after. Others grew in importance as the war went on, notably those concerned with planning for peace: 'Post-War Reconstruction' thus met just four times in 1941, when the subject was not a great priority, but met over 100 times in 1944.

As historian Richard Overy writes, the committee system was critical to Allied victory:

> No one man could hope to master every area of activity; delegation was an absolute necessity. The Western war effort was run by large committees staffed by both Allies. These committees formed the apex of a pyramid of staffs and offices where the routine work of the war effort was conducted. The war was not so much led as administered ... Behind each leader there emerged a cohort of military managers and civilian officials who took on the real responsibility of running the war.[64]

The Second World War, still more than the first, required a massive expansion of government authority and reach. Historian Robert Tombs comments that the British war effort 'matched totalitarian levels of mobilization without using totalitarian methods'.[65]

In 1940 and 1941, the Defence Committee met very frequently, chaired by Churchill. Thereafter, the Chiefs of Staff Committee effectively took over, meeting daily at 10.30 a.m., and holding some 2,000 meetings during the war. None of the Chiefs of Staff was more frequently exasperated by Churchill than Alan Brooke, Chief of the Imperial General Staff, whose diaries are peppered with irritation. Brooke was a powerful influencer of military strategy; and, like Hankey, he was wont to make pungent judgements in his diary. 'Temperamental like a film star' and 'peevish like a spoilt child' are two such jibes about Churchill. More damning still: 'I just cannot get him to face the true facts!' He had 'no long term vision ... In all his plans he lives from hand to mouth. He can never grasp a whole plan ... My God how tired I am of working for him.' He encapsulated his divided feelings about the Prime Minister in a diary entry in 1941: 'God knows where we would be without him, but God knows where we shall go with him.'[66]

Historian Andrew Roberts probes Churchill's determination to avoid the 'dangerous dissensions between the "Frocks" [politicians] and the "Brass Hats" [soldiers]' that had characterised the government during the First World War.[67] He achieved this, to the extent that he did, by 'working on all strategic problems with and through the Chiefs of Staff, however frustrating they all found it at times'.[68] Churchill had insisted on becoming Minister of Defence in 1940 as well as Prime Minister to insert himself into the heart of military strategy. He later wrote in his memoirs on the Second World War, which rival Lloyd George's in length and subjectivity:

> The key change … on my taking over was of course the supervision and direction of the Chiefs of Staff Committee by a Minister of Defence with undefined powers. As this minister was also the Prime Minister, he had all the rights inherent in that office, including very wide powers of selection and removal of all professional and political personages.[69]

The Cabinet Office would play a vital role during the Second World War in the organisation of the international conferences to coordinate the Allied war effort, an echo of the niche Hankey had carved out for it during and after the First World War. Cabinet Office staff thus accompanied Churchill to conferences in Washington in 1941 and 1942, Moscow in 1942, Quebec and Tehran in 1943, and Yalta and Potsdam in 1945. Winnifrith, who attended some of these, noted the puzzlement of the Americans at the civilian Cabinet Office team:

> The Americans just couldn't get over the spectacle of our staff coming off the ship or off the aeroplane, all our typists and clerks [were] girls dressed in civilian dress, with the Americans – all of them – in uniforms. They speedily learned, though, to respect the skill and energy of our civilian staff, and our military officers were proud of their civilian subordinates.[70]

The risks and demanding nature of international travel in cold and slow propeller planes notwithstanding, the Cabinet Office's standards were upheld by Bridges: 'travelling with Winston, for example, going to Moscow etc., one would do minutes on the plane. Everything had to be up to date.'[71] The 'Combined Chiefs of Staff', set up with the Americans in January 1942, was also serviced by the War Cabinet Office. From June 1941, the British Joint Staff Mission liaised with the American Joint Chiefs of Staff, while the British Civil Secretariat, set up in 1943, supported British Ambassador Lord Halifax and other senior diplomats in the United States.[72] By 1945, some twenty-four Cabinet Office staff were permanently stationed in Washington.[73]

Back in London, the decision had been taken in December 1940 to move the Cabinet Office from Richmond Terrace, which was aged and vulnerable to bombs, to the nearby Government Offices on Great George Street (GOGGS) bordering Parliament Square. Beneath GOGGS, the Cabinet War Rooms had been carefully constructed, with a reinforced bunker providing physical protection for Churchill, his family, and other key staff. Considerable work had taken place throughout 1939 and 1940, strengthening the floor with ferrous concrete capable of withstanding a direct hit from the skies. This reinforced area was 'intended to be the last resort in the event of a devastating attack on London by the *Luftwaffe*, or other German forces. Provision was therefore made for key personnel to be housed in this accommodation.'[74] The building, nevertheless, was still vulnerable: if a bomb fell at an angle, it could penetrate the side wall which had not been reinforced. With gallows' humour, the office staff, deploying a cricket term, joked about the 'in-swinger' that would kill them all. In fact, neither the Great George Street building, nor the Foreign Office, nor indeed Richmond Terrace, ever received a direct hit in the war. By contrast, 10 Downing Street and 70 Whitehall were severely damaged by bombs falling nearby.

Life had to go on. The Cabinet Office was in operation twenty-four hours a day, 365 days a year. Staff slept in War Cabinet rooms; one remembers the conditions as 'very stuffy ... We had tin beds, army type.'[75] But there were compensations: '[T]here was a luncheon club in the Ministry of Agriculture and Fisheries, and we had some subsidised bonds. I think we used to pay something like a pence and two shillings for our lunch. It was quite good. Well, it supplemented the rations.'[76]

The Cabinet War Room 'bulletin', an update of secret news, had to be prepared every day and be taken by the leading 'map room officer' to George VI at Buckingham Palace. Staff vividly remember bulletins discussing the losses of merchant shipping, which rose to terrifying heights in 1942.[77] Morale, though, seemed to remain high. Bridges recalled:

> [W]e all worked very long hours, many of us for years with very little let-up. But it didn't even in the least occur to any of us to regard this as a hardship, less so to feel any kind of resentment. Certainly I never remember anybody who worked in those years wishing to leave.[78]

Leadership and example from the top were all-important in the maintenance of morale under such relentless conditions. If the Cabinet Office was a naval vessel, Bridges was said to be its captain. 'Nobody complained, because in war it is drive and inspiration which are needed at the top,' wrote Colville. 'Without the unruffled competence of the Cabinet Office, which became, under Sir Edward Bridges, the powerful organisation it has ever since remained, and the patient diplomacy of General Ismay's Office of the Minister of Defence, the machinery of government would have broken under the strain.'[79]

THE EVOLUTION OF THE WAR CABINET OFFICE

The months leading up to D-Day on 6 June 1944 were particularly intense, but once the invasion had been successfully launched, Bridges's mind could roam more widely. In September 1944, he sought to clarify the separate functions of the modern Cabinet Office in a single document which, as he tellingly noted, 'have never been defined in any legal instrument, or other formal document'. Three distinct activities, he said, predominated. First was 'Normal Secretarial Duties', second 'Preparation of Material and Collation of Information on Matters Affecting Several Departments', while the third was, more prosaically, 'duties involving correspondence'.

'Normal secretarial duties' were the heart of the Secretariat's work, as had been pursued by Hankey ever since December 1916:

- The arrangement of meetings.
- The reproduction and circulation of agenda, memoranda and other documents.

- The drafting and circulation of minutes and conclusions.
- Follow-up action on conclusions to make sure that they are carried out.
- The drafting of reports.
- The custody and indexing of records.

The second function, i.e. 'preparation of material and collation of information on matters affecting several departments', was establishing some new ground. Bridges went back through the historical records to find antecedents for the centre coordinating Whitehall. He alighted upon a Treasury minute from 1904 that listed, as one of the duties of the Committee of Imperial Defence, the 'collation and coordination of information of relevance to the Committee'. The Cabinet Office's future role as the locus for a variety of central functions for Whitehall departments had clear antecedents with the approach taken by the CID, and explains how, like a gathering snowball, it gradually brought into its orbit, especially during war, a variety of diverse operators, including the Economic Section, the Central Statistical Office and the collation of research and intelligence for Whitehall. Bridges's document spoke thus about '[t]he collation of information ... from several departments in the form of draft memoranda or telegrams for consideration ... a natural development of normal secretarial duties, and as such is performed to greater or lesser extent by all committee secretaries'.[80]

'Correspondence', the third function, referred to communications with institutions or individuals, in Britain or abroad, not already the responsibility of any one single departmental minister. Under this heading are listed: communication between the government and the League of Nations; correspondence on intelligence with commanders-in-chief and other senior figures abroad; and correspondence with secretariats responsible for North American Supply, African Economic Affairs, and Allied Supplies. Here spelt out was justification for the major postwar responsibility the Cabinet Office was to acquire for the Commonwealth, and later Europe. No document better delineated the function and the role of the Cabinet Office, or foresaw the way that it would develop in the postwar world, including the formation of the National Security Council in 2010. Bridges was already alert to the risk of shifting too much responsibility to the Cabinet Office away from individual ministers, with a possibly detrimental impact on ministerial responsibility:

'[F]or this reason the conduct of correspondence on behalf of the Cabinet Committee is a development which requires to be closely watched.'[81]

Bridges's approach towards the writing of Cabinet minutes contrasts to Hankey, who, 'in general, recorded the individual statements of all Ministers who contributed to the discussion'. Bridges's system, in contrast, 'was to marshal the arguments which had emerged, pro and con, without attributing them to any individual, except when a Minister had so obviously expressed an individual opinion of considerable significance that its attribution to him was desirable'.[82] Indeed, Bridges expanded on the topic of how Cabinet minutes were to be written in 1943:

[I]t is an instruction of the Secretary, in drafting War Cabinet Conclusions, to avoid, so far as practicable, reference to opinions expressed by particular Ministers. The record in respect of each item will be limited to the decision of the War Cabinet together with such a summary of the discussion as may be necessary.[83]

Harold Wilson, the later Prime Minister, but then a Whitehall statistician who had joined from academic life in 1939, recalled an encounter with Bridges over the minutes:

In 1940, on a famous occasion, I recorded the Cabinet minutes, at the age of twenty-four. Sir Edward Bridges, Secretary of the Cabinet, came into my room – a gross breach of protocol: he should have sent for me – and said 'I want you to write the Cabinet minutes. I can't make head or tail of the discussion.' I stuttered that I had not been there and did not know what they had said. He said if I had been, I would not have been any better informed than he was. I tried vainly to excuse myself, and he thrust his notes across the table and asked me to read them. I was still no better informed. In the event he ordered me to produce the minutes in one hour, saying: 'This is your subject. You know what they ought to have decided, presumably. Write the minutes on those lines, and no one will ever question it.' He was right. They didn't.[84]

Wilson's portrait of a remote Bridges is not a typical one: but Wilson was no lover of the Treasury or its one-time mandarins, which was to become a theme of his premiership.

THE END OF THE WAR

Bridges's mind, as the war moved towards a conclusion, became increasingly engaged thinking about the postwar era at home and abroad. Regarding the latter, he looked at the Allied plan of dividing up Germany into American, British and Soviet sections. On 1 November 1944, he wrote to one of his senior officials in vivid prose, if not necessarily correct in his foreboding:

> Horrid thoughts. I know the proposal to have three high ranking officials [in postwar Germany], one from each power, at the head of the main divisions of the control staffs has been under consideration for a long time and is now virtually agreed. But I must say this vision of a whole series of three-headed monsters strikes me as one of Satan's happiest thoughts. I cannot conceive that such a series of bodies could possibly work effectively, unless it is arranged that one of the three heads is a nonentity and the second is always drunk. But I suppose this is past praying for![85]

George VI was one of many to appreciate the seminal importance of the Ismay and Bridges combination, highlighting their role in the celebrations of Allied victory. Ismay wrote: '[A]fter several group portraits had been taken, His Majesty remarked that he and Bridges and I ought to be taken together as the only three who kept our jobs throughout the war. But alas the proposal was not passed.'[86] If Bridges gave a speech to congratulate Cabinet Office staff as Hankey had done in November 1918, which he surely must have, no record of it appears to be in the archives. But his praise for their work was genuine. By the time the war ended in 1945, the Cabinet Office consisted of 123 senior staff, 453 'subordinates', making 576 in total.[87] There was very little time for celebration anyway. Shortly after VE Day on 7 May, Bridges oversaw the winding up of the war coalition government on 23 May 1945, and its replacement by the caretaker Conservative government headed again by Churchill, and its replacement two months later following the July general election by the Labour government under Clement Attlee, the first to have a full majority in Parliament. Attlee was exceedingly content to work with Bridges, a man with whom he shared many similar principles; as historian Kenneth O. Morgan testifies, 'the admiration was mutual'.[88]

Bridges's attention was preoccupied with the war in Japan, with no time to ease up. On 14 August, he recorded: 'The Cabinet met at 10:50 p.m. to discuss the Japanese surrender'. Foreign Secretary Ernest Bevin wrote out a message. The minutes record: 'Propose 6:30 Washington time, proceed for 7 p.m., W at midnight'. Attlee asked: 'Is this satisfactory?', to which Bevin replied that he wanted to get it checked with the State Department. Attlee responded: 'Assuming that it is OK, he would [broadcast] at 12 m-night. Send warning flash in advance.' That night, Attlee spoke to the nation from the Cabinet Room to say that the war with Japan was over and that the following day, 15 August, would be VJ Day.[89] Two weeks later, on 28 August 1945, Attlee wrote a memo on the atomic bombs which had so recently been dropped on Hiroshima and Nagasaki: 'We should declare that this invention has made it essential to end wars. The new World Order must start now … The time is short … I believe only a bold course can save civilisation.'[90]

Bridges had been unstinting for seven years, and was deeply fatigued. His lot was eased when Norman Brook joined as 'Additional Cabinet Secretary'. As historian John Bew observes, 'Attlee got on as well with … Brook.'[91] It would be Bridges, though, who was entrusted to go to Washington in December 1945 on the vital mission with Keynes to meet with American officials to secure a huge loan for postwar Britain. Bridges was deeply respected in Washington, and his role was to add further authority to the final stages of the negotiations. Eventually, a deal was reached that could be sent to the ministers in London; 'They will grumble but accept,' predicted Bridges.[92] He was correct: the loan agreement was signed on 6 December 1945, with Bridges benignly looking on. Bridges was the only Cabinet Secretary to go on to another position in the Civil Service. He continued to serve with distinction as Permanent Secretary at the Treasury, with perhaps less impact as Head of the Civil Service, until his retirement in 1956 at the unusual age of sixty-three. He led a quiet life subsequently, receiving a peerage in 1957, following the careers of his children with pride, including his son Tom, a diplomat who was to serve in No. 10 under Heath. Academic life, too, captivated Bridges during the final years of his life. He took great pleasure in being the Chancellor of the University of Reading.

In 1965, when Churchill died, Bridges would be one of the ceremonial pallbearers at his funeral, greeting the flag-draped coffin as it arrived at St Paul's and escorting it into the cathedral. Other Cabinet Office figures Ismay and Brook were among the pallbearers. A stickler for correct form, Bridges remained to the end a passionate believer in government secrecy, keeping no personal papers of historic consequence. Nevertheless, he felt moved to write just once, following the publication of a book by Churchill's doctor, Lord Moran, in 1956, entitled *Winston Churchill: The Struggle for Survival*. Bridges felt Moran had betrayed his confidentiality and had given an inaccurate version of Churchill, as indeed had Churchill's friend Violet Bonham Carter in her book *Winston Churchill: As I Knew Him*. To counterbalance these misrepresentations, he agreed to contribute to a book edited by historian John Wheeler-Bennett called *Action this Day*.[93]

When he died in August 1969, he was two-thirds of the way through working on his father's papers. A meticulous notetaker until the end, his sitting room was full of little postcards covered with his writing. Bridges was trying to bring order to his father's disordered papers, just as he had brought order to Britain's government during its great trial during the Second World War.

NORMAN BROOK, PHOTOGRAPHED IN HIS OFFICE IN 1956

CHAPTER 5

NORMAN BROOK: COMMANDER OF THE MID-TWENTIETH CENTURY, 1946–63

When you write the Cabinet minutes
You write not what they said,
Nor what they thought they said,
But what they would have said
If they had thought what they were saying[1]

BROOK'S CAREER AND CHARACTER

NORMAN BROOK WAS born in April 1902, a month before the Boer War ended, so just missed fighting in the First World War, though all the Prime Ministers he served had. He died in June 1967, aged just sixty-five, the month after the Beatles released their album *Sergeant Pepper's Lonely Hearts Club Band*. Yet, for the middle years of this century, he piloted the ship of the British state, steering one Labour and three Conservative Prime Ministers through the growth of the welfare state, the decline of empire and Britain as a world power, and the rise of government intervention in the economy.

In contrast to Bridges, Brook had a traditional, suburban upbringing, and was a much more conventional man. The son of Frederick Brook, a Bristol school teacher and inspector, he attended Wolverhampton Grammar School. Certainly, at school he was a high flyer: captaining the cricket team, in the first eleven of the football team, a prefect, debating laureate, a sergeant in the Officer Training Corps, editor of the *Wulfrunian*, a clarinettist in the orchestra,[2] and the recipient of a scholarship to Wadham College, Oxford. He obtained a First in Mods (the first part of the degree course) but, strangely given his intellect, only a Second in Finals. He married Ida Goshawk; there were no children. A career in the Civil Service seemed a natural choice for a young man from his background, and he was placed third in the HCS exams in 1925, being appointed to the Home Office. His solid-starting career was accelerated sharply by his catching the eye of John Anderson, Permanent Secretary of the Home Office (1922–32), who was one of the four dominant home civil servants in the interwar years, alongside Maurice Hankey, Warren Fisher and Horace Wilson.

On Anderson's retirement from the Home Office in 1932 he was appointed Governor of Bengal, but on his return from India he accepted Chamberlain's invitation to become Lord Privy Seal, a rare switch for a former official to ministerial office. He had no hesitation in picking out Brook as his PPS. Brook was to play an important role in helping prepare the country for war: when Anderson became Home Secretary in September 1939, he took Brook back to the Home Office with a brief to integrate air raid precautions into the wider responsibilities of the Home Secretary. When Churchill appointed Anderson Lord President in October 1940, succeeding Neville Chamberlain, Brook again followed him as his personal assistant. The Lord President's brief was wide-ranging, overseeing Cabinet Committees across the domestic front. Here, Brook had a penetrating insight into the entire Whitehall system. He excelled as head of Anderson's team and the relationship they cemented in these years was to endure until Anderson's death in January 1958.

When Rupert Howorth retired as Deputy Secretary (Civil) to the War Cabinet in March 1942, Brook was his natural successor. In November 1943, Churchill appointed Lord Woolton to the new Ministry of Reconstruction (a predecessor department had been created by Lloyd George in 1917); Woolton asked the greatly admired Brook to join him as Permanent Secretary. When, in July 1945, the department was abolished, Brook became the 'Additional' Cabinet Secretary working alongside Bridges, before becoming the sole Cabinet Secretary when Bridges went back to the Treasury in January 1947.

Physically, Brook was an imposing man, with a large head and heavy eyes. His voice was slow and, as with his writing, he considered every word. Not a hair was out of place on his tidy head, nor a paper on his desk, nor a thought in his mind. Everything about him was meticulous: his punctuality, his temperament, his judgement. He enjoyed travel, occasional golf and carpentry at home, which led to predictable jokes about his 'Cabinet making'. But his real hobby and joy was his career; he lived and breathed for his work. To Burke Trend (Cabinet Secretary 1962–73), he was classic Whitehall: 'essentially regulatory, rather than innovative in character ... his natural inclination was that of the Coordinator', ironing out differences between departments.[3] Subordinates found him austere: 'Brook was respected but feared,' recalled Armstrong, 'and not much sense of humour.'[4] Historian Kevin Theakston said Brook could be very formal, 'buttoned up', and genuine friendships developed with only a few intimates.[5] One of his colleagues, Lord Sherfield, formerly Roger Makins, described him as personally 'very warm, charming', 'not a ruthless administrator [but] a very firm administrator'.[6] Unsurprisingly, to the press, he was dubbed 'the man of secrets'. Our understanding of the years 1945–62 would be infinitely richer had he consented to a long and candid interview, kept a diary like Hankey or Cadogan, or written discursive letters; but he never did, nor did he write memoirs beyond his contribution to *Action this Day* about working with Churchill.

Humanity certainly lurked beneath the surface. Harold Evans, Macmillan's press secretary, artfully described him at one point as 'an Olympian figure whose aloof demeanour only partly concealed an amiable disposition and a dry sense of humour'.[7] Churchill's doctor Lord Moran thought that Brook was more approachable than Bridges: '[It] is easy to understand how the Cabinet rely on him and trust him.'[8] Brook on one level was a dry, professional mandarin, with chameleon-like gifts for serving different Prime Ministers and accommodating himself to the different Cabinets. Conservative constitutionally and politically, he had a passion for the Commonwealth and the traditions of British history. He accommodated himself to advancing social reform but was not forward-thinking when it came to issues of gender and racial equality.

His influence, indeed, was all-pervasive throughout his seventeen years as

Cabinet Secretary. You find his fingerprints 'almost everywhere you look in the Cabinet and premiership files of the period, including the most sensitive intelligence, nuclear and war planning areas', states Peter Hennessy.[9] His approach to the job has not, however, escaped criticism: 'Traditionalists could say with some justification that at times he seemed to fall into the trap of over-identification with the Prime Minister and government of the day,' wrote Theakston.[10] The position he came to occupy was akin to a 'chief of staff', as foreshadowed by Horace Wilson with Chamberlain in the 1930s, or William Armstrong with Ted Heath later in the early 1970s. Unlike these figures, he avoided the allure of over-identification, though he perhaps allowed himself to be overly captivated by the aura of Churchill and was overly protective of him.[11]

Working for Attlee, 1945–51

Brook had worked very closely with Attlee during the war and both men were pleased to find themselves working with each other again. His government was notable for 'the big beasts', who had been blooded with departmental responsibilities during the Second World War; notably, Ernest Bevin, Herbert Morrison, Hugh Dalton and Stafford Cripps. Attlee was a far more systematic, consistent politician than Churchill, with a much clearer ideological stance, informed by his clear socialist agenda. Douglas Jay, a junior Treasury minister, summed him up as 'a straightforward Victorian Christian, who believed one should do one's job and one's duty, whether as an army officer or member of Parliament, or Prime Minister'.[12]

A thorough shake-up of Cabinet and its committees had been anticipated in 1945, as after 1918, when the country last transitioned to peace. Attlee was conservative organisationally, and was keen to maintain the system he had seen working well during the war. He retained Cabinet Committees, but conducted them in a far more business-like manner. Kenneth Harris, one of his biographers, was impressed by his 'object, visible from the opening of business, [which] was to get the meeting over as soon as possible'.[13] An added blessing for Brook and his team of scribes was that Attlee's Cabinet meetings were easy to minute, aided by the concise and concrete way he summed his meetings up. There were downsides for officials: Attlee could be abrupt and openly critical: '[I]t is no good you coming here so ill-prepared and wasting everyone's time,' Deputy Cabinet Secretary Mallaby later recalled. He added: '[I] had never ... seen Churchill talk to his officials in such a manner.'[14] In truth, though, Churchill could be far more curt.

Jock Colville, who stayed on in the Private Office after Churchill departed in July 1945, thought Attlee had less of an ego than any other twentieth-century Prime Minister apart from Alec Douglas-Home (1963–64). But his ego could flare up under certain provocations. He was particularly riled when his colleagues criticised the army. This did not go down well with a man who attended the public school Haileybury and served as an officer in the First World War. Suddenly, startled colleagues would hear him snap back: 'What the hell do you mean?', or, 'You could keep your bloody sneers to yourself.'[15]

Never in the twentieth century had a new Prime Minister been better pre-pared for the job, having been an all-encompassing Deputy Prime Minister to Churchill since February 1942. From his earliest days at No. 10 after July 1945, difficult decisions had to be taken on a long list of major issues: the recovery of the economy, the occupation of Germany and Austria, policy towards Stalin, the building of a British atomic bomb and the transition from a wartime to a peacetime society. Brook's presence was felt at the heart of every major decision.

With Attlee's willing support, Brook after 1945 consolidated the Cabinet Committee structure that Bridges had built during the war, with the prin-cipal standing committees being 'Defence', 'Economic Policy and Home Affairs', and 'Legislation', a model that was to endure for fifty years. 'These committees', Brook said, 'take a great deal of weight off the Cabinet; they have settled quite a lot of things without reference to the Cabinet by virtue of ... devolution of authority.'[16] Brook wanted to codify and regularise not only Cabinet Committees, but also how ministers were to act, drafting the first 'Questions of Procedure for Ministers' in 1946 for Attlee to circulate, which was regularly updated by subsequent Prime Ministers.

Brook was effectively running the Cabinet Office alone for the first eight-een months even while nominally working in partnership with Bridges. From early on, he could be forceful with the most senior figures in Attlee's government. In November 1947, Chancellor of the Exchequer Dalton divulged information about tax changes to a journalist while walking into the Commons chamber before delivering his Budget speech. Brook was furious. The story was printed in the early edition of the evening papers before the Budget speech had been completed (an early example of real-time news). Brook wrote Attlee a 'damning' note about Dalton, stating that his comments 'off the record' were unacceptable: he had made 'a premature disclosure on the budget to which he had no right'.[17] Dalton was eventually forced to resign and, though the Lynskey Tribunal exonerated him, he returned to Cabinet a diminished figure.

Brook's strength can be seen in standing up to Aneurin Bevan, who was deeply opposed to Chancellor Gaitskell's (1950–51) plan to introduce prescription charges to help pay for the Korean War. Brook had written in a briefing note to the Prime Minister saying that 'the Cabinet will be asked on Monday to make a decision of principle ... To the Cabinet the question will presumably present itself in the form – Is it politically possible for the Government to abandon the principle of a free and universal health service?'[18] Bevan had been responsible for establishing the NHS, and was adamant the service should remain free. He wanted his dissent from the policy recorded in Cabinet minutes. Brook told him on 19 August 1950 that since the decision had to be a collective one, recording his dissent would be a breach of collective responsibility:

> When a minister who dislikes a particular proposal has deployed all his arguments against it and has failed to convince his colleagues, I believe that the doctrine of collective responsibility requires him to acquiesce in the decision taken ... He must either subordinate his view to that of his colleagues or part company with them.[19]

The debate rumbled on for nine months until 19 April 1951, when Brook's Cabinet notebooks record Bevan stating: 'I shall not vote in favour of N. Health Bill, if there is a vote. I shall resign after Third Rdg. I want this recorded.'[20] Bevan duly left the government four days later; a key turning point in the history of Attlee's government, and a sign of the deepening philosophical division in the Labour Party.

Brook was an utter stickler for both Cabinet collective responsibility and 'individual ministerial responsibility', which states the minister is responsible to Parliament for the policy and administration of his department. He dilated on the subject in one of his rare public pronouncements, a lecture given at his former department, the Home Office, in June 1959. He argued that the doctrine of collective responsibility predated the foundation of the Cabinet Office in 1916. In the eighteenth and nineteenth centuries, he said, it had been possible to reach a collective decision because topics under discussion were less complex, and were primarily political, 'which ministers understood, [rather than] economic questions which they did not'. Decisions then were more likely to be confined to a single department without cross-Whitehall implications. Additionally, ministers, too, were a different breed then, he said, and far more likely to meet 'socially, in the great houses with the political hostesses ... A lot of business was [efficiently] transacted in that fashion.'[21]

Brook then asserted that the need for ministers adhering to collective responsibility had become all the greater because of the developments since 1900, above all the growth of the welfare state, which he dated back to the National Insurance Act of 1911. The great expansion of government welfare and the economy since 1945 had made the task of achieving collective responsibility vastly more complex, though it could still be reached through a variety of devices, including the circulation of minutes to all ministers, ministers attending full Cabinet when their departmental responsibilities were being discussed, and the use of committees to ensure ministers with relevant interests were included in discussions and conclusions.

RETURN OF CHURCHILL, 1951–55

Brook was being lined up to be the Permanent Secretary of the Treasury, and Head of the HCS as Bridges's successor (Bridges was sixty in August 1952). In preparation, Attlee appointed Brook, who had never worked in the Treasury, in 1951 to be 'second Secretary' there, giving him experience of the dominant domestic department before the handover. The plan had not bargained for the return of Winston Churchill as Prime Minister in

October 1951. Churchill did not relish the prospect of working with Thomas Padmore, a high-ranking Treasury official selected to be the new Cabinet Secretary, whom he nicknamed 'Mr Podsnap'. Churchill, just a month off his seventy-second birthday, did not relish working with new and uncongenial faces. But he did know Brook, and had a high opinion of him from his eighteen months as Deputy Secretary of the Cabinet Office (1942–43). Why should he submit to the imposition of new staff? He flatly demanded that Brook remain in office. Brook was not unhappy; he liked and admired Churchill, seeing him as a fellow patriot and romantic about British history. Besides, the post of Cabinet Secretary had entrenched itself after 1945 as *the* key position in the Civil Service. Why would he want to leave the fount of power?

Brook had kept in touch with Churchill during 1945–51, when he had been Leader of the Opposition, not least over his memoirs of the Second World War. Attlee had agreed to let Churchill and his research team access government archives, as long as official secrets were not revealed, no party political gain was sought, and the Cabinet Office vetted the text. Brook personally rewrote several sections of the work, published in six volumes from 1948 to 1953. Brook ensured secrets, including Bletchley Park, were omitted. Brook possessed a deep understanding of Churchill's methods and frailties, and saw it as his duty to manage the ageing Prime Minister to the best of his ability, shielding him from the public gaze, and from the jibes of an antagonistic Cabinet. He believed that Churchill was as formidable in his first two years back at No. 10 as he had been during the war: '[T]he personal minutes still went out; but there were fewer of them and none now carried the old label "ACTION THIS DAY".'[22] But the rot set in after his stroke in June 1953. Brook's intimacy with Churchill came at the cost of closeness to Bridges, who had been unsuccessful in establishing a natural, close relationship as Churchill's Cabinet Secretary, even during the war, unlike his contemporaries Ismay, Jacobs and Colville. But Bridges and Brook had been close colleagues during the war, 'always in and out of each other's rooms, and close personal friends', as I wrote in *Churchill's Indian Summer*.[23] The initial fissures in their relationship began to emerge in the first eighteen months of the Attlee government, when Brook, fortified from his stint as a Permanent Secretary (at Reconstruction), wanted very much to run his own show at the Cabinet

Office. He resented Bridges, whom he saw as hanging around and holding onto the role, sensing perhaps that it was emerging as the more central
and influential post, rather than head of the Treasury or Civil Service.[24]
Differences between these Whitehall big beasts emerged over Civil Service
reform, which Bridges saw himself as driving, and over-embedding the new
army of technical specialists, economists, scientists and statisticians at the
heart of Whitehall. Brook believed the natural locus for these new adjuncts
should be in the Cabinet Office, not the Treasury.

Bridges and Brook were to unite in 1951 briefly on one subject – opposition to Churchill's attempts to remodel the centre of government with his
'overlord' system. But they quickly fell out again over Churchill's demand
that Brook remain for the duration of his premiership. (Could this have
been a factor in Brook's fighting so hard to keep Churchill in power for so
long?) Bridges was becoming an isolated figure at the Treasury, finding his
attempts at reforming Whitehall were thwarted. In March 1952, he wrote
in desperation to Brook: '… if those of us who have lived all our working
lives in Whitehall and have studied the Whitehall organisation give up as
hopeless all attempts to reform it from the inside, then what hope is there
of any reform in our time?'[25] Obstructed in his work, cut off from the Prime
Minister, on the losing side of decisions including Churchill's honours
list, and seeing his one-time subordinate usurping his position, inevitably
relations between the two men became cool. Bridges was certainly jealous
of Brook's influence: he may also have disapproved of a blurring of Civil
Service and ministerial lines. The coolness intensified in the run-up to the
Suez invasion by Eden in 1956, when Bridges felt excluded, as indeed he
had become. The tensions between the positions of Cabinet Secretary and
Head of the Civil Service were laid bare in the early 1950s as never before,
justifying in Brook's mind the need to unify both positions as soon as
politically possible.[26]

A totem of Churchill's preference for the company of Brook over
Bridges came in a rare honour he afforded Brook. As Colville recorded:
'Sir Norman Brook, whose wisdom and diligence he [Churchill] esteemed
and whose company he found so agreeable that he elected him to the
"Other Club".'[27] (The club had been founded by Churchill and F. E. Smith
in 1911, and dined fortnightly in the Savoy Hotel.) That was the highest

personal honour he could confer, and not one offered to either of Norman Brook's predecessors.[28]

So speedily did Brook re-establish his relationship with Churchill after his return that he was invited to the party that sailed to Washington to see President Truman just after Christmas Day 1951. Brook was one of the inner group gathered in Churchill's sitting room to toast the New Year. As Moran recorded: '[A]s the clock struck twelve times, his thoughts seemed a long way off. He pulled himself out of his chair, and put down his glass, crossing his arms, began to sing *Auld Lang Syne*. When this had been sung, he began to sing "God save the King". Then [Churchill] resumed his seat as if that part of the proceedings had been accomplished.'[29] Within no time, Churchill was asking for Brook's opinion on all kinds of issues, ministerial and Civil Service appointments, and how to handle difficult policy and negotiations, straying into Civil Service domain that was clearly Bridges's. Brook became a frequent weekend visitor to Chartwell, Churchill's home in Kent, and to Chequers, and almost invariably went on overseas trips with him: '[T]his was not on account of his expertise in foreign affairs but because Churchill found his calm judgement and advice indispensable.'[30]

Brook could be fierce in standing up to Churchill. After all, he had total job security, and nothing to lose. Their first fight came over Churchill's conviction that Whitehall needed to be 'cut down to size'. Brook drew up an organisation chart, featuring sixty committees, forty-seven sub-committees and seventeen working parties, which he showed Churchill. Churchill was not impressed. He wanted Cabinet Committees slashed and even terminated. He wanted to take personal charge over every facet of government, and feared the labyrinthine Cabinet Committee system would defeat him. Brook's response was to offer up nine committees that he could abolish or merge: but this failed to satisfy Churchill, whose response was that Brook: 'seemed to put very few birds out of this enormous covey'.[31] He told Brook: 'Pray let me have a list of the ones that you say could now be dispensed with so that at least we can make a beginning.'[32] Within a few days, Brook earmarked five more committees to satisfy Churchill's passion for economy.

Churchill won some minor battles in his desire to slim down the Cabinet Committees system: but Brook won the war. Within no time, the principal committees were continuing as under Attlee, with Churchill himself chairing the Defence Committee, with Chancellor Rab Butler chairing the Economic Committee, Lord President Salisbury the Home Affairs Committee, and Home Secretary David Maxwell Fyfe the Legislation Committee. Foreign affairs tended to be discussed in full Cabinet.[33] Churchill then turned his venom on Cabinet Committees consisting just of officials. He kept up pressure on Brook for them to be cut, on one occasion demanding that twenty be axed immediately. Before long, the senior mandarins began to complain to Brook that their neat system for coordinating Whitehall departments was in disarray. They compensated by increasingly meeting in their Whitehall clubs and in the Cabinet Office over lunch, ensuring government business was properly transacted in the absence of their official committees.[34]

The major Churchill–Brook dispute came over Churchill's enthusiasm for creating a system of 'overlord' ministers to oversee a number of departments, dispensing with the need for Cabinet Committees. Brook found a ready ally in his former masters, Labour, who were similarly incandescent about Churchill's hare-brained scheme, arguing in November 1951 and again in April 1952 that coordination had previously taken place by the chairmen of committees in secret, whereas now the identity of the coordinating ministers would obviously be public.[35] Did Brook and fellow mandarins work to undermine the scheme by withholding their full support? It is unknown. The overlord system never worked well though, and 'within a year the former pattern of ministerial and official committees began to exert itself, as Churchill's attention moved away from the machinery of government'.[36] In August 1953, Churchill minuted Bridges, in his capacity as Head of the HCS, asking for a 'statement, admitting that the experiment should be wound up: a statement should be prepared on how necessary this was and how what has been achieved justifies the means [a] having created, and [b] abolishing the post in question. This might extend to 500 words.'[37] Which, as master Whitehall watcher Peter Hennessy observes, had 'a delicious ironic touch'.[38]

Despite Churchill's efforts, the total number of Cabinet meetings increased in 1952, with 108 sessions, as opposed to eighty-seven under Attlee in 1950. The Economic Policy, Home Affairs and Legislation standing committees met similarly or more frequently, while the Defence committee met slightly less.[39] The following year, Brook wrote to Churchill, perhaps with a hint of satisfaction, to say there had been no substantial reduction in Cabinet meetings or committees in 1953.[40] Churchill was also keen on brevity in official papers, and Brook encouraged him to reissue a 1940 instruction he sent around Whitehall in November 1951.[41] A few days later, Churchill did just that, with an attached note: 'Official papers are too long and too diffuse. In 1940 I called for brevity. Evidently I must do so again.'[42]

Brook always prevailed over Churchill in retaining his full complement of Cabinet Office staff, all seconded on short-term contracts from other departments. Brook liked to retain a small number of officials he considered particularly effective for longer periods, though he never found one particular protégé, as he had been to John Anderson. Beneath him was a Deputy Secretary, Ian Jacob, who oversaw the Defence Committee for a period, to Churchill's delight and encouragement. On the civil side, he had two Under Secretaries, one being George Mallaby (1950–54), who very unusually had been a headmaster and, even more unheard of for an official in the Cabinet Office, went on to write two books.[43]

Brook would sit by Churchill's side at Cabinet meetings, with Under Secretaries taking notes. He himself would make a note of the most important items, in crisp writing about two-thirds of a page in length, conforming closely to the final printed minutes that were circulated to ministers. The minutes written by his staff had to be finished by 4 p.m. on the afternoon of the Cabinet Meeting. Names of individual ministers were not usually to be mentioned, and he insisted final minutes should be brief and 'to the point'. The one occasion where a minister could be mentioned was when he or she specifically requested it, and when they did not contest the conclusion. Mallaby recorded Brook's iron routine, how we 'went back to the Cabinet Office after the meeting ... then we examined our notes very carefully and the determination was that we should not miss any point of importance that had been made in the discussion ... we should not expose anything that distorted the collective responsibility of the Cabinet.'[44]

The conclusions of Brook's Cabinets might have satisfied the requirements of collective responsibility. However, they did not satisfy all ministers, especially not those with historical minds. Harold Macmillan, then Minister of Housing, memorably told Mallaby he thought Cabinet officials were falsifying the truth:

Historians reading this in 50 or 100 years hence will get a false picture. They will be filled with admiration and surprise to find the Cabinet were so intellectually disciplined that they argued each issue methodically and logically through a set of neat and precise conclusions. It isn't like that at all [and] you know it.[45]

The Cabinet Office's defence was that it was perfectly aware of the risk of falsifying history, but more prosaic concerns were given higher priority: '[T]he form of minutes preferred by Brook, and perfected by him, was the best way of getting action taken.'[46]

Brook expended considerable energy drafting the agenda for Cabinet, for which he gave Churchill increasingly directed handling advice. The Cabinet Office would collate agenda ideas from ministers and officials, more rarely from Churchill himself, often with Brook providing them himself because he knew the various topics that most needed to be discussed.[47] But it could not stop Churchill interfering with his good order. At the start of the meeting he would announce that 'item X' was the one that really mattered and should be taken first. As Hankey found with Lloyd George, Churchill's idiosyncrasy played havoc with Brook's detailed preparations, including notifying the non-Cabinet ministers waiting outside in the ante-room precisely at the right moment they were to enter. On other occasions, Churchill would become confused, and when Brook's officials pointed out that he had missed an item on the agenda, he would retort angrily: 'What is it you are doing? I am well aware of the business. You should hold your tongue and attend to your menial task.'[48]

Churchill was content to take rebukes from Brook he would from no one else. In March 1952, Churchill wrote a note to him to say he strongly disliked the American expression 'Top Secret', and much preferred the traditional English phrase 'Most Secret', which he wanted readopted. With quicksilver pen, Brook shot back: 'I share your dislike of the term top secret and wish we had never had to adopt it', but went on to say that the expression was now in use by NATO, Commonwealth countries and the United States, and returning to the old style would cause immense upheaval. Moreover, as he delicately slipped in: '… it was introduced with your approval in 1944.' Churchill responded two days later: 'I surrender.'[49]

Brook played a sensitive and controversial role in ensuring efficient government continued after the Prime Minister had a stroke on 23 June 1953. Brook worked with Colville, whom he also insisted return in 1951 as his PPS, and with his *Parliamentary* Private Secretary Christopher Soames (the husband to his youngest child, Mary) to ensure the news of the stroke was kept from the public, a feat that would have been impossible to achieve in recent times. To compound the problem, Anthony Eden, Churchill's designated successor, had had an operation on 10 June in Boston, USA, to repair the damage from botched bile duct operations in the UK, and was on long-term convalescence.[50] Churchill had little confidence in the next in line after Eden, Rab Butler. Every ounce of Brook's discretion, tact and judgement was required to keep the government on the rails.

Churchill was smuggled down to Chartwell, and the inner team milked Churchill's friendships with the press barons: soon stories circulated about him being temporarily unwell, but the government continued to function. Brook had to overcome several qualms including allowing Soames, who was not a government minister, on Colville's insistence, to see secret papers. By mid-August, Churchill was starting to feel better: 'I am going to have my lunch today while Norman Brook tells me the agenda for the Cabinet,' he chirpily told his doctor on 18 August.[51] 'I am astonished by the speed of his recovery,' stated a relieved Brook.[52]

Accordingly, he advised Churchill, against the views of most of the Cabinet, that he should stay on if he wished. To the chagrin of his Cabinet colleagues, who hoped his withdrawal would be a prelude to his departure, he shot off for a long holiday in September. They were still more irritated when he announced at the annual Conservative Party Conference in October that he would be staying on as Prime Minister to fulfil vital international work. Junior whip Ted Heath rose to the platform to praise his 'inspirational leadership' and 'magnificent speech'.[53] Churchill's vigour, however, declined after that autumn: '[H]e initially struggled to preserve his life and then struggled to remain in office,' wrote Brook.[54] That December, Moran and Brook had a critical discussion about the future, with the physician praising the skills of the mandarin as those of a high-grade medic: 'I value Brook's opinion,' Moran wrote. He recorded verbatim their quasi-medical assessment of Churchill's continued fitness for office: 'During the

War', he wrote, 'the Prime Minister had a gift for picking out two or three things and getting them up in detail – that was his strength. He made no attempt in those days to keep up with lots of things. Now, of course, he is a lazy Prime Minister; he reads novels after breakfast. But it is much better from the country's point of view that he should stay on.'[55] Why did Brook believe in keeping on a seriously ill 79-year-old rather than letting natural political processes take their course, and to make way for Eden, his anointed successor, waiting impatiently in the wings? It is difficult to know precisely. We do know he blocked Eden using the title 'Deputy Prime Minister, agreeing with George VI's Private Secretary, Alan Lascelles, that doing so would have compromised the King's prerogative to choose the new Prime Minister'.[56] We do know Churchill had increasing doubts about Eden's temperamental nature, and whether he would be an effective Prime Minister. Colville told me so several times. Were Churchill's reservations shared by Brook? If Brook had such inner doubts, we know he would never have shared them with anyone, any more than he would have told anyone why he was propping up Churchill.

Delay would only postpone inevitable succession. Brook still thought that Churchill was managing Cabinet satisfactorily in December 1953 and retained this belief as late as July 1954, after a bruising seven months since Christmas.[57] Not all have agreed with Brook's judgement: historian John Grigg, the son of Churchill's wartime minister Edward Grigg, wrote an article in *Encounter* condemning the handling of the stroke and Churchill's continuance in power after 1953.[58]

Churchill stood firm, determined to remain in office until he had reached an understanding with the Soviet Union, in what he regarded as newly promising conditions following the death of Stalin in March 1953. On 11 May, Churchill with Colville's support, had outwitted the Foreign Office in Eden's absence, delivering a powerful speech against their advice calling for talks with the USSR. Brook's loyalties were now deeply divided. Disagreement over the prospect of talks regularly broke out in Cabinet, with Eden and Salisbury providing the main dissent from Churchill's scheme. Churchill argued in Cabinet in July 1954 that it was his right as Prime Minister to conduct negotiations with foreign leaders, to which Salisbury replied that if Churchill felt that way, 'we should have to consider our position also'. Churchill conceded that 'I may have exaggerated my hope for strengthening world peace'.[59]

Divisions flared up again in mid-March 1955, shortly before his resignation. Churchill seized on his hope of a forthcoming visit to Europe by President Eisenhower to delay his departure again. The idea of another delay was greeted with dismay by Cabinet. Eden was already planning an early general election for May 1955, and was worried about how such a visit would be perceived. Churchill said: 'Suppose it were said we had discouraged visit by E[isenhower] to Europe in order that we might be able to seize Party advantage in a snap election.'[60] Cabinet debated the possible date of polling day, and the risk of capitalising on or deterring a visit from Eisenhower. Eden asked Churchill: 'Are the PM's plans off if E[isenhower] is likely to come to Europe later in the summer?' Churchill responded: 'A new sit[uation] I sh[ould] have to consider my public duty.' Eden, by now clearly furious, responded: 'If I am not competent to meet E[isenhower] then as Prime Minister, that w[ould] rule for all time.'[61]

Brook faced the possibility of a deeply revered Prime Minister, who had just had his eightieth birthday to national acclaim, resigning in anger, dividing the Conservative Party and country. Inaction was also risky: if Churchill stayed on, Cabinet resignations were likely. In the end, Brook helped coax both parties to the 'right decision'. 'On the whole', Moran thought, 'Eden had behaved well under provocation.' Brook admitted that the final days for Churchill had been 'rather sad'.[62] Churchill eventually went to the Palace to see the new Queen Elizabeth II on 5 April 1955. A day later, in line with the Royal Prerogative, Eden went to the Palace and emerged as Prime Minister; a job he had anticipated for fifteen years and more, the frustrations of delay not helping his own physical and mental health.

EDEN AND SUEZ, 1955–57

If Brook doubted Eden's suitability to be Prime Minister, due to his inexperience with domestic policy, he shared them with no one. Eden's biographer, Richard Thorpe, is clear: 'Norman Brook was intensely loyal to Eden, and in no way thought he was not up to it.'[63] If Churchill's stroke and continued questionable capacity to remain as Prime Minister had dragged Brook into a moral dilemma, Eden was about to drag Brook into the greatest moral crisis of his career. This was the Suez Crisis, precipitated by the Egyptian President Colonel Nasser's decision for his forces to seize control and nationalise the Anglo-French canal on 26 July 1956. Eden was hosting a dinner for the King and Prime Minister of Iraq when he heard the news: both advised Eden to hit Nasser hard, soon, and alone.

Brook had long been alert to the possibility of trouble in the Middle East. In 1954, he wrote to Eden to express his concern about confusion with Washington over British policy in the region. Even as Foreign Secretary, Eden had learnt he could rely on counsel from Brook, as in discussions with Eisenhower on handling Egypt: 'We can have no confidence in the regime in Egypt,' Brook declared.[64] In April 1956, one year precisely after Eden became Prime Minister, Brook wrote to Eden reminding him of a paper that he had circulated as Cabinet Secretary in February 1953, which concluded that

> it would be a delusion to suppose that in Egypt, or elsewhere in the Middle East, opinion would tolerate American or French forces any more than the Egyptians put up with the British garrison on the canal … if we are to maintain influence in this area we must harness [nationalist] movements.[65]

Eden pondered this advice. When the crisis came, though, he made it explicitly a head-on clash between him and the Arab nationalist Nasser.

During the summer of 1956, Brook became increasingly concerned by the direction of Eden's thinking, and by the growing opposition to a British retaliation at home and abroad. In August, he gave Eden unambiguous advice:

> All the members of the Cabinet, without exception, are solidly in agreement that we cannot afford to let Nasser get away with this, – for if he succeeds we lose our oil and with it our standard of life in this country, not to mention our position in the Middle East and our influence as a

World Power. The Cabinet are therefore agreed that we must stop this at all costs and that, in the last resort if all other methods fail, we must be ready to use force ... But some in various degrees, think that, before we resort to force, we must be able to show that we have made an honest effort to reach a settlement by peaceful means and have exhausted all the 'other methods'.[66]

He added: 'Some ministers are less certain than others about the extent to which "middle" opinion in this country would support forceful action at this stage.'[67] His counsel was that it would require a *further* provocative act from Nasser and that an international agreement from the UN might well be vital. John Hunt, the future Cabinet Secretary (1973–79), was then Private Secretary to Brook: he later maintained that Brook was so secretive about Suez that he knew little to nothing of what was going on.[68] But Brook knew it all. He was secretary to the Egypt Committee, chair of the Egypt (official) Committee and of the Defence (Transition) Committee overseeing Suez. He knew every single Suez secret, even the worst.

At Cabinet on 23 October, Eden reminded ministers that the British and French governments were presented with the choice of prolonged negotiations or early military intervention, but the latter was difficult to delay indefinitely because 'neither we or the French could be seen to keep our military in a state of readiness'. If it was this option that had to be pursued, he concluded that 'brave decisions would have to be taken by the Cabinet'.[69] What Eden did not share with his Cabinet colleagues was that Israeli Prime Minister David Ben Gurion and Patrick Dean from the Foreign Office had travelled secretly to France to meet with senior political and military French officials the day before. Together they plotted a course of action in which Israel would attack Egypt, and Britain and France would intervene ostensibly to protect the canal as peacekeepers. The secret agreement was called the 'Protocol of Sèvres', after the commune in the south-west of Paris where the talks took place, also the location of peace treaty talks with Turkey in 1920.

When Dean returned to London, he went to see Eden and showed him the Protocol. Eden was horrified, said that he had not agreed to it and demanded that Dean destroy all the evidence of any records. He sent the hapless Dean back to Paris to convince the French to destroy their record too. The French were thrown: Dean was ushered into a room and the door was locked. Held without food or drink for four hours, an official later came to tell him that the French refused to destroy their record. Besides, he was reminded, the Israelis had a copy themselves.

On 29 October, the Protocol was put into action. Israel invaded Egypt: Britain and France vetoed an American Resolution at the UN Security Council calling for an end to the Israeli actions. Britain requested Egypt leave the Suez Canal and, when this request was refused, Britain and France launched their invasion. Cabinet met on 30 October with the sole topic of the Suez Canal. Brook wrote the bald words 'note not taken' in his notebook.[70]

The Egyptian military was swiftly defeated, but not before they had blocked the very canal that Eden was intervening to keep open. Eisenhower, on the cusp of his presidential re-election on 6 November, reacted sharply. He had warned Eden strongly not to invade and he threatened retaliation against British finances. At home, violent debate took place in the House of Commons and across the country, with Labour leader Hugh Gaitskell calling the invasion 'an act of disastrous folly'.[71] With a vote in the UN 64:5 against the military invasion, Cabinet divided, sterling falling dramatically, Eden was forced to end military operations after capturing only twenty-three miles of canal.

On 20 December 1956, seven weeks later, Edward Heath (by now Chief Whip) was talking to Eden's PPS Frederick Bishop outside the Cabinet. According to Heath:

Sir Norman Brook, the Cabinet Secretary, came through the door from the Cabinet Room, where he had been seeing the Prime Minister, looking like an old Samurai who had just been asked to fall on his sword. We paused, as Brook said: 'He's told me to destroy all the relevant documents. I must go and get it done.' With that, Sir Norman, loyal as always to his Prime Minister, went off to destroy the Sèvres Protocol and other documents which confirmed the collusion between Britain, France and Israel over Suez. Anthony Eden always denied that any such agreement had ever existed … he never changed his position.[72]

Brook was doubly at fault over Suez: for not preventing Eden on 20 December from lying to the House of Commons ('there was not foreknowledge that Israel would attack Egypt') and for destroying the documents. When, in the 1980s, the files were being reviewed in Whitehall before release to the National Archives, the then Cabinet Secretary Robert Armstrong (1979–87) wrote that Brook was 'known to have destroyed a file of private papers which he had relating to the Suez affair'.[73] Brook was alleged to have said that he took 'damn good care that the truth does not come out'. Later Cabinet Secretaries condemned his action. Bridges was scathing, saying that if he had been Cabinet Secretary, 'Suez would never had [*sic*] happened.'[74] This is a significant indictment. Never before or since has a Cabinet Secretary been so critical of another. It highlights the extent of Brook's folly and misplaced loyalty. Had indeed Bridges still been Cabinet Secretary, the deception may have come to light and the Suez invasion, with all the damage it did to Britain's reputation in the region, might not have occurred. Robert Armstrong paused for a long time when I asked him if he would have destroyed documents at the request of the Prime Minister. He admitted quietly that he hoped that he would not have done so, but that, if he had not, he would have put the document away in a very secret place, where it would be opened only by the Cabinet Secretary of the day.[75] Richard Wilson (1998–2002) said that if he had been confronted by similar actions he hoped he would not have acted as Brook had done, while Andrew Turnbull (2002–05) called Brook's actions 'reprehensible'.[76] Armstrong wonders whether Brook might have reflected that it did not matter very much what he did: the French and Israeli governments after all had their own copies of the protocol. Comparison must be drawn to Churchill's destruction of sensitive documents at the end of the war.

Brook's relationship with Bridges was over, but he retained a special bond to Eden even after he resigned as Prime Minister on 9 January 1957. In March 1957, he prepared a document for his successor Harold Macmillan, who was to pay a visit to him – a delicate matter as Eden was such a damaged predecessor: no other Prime Minister had left No. 10 that century, not Lloyd George nor Chamberlain, with his credibility at such a low ebb. The note shows Brook's almost feline insight into Eden's preoccupations and agitated state of mind. The former Prime Minister would want to talk, he advised his new boss, about nuclear weapons, where he was becoming concerned about the growing antipathy, with the Campaign for Nuclear Disarmament (CND) formed in 1957. Eden's belief was that it stemmed from the decision to allow the US to station nuclear missiles in Britain. Brook said that Eden 'wondered why this was necessary ... he thought the state of public opinion was due to fear, and partly due to anti American feelings'.[77] Eden would also want to discuss oil, where he believed Nasser's aim was to gain control of Saudi Arabia and its oil supply. It would thus be wise to build up an alternative supply.

Brook said Eden would also want to raise the topic of his memoirs, which he was anxious to see published, in part to see his record vindicated (he continued to deny collusion), and in part to raise money (he was paid a £100,000 advance by *The Times*). Eden hoped that Macmillan and the Cabinet Office would allow him access to the public records, as Churchill had enjoyed for his six-volume war history of the Second World War. Eden's first volume, *Full Circle* (1960), dealt with his postwar career, including Suez. Eden would eventually confront the truth in a private interview in 1967, which he said could not be used until after his death. He at last acknowledged collusion but offered a defence: '[T]he joint enterprise and the preparation for it were justified in the light of the wrongs it was designed to prevent. I have no apologies to offer.'[78]

Eden continued to blame his colleagues, especially Rab Butler. In the private papers of Eden's wife, Clarissa, records exist of a memo Eden wrote on 9 September 1968 purporting to show Brook a secret Suez sympathiser:

Norman Brook remarked to me when I saw him in his house in London today, as he had done before, that it was a calamity that we had had to adapt our views over the Suez business to allay the qualms of the weaker brethren of whom Rab mattered the most. They were not prepared to face direct action against Egypt by the time our military preparations were ready. On the other hand they were prepared to go along with more devious arrangements which obscured this. Yet Rab was the one member of the Cabinet who since then had spoken in half-truths and criticism of all that happened. In other words, those for whom we had bent our tactics proved the least loyal.

Rab was kept closely informed by me of every development in the Suez business from the beginning to the end. He missed no important Cabinet and when, as sometimes happened, he arrived late, we waited for him. Norman Brook told me that Rab had also attended a number of the meetings of our Cabinet Committee on Suez, on one occasion he had presided over it.

Norman Brook told me that he had looked up the composition of our Cabinet Committee. The committee was at my decision set up and its members chosen by the Cabinet itself in session.

I mentioned to Norman Brook the tale which I understood was to appear in the *Sunday Times* [in the forthcoming Lacey serialisation] that the Queen, as a result of the promptings of Mountbatten, had telephoned her concern to me during the Suez crisis. There was of course not a word of truth in this. Norman Brook told me that he was sure that there was not.[79]

MACMILLAN, 1957–62

Macmillan, the last Prime Minister of four in succession to have served in the First World War, was admirably qualified to become Prime Minister, having been both Chancellor and Foreign Secretary, albeit briefly, in 1955–57. He was one of those Conservative Prime Ministers – Heath and Major were others – who were happier working with civil servants than fellow politicians. Macmillan was extraordinarily close to four: Frederick Bishop, Tim Bligh, Philip de Zulueta and, of course, Norman Brook. Bishop had been an Assistant Secretary at the Cabinet Office, hence Brook's recommendation that he become Eden's PPS in 1956. Macmillan kept him on and used his services extensively, notably sending him to Washington to help repair the Anglo-US relationship in early 1957 post-Suez, and going with Macmillan on a critical visit to see Soviet leader Nikita Khrushchev in 1959. During the general election that year, Macmillan practised his speeches in Bishop's garden in East Grinstead, Sussex. Even after Bishop returned to the Cabinet Office as Deputy Secretary at the end of that year, he continued to advise Macmillan on foreign affairs. Macmillan became equally close to Bishop's successor Bligh as PPS, who quickly came to see his primary loyalty not to the Civil Service but to the Prime Minister, becoming part of the tight family group that surrounded him.[80] Macmillan wanted Bligh with him on his epic African tour in January and February 1960, which lasted six weeks, and kept him by his side until the end of his premiership in October 1963. He leaned heavily on his foreign affairs Private Secretary, Guy Millard, and after he departed in 1957, Philip de Zulueta, who for the next six years worked intensely with Macmillan. Not insignificantly, Bishop, Bligh and de Zulueta all left the Civil Service prematurely, unable to adjust to Whitehall life after leaving the intensity and power of No. 10.

Brook had already tolerated the irregular position that Colville had enjoyed, who left the Civil Service with Churchill in 1955. He does not appear to have been exercised, as subsequent Cabinet Secretaries were, when officials became too identified with their Prime Minister, losing their impartiality in the process. None, indeed, surpassed the influence of Brook, who was described as Macmillan's 'chief of staff', a title his successors would have baulked at. This was the position that was to be officially created by Tony Blair in 1997, when he appointed former Foreign Office diplomat Jonathan Powell at the apex of his No. 10 staff.[81] Macmillan's own description of the Cabinet Office is illuminating:

> Parallel to Downing Street staff, but not exclusive to the service of the Prime Minister, is the Cabinet Office. Its head acts as Secretary to the Cabinet, and he and his colleagues serve all Ministers alike. But necessarily since all Cabinet papers are circulated by permission of the Prime Minister and since all various committees of Ministers, permanent and temporary, are set up only with the approval of the Prime Minister, the Secretary to the Cabinet acts in effect both as co-ordinator and friend in a very special degree. It was my good fortune to have from the beginning the outstanding services of Sir Norman Brook.[82]

The term 'friend in a very special degree' is one at which we might cavil. The successors did not attain 'very special' friend stature with their Prime Ministers, but neither did they seek it or think it appropriate.

Another insight from his diary comes in 1959, when Macmillan is reading

Lloyd George's *War Memoirs*. Macmillan reflects on how much better he himself is supported: 'The contrast today is very great. I am admirably served in the Private Office. The Cabinet Secretariat has become a very efficient machine.'[83] The comparison is odd not the least because Lloyd George enjoyed more support, with Cabinet Secretariat and Prime Minister's Secretariat, than any predecessor in history. It may well be that Macmillan knew little about this: it is a constant surprise how little most Prime Ministers know about the working lives of their predecessors.

Cabinet under Macmillan saw more free-flowing discussion than under Eden, and was a more structured environment than under Churchill. Lord Muirshiel, who as John Maclay was Scottish Secretary, remembered Macmillan as 'a delight as a Chairman of Cabinet' and the meetings were always 'a very pleasant experience, even if one wasn't always getting one's entire way oneself'.[84] Macmillan's habit, though, was to avoid problems rather than confront them, a common and understandable Prime Ministerial trait. Alec Douglas-Home later related one particular episode of avoidance:

> One morning I came into the Cabinet room rather early and found the Cabinet Secretary, Sir Norman Brook, changing all our places. I asked what had happened – Had there been a shuffle? – or had one of us died in the night? 'Oh no,' said Sir Norman, 'it's nothing like that. The Prime Minister cannot stand Enoch Powell's steely and accusing eye looking at him across the table any more, and I've had to move him down to the side.'[85]

Macmillan held eighty-six meetings of Cabinet in 1957, sixty-five in 1960, but just sixty in 1961. Brook sent Macmillan a memo in 1961, commenting on the decline, saying it would 'seem that we are doing less of our collective business as a Cabinet'.[86] Macmillan wrote on the bottom of the memo in red ink: '[O]n the whole, I think Ministers feel ... in the picture.'[87] The exact time varied between Tuesday and Thursdays at either 10.30 or 11 a.m. The place changed too, with 10 Downing Street under renovation from the second half of the year, nearby Admiralty House being used instead. New Cabinet posts were in the process of being created too, such as Secretary of State for Defence, while old positions like Secretary for War, First Lord of the Admiralty, and Minister of Supply were disappearing.[88] Cabinet under

Macmillan would often confirm decisions taken by individual ministers in committees, and discord was rare. An exception came over a debate on 13 July 1960 on Britain's entry to the European Economic Community. Macmillan concluded the discussion by saying that he would tell the House of Commons that 'insuperable difficulties [stood] in the way of our accepting membership of the Community'.[89]

Below the level of Cabinet, the committee system was changing. The Defence and Overseas Policy Committee was created by merging the former Defence Committee with the Foreign Affairs Committee. The Home Affairs Committee continued to discuss all domestic issues, still occasionally known by its name from the war, 'the Lord President's Committee'. Other standing committees had been created including Future Legislation, Economic Policy and Atomic Energy, though the last was disposed of during the early 1960s. Below committees were subcommittees, referred to as 'miscellaneous' (MISC) or 'general' (GEN). They discussed specific subjects, such as the one set up in 1959 to focus on expanding higher education, or the one set up in 1960 to discuss military assistance to Oman. As time passed, and imperceptibly from the 1950s on, Cabinet was increasingly willing to accept the decisions of these subordinate bodies, even if it retained the final say.[90]

Macmillan provided a stability and consistency that No. 10 had not seen since Attlee, daunting though the task confronting him was post-Suez. But he was taken aback by the job. On 11 March 1958, Cabinet had a wide-ranging discussion about the domestic problems facing government in the late 1950s. Macmillan opened discussions by saying that the government had done well to weather the political storms of the year since 1956, but 'that he could not remember a time when a government was faced with so many intractable problems'. Ministers nodded their heads at this portentous statement. Such a declaration is uttered by every Prime Minister a year or so after taking office, comprehending for the first time how overwhelming the job is and how impervious to easy solutions.[91]

Sensing an opportunity to cement his relationship with the still-learning Prime Minister, Brook wrote to him after the discussion with suggestions 'that had occurred to me'.[92] The Brook note is masterly in the way it steers and tutors Macmillan. To meet his anxiety that ministers are not giving themselves enough time to think strategically, Brook suggests the solution that a number of ministers meet together with him, adding 'it might help if I might speak to their permanent secretaries'.[93] He offered some ideas about how the legislative programme in the following year, 1958–59, might be optimised, with some attractive ideas in the run-up to the general election. Equally, with the Budget in 1959 to be the last one pre-election, Brook offered some thoughts about ensuring nothing was done during 1958 which would preclude them having a popular Budget in 1959. On the growth of CND and anti-war nuclear protests, Brook suggested how ministers might be asked to devise their own campaigns to counter the 'wave of hysteria' about nuclear weapons.[94]

Macmillan, like Churchill before him, wanted Brook to travel with him on overseas trips. The Cabinet Secretary proved his worth from the very outset, when Macmillan flew out to Bermuda to meet with President Eisenhower: Brook's briefing note warned Macmillan that Eisenhower was 'ageing' and increasingly dealt in terms of 'dealing with generalities'.[95] Brook would work long hours on overseas trips, keeping in touch with Whitehall developments by telegram and by far from reliable telephone lines, while keeping Macmillan on track for his deliberations abroad. In April 1961, Macmillan's press secretary, Harold Evans, recorded in his diary a vignette of the Cabinet Secretary in action on a return flight from Ottawa to London: '[O]nly two hours to go and the aircraft is hot and stuffy, Norman Brook sits opposite in a navy blue cardigan dictating at length.'[96] His work did not go unnoticed abroad. A secret briefing for new President Kennedy from the US State Department in 1961 described Brook as having 'the best mind in the Civil Service'. It added that his 'years as Secretary of the Cabinet have given him a unique knowledge of government secrets, and he is believed to have exercised considerable influence in a quiet way'.[97]

Few Whitehall mandarins rivalled Brook's understanding of postwar Britain. A report that Macmillan asked him to write about Britain's position in the world after the Suez Crisis was described by Hennessy as the first real cost/benefits analysis of Britain's empire.[98]

Brook's central position in the conduct of international affairs owed much to Macmillan, who, as a past Defence and Foreign Secretary, wanted to conduct his own foreign policy, and had biddable Foreign Secretaries, notably Selwyn Lloyd (1955–60), to ensure it.

Macmillan's reliance on Brook can be seen in the crisis in July 1958 in Iraq, when a military coup saw the overthrow of the pro-Western Hashemite monarchy established by King Faisal in 1921. The Eisenhower administration was taken aback, with the CIA director Allen Dulles telling the President that Nasser was behind the coup. Washington was worried that a chain reaction would occur in the region, with pro-Western governments falling in Jordan and elsewhere across the Middle East. Should the West intervene? Was there anything the government could do? Macmillan's diary picks up the story:

16 July 1958
Finally, I asked for 10 minutes by myself. I went with Rab and Norman Brook into another room, and tried to make my decision. We all thought the Cabinet were determined to do this rather 'quixotic act' and that we wd not forgive ourselves if the King were murdered tomorrow ... Moreover, the Arab world (on the Gulf etc) might be moved by our inaction than by some reaction to the loss of all our friends in Iraq.

I came back into my room – where all were assembled – I tried to sum it up again – pro and con. Then I went round the room. All were 'for'. So I said 'So be it'. The Cabinet dispersed about 3am ... Norman Brook undertook to coordinate the work. In fact, he did not go to bed at all that night. I got to bed around 3:30 a.m., having been assured that everything would be done that needed to be done.

17 July
... What was I to say in the House? I must announce the facts at least, at 3:30. But what were the facts? No one seemed to know. I waited throughout the morning in my study trying to deal with the other work and hide my sickening anxiety. All we knew was that the Israeli Govt was still sitting. Brook (who thought it was his fault) was almost in tears. F Bishop and the other PS's were very kind and sympathetic...[99]

The July 1958 revolution saw King Faisal II, the Regent and Crown Prince, and the Prime Minister, all assassinated, and an Arab nationalist Republic of Iraq established, which ended its alliances with the West. An intolerant regime was initiated that led to hundreds of thousands of Iraqis fleeing the country, and later to Saddam Hussein emerging as Iraq's leader in the 1970s, before becoming President in July 1979.

Decolonisation was a major preoccupation for British Prime Ministers after the Second World War. The process was accelerated by Britain's reluctance to retain a distant empire by force, the rise of anti-colonial movements, and the Cold War, with the US unsympathetic to the maintenance of the British Empire. The Colonial Office oversaw the detail of decolonisation that followed Indian Independence in 1947, but the Cabinet Office played a vital role in coordination. The pace of decolonisation sped up after the Suez Crisis, which confirmed Britain's loss of standing on the world stage, with Ghana receiving its independence in 1957, and Nigeria and Tanzania in 1960. Macmillan wanted the process of decolonisation to be orderly, and to lead to voluntary membership of the Commonwealth, in which Brook took such pride, as did Trend after him.

Brook accompanied Macmillan on his celebrated tour of Africa in January and February 1960. He looked, as one of the party wrote, 'like a casual tourist who happened to be following … and few of the [local officials] realised that he was the central cog in the British government machine'.[100] Throughout the lengthy procession, providing such a stark contrast to the modern Prime Minister's day-long international visits, Brook provided constant support to all, on one occasion outlining the work of the British Cabinet to the Nigerian Council. Brook helped to shape Macmillan's centrepiece 'Winds of Change' speech, delivered to the South African Parliament in Cape Town on 3 February. Macmillan told them 'the wind of change is blowing through this continent. Whether we like it or not, this growth of national consciousness is a political fact,' criticising South Africa's apartheid policies. He made it clear that Britain wanted to avoid the poisonous type of colonial war that France was fighting in Algeria. Parts of the speech were received by 'total silence' from the audience, and only a smattering of applause when finished.[101] Given the tensions in Cape Town, when they finally boarded the *Capetown Castle* to return home on 5 February, 'an atmosphere of the carefree pleasure cruise' was understandable. 'The stately Norman Brook was teased at finding lipstick on the lapels of his white dinner jacket after dancing too closely with the ladies of the court,' records Macmillan biographer Alistair Horne.[102]

Hankey had immersed himself much in the Dominions, Bridges less so. Brook ensured the Cabinet Office became the overseer of the Commonwealth and its regular conferences rather than the Commonwealth Relations Office (which merged with the Foreign Office in 1968 to become the FCO). Between 1946 and 1962, he acted as secretary to eleven full-scale conferences for its Prime Ministers held in London. His long service and the relations he built up with politicians across the Commonwealth, and his intrinsic understanding of the problems faced by them, made him a much-trusted figure across the Commonwealth.

The origins of the regular meetings lay in the meetings of colonial Prime Ministers, which were held regularly from 1887, and the 'Imperial Conferences', which started in 1911. Difficulties emerged when colonies became independent. If they chose to become republics could they remain within the Commonwealth family? This created a constitutional conundrum; could republics become members of the Commonwealth given that it was united by an acceptance of the monarch as head of state? Brook was sent on sensitive visits to New Zealand, Australia and Canada in 1948 as the Prime Minister's envoy to find a common way forward or whether a newly independent and Republican India could remain in the club. George VI was much exercised on what might happen to the Commonwealth: Brook wrote to his Private Secretary from the trip in August: 'My dear Lascelles, your letter reached me while I was in Ottawa ... I am now writing in the aircraft en route to Australia.'[103] Brook told him that, in discussions with ministers in Canada, 'their approach ... is the same as our own – they wish to see the existing members of the Commonwealth together as a free association of independent people ... they are alive to keeping the word "dominion"'. In 1949, under the London Declaration, India declared that it would become a republic in 1950 and would still continue as a member of the Commonwealth, albeit no longer under the Crown.

Brook was intimately involved in the emergence of Britain as a nuclear power after the Second World War, overseeing the Cabinet Committee meeting in 1946, when Foreign Secretary Ernest Bevin insisted that Britain develop its own atomic bomb, famously declaring: '[W]e have got to have this ... we had to have the bloody Union Jack on it.'[104] Britain exploded its own atomic bomb in October 1952, but when the US detonated its first thermonuclear 'H' bomb, which was considerably more powerful, Britain was faced with another dilemma: should it build its own H bomb? Could it afford to do so? Brook chaired a committee codenamed 'GEN 465': it met in his office on 12 March 1954 to discuss the ramifications. As cooperation with the US had been severely restricted following the US McMahon Act of 1946, Britain would have to act alone.[105] Brook's notes reveal that Churchill spoke to ministers about proceeding with the nuclear programme on 7 July, beginning: 'CAB must decide … what we should go with … [we] must be able to make it clear to [Russia] that they cannot stop effective retaliation … [it is essential that we] make the H-Bomb and play our part.'[106]

The subject was raised in Cabinet again on 8 July, and would prove controversial. Some ministers wanted more time to contemplate something so momentous. Churchill's view was that it was 'mainly a moral question' whether they should build it or not. Eden's view was that the moral question had been answered by the Labour government's decision to build the atomic bomb.[107] The decision was taken to proceed. Instructions were given to begin work to develop the British H-bomb, work that was handicapped by the lack of fuel and cooperation by the US. Prototype bombs were tested successfully in September 1958.

For several years, Brook had been turning over how the structure of government would work in case of nuclear war. His interest in this area dated back twenty years to the mid-1930s, when he had headed the division of the Home Office overseeing civil emergencies, the 'war book', and defence preparations. In early 1955, he was one of the very small number of people who saw a report from the Strath Committee which estimated that some twelve million would be killed outright, and four million injured, and that Britain would need to adopt a military dictatorship. Brook greeted Eden as Prime Minister in May 1955 with the report, which would then be classified until 2000.[108]

Macmillan was in power for two of the most serious incidents of the Cold War, including the Berlin crisis in 1961, when the Berlin Wall was erected, and the Cuban Missile Crisis in 1962. The popularity of CND was reaching an all-time high before it waned from 1963 and, for many in the public, using nuclear weapons and a third world war seemed a real possibility. Brook wrote to Macmillan about what might happen:

I undertook to prepare lists of the Ministers who, in such an emergency, would (i) stay in London, (ii) proceed to Regional Headquarters and (iii) go to Burlington ... I now attach a list showing a possible distribution of senior Ministers on this basis. The appendix gives a list of junior ministers who would either remain in London or be available, if necessary, for other duties. In compiling this I have assumed that the Leader of the House must remain in Whitehall and that one of the Ministers who would be nominated as one of your deputies for the purpose of authorizing nuclear retaliation would go to Burlington. I have also assumed that the Secretary of State for Scotland would be in Scotland.[109]

'Burlington' referred to the nuclear underground bunker in Wiltshire. Were nuclear war to break out, Brook was to be evacuated by helicopter from Horse Guards Parade with the Prime Minister and twelve ministers, along with the chiefs of staff and a small number of select officials to the safety of the bunker.[110]

More peaceable uses of science were also being considered at this time. The Cabinet Office has been involved in science throughout its existence, born as it was in the midst of a world war in which government explored every facet of science to find ways to win. Churchill's systematic use of Professor Frederick Lindemann (later Lord Cherwell) constitutes the first de facto Chief Scientific Adviser, who provided frequent if controversial advice. When in 1951 he became Prime Minister again, he reappointed Lindemann. David Edgerton, the historian of science, highlights the failure in the literature to distinguish between advisers, like Lindemann, and executives, the chief scientists who increasingly worked across Whitehall departments, as the twentieth century progressed.[111]

Solly Zuckerman was the first fully recognised Chief Scientific Adviser appointed by Macmillan in 1960, followed by ten others to date. Zuckerman, significantly, was not a military or nuclear specialist, as were powerful government scientists like Henry Tizard and William Penny, but a zoologist chosen specifically because of his ability to offer general scientific advice to the Prime Minister and government across the field. The job of Chief Scientific Adviser was in the Cabinet Office until 1995, when it was transferred to the Department of Trade and Industry.

The Cabinet Secretary's job overseeing intelligence was extended under Brook, though oversight did not come fully under the incumbent until Trend succeeded him in 1962. Brook had kept a hawk eye on intelligence from Attlee onwards, introducing major changes to the vetting of new employees in the Civil Service from 1951. His apprehensions of major trouble were heightened when Guy Burgess and Donald Maclean defected to the Soviet Union in 1951, with concerns reaching a new high point when Kim Philby, the alleged 'third man', was named in the press in 1955 as a possible spy.

Brook was alarmed by the evidence that came out into the open, but wrote in private to Eden in October 1955 to dissuade him from conducting an inquiry (which Macmillan, the Foreign Secretary, was urging). Brook was worried a wide-ranging inquiry into security concerns among public officials might infringe personal freedom: '[M]ost of us are not prepared to abandon civil liberties which we fought so hard to preserve.'[112] In October 1955, Philby was officially cleared by Macmillan when he told the Commons: 'I have no reason to conclude that Mr Philby has at any time betrayed the interests of his country.'[113] Macmillan, Brook and the entire establishment had been taken for a ride: Philby was indeed a spy and defected from Beirut to the Soviet Union in January 1963. Brook had shown himself ultimately to be naive, without the subtlety of mind to penetrate to the heart of corruption within the intelligence services. Prime responsibility, though, lay with the leadership of the security services: Brook was instrumental in the appointment of MI5 head Dick White to run the Secret Intelligence Service (MI6) in 1956 with a brief to shake it up.[114]

Brook had been anxious for several years to see the Joint Intelligence Committee (JIC) founded in 1936 transferred from the Foreign Office, facilitated by his appointment as Head of the HCS in 1956. The detail was confirmed in an agreement with Foreign Office diplomat Patrick Dean, who was now chair of the JIC,[115] who agreed that the secretariat for the JIC would be provided by the Cabinet Office. Brook took pains drawing up a detailed organisation chart, showing the JIC at the centre of an elaborate structure, with information coming to it from the Foreign Office, MI5 and MI6, with JIC reporting up through the Chiefs of Staff Committee to the Cabinet Defence Committee.[116] The new system meant that the Prime Minister, and therefore the Cabinet Secretary, had more direct control

The Old Treasury, and entrance to Downing Street from Whitehall, taken during the late nineteenth century, and the site of the Cabinet Office from 1963.

The Derby Cabinet discussing the Abyssinian Expedition, 1867.

The Gladstone Cabinet, in 1868, in the Cabinet Room.

The War Cabinet Secretariat at the end of the First World War in 1918.

Maurice Hankey arriving with Lord Haldane (left) for a Cabinet meeting at 10 Downing Street.

Three Cabinet Secretaries: John Hunt, Robert Armstrong and Burke Trend, in the 1980s.

War Cabinet, 1941. Edward Bridges is on the extreme left.

Commonwealth Conference – officials and Cabinet members, London 1948. Norman Brook is on the extreme left.

over intelligence reports, with the Prime Ministerial 'red book' replacing the old 'CX' intelligence reports.[117]

Macmillan's final period in power, and thus Brook's, was overshadowed by a series of spy scandals. In August 1961, Brook warned Minister of War John Profumo about his contact with Stephen Ward, a private osteopath, because of Ward's associations with the Soviet naval attaché. Profumo thought that Brook was tacitly warning him to break off his affair with nineteen-year-old nightclub model Christine Keeler, which he quickly did. However, Brook did not know about Keeler, nor did he bring the issue of Ward and Profumo to the attention of Macmillan.[118] The subsequent scandal deeply tarnished Macmillan's government and damaged Macmillan's reputation for sound judgement, as he chose to believe Profumo. The Denning Report also revealed that Brook warned another unnamed Cabinet minister away from Ward, but did not criticise him for not telling Macmillan about his warning to Profumo.[119]

In the spring of 1962, the so-called 'Vassall affair' broke out. Brook warned Macmillan that Vassall, a clerk at MI5, was selling state secrets in clubs around Victoria. 'Nonsense,' replied Macmillan, 'there are no clubs around Victoria.'[120] In September 1962, Macmillan recorded in a meeting with Lord Carrington that

[t]here has been another 'espionage' case – and a very bad one in the Admiralty. An executive officer, homosexual, entrapped by the Russian embassy spies and giving away material (of varying value) for five or six years. He was only caught by the help of a Russian 'defector'. There will be another big row, worked up by the Press over this...[121]

Macmillan found it difficult to comprehend the sexual mores of those who thought and acted very differently to himself, and seemed in the early 1960s to be increasingly out of touch with modern life. It was beyond the powers of Brook, increasingly fatigued as he was becoming, to make Macmillan comprehend the actions of ministers and officials for whom he was responsible.

Cabinet Secretaries regularly advise Prime Ministers on reshuffles as part of their responsibility for machinery of government; they will often know far better than the Prime Minister through the Whitehall grapevine which ministers are good and ripe for advancement, or ready for the chop. Brook became very close (again, one has to ask – too close?) to Macmillan on appointments. In his major reshuffle in July 1962, the so-called 'Night of the Long Knives', when he dismissed seven Cabinet ministers, Brook was by his side throughout, in particular urging him to dismiss Selwyn Lloyd, the Chancellor.[122] Eden made headlines when he said that Lloyd had been 'badly treated'. Eden's ongoing spat with his successor foreshadowed Heath's with Thatcher, and matched it even in venom, if not public awareness nor duration. Eden wanted to return to active politics but thought, rightly, that Macmillan was not supportive of him finding a seat. He was livid that Macmillan only offered him a Viscountcy rather than an Earldom, though under pressure he relented, and Eden entered the House of Lords as the Earl of Avon in 1961.

Brook retired in December 1962 when the Cabinet Office was moving out of the Great George Street offices into 70 Whitehall. Macmillan gave instructions that the job was to be broken up, with the Treasury gaining in authority. The union of the post of Cabinet Secretary and Head of Civil Service, on Bridges's retirement in October 1956, had made perfect organisational sense, given Brook's Olympian command of the Whitehall scene. But it was to become too much for even Brook's prodigious work ethic. Much more could have been done by him to improve and modernise the Civil Service. Though the headship of the Treasury's economic and financial work was given to a joint Permanent Secretary, initially Roger Makins, then Frank Lee, it was still too much for Brook. On top of trying to run the Civil Service, he had also to do the regular Cabinet Secretary job as the Prime Minister's chief adviser, head the Secretariat, oversee propriety and ethics, intelligence, the Commonwealth, and be the Prime Minister's chief foreign policy adviser. In the new dispensation after 1962, there would be two Permanent Secretaries, but both would work at the Treasury, one looking after the economic and financial work, while the other, Head of the HCS, would oversee the management of personnel and Whitehall departments.

Brook's obituary in June 1967 said that he was 'greatly liked and trusted by all his colleagues'.[123] This was true in part, even if he was not adept at creating a sense of camaraderie, or winning round the old or new guard among the mandarins. Robert Armstrong said: 'I never heard anyone express affection for Norman Brook but he was held in great respect ... he exuded authority.'[124] In January 1963, he was honoured as 'Lord Normanbrook', and on 13 February 1963, Macmillan hosted an unusual farewell party for him at Admiralty House, where the Prime Minister was still living as the renovation of No. 10 was completed. He invited all the Prime Ministers and the former ministers who had served in the Cabinet during Brook's long tenure, as *The Times* recorded.[125] Brook was already a tired man, and far from well. In May 1964, he was appointed, oddly perhaps, as chairman of the BBC, an unsuitable choice for the job at a near impossible time. No other former Cabinet Secretary would have picked up such a gauntlet. It was not a success. He struggled to adapt to the alien environment. He had little time to enjoy his hard-earned retirement, or revel in his substantial achievements. Did he come in his brief retirement to accept that he had, in his desire to serve, departed too far from Civil Service neutrality? We will never know. He died at his home in Chelsea in June 1967, the only Cabinet Secretary to die as young as sixty-five.

1–3 WHITEHALL GARDENS, ELEVATION FROM LAWN,
PHOTOGRAPHED IN 1912

CHAPTER 6

Housing the Cabinet Office, 1916–2016

T HE CABINET SECRETARY and his staff, like the office of the
Prime Minister, has never enjoyed purpose-built accommodation.
We take time out then from the consideration of the Cabinet
Secretaries in history to peer inside the offices they and their staff occupied. During its first fifty years, it had a variety of homes, before alighting
on its current residence in the heart of Whitehall, symbolically closer than
the Treasury to No. 10, umbilically joined by the most powerful and mys-
terious interconnecting door in Britain.

2 Whitehall Gardens

Appropriately, the first home of the Cabinet Office was situated on land
previously occupied by the great rambling residence of the Tudor and Stuart
monarchs, Whitehall Palace, between what is now Whitehall Road and the
River Thames. Three houses in Whitehall Gardens (1–3) were constructed in
1806–07 at the height of the Napoleonic Wars, on land hitherto occupied
by the Duke of Portland. Three remaining houses (4–6) were built when
the lease on the land expired in 1824.[1] The row of six houses were of uni-
form design with basements, four storeys above, with an attic in a slated
mansard roof. The elevations were an elegant mix of brick with stuccoed

dressings, and the entrance doorways had porticos with Doric columns. Inside, the main staircase was of stone, and illuminated by elliptical skylights. The attraction of the houses was enhanced by their proximity to the River Thames, though when the river became more polluted and unhealthy during the Victorian era, it became a mixed benefit.

Benjamin Disraeli had lived at 2 Whitehall Gardens in the latter years of his life, and moved across the road into Downing Street partly because he found it tiring going up the staircases. Robert Blake, his biographer, describes how Disraeli had found the house at the last minute before being asked to form his new government by Queen Victoria in February 1874, and it was here that he composed his first Cabinet 'in reasonable comfort'.[2]

Forty-two years later, Maurice Hankey spied 2 Whitehall Gardens as the ideal location when he had to find premises at short notice for the new Cabinet Secretariat. He wanted more space, however. Blessed with unlimited powers from Prime Minister Lloyd George, the resourceful Hankey demanded the Office of Works 'commandeer' the houses on either side of 2 Whitehall Gardens, i.e. Nos. 1–3. Barely had the residents (the National Club in No. 1, government offices in No. 3) had time to pack before he had given instructions that holes should be knocked through their walls, creating more open office space. Despite occupying all three houses, it retained as its working address '2 Whitehall Gardens'. Hankey recorded the pandemonium of the early days in his diary:

> Then began a terrible turmoil of knocking holes in walls and re-arranging accommodation to take the new office. How my staff managed to carry on in those days is still a mystery. Working three or four in a room, one would be dictating, trying to make his voice heard above the din of hammering and sawing; another conducting a business interview on some high matter of State; a third trying to compile a Memorandum. They were a loyal and enthusiastic team or they never could have done it.[3]

Hankey offered a retrospective portrait of the drama when addressing the Cabinet Secretariat after the armistice in November 1918:

There was hardly any accommodation; we just had this little house we are standing in now and we had a very small staff, but ... a very efficient one. There was a small nucleus of loyal stalwarts to help me ... They all did absolute yeoman work in conditions of the greatest discomfort and overcrowding. It was a bitterly cold winter, and ... we only had this little house to start with ... The typists and distributing clerks worked in cellars and attics and anywhere they could ... There was hammering and din and dirt everywhere and the place was full of workmen.[4]

Hankey returned to the subject of the location of the Cabinet Office during the hiatus following the fall of Lloyd George in October 1922. His suspicions were aroused when the powerful Permanent Secretary of the Treasury, Warren Fisher (1919–39), had moved from Whitehall Gardens to Downing Street to be 'under the same roof as the Prime Minister'.[5] This was achieved by moving the Privy Council out of the rooms it was occupying in Downing Street into the Soane/Barry building, now 70 Whitehall. Hankey and Fisher had very different conceptions of the future of the Cabinet Secretariat after the departure of its champion Lloyd George. Hankey wanted to retain its full independence: Fisher to submerge it within the Treasury, thus gaining a foothold for the Treasury close to the very heart of the Prime Minister's Office itself. The Cabinet Office did not move in 1922, though Hankey noted: 'I anticipate ... that we shall cross the road [i.e. Whitehall] before long and, in this event, may eventually pool some of our clerical and messenger services with those of the Treasury.'[6]

By the 1920s, Whitehall Gardens was beginning to show its age, though the staff were content enough with their 100-year-old office. Margaret Walker, who worked in the interwar Cabinet Office, remembers the now-vanished offices: 'You couldn't see them from [Whitehall]. It was called Whitehall Gardens and from the front of our house, we would look onto the Embankment, and in the Embankment there were three lovely gardens outside.'[7]

A government report, with Philistine insensitivity, described the area as full of

old and unsatisfactory buildings. [The area] is very much under-developed and there can be no justification for any further delay in replacing these obsolete premises with modern office buildings which are, and have been for some time, urgently required to enable the demands for centralised Headquarters accommodation in the Whitehall area, which have been growing with increasing intensity in recent years, to be properly satisfied.[8]

The first of the three major buildings to be constructed in Whitehall was the Foreign Office, designed by George Gilbert Scott, and built from 1861 to 1868 to house the India Office, Colonial Office and Home Office. The Foreign Office itself had been formed in 1782 from the merger of the Northern and Southern Departments. Originally based in terraced houses on the opposite side of Downing Street to No. 10, its buildings were in a poor state of repair. Indeed, in 1852, part of the ceiling of the Foreign Secretary's room fell onto his desk.

The great expansion in the size of government during and after the First World War meant that space was urgently needed in the area of Whitehall for the new Air Ministry (formed in 1918) and the Board of Trade, as well as for the Ministries of Labour (1916), Transport (1919) and Health (1919), which had already outgrown the recently finished Government Offices on Great George Street (GOGGS), the subsequent home for the Treasury during much of the twentieth century.

Neighbouring the Foreign Office are the Government Offices on Great George Street (GOGGS), the second of the major government buildings to be erected, which were designed by John Brydon and based substantially on Inigo Jones's unrealised seventeenth-century design for a remodelled Whitehall Palace, in place of the disjointed buildings that had been erected over the years. Construction of GOGGS began at the beginning of the twentieth century, with the west end, looking out over St James's Park, opened in 1908, and the east end, facing Parliament, in 1917. Conceived as the domestic equivalent of the Foreign Office, it was built on a site which contained narrow streets and historic houses, some dating back to before Whitehall Palace was finally destroyed by fire in 1698. The plan was for it to accommodate the Board of Education, the Ministry of Works and the Local Government Board. The Treasury itself was housed in the Old Kent building beside Downing Street, until it moved to GOGGS in 1940.

The aim for GOGGS was to build light, reasonably open offices around perimeter walls, including three large internal courtyards. Brydon, a successful if not distinguished architect, known for Chelsea Town Hall and the Victoria Art Gallery in Bath, chose to clad GOGGS in Portland stone. Happy indeed was the decision to base the design on Inigo Jones: one shudders to imagine what might have been built on the site in the mid-twentieth century. Originally named the 'New Public Offices', as opposed to 'Old Public Offices', i.e. the Foreign Office, it originally housed Education, Local Government and the Works Office, joined shortly after by Health.

The new Ministry of Health had not been part of the original plan for housing in GOGGS, but had been located there for want of any other central accommodation. Internal documents from 1929 deplore the lack of space within GOGGS, less than a decade after its completion, which necessitated staff having to be crammed into wholly unsuitable accommodation, including 'basements, never intended for anything else but stores.' The archives record how 'everything possible had been done in terms of artificial lighting and ventilation to make this accommodation reasonably satisfactory. But it cannot be denied that no government would voluntarily place their staff in such a cellar-like accommodation'.[9] Almost as soon as the giant GOGGS had been completed, it became apparent that, with the size of government expanding rapidly as it was, neither it nor the Gilbert Scott Foreign Office building were big enough to accommodate all the office space that was needed, and further large spaces were required.

Vincent Harris, a classical architect who had designed the Board of Trade (1914), was chosen to design a new building bordering the River Thames, in neoclassical style, which was to be opened in 1938 before the Second World War, but took a further twenty-one years to be fully completed. This is what we know today as the Ministry of Defence building. It eclipsed the GOGGS and Foreign Office buildings in size, with up to three times the number of floors. Its construction required the demolition of Whitehall Gardens, and other fine historic houses equally dismissed as of little consequence. As the buildings were gradually emptied out from the mid-1930s onwards, the Cabinet Office staff at 2 Whitehall Gardens were the last to remain before demolition. A letter to the Treasury from the Office of Works in December 1937 asked for speedy approval of the move of the Cabinet Office, to be relocated to nearby Richmond Terrace, noting that 'a considerable amount of work will have to be done before the Cabinet Secretariat can enter in to occupation'.[10] The letter went on to say that 'the differences in size between the rooms occupied by the Cabinet Secretariat staff in Whitehall Gardens and the room that they occupied in Richmond Terrace will result in a greater supply of furniture and floor coverings than is usual in a change of occupation'.[11] The Cabinet Office asked the Treasury for £11,690 for the move, concluding with an expression of their 'desire to start the work as soon as possible'.[12] J. A. Barlow responded from the Treasury saying that he would authorise the move for a 'revised total estimate expenditure … of £10,110 – £1,580 less than the amount previously authorised'.[13]

RICHMOND TERRACE

The entrance to Richmond Terrace is directly opposite Downing Street, going eastwards in a straight line towards the River Thames. The whole area was once a part of Whitehall Palace. Diarist Samuel Pepys referred to buildings in the street when he wrote about King Charles II and Catherine of Braganza arriving at the palace:

> So we fairly walked it to White Hall and through my Lord's lodgings we got into White Hall garden, and so to the Bowling green, and up to the top of the new Banqueting House there, over the Thames, which was a most pleasant place as any I could have got.[14]

The Duke of Richmond had taken possession of the land, and had the existing house demolished in 1738 to be replaced by another Richmond House, only for it to burn down in 1791. This was in turn replaced in the 1820s by the finely proportioned row of eight houses on what became Richmond Terrace, described thus in the *Survey of London*:

> Eight residences of the first class, and appropriate domestic and stable offices thereto, with a terrace at the north front of the houses and a mews in the rear of the stabling, besides allotting a considerable portion of pleasure ground next the river for the enjoyment of the occupiers of the

new residences, and a suitable lodge and gates at the north-west angle of the ground, where the general access to the said terrace is to be made.[15]

By the 1930s, Nos. 2 and 3 became available for government use, for general offices, and Nos. 6, 7 and 8 went to the Cabinet Office, while Nos. 4 and 5 remained in private occupation.[16] The buildings still stand today: a rare example of early nineteenth-century domestic dwellings in the whole Whitehall vicinity, and a suggestion of what it would have looked like in the nineteenth century.

The move meant breaking up some of the functions acquired by the Cabinet Office during its first twenty years. The Historical Section was moved into Gwydyr House on Whitehall next to the Banqueting House, today occupied by the Welsh Office. Constructed in the 1770s on space originally part of Whitehall Palace, the lease of Gwydyr House expired in the nineteenth century, reverting back to the control of the Crown; the Reform Club leased it temporarily while its new premises were being built in 1837–41.

The Cabinet Office remained in its new premises in Richmond Terrace for just two years before the pressure of the Second World War demanded a change. With the greatly expanded role of the government in wartime, it moved even closer to the centre of power, to the Great George Street Offices, a move completed by the end of 1940. The new premises were safer from the anticipated menace of massive aerial bombardment. News of the relocation was greeted with relief in some quarters, as Ian Jacob indicates:

> For a long time it had been felt that Richmond Terrace was much too dangerous. It was a flimsy building. The basements had been strengthened with timber baulks and that sort of thing, and I remember going down there right at the beginning of war and spending one or two nights.[17]

GOVERNMENT OFFICES ON GREAT GEORGE STREET (GOGGS)

It was the more recently constructed half of GOGGS with the concrete foundations that was seized upon by officials hunting for secure locations for vital government offices as war approached. The basement was selected as a secure alternative Cabinet Room, with the space also accommodating the Air Ministry, the Joint Intelligence Chiefs and the Allied military staffs. Defences were constructed:

> A thick bomb-proof concrete slab was constructed at ground level to protect the activities within the basement, and a large torpedo net was slung across the western courtyard to catch falling bombs. Special measures were taken to filter the air in the event of attacks by bombs carrying poisonous gases.[18]

Ground floor space that was hitherto occupied by the Board of Trade was selected as suitable for the Cabinet Office. Some 300 staff moved into GOGGS from Richmond Terrace, Gwydyr House and other central locations into which Hankey's sprawling Cabinet Office had spread. Preparation was extensive: it included, as contemporary documents reveal:

> the work of repairing the accommodation and the new public offices to meet the requirements of all Cabinet [Office] staff, included the bricking up of windows on the sub-ground floor to give lateral protection ... the fitting up of the cafeteria transferred from Richmond Terrace under thorough overhaul of the blackout arrangements.

Work included the partitioning of space in the basement to form sleeping cubicles for those on overnight shifts. The total cost of this work was £54,905, a sum that the Treasury decreed, when sanctioning the expenditure, as 'moderate for the job'.[19]

The Cabinet Office remained in the Treasury building, as it came to be known throughout Norman Brook's tenure, until the early 1960s, though parts of the Cabinet Office remain there to this day.

70 WHITEHALL

Repair work to the bomb damage in Downing Street was painfully slow after 1945. Three Prime Ministers – Attlee, Churchill and Eden – came and went with little progress made. After Eden left in January 1957, it fell to Macmillan to bite the bullet. He pondered whether the Treasury would ever be able to move back into the Old Treasury in the Kent Building, 'which [the Chancellor] had used for over 200 years'. It would only be possible, he considered, if the Treasury was to secure an adjoining building as an annex to accommodate the physical requirements of a much expanded Treasury. He realised, however, that 'even after the bombed section had been replaced, [it] is far too small to house them'. So he came to the conclusion that the Treasury should remain in GOGGS, while the Cabinet Office should move into the Old Treasury. As he wrote, 'I suggest therefore that the plans for the use of the Old Treasury, after the completion of the work to be done in making good the bomb damage, should provide for its use for the Cabinet Office.'[20] Two weeks later a positive reply arrived from the Minister of Works, saying, '[M]y own view is that this is a very attractive idea if it can be worked out.'[21]

The cluster of buildings to the east of Downing Street, including the Soane-Barry building on Whitehall itself, the Kent Treasury and the buildings along Downing Street, were to be occupied by the Cabinet Office, as was a small part of the Treasury; while the Privy Council, the Lord President's Office and Judicial Committee were to be left in their present offices in the building. The essential requirements for the Cabinet Office, apart from office space, according to contemporary documents, would be adequate conference rooms for committee meetings, access for distribution vans to take key documents around Whitehall in those pre-email days, and the guarantee of security. Four rooms were designated for use by committees, including the Treasury boardroom and the old Financial Secretary's room. Distribution of paperwork would be via the rear of the building, with a new, single-carriage roadway to be built diagonally across Treasury Green.[22]

The profoundly historical nature of the site weighed heavily on the minds of the planners: 'It is essential that [with] any adaptation, the utmost care should be taken to preserve the few antiquities which still remain.' In particular, 'the whole of the Tudor structure on the sub-ground, ground, first and second floors on the site of Cockpit passage should be preserved intact, and no new buildings added which will obscure them'.[23] Considerable effort was taken to preserve the remnants of Whitehall Palace. The architects were duly told of the priority given to preservation. 'I understand you are in favour of retaining what, in the main, seems to be a Tudor wall for the tennis court,' a Ministry of Works official wrote to John Charlton, one of the architects, in October 1960.[24] 'I recommend most strongly the retention of the angle-buttress, basement window and the best preserved bay of the Tudor structure: marked respectively A, B and C on the annexe to drawing,' he replied.[25]

Contemporary drawings show how the plan integrated all the separate elements into the new building at 70 Whitehall. They include: the judicial wing, built by Soane in 1827 with minor alterations by Barry; the long office structure facing Whitehall, which Barry heavily remodelled in 1847; and the Barry extension of 1847 to what had been the Duke of Monmouth's lodging, originally adapted from Henry VIII's tennis court. The entrance area of 70 Whitehall was designed cleverly to embrace the entrance to the Cockpit and Treasury, showcasing much of the remaining structures from Whitehall Palace. Also included is Dorset House, a small structure at the edge of the complex facing Horse Guards Parade, named after the Duke of Dorset, who had lived there in the eighteenth century.

The possibility of linking No. 10 *internally* to the Kent Treasury had been raised by Macmillan's PPS, Tim Bligh, in late 1961. Frederick Bishop, Deputy Secretary in the Cabinet Office, who as Bligh's predecessor knew No. 10 inside out, wrote to him to say:

> [Norman] Brook agrees that the course you suggest in your letter of 17th November about accessing the Treasury buildings, Whitehall and No. 10 is the right one. We will make plans on the basis you suggest, i.e. a locked door between No. 10 and the Old Treasury building with a system of keys for senior staff and ministers. I do not think we need to discuss this as we are in agreement.[26]

Hence was created the most famous internal doorway in Whitehall.

The interconnecting door gave Cabinet Secretaries from Burke Trend in 1963 onwards unprecedented access to the Prime Minister, if allowed to gain access, which was periodically denied to Trend's successor, John Hunt (1973–79). Robert Armstrong was one of those to avail himself of the opportunities it offered: 'I timed it. It took me fifty-three seconds to get from my desk [in the Cabinet Office] to the Prime Minister in No. 10. And if your relationship with the Prime Minister is good, the Prime Minister can say, "Get Robert over!"'[27] As Macmillan's Press Secretary, Harold Evans, put it in his diaries: 'At No. 10, as in love, proximity is everything – that and the instinct that takes you to the right place at the right time.'[28] The connecting door also offered Prime Ministers a windfall. Blick and Jones record:

> Utilising [the interconnecting door] for their specific purposes became practically easier. Over the decades that followed, Premiers used the Cabinet Office as a physical space in which to house their staff, for whom room was not available in No. 10, and drew upon the support of staff in the location of the Cabinet Office.[29]

Richard Wilson (1998–2002) notes how proximity was of particular advantage in moments of crisis:

> 9/11, for instance, was a very difficult moment. I remember being in my room in the Cabinet Office round the corner from No. 10 … I was ringing up all the people we needed to mobilise to help with contingencies in London, watching in real time what was happening on television, and thinking this was an absolute nightmare. I think that was probably the most difficult time.[30]

Power has resided for 500 years in the same precise area of London. It took the Cabinet Office three moves in its 100-year history to find the perfect location: seconds from No. 10, on the very same location from where the great secretaries of the realm once guided the heads of state, and where now the great secretaries guide the head of government.

BURKE TREND,
PHOTOGRAPHED IN 1973

JOHN HUNT,
PHOTOGRAPHED IN 1975 ON
LONDON'S STRAND

CHAPTER 7

BURKE TREND AND JOHN HUNT: ADJUSTING TO THE MODERN ERA, 1963–79

THE SIXTEEN YEARS from 1963 to 1979 were years of satire and irreverence, with the establishment – a term coined only in 1955 by Henry Fairlie – no longer able to command an automatic respect, and with the 'man in Whitehall' becoming a figure of ridicule. The period opened with the launch of *Private Eye* in 1961 and concluded with television's *Yes, Minister*, first screened in February 1980. The years saw very considerable economic and social turbulence, which threw up a slew of new problems for the Cabinet Office to oversee. The years were not easy ones for government, and suspicion of the Civil Service played its part in a reduction of the authority of the Cabinet Secretary, with the donnish Burke Trend (1963–73) finding it difficult to establish a close relationship with Harold Wilson (1964–70, 1974–76) and subsequently Edward Heath (1970–74). How would the less subtle John Hunt (1973–79) fare when serving his four Prime Ministers in six years, the most any Cabinet Secretary worked with in such a short period of time? Would he restore the lost authority, or would ultimate control pass to that other big beast roaming Whitehall – The Head of the HCS? No longer was it ensconced in the Treasury. From November 1968, it was at the apex of the new Civil Service Department.

BURKE TREND

Trend was born into a middle-class family in Greenwich, and attended Whitgift School in South Croydon before going on to Merton College at Oxford, where he achieved a first-class degree in Classics in 1936.[1] He entered the Civil Service directly after finals and was appointed to the Ministry of Education, though he was headhunted for a role in the Treasury a year later, where he remained for the following twenty-five years, earning a reputation as a brilliant, meticulous and tireless administrator. In his early years in the Treasury, he focused on defence, a lifelong interest, before being appointed a junior Private Secretary to the Chancellor of the Exchequer John Simon in 1939. After he left the Private Office in 1941, he oversaw problems of defence equipment within the Treasury for much of the rest of the war. His reputation as one of the brightest and best among the Treasury led to his being appointed PPS to the Chancellor (Dalton, then Cripps) from 1945 to 1949 (when he was succeeded by another rising star, William Armstrong). Trend then returned to mainstream work, overseeing home finance before joining the central economic planning staff. Brook was an admirer and in 1953 moved him to the Cabinet Office as Deputy Secretary, but he returned to the Treasury in 1956 where he was swiftly promoted to Second Secretary.

The 1950s and 1960s were not a golden era for the Treasury. Bridges remained as Permanent Secretary for too long and was overly deferential to the pedestrian Second Secretaries, in the view of economics adviser Robert Hall.[2] Rab Butler, apt to be very indiscreet, told Hall regularly: '[T]hese top people in the Treasury are not up to the job!'[3] Lack of a suitable successor in part explains why Bridges stayed long after his sixtieth birthday in August 1952. Eventually, Butler chose the intellectually brilliant Ambassador to the US, Roger Makins, who became Permanent Secretary of the Treasury in 1956. Douglas Allen, another of the rising stars at the Treasury, was one of many who thought the arrangement did not work: 'He had no experience of the Home Civil Service, which was not good in itself, while Brook ... was too tied up with Cabinet to have time to devote to the functions of the Head of the Home Civil Service.'[4]

Senior Treasury officials were again passed over for the top job when Makins retired in 1960, with the job going to Frank Lee, Permanent

Secretary at the Board of Trade. Yet again, after his stroke in 1962, prefer-
ment went to comparative youngster William Armstrong. Then, in October
1964, Wilson, acting on a long-held mistrust of the Treasury, took away
some of its powers and put them into the new Department of Economic
Affairs; a failed experiment which lasted only five years, killed off in part
by a resurgent Treasury.

Brook saw Trend as his natural successor as Cabinet Secretary in January
1963. Macmillan was only too happy to agree, but then decided that the job
had to be split again, as it had been up to 1956, with the headship of the
HCS reverting to one of the joint Permanent Secretaries at the Treasury.
Thus was Laurence Helsby appointed, a curious choice that baffled insiders;
an economics lecturer who joined the Civil Service from Durham University
in 1945, aged thirty-seven, and who was catapulted after only two years into
the post of PPS to Attlee from 1947–50. He in turn was succeeded in 1968
by William Armstrong. Neither Helsby nor even Armstrong were fulfilled
as Head of the Home Civil Service, finding themselves cut off and with less
access to the Prime Minister than the Cabinet Secretary enjoyed. Life was at
least eased for William Armstrong by his relationship with Trend. As Robert
Armstrong said: 'William and Burke had been close friends in the Treasury,
and William hoped that a partnership between him at the Treasury and
Burke at the Cabinet Office would minimise friction and dissent between
both offices.'[5] His hopes were substantially fulfilled.

Trend was excited by his appointment, regarding the post as the apex of
a civil servant's career. He relished his time in the early years. An avid reader
of John le Carré novels, he possessed a deep interest in the security services,[6]
and was particularly captivated by that dimension of the job, as he was
by relations with the Johnson and Nixon administrations in Washington,
and by oversight of the Commonwealth. Domestic policy he enjoyed less,
as he did the machinations of a very political court surrounding Harold
Wilson after 1964. Trend was a great protégé of Bridges, who exemplified all
he admired. He emulated Bridges's immense thoroughness, the warmth he
displayed to his colleagues, and the observation of the correct delineation
of the job of a civil servant.[7] Heath (Prime Minister 1970–74), to whom he
was not close, nevertheless wrote a laudatory entry on him in the *Dictionary
of National Biography*:

Trend had a formidable intellect which he used to penetrate at once to the heart of any problem. ... He never gave the least indication to those present, either by word or by facial expression, of his personal views or feelings. Tall and serious, he responded to the humour of others but seldom followed it up with his own. Everyone who dealt with him knew that in all circumstances his conduct would undeniably be correct.[8]

Trend described the role of Cabinet Secretary thus:

> He is not the Prime Minister's exclusive servant ... there has to be a central official that the machine can come around ... He has got to be a bit more detached: not taking sides in departmental squabbles, ensuring they all got a fair hearing. And he has to deal with the endless upset of business, driving it down as much as he can.[9]

Trend's briefs for Prime Ministers were 'balanced thorough expositions', Armstrong explained:

> If he minuted a possible conclusion, ... it was for the purpose of suggesting to the Prime Minister what decisions might flow through those conclusions. Every [piece of] written advice to the Prime Minister from the Cabinet Office had to get his signature. At the same time, he was acutely conscious that, as the Secretary of the Cabinet, he was responsible to every member of the Cabinet, especially to the Prime Minister as his chairman.[10]

John Chilcot, later to be a Whitehall luminary himself, worked with Trend, and greatly admired his talent for being able to 'distil and articulate, in a very lucid and compressed fashion, very complex ideas or systems of thinking ... he was an extraordinarily gifted "Mandarin" draughtsman'.[11] Henry Kissinger, later to be US Secretary of State, often spoke to Trend, describing him as 'imperturbable, well-informed, discreet, tactful, [and] quite charming'.[12]

As the epitome of correctness, he chimed perfectly with his first two Prime Ministers, Macmillan (1957–63) and Douglas-Home (1963–64). He suited Wilson less, who ultimately wanted somebody more malleable and on his own wavelength; likewise, Heath (1970–74), who wanted a loyal 'doer' and less of a cerebral thinker.

WORKING FOR MACMILLAN AND DOUGLAS-HOME, 1963–64

Macmillan, who disliked change among his staff, was very sorry to bid farewell to Brook, tired though he was. But he knew Trend well, and had grown to like and trust him from his time as Deputy Secretary to the Cabinet. Macmillan's biographer Richard Thorpe captures the truth when he says 'Macmillan found Trend full of probity'.[13] In November 1962, as incoming Cabinet Secretary, he had a long conversation with Macmillan, where they discussed five main problems that they would work on after he took over in the new year: progress in negotiations for joining Europe; the economy; the unification of the Ministry of Defence; 'modernisation' of Britain; and Britain's role in the Cold War following the Cuban Missile Crisis. Macmillan confessed to him: 'I feel that Sir N. Brook has [been unable] to give me full time.'[14] Under the new arrangement they discussed, Trend was to be Macmillan's '*Chef de Cabinet*'. Macmillan's subsequent diary entries were fuller on Trend than they had been about Brook, dwelling at length on matters concerning spies and intelligence.[15]

Before Trend's first month in office was over, French President Charles de Gaulle vetoed Britain's application to join the EEC. It was a severe body blow for Macmillan's premiership. His 'strategy lay in ruins', wrote Thorpe, leaving him looking for a 'graceful exit'.[16] Pressure mounted after the Denning report into the Profumo Affair was published in September, and his illness just before the party conference gave him a pretext to leave. Trend was intimately involved in every stage, observing the strictest code of impartiality throughout. Brook might have engineered for Macmillan to stay on in office, as he did Churchill, but not Trend. The Queen came to his hospital bed on 18 October for the resignation audience.

With Alec Douglas-Home, Trend was at his happiest. He found here a civilised, orderly and scrupulous Prime Minister. Unsurprisingly, of all the four Prime Ministers Trend served, Home was the one he preferred, considering him the most underrated of all Prime Ministers.[17] Trend admired Home's 'dispatch of government business' and his conduct of Cabinet: '[T]he agenda was crisp and rounded monologues were cut short.'[18] It was Trend's loss that they had such a short time working together: his premiership lasted just two days short of a year. Home came within a whisker of winning the October 1964 general election – all the 'garden room girls' in No. 10 were rooting for him – but Labour won with a majority of five.[19] The Cabinet Office had prepared detailed plans for enacting Conservative manifesto policies, as they had to for major parties at all elections: but imagining a Home-led Conservative government in the mid to late 1960s seemed particularly hard.

Home deeply respected Trend and his oversight of Cabinet Committees, crucial to the smooth conduct of government. He later said:

> [The] proper use of Cabinet's committees is really the secret of a success-ful Government. And the Cabinet Secretary can do an enormous amount. He can say to whoever is chairing a particular Cabinet Committee, 'Well look, that oughtn't to come to the Prime Minister and the Cabinet in that form. You must get it better before it does.'[20]

To Home, his short premiership seemed to be dominated by one major item of legislation: the abolition of resale price maintenance. Near the end of his life, in a rare interview that he deliberately asked to be closed until after 2000, he called it a 'ridiculous thing' which helped lose him the general election, squarely blaming Ted Heath for insisting on it.[21] Trend, meanwhile, found much of his time taken by another matter: the publica-tion of Lord Kilmuir's memoirs, *Political Adventure*, which he submitted to the Cabinet Office for approval after the summer in 1963. As David Maxwell Fyfe, he had been Home Secretary from 1951, and from 1954 an unusually long-serving Lord Chancellor until he was sacked by Macmillan in 1962. Trend was immediately alarmed, as was Home. 'There are three sections of the book which, for different reasons, give me concern,' wrote Trend, namely: Suez, Eden's resignation in 1957 and the 'Night of the Long Knives' reshuffle in 1962.[22] Kennedy's funeral in Washington, following his assassination on 22 November, took both Home and Trend's time and delayed their consideration of the book, to Kilmuir's irritation. Home was most vexed about the criticisms of Cabinet ministers still serving, especially with a general election only months away, and a newly invigorated Labour Party under Harold Wilson hungry for passages they could capitalise on. Home and Trend presumed Kilmuir was venting his anger and frustration at the way he had been dismissed in the 1962 reshuffle, and was seeking to achieve large sales and serialisation royalties from a controversial book. Home was most worried about the criticisms of Butler and Selwyn Lloyd, while Trend was more exercised by the disclosing of details of Cabinet Committees during the Suez Crisis.

They agreed that Kilmuir should come in to meet Home and go through drafts specially marked up with concerns. He came in on 5 December, but the former Lord Chancellor was in a defiant mood, agreeing to some minor modifications about naming Cabinet Committees, but arguing hard against other changes. Home reminded him that 'he was writing about people who were not only members of the government, but were also for a long time his ministerial colleagues'.[23] He offered his former colleague some pointed advice, saying that he 'just thought it right that [he] should bear in mind the high reputation he at present enjoyed for being a fair-minded man'.[24]

At a time when the 'fifty-year rule' was in operation, and mindful of the risks of opening the sluice gates to future books capitalising on privileged access, Trend fought hard. The book was published in early 1964 with only minor modifications, and was serialised in *The Spectator*. Leaks, which came of age in the 1960s, were rife, and Home had to face uncomfortable questions in the House about whether the government had exerted pressure on Kilmuir. The public mood had turned sharply against attempts by the establishment to maintain official secrecy. But nothing prepared Trend for the challenges to the long-standing conventions that he confronted from Wilson's Labour government, which swept the Conservatives aside in October 1964.

TREND AND HAROLD WILSON, 1964–70

The contrast between the aristocratic Etonian Douglas-Home, one-time Parliamentary Private Secretary (as Lord Dunglass) to Prime Minister

Neville Chamberlain, and the state-schooled Harold Wilson, desperate to bring his scientific and modernising revolution to the world, could not have been starker. Wilson's biographer, Ben Pimlott, describes his first halcyon day after bringing Labour back to power for the first time in thirteen years in the general election of October 1964:

> At forty-eight he was the youngest Prime Minister of the century, at the peak of his energy and ability, filled with wonder at his success after only a year and a half as opposition leader, and with a terrific sense of what he might yet achieve. He clearly believed in himself; he believed in the programme on which his party had been elected. He had a clear idea of how he might set about implementing it.[25]

Wilson burst on the Whitehall scene with a dynamic 'First Hundred Days' plan in emulation of President Roosevelt after he came to power in March 1933. He wanted Trend to be an integral part of his ambitious programme, seeing the job of Cabinet Secretary as more than just 'provid[ing] secretaries for the Cabinet Committees and see[ing] that the papers are properly circulated'. Wilson was the only Prime Minister who had worked in the Civil Service, rising to be Director of Economics and Statistics at the Ministry of Fuel in 1943–44, and had clear ideas about how it should work. In an interview shortly before he became Prime Minister, Wilson said he foresaw the Cabinet Secretary

> briefing the Prime Minister, not only … on the machinery of government and … on the work of any Cabinet Committee, but also providing a briefing agency, so that he is right up-to-date and on top of the job … My conception of the Prime Minister is that, if he's not a managing director, he is at any rate and should be very much a full-time executive chairman.[26]

In 1967, he added fresh thoughts:

> [T]he Cabinet Secretariat is the private department of the Prime Minister. [The Cabinet Secretary] is a servant to the whole Cabinet and attends all its meetings, but he is also my personal secretary/chief adviser.

He advises me, briefs me, not only for Cabinet meetings and other Cabinet Committees over which I preside, but for the general running of the government so far as policy is concerned.[27]

Trend's relationship with his new Prime Minister started out very well: Wilson told Barbara Castle, initially Minister for Overseas Development, that Trend 'was the best civil servant I have ever known'.[28] Philip Ziegler, Wilson's official biographer, says Wilson possessed a vast respect for Trend, tinged with a degree of suspicion.[29] Widespread foreboding had permeated No. 10 and Whitehall about what a Wilson government might mean: rumours circulated of a purge of officials deemed to have been too close to the despised Tories. Trend was a model of calm reassurance, pacifying feverish officials while speedily gaining the trust of the incoming administration. He handled the transition with impressive assurance and authority, a model of how to do it.

Trend wrote a typical brief for Wilson before his first Cabinet on 20 October, making tactful suggestions while avoiding condescension:

As the first item of the agenda you may wish to say a few words to your colleagues on the general heading of 'procedure',

If so I suggest that these might include the following items –

A word of welcome and congratulations.

A reminder about the main principles which should govern the conduct of public business. Most of these are summarised in the note on 'Questions of Procedure for Ministers', which is being circulated with your approval and will, I hope, be in Ministers' hands by the time of the first Cabinet meeting. You may think it worthwhile referring to it and asking your colleagues to study, with care and attention, a codification of past experience which has been tested by time and has occasionally been purchased only at rather bitter cost ...

a) Devolution

As much as possible should be settled by direct dealing between the Ministers concerned. Issues requiring collective consideration should always be referred initially to the appropriate committee. Only the most important or urgent matters should be submitted to Cabinet ...

(b) Brevity

Both memoranda and oral contribution to discussions should be as brief as possible. It is hard to observe this principle in practice; but the dividends are considerable.

(c) Confidentiality

It is not an accident that the words 'confidence' and 'confidential' have the same root: and the mutual trust which is the foundation of collective responsibility depends not a little on the ability of a Government to safeguard the private nature of its deliberation, particularly in Cabinet. It is becoming progressively more difficult to observe this principle in the face of the increasingly sophisticated pressure of the press, television and so forth. But the damage which may result from its neglect can be very serious. You may like, at this point, to give your colleagues the warning that at least for some weeks and until the Government have taken stock of the very formidable problems which face them – they should be 'seen but not heard'.

(d) The Cabinet Office

I hope that you will also spare a moment to tell the Cabinet that the Cabinet Office exists to serve the Government as a whole and to assist Ministers in the discharge of their collective responsibility. We will do our best to help them; and, if there is anything that we can do to assist any individual Minister, I hope that he will not hesitate to let me know…

Finally – on a lighter note! – a clear rule about smoking (or not smoking) during Cabinet is always helpful. In making up your mind you will remember that the Cabinet room tends to be also your own personal working room for a large part of the day.[30]

Trend's final paragraph should be savoured for a moment, offering the recipient a clear choice while steering him subtly toward what he believes to be the right conclusion.

An early skirmish between Wilson and Trend emerged in July 1965 over the Prime Minister's desire to shrink the Cabinet. Wilson decided he wanted 'a smaller nucleus' to which 'other members and officials would be added as the nature of the meeting required'.[31] Trend did not like the sound of it one bit, and convinced Wilson it was not workable. It was a harbinger of what was to come.

After Britain became a nuclear power in the 1950s, new responsibilities fell to the Cabinet Secretary. One of his earliest jobs was to brief the Prime Minister on nuclear weapons, a topic illuminated by the work of Peter Hennessy. Wilson was mesmerised by the briefing Trend gave him 'on the intricacies of the JIC, espionage tradecraft, and the perils of hostile audio surveillance and bugging'.[32] Trend patiently explained to Wilson Britain's new geopolitical reality since the Suez Crisis, with the diminution of Britain's power on the world stage. It now had to rely less on raw military force than on intelligence and diplomatic power: thus 'political intelligence henceforth would be as important as military intelligence if not more so'.[33]

Overseeing the process of appointing nuclear deputies for the Prime Minister was another of the Cabinet Secretary's responsibilities. As he put it to Alec Douglas-Home in a Christmas Eve letter, with as much delicacy as he could muster, these are the people 'who would be empowered to authorise nuclear retaliation if, at the critical moment, you were not available'.[34]

The Cabinet Secretary thus had a crucial role in a nuclear war.[35] It was down to him, for example, to inform the Chiefs of Staff, Fleet Commander and RAF officers of the identities of the first and second nuclear deputies to the Prime Minister. He was then responsible for reminding Cabinet of steps that had to be taken to ensure the readiness of the RAF strike force and submarine Polaris force, and, in consultation with the PPS to the Prime Minister, would arrange for the Prime Minister to speak to the President of the United States.[36] Throughout the Cold War, a special cupboard in the Cabinet Office contained the government's war plans, along with blank Royal Warrants that could be used to appoint Regional Commissioners in the bleak aftermath of a nuclear attack.[37]

Trend began to arouse the suspicion of ministers in part because his enthusiasms for intelligence, nuclear security, for Washington and the Commonwealth were not shared by many in government, whose priorities lay principally in economic and social policy. The Commonwealth became a particular passion of Trend, and even after a Secretary-General was appointed in 1965, and conferences ceased to be held in London, he continued to be the lynchpin and to mentor the organisation.

Wilson himself had no abiding interest in the Commonwealth and empire, but was dragged headlong into it. When the British colony of Rhodesia declared unilateral independence in November 1965 under a white supremacist government led by Ian Smith, it expressly rejected London's demand that it consent to black majority rule. Wilson's response was to institute sanctions, coordinated by the Cabinet Office. Unbeknown to them, a typist among the celebrated 'garden room girls' in Downing Street was passing information to the Rhodesian government between 1966–67, the only known occasion when anyone in this estimable group acted in this way.[38]

By early 1966, Wilson was tiring of his tiny majority and triggered a general election. His gamble after just a year and a half paid off. Labour defeated the Tories in style on 31 March, picking up forty-eight seats and boosting their majority to ninety-six – Labour's second biggest tally after 1945. After the result, Trend penned an unambiguous note to Wilson, entitled 'Post-Election Strategy', reminding him of a desire he had expressed to be a more effective administrator:

> I have borne in mind your intention to moderate the pace of work under the new government to a rather gentler 'rate of striking' – which I take to mean, essentially, more effective discussion of issues before they come to Cabinet; perhaps rather fewer Cabinets and certainly less pressure to reach decisions against the clock. This means a more systematic structure of committees, both ministerial and official; a more thorough and unhurried use of these Committees (including regular stock takings of their work and their rate of progress); and a careful choice of the ministers to fill the 'sinecure' posts in Cabinet, who tend to be the natural choice for Committee Chairmen in a good many cases.[39]

He then returned to a regular theme, cautioning Wilson against his oft-stated desire to create a smaller, inner Cabinet:

> Although the pre-Election Cabinet was perhaps rather too large and unwieldy, size is a relative concept. 'Small' Cabinets have often been advocated and have occasionally been tried. But, apart from periods of war, they have not been found to have sufficient advantages to compensate

for their drawbacks, namely that they tend to undermine the sense of collective responsibility, that they place too heavy a burden on the Ministers who are members, and, above all, that they may not give a Prime Minister sufficiently broad a representative 'political base' from which to operate. I am sceptical about excessive federalisation of departments – and for reasons which are basically the same in both cases, namely that units which are too large in size and too few in number are liable not only to become unmanageable as separate administrative entities, but also to make it difficult to maintain a reasonable balance of collective power. Anyone who has sat through a really thorough and closely argued Cabinet discussion will know what I mean.[40]

Trend wanted to ensure that Wilson's second government would be a much tidier ship. He had become concerned by an excessive number of meetings, and by their lack of rigour. He told Wilson that, in 1965, the Cabinet Office had circulated 1,591 memoranda and serviced 546 meetings of Cabinet and committees. Too many, he said, and too great a pressure placed on Cabinet Office officials: 'I am anxious that the Cabinet Office should not become too large, and we shall continue to staff it as economically as we possibly can.'[41] Wilson's lackadaisical style of managing meetings, so different from Attlee, helped give licence for his ministers to ramble, and for meetings to become mere talking shops.[42]

The diaries of Richard Crossman provide a rich, if partisan, insight into the Cabinets of the Wilson years. Crossman, an Oxford philosophy don before the war, held a succession of Cabinet posts from 1964 to 1970, including Leader of the House of Commons (1966–68). A left-winger who never lost the detached stance of the academic commentator, he was highly critical of Trend and the Whitehall machine. Cabinet colleague Lord Shackleton said Crossman talked more than anyone else in Wilson's Cabinet and 'acted as the sort of critic', though he was not the most influential voice, which he said belonged to 'Tony Crosland, Roy Jenkins, George Brown and Denis Healey'.[43] Crossman came to believe, nevertheless, in the words of Theakston, that 'Trend helped water down Wilson's radicalism and that he cooked the Cabinet minutes'.[44] Cabinet Committees were a particular bête noire of Crossman. On joining the government in 1964, he was surprised to find in addition to the Cabinet Committees which only ministers normally attend, there is a full network of official committees; and the work of the ministers is therefore strictly and completely paralleled at the official level. This means that very often the whole job is pre-cooked in the official committee to a point from which it is extremely difficult to reach any other conclusion than that already determined by the officials in advance.[45]

Crossman wrote dismissively in his diary: '[I]t's important to remember how little historians can trust Cabinet minutes to tell what really went on. What they do tell is what went on according to the officials and the official briefs.'[46] What Crossman wanted to see was power and oversight rebalanced from the executive to the legislative. Crossman and Trend talked this over, and appear to have been reconciled in late 1966 over Crossman's idea for strengthening Parliament's committee system. But any accord was short-lived, and they clashed increasingly from 1967, even on more minor matters. That September, Wilson's team assembled for the traditional post-summer conference at Chequers. Crossman wanted to stay in the nearby town of Aylesbury instead of at the house. When Trend discovered his intentions, he made a 'terrible fuss'. 'That's impossible', Trend had said, 'because if the Lord President is seen in Aylesbury with officials from the House of Lords, the journalists will realise you are holding a secret meeting and conclude you're discussing House of Lords reform.'[47] In April 1970, shortly before the general election, they had another disagreement, over the Official Secrets Act, and whether authors could be prosecuted for breaching it. Crossman naturally thought they could not, and should not.

Trend became increasingly perturbed by Crossman's attacks. He believed that Crossman had failed to understand the way that the Cabinet Office and modern Civil Service operated.[48] Trend maintained that the structures of committees were there to serve ministers and help them achieve their wishes, not to thwart them. But he could not convince the sceptics. In his biography on Crossman, for example, Tam Dalyell concludes that Trend's Cabinet minutes 'failed to describe the real struggle which according to Callaghan and Barbara Castle, off the record, had in fact taken place'.[49] He found it harder and harder to convince ministers of the merits of his way of doing business. His critics in the Cabinet increasingly blamed him, no doubt unfairly, for Labour's failure to make more progress on its ambitious policies. Ministers of all parties indeed have been wont to blame the Whitehall machine over the years if their policies are not gaining traction.

Damage to Trend's relationship with Cabinet had come quite early on. The *Daily Express* published an article by journalist Chapman Pincher, which claimed that 'thousands of telegrams sent out by the post office or commercial cable are made available to security services',[50] suggesting the government was intercepting secure cable messages on an industrial scale. The government tried to impose a 'D-Notice' to stop him: such notices advised the press not to publish material considered a risk to national security. A question was tabled in the House of Commons about the number of D-Notices issued in secret to the press under Wilson. Trend advised the Prime Minister not to overreact. Wilson ignored his advice, and instead he laid into the *Daily Express* for publishing a 'sensationalised and inaccurate story'.[51]

Wilson became embroiled in a week-long confrontation, which gave Heath, the opposition leader, an opportunity to demand that a committee of privy councillors be appointed to investigate the government. Wilson's refusal to accept its findings prompted press outrage and the resignation of the D-Notice Committee's secretary.[52] Trend took the blame in some quarters for the debacle. 'I suspected that Harold never trusted [Trend] quite so much since the D-Notice mess for which Burke was responsible, and they had grown much more distant,' Crossman recorded in his diary. Wilson knew Crossman was critical of Trend, and confided in him: '[Y]ou know, Burke is not all that close to me. He is such an establishment figure, and the Cabinet Secretariat is very much an independent force, standing on its own.'[53] In his diary, Crossman privately reflected on this exchange: 'I think that although Harold doesn't feel Burke is very close to him, Burke feels his loyalty is to the Prime Minister and to strengthening his position, a loyalty which he doesn't feel to other Ministers.'[54]

Trend's advice nevertheless remained important across the board. In 1967, he guided Wilson towards another decision, when he counselled Wilson to devalue the pound. Britain had pursued an exchange rate of £1 to $2.80 since 1947, the strong pound being seen as important for the maintenance of living standards and national prestige. But the trade deficit that persisted throughout many of the postwar years required using up foreign exchange to finance it. Trend wrote to Wilson to say that

we have not succeeded in relieving the balance of payments. The inflationary pressure (which appears in the balance of payments context as an excess of imports) persists at too high a level; and the world is aware of this. As a result, we have not yet restored international confidence in our ability to maintain the value of the pound. When there is a basic unsoundness of this sort, anything (however irrational) can [instigate] … a run on a currency without notice – as we know, since we are now experiencing it for the third or fourth time.[55]

In October and November 1967, the Bank of England increased the interest rate by 1 per cent, not confident that the government was doing enough to protect the pound. But Wilson devalued the pound in mid-November to $2.40 (i.e. by 14 per cent). On 18 November, he delivered a nationally televised address intended to reassure the public, stating that the 'pound in your pocket' would not lose 14 per cent of its value, and that the economy would recover. Wilson's credibility and the Labour government never fully recovered.

Trend's influence over Wilson dwindled in the latter 1960s. Lord Shackleton, who had become minister in charge of the Civil Service Department, said: 'Burke was a very nice and very wise man. But it was very difficult to know what his role was. [Beyond Cabinet minutes] one was not conscious of his influence.'[56] This does not do justice to Trend's role, which was strengthened because Wilson's PPS, Michael Halls (1966–70), was struggling, so creating an opening for Trend to fill. It is a mark of Trend's ability that he kept the system of Cabinet government fully operational and intact throughout, overseeing considerable expansion in the size of government, with public expenditure rising from 34 per cent of GDP in 1964–65 to 38 per cent in 1969–70. The government introduced a wide range of liberal reforms, which Trend facilitated even if he did not always find them congenial. He served the government loyally through a difficult final year, with clashes with the unions over Castle's White Paper 'In Place of Strife' until the general election in June 1970.

Wilson might well have won it, his team thought, if he had not delayed the date from 11 to 18 June, by which time bad trade figures were published which damaged the government's reputation for economic competence.[57] Wilson was not finished with Trend yet. Wilson left office in June 1970 £14,000 in debt, with a large office to maintain. He fell back on the idea of memoirs, for which the *Sunday Times* paid him £240,000. The book, mostly written by his Press Secretary, Joe Haines (1969–76), had to be vetted by Trend, who insisted on passages about China being amended.[58]

TREND AND HEATH, 1970–73

Trend was rejuvenated by the arrival of a new Prime Minister in the shape of the Conservative, Edward Heath, who won the general election with a majority of thirty-one.[59] He had encountered Heath when he had been Chief Whip under Eden, and seen much more of him after he became Cabinet Secretary. Trend was looking forward to working with Heath, but differences emerged from the start. Heath had looked with increasing disgust at Wilson's shambolic premiership, and entered Downing Street convinced 'that we needed to change the structure of government … a subject which engrossed me … because I was concerned that ministers spent too much time on day-to-day matters, instead of on strategic thinking'.[60] This might have chimed with Trend's own thinking, but Heath wanted fewer Cabinet Committees and to make Cabinet itself much smaller.

Trend had sweated blood to evolve a tight and effective Cabinet Committee system under Wilson, in the way he believed right for good government, and tried to tell Heath it had improved considerably since the Tories left office in 1964. Above all, he said, the system relied upon a number of Cabinet ministers with no departmental responsibility (notably the Lord President) to chair the Cabinet Committees, as they had 'no personal axe to grind'.[61] Trend had built up considerable understanding under three very different Prime Ministers of what worked and what did not. He met Heath before the election to talk it over, but Heath, not the most flexible of men, would have none of it. He was adamant he would forge ahead, creating two new 'super-ministries'. Cabinet was reduced from Wilson's twenty-one down to eighteen. Trend remained unhappy, writing:

[I]t would be a pity if the result were to disinterest other ministers in the work of some of their colleagues; and it could be damaging if questions which are either important on merits or politically sensitive did not emerge for collective inspection until it was almost too late to affect the outcome.[62]

So Trend noted with wry satisfaction that, by 1973, the number in Cabinet had crept back up to twenty-one again.

The Central Policy Review Staff (CPRS) was one innovation he did not contest, which had been foreshadowed in the White Paper authored by Heath entitled 'The Reorganisation of Central Government', published in 1970.[63] Trend equally had had no option but to swallow the introduction of a 'Political Office' in 1964 by Wilson, headed by Marcia Williams. But he could see much more constitutional sense in the CPRS, and proposed Victor Rothschild, the banker, scientist and former intelligence officer as its first head.[64] Trend was less content with the nickname soon ascribed to the new body: 'It became known as the Think-Tank,' he told Hennessy regretfully:

I remember scratching my head and sucking my pencil and thinking 'what on earth are we going to call this thing?' And then it seemed to me that if you took the words which we finally did adopt, they came as near as I could come to being accurate about it. It was central; it was concerned with policy; and it was concerned with reviewing policy centrally and it consisted of staff, not a political unit.[65]

It continued to operate under both its 'Think-Tank' and CPRS names until Margaret Thatcher killed it off in 1983.

Rothschild duly became the first, and most successful, head in 1971. He recruited a prodigiously bright team, a mix of Whitehall officials on secondment and outsiders from the private sector (several from Shell, where Rothschild had been head of research). Inevitably, once they began their work, it ruffled Whitehall feathers. Rothschild recalled a difficult moment in May 1972:

Sir Burke Trend called a meeting of the permanent secretaries this morning to review the activities of the CPRS, of whom four were present. I am too insensitive to appreciate nuances but the other three members of the CPRS who were present respectively thought that the permanent secretaries put the boot in; that they put the shoe in; that our shin pads were thick enough to cope with these eventualities.

He concluded sardonically, 'Sir Burke, needless to say, was neutral.'[66]

Heath remained a strong believer in the value of the CPRS nevertheless, writing in his memoirs: '[T]heir work was thoroughly researched and presented. I regard the CPRS as one of the best innovations of my time at No. 10.'[67] British government has been notoriously under-powered in thinking beyond the timeframe of the next general election, and the idea of establishing an office to think longer-term was a good one, which explains various attempts after 1983, including Blair's Strategy Unit, to corral very bright minds in Whitehall to think beyond the horizon of the next general election. In the end, though, the CPRS ended up punching below its weight.[68] The immediate and the political in Whitehall, as in all democracies, tends to trump the long term.

Heath's relationship with Trend was not always fraught. The National Archives show many helpful and wide-ranging papers by Trend designed to support Heath, and make the government's work easier. A typical example is a confidential minute he sent Heath in early August 1970:

> I have been reviewing the main issues which we are likely to have to deal with from now until the party conference; you may like to have this brief picture of what seems to lay ahead ... [T]here may be trouble in Northern Ireland, the month is also the time of the year where there is a periodical risk of tidal flooding in London. In the near future – we must rely on ad hoc measures.[69]

In September, Trend warned Heath of difficult issues which might cause trouble, including 'arms for South Africa', 'protection of the seas in the southern half of the Indian Ocean', and whether to proceed with the Concorde supersonic airliner following disappointing sales. The need for decisions on public expenditure was another concern he flagged, suggesting that the crisis would come in the middle or end of the following month.

'At the two critical periods that I have mentioned, the Cabinet will have to work very hard!' he counselled the new Prime Minister.[70]

Trend achieved success in persuading Heath to agree to important reforms to strengthen the Cabinet Office's capacity for managing emergencies, reforms which he had failed to sell to Wilson in 1969. He told Heath about his concern that

> there was no central government organisation for collating and presenting background information necessary to enable you, other ministers, and … officials, to take timely and informed decisions on the complicated problems arising in a period of tension, which might extend from the stage of 'transition to war' right into the preliminaries to the nuclear exchange and even, perhaps, the nuclear exchange itself.[71]

Heath was happy for Trend to take the initiative and convene meetings with the heads of the three main Whitehall departments concerned: the FCO, the Ministry of Defence and Home Office. What was needed, he said, was

> a new crisis management centre to be known as the Whitehall Situation Centre. This centre should collect, collate and display political, home defence and military information provided by appropriate departments in order to enable Ministers and, where appropriate, senior officials, to take prompt decisions based on information which is up to date and made simultaneously available to all those concerned.[72]

He envisaged a conference room in the Cabinet Office where ministers and officials could meet for direct briefings using closed circuit television with the FCO, MoD and Home Office and other expert opinion joining. Created in 1972, and known as 'the winter emergency committee', it morphed into Cabinet Office Briefing Room [known as COBR]. The Home Office had traditionally overseen this area under the Emergency Powers Act of 1920, and from 1935 to 1971 it was organised by a 'Civil Defence Department'. The first meeting in the COBR room took place in 1972 to coordinate the government's response to the National Union of Mineworkers (NUM) strikes.[73] Thereafter, it was used for a variety of purposes, including counter-terrorism, and as part of contingency planning for nuclear war.[74] Even after COBR was set up within the Cabinet Office, emergency planning and civil defence remained in the Home Office in the renamed 'Emergency Planning Division'. In 2001, under Blair, the Cabinet Office took over responsibility for all crisis planning for both civil and military eventualities, in the Civil Contingency Secretariat.

The changes were timely, because Heath's government was to be more crisis-ridden than any other postwar government. Northern Ireland, mostly quiet following the Lloyd George settlement in the early 1920s, was already in a feverish state when Heath came into power. Only three days into office, Trend warned him that the province would take a 'miracle' to see any improvement. The position, he cautioned, 'could get worse', and he 'must be prepared ... to suspend the Parliament of Stormont [the Northern Ireland Parliament] ... and to place the executive government of Ulster in the hands of nominee of our own'.[75] The following year, Trend advised Heath against the implementation of an internment policy; advice Heath reluctantly disregarded. The Cabinet Northern Ireland Committee met on 11 January 1972, Trend's brief for Heath expressing pessimism whether talks would lead anywhere. In March, Heath suspended Stormont, and direct rule of Northern Ireland from London resumed. Ultimately, Northern Ireland proved to be, Hennessy thought, 'one of the top three, and possibly the greatest absorber of high-level Prime Ministerial time, over the life of the government as a whole'.[76]

The other great domestic concern was economic and industrial policy. Heath was in almost constant battle against the trade unions, inflamed by his Industrial Relations Act of 1971, which sought to introduce new law and regulations into union activity, resulting in the imprisonment of workers who embarked on a series of strikes. Not since the 1926 General Strike had union relations been so inflamed. The miners' strike of 1972 was the first official strike by miners since 1926. The NUM went back to work in February, but in 1973 it became more militant still after the radical left-winger Michael McGahey was elected Vice-President. A desperate Heath asked Trend to increase surveillance of miners' and other militant forces, and Heath was furious when MI5 told him that his request to have advance warning of strikes was not permissible. Heath kept up the pressure, believing the security services could be doing more to tackle the left-wing radical challenge. MI5 is said to have agreed to monitor industrial 'subversives', with Trend reassuring Heath that 'the operations are carried out with very great care'.[77]

Trend's heart remained with his staples, above all Anglo-American policy. National Security Adviser Henry Kissinger believed Trend was distressed by Wilson's 'cavalier' neglect of this special relationship, which had been ranked so highly under Churchill and Macmillan.[78] Certainly, the situation did not improve much when Edward Heath came to power in 1970, determined to take Britain into the European Community. As a result, Trend found himself, somewhat to his surprise and certainly not to his displeasure, one of the foremost Atlanticists in Whitehall, which did not go unnoticed in Washington DC.

An insight into the unique relationship between Trend and his counterpart Kissinger can be found in an account of a meeting between the two in April 1973. Trend described Kissinger as 'a man in a hurry', above all, he thought, because of the Watergate Affair, which, as the American noted, 'could pre-empt quite a large part [of Nixon's] remaining three years'. Trend was surprised that Kissinger did not mention the subject of Vietnam and the wider Indo-China region once during the entire meeting, but instead emphasised his wish for a close working relationship with Britain, including a series of working parties 'held together by a top level steering group meeting once a month … to give some formal study of the future of the Atlantic relationship'. Kissinger was content to work solely with Britain, but Trend argued that 'the process could not go far without involving the German or the French at an early stage', and suggested that Heath explore the topic on his visit to Paris, when he was due to meet French President George Pompidou. Kissinger appeared irritated by Europe's unwillingness 'to speak with one voice on any one subject'.[79]

In addition to set piece encounters, Kissinger and Trend spoke regularly on all manner of subjects. Kissinger said this of their relationship, an important summation of the state of Anglo-American relations at the time:

We had frequent exchanges of impressions about either leaders or problems. Between the British Government and American Government, the relationship was not very formalised. So if we had a problem that we wanted advice on, I would call Burke Trend and he would then involve the right British agency or he would find the answer himself.[80]

Kissinger had a soft spot for Trend, and phoned his celebrity friends, the actor Douglas Fairbanks Jr and the publisher of the *Washington Post*, Kay Graham, to ask them to join him for dinner with 'the British Cabinet Secretary'.[81] Kissinger offered Graham an intriguing description of the Cabinet Secretary: 'He is ... sort of my equivalent in job, except he is permanent,' continuing that he thought Trend 'an outstanding man – really a fine person'.[82] Both celebrity figures appear to have been delighted to accept, though regrettably there is no record of what was discussed during this improbable gathering.

After a meeting in January 1973 between Trend and Kissinger, Kissinger reported to President Richard Nixon (1969–74) that Trend was apparently 'delighted' with US policy in Vietnam, and commented that 'they never said anything while it was going on'.[83] He was very likely referring to 'Operation Linebacker II', the US heavy bomber offensive in December 1972 against North Vietnam, which the US terminated early. Kissinger adds: 'He's strongly for it. If anything, his instinct is like yours, he would have liked to have won,' to which Nixon responded, 'Well, you and I know we couldn't do that.' Kissinger returned to the theme soon after: '[H]e thinks that Europe will be thankful to you someday for what you did. I told him that ... what the Europeans [did] ... had done more to undermine the NATO alliance.'[84]

Even Nixon seems to have held Trend in high regard. In January 1970, he insisted that 'Trent' be given notes of an NSC meeting that Harold Wilson had recently attended, 'I thought he should have been at the meeting and I didn't realise he was not there'.[85] Later, in July 1973, Nixon remembered 'Trent's' name as part of a 'British group' Kissinger was meeting, and asked him to 'unless he is being difficult ... give him [Trend] my personal best and if he's being bad in any other way just give him my worst'.[86] That the British Cabinet Secretary's name would be (mostly) remembered, and praised, by a beleaguered President Nixon gives an indication of how much he was respected by American policymakers.

Relations between Wilson and Heath and their counterparts in the White House in contrast were difficult. They deteriorated further after Heath began focusing more heavily on European, rather than Atlantic, affairs. Kissinger later reflected that

> Ted Heath was not the easiest man in the world to deal with. It was never a broken relationship, but when the Prime Minister was not as ready to communicate as one would think, Burke provided the bridge to make sure it would operate efficiently and correctly … a temporary bridge, not as an exclusive bridge … to smooth things over.[87]

In July 1971, Kissinger visited China under conditions of great secrecy. Because China had been ostracized since 1949, following the communist takeover on the mainland, Kissinger's trip was particularly sensitive and it paved the way for Nixon's historic visit the following year. Heath had long taken a special interest in China, but Kissinger chose not to inform him ahead of time. Always sensitive to perceived snubs, Heath responded by cutting off formal communications between No. 10 and the US administration. It fell to Trend to pick up the pieces. As Kissinger recalled: 'I called Burke Trend and said, "what the hell is going on here?" And he said, "I just can't tell you on the phone, but I'll tell you when I come over in another week and we'll fix it then."'[88] Communications were duly restored.

Heath believed firmly that Britain's destiny lay in Europe and, as his premiership evolved, he sought to distance the UK from the Americans. In July 1973, British officials informed their American counterparts that, henceforth, the Heath government would seek to conduct multilateral negotiations (including the Europeans) with the US rather than the traditional UK–US bilateral consultations that had become the hallmark of the 'special relationship'. Trend told Kissinger on the phone that 'I thought today was terribly sad,' to which Kissinger responded: '[W]ell, it is a sad day in the history of our two countries.' Kissinger said to Trend: '[Y]ou and I are going to remain personal friends as far as I'm concern[ed],' and Trend replied: 'I would hate it otherwise.'[89]

Europe was the more serious issue dividing Prime Minister from his Cabinet Secretary than differences over the US. It was the greatest theme in his premiership, and Heath was disappointed that Trend's Atlanticism and love of the Commonwealth meant he could not share in his enthusiasm for Europe. He ploughed ahead with his crusade nevertheless, despite having a majority of only twenty-five and forty Eurosceptic MPs with whom to reckon. The legislation was driven through Parliament with no less than 105 divisions. The European Community Act was passed in October 1972, and Britain joined in January 1973.

Despite Trend's own beliefs, which he kept to himself, the Cabinet Office played the central role in coordinating Britain's European policy 'both during the accession negotiations themselves, and subsequently'.[90] Trend was indeed pleased that the Cabinet Office rather than another department became the locus for the work. Machinery had originally been set up in 1961, with most of the work carried out by the Treasury, but was mothballed when Macmillan's bid to join failed in 1963. When reinstated from 1971, there was a question about whether it should return there, or go to the FCO. The Cabinet Office won out due to its reputation for cross-departmental coordination, and no subject required more intra-Whitehall debate, *sanspareil* by the early 1970s.[91] Thus was born the European Secretariat, which Hennessy argues 'acquired a (deserved) reputation for ... having the most effective arrangements of European policy compared to any member state'.[92] Indeed, civil servant Sir Antony Part said the Cabinet Office's coordination of Whitehall allowed the government to put together a 'first eleven' negotiating team led by diplomat Michael Palliser.[93]

With Trend disengaged from him on a personal level, Heath came to rely much more closely on his PPS, Robert Armstrong, with whom he shared a love of music. Equally, he found Head of the HCS William Armstrong (no relation to Robert Armstrong) a far more productive adviser than Trend, and the fact that he was sympathetic to Heath's style of government was an added boon. As early as the spring of 1971, Heath and William Armstrong were meeting regularly, and that autumn he was appointed to a confidential task force developing a response to the rising unemployment, an area of particular expertise.

Heath, a lover of Europe to his fingertips, was very impressed by the French Civil Service model, where officials were far more active politically and less nuanced, as opposed to traditional Whitehall mandarins, whose style was to outline a range of options to him, while being reluctant to make strong recommendations of their own.[94] As a whole series of crises unfolded – economic, industrial, security, Ireland and Northern Ireland – he grew to lean on William Armstrong. 'Armstrong in effect became Heath's *chef de cabinet* and acquired a "political" influence. This resulted in him being dubbed "Deputy Prime Minister" in 1973,' said historian Rodney Lowe.[95] Heath 'came to lean increasingly, and in the end dangerously, on officials who could pose no threat to him. Although his political colleagues were outstandingly loyal, they all had careers and constituencies and interests of their own, whereas his officials were devoted exclusively to serving him,' wrote Heath's biographer John Campbell, with William Armstrong expressly in mind. He concludes tellingly about Heath that 'senior civil servants felt that he was at heart one of them'.[96]

Douglas Hurd, a former diplomat at the FCO (1952–66), was another who came into No. 10 as a core member of Heath's team, as his Private Secretary. As Heath's premiership continued, he articulated Heath's frustration at Trend's contribution. Hurd complained that the ministers were let down at three crucial moments by officials: the aftermath of the 'Bloody Sunday' shootings by British soldiers in January 1972, in discussions on inflation strategy in 1973, and preparation for a confrontation with the NUM in late 1973.[97] But was Trend necessarily at fault for not playing the game that Heath wanted? Rather he deserves credit for abiding by his Civil Service code and personal credo, and refusing to be overly drawn into the cauldron.

Heath's disillusion with Trend was becoming common knowledge. William Plowden, a CPRS member, was one of those who believed Trend's Cabinet Office was not doing enough to help. According to his son, Michael, Trend began looking for an exit. Robert Armstrong later said that Burke Trend had dual motivations for leaving: 'he thought that ten years was enough', and he ran 'out of sympathy with Heath's European direction of international policy'.[98] In September 1973, just before he finally left office to become Rector of Lincoln College, Oxford, the only Cabinet Secretary to retire early, he received a message from Kissinger: 'I confess a certain envy seeing you re-enter the groves of academe. You take with you the respect and esteem of your colleagues everywhere, and I extend my very best wishes.'[99] His premature departure was a poignant end to the career of a great public servant.

JOHN HUNT AND HEATH

With Trend clearly on his way out, John Hunt was brought into the Cabinet Office as his deputy, poised to take over. Hunt was born in 1919, son of a Royal Artillery officer who fought in the Great War. His parents were Roman Catholic, so sent him to Downside public school, where he excelled academically and at sport. He won a place at Magdalene College, Cambridge, leaving after just two years to join the Royal Navy, with a second-class degree.[100] The only Cabinet Secretary to serve in the Second World War, he always had the air of a military man about him, and was always eager to support the services. During the war, he had been deployed on convoy escorts, qualifying as a signals officer. In 1944, he was transferred to the Far East, where, at the age of twenty-four, he took the surrender of a Japanese garrison. He married Mary Robinson, who gave birth to the first of their three children in 1942 and died in 1971. Hunt was released from the navy in 1946 and, with his newfound fascination for the Far East, chose to join the Dominions Office in the Civil Service, then a high-ranking department. Promotion was swift and he became Private Secretary to a dynamic junior minister, Patrick Gordon Walker, later Foreign Secretary under Wilson. Hunt's sangfroid had made a clear impression on Walker. On a visit to Sri Lanka, they would swim together: '[T]here were said to be sharks about, so I always sent him in ahead of me: he never seemed to mind!'[101]

Luck – specifically, being in the right place at the right time – played a role in the promotion of all Cabinet Secretaries. Hunt was fortunate to be the First Secretary at the British High Commission in Ottawa when Brook spotted him, and in 1956 invited him to become his Private Secretary. Brook was impressed by Hunt, becoming his mentor and inspiration, as Bridges had been to Trend. Brook brought Hunt back again into the Cabinet Office in 1960, after a spell as secretary to the JIC. When he left, the Committee recorded its 'warmest thanks for the magnificent work Mr Hunt had done'.[102]

179

Hunt was clearly destined for the top. In 1962, he joined the Treasury, becoming the Deputy Secretary, and First Civil Service Commissioner in the new Civil Service Department from 1968 to 1971. He soon established a reputation as a staunch defender of the Civil Service against its critics, notably the Fulton Committee, which had been set up by Wilson in 1966 to review its operation. He was promoted again in 1971 to Third Secretary, and from 1972 he was brought into the Cabinet Office as Second Permanent Secretary. Hunt had worked closely at the Treasury with William Armstrong, where the two men shared a similar outlook on government.

In 1973, Heath invited Hunt to conduct an audit of the Cabinet Office, while Trend was still in situ, and to make recommendations for improving it after he departed. Hunt scrutinised the various minutes that Heath had sent Trend on improving Cabinet Committee meetings, and spoke to over fifty ministers to garner their views. His diagnosis was damning. There were far too many committees he said (forty-six ministerial and twelve official), and they failed to distinguish sufficiently between those with collective responsibility and those merely coordinating low-level departmental business. Further, he found the system too passive and reactive, leaving insufficient time to explore major policy issues.[103]

Hunt scrupulously avoided criticising Trend personally, maintaining that all changes must await his retirement, but he nevertheless pinpointed several inadequacies in the Cabinet Office's organisation: '[W]e should be less a house of scribes and more of a place for seeing that government business is run properly.'[104] Lessons could be learnt, he believed, from the dynamism of the new European Secretariat which had impressed everyone in its short life dealing with Whitehall and the European Community. The Cabinet Office, furthermore, needed to be a 'more rewarding place to work' and this would 'help us get the best quality people'.[105] The Cabinet Office, he thought, had lost some of its role as an 'active bridge between the Prime Minister and ministers on one hand and the Whitehall machine on the other'. His solution to curing the Cabinet Office malaise and making it more dynamic was bringing in better quality personnel, and upgrading the deputy secretaries, which would help make it the best-informed department in Whitehall. Internally, improved coordination was needed between the diverse elements that made up the Cabinet Office. Hunt proposed a weekly strategic meeting, which he wanted Robert Armstrong to join from No. 10, which 'would do much to offset the reactive criticism of the committees' system'. Hunt was finally clear that if he was to do the job properly he would need to free himself of some of 'Sir Burke Trend's current preoccupations … in order to concentrate on things where I can be of more help to you'.[106] This included delegating more of the work, particularly on the economic side. Hunt, the master tactician, took the sensible precaution of securing the agreement of William Armstrong to his proposals before he sent them to Heath.

So, even before he took over, Hunt had made a favourable impression on Heath. He sent Heath a private letter to thank him 'for the confidence you have shown in me … It would be a pleasure to serve you as Secretary to the Cabinet.'[107] He also wrote to thank Heath for inviting him, together with his daughter Charlotte and youngest son Martin, to watch the Trooping of the Colour from No. 10, a very thoughtful gesture. Hunt married his second wife Madeleine in 1973, the widowed sister of Cardinal Basil Hume. The first Catholic to be appointed Cabinet Secretary, he was said to be the most senior Catholic openly operating in Whitehall since Henry VIII disposed of the services of Chancellor Thomas Wolsey in 1529.

Hunt's honeymoon with Heath was never going to last. Impatience soon took over. He was soon jibing away to Hunt about pruning Cabinet Committees: '[C]an we not abolish a whole lot more? It still leaves 113 committees.'[108] Hunt wrote back to point out that the fifty-three committees he had abolished already had predominantly been unnecessary, but those remaining all served vital roles, consisting largely of the committees of officials. Only twenty-five ministerial committees (including sub-committees) remained, he said, and seven major standing committees, signified by the acronym 'GEN'. Hunt reassured Heath that 'nevertheless, I will remain on the war path'.[109] Robert Armstrong wrote back diplomatically that 'the Prime Minister is happy to know you will remain on the warpath, and hopes that you will be able to add to your collection', adding, with a flourish: '[T]here ought to be a sort of capitation reward – the opposite of a productivity bonus.'[110] Pruning Cabinet Committees was a constant obsession of Prime Ministers, and hence became a constant preoccupation of Cabinet Secretaries.

Hunt's four months with Heath proved a baptism of fire. In a less feverish time at No. 10, Hunt might have worked well with him. As Theakston wrote, compared to Trend, Hunt was 'more in the mould of dynamic and active "doers" favoured by Heath'.[111] Heath definitely preferred his crisp style of briefs to Trend's noncommittal, academic submissions. With Hunt, briefs followed a common format: section one provided the background and listed the options, section two outlined the likely problems, while section three offered decisions with his own advice.[112] But we can exaggerate Hunt's importance. Campbell believes that Hunt would never have supplanted William Armstrong as Heath's key strategic adviser on the multiple crises assaulting Downing Street.[113] William Armstrong's health collapsed under multiple pressures, from which he soon recovered, enjoying success as chairman of the Midland Bank before dying suddenly aged sixty-five.[114] His decision to leave the Civil Service to take up such a senior position in a clearing bank, so soon after helping oversee the government's economic policy, aroused some concern, until Prime Minister Harold Wilson gave a green light. William Armstrong is one of those Whitehall giants who never made it to Cabinet Secretary, but might well have done bar the crucial question of timing. Had he become Cabinet Secretary, he would have been more in the Hankey than Bridges mould.

HUNT AND WILSON, 1974-76

Heath called an election for 28 February, posing the question 'Who runs Britain? The government or the unions?' The Conservatives won 297 seats to Labour's 301 and the Liberals' fourteen. Hunt was closely involved in Heath's delicate and abortive attempt to form a Liberal–Conservative coalition, liaising closely with the Queen's Private Secretary Martin Charteris throughout. But it was not to be, and Wilson returned to Downing Street again on 4 March.[115] For Hunt, it was out of the frying pan and into the fire. It was perhaps fortunate for him that he was older and more robust, aged fifty-five, when he succeeded Trend, making him the third oldest of the eleven Cabinet Secretaries on taking office. In contrast, Wilson was a much reduced, feebler figure than he had been in 1964–70. Joe Haines said he was 'significantly' weaker physically, with an array of physical ailments, explaining his wish to be a 'centre half rather than a centre forward' as in the 1960s.[116] His ailments were in part alcohol-related. Kenneth Stowe, Armstrong's successor as PPS, said 'that it could be pointless [because of drink] to get a decision out of him after 6 p.m.'.[117] Another aide said that PMQ days were the worst, when he needed brandies to fortify him before, and more brandies to celebrate after.[118] Wilson may also have been suffering from the early signs of the dementia that was to afflict him in retirement. Either way, Wilson's great political career was ending with a whimper, not a bang.

Barbara Castle, now Health Secretary, thought Hunt 'far less intrusive then his predecessor but ... [with] less charisma and so I think he will fit better into the new mood'.[119] Hunt was the supreme technician – less cerebral then Trend or Brook – but a master at getting the job done, and in comprehending the electric currents of power that surged back and forth between the big political beasts. Henry Kissinger considered that 'Hunt was more formal than Burke Trend and stayed more strictly within the defined confines of a Cabinet Secretary. We [the White House] got less informal advice – but it was also less needed.'[120] Ian Beesley, the Cabinet Office historian, described Hunt as 'courteous and often kind, but at first sight he could appear off-putting and unapproachable ... [Though] some senior colleagues never felt they got close to him.'[121]

To Wilson's Praetorian Guard, Joe Haines and Bernard Donoughue, Hunt was an imperialist who wanted a central No. 10 and to bring it within his empire. Even Stowe said: 'John wants us as one of his colonies and we won't do it'.[122]

Chairing meetings was one of his signature skills. Like all good chairs, he knew exactly what he wanted the meeting to achieve, and how to steer it towards the right conclusion. He distilled his approach into a manual, 'The Dos and Don'ts of Chairmanship', published in *Management Services and Government*, the Civil Service journal, in 1977. 'Don't appeal ever for moderation', he cautioned, if 'things get sticky. Rather:

1. Introduce a totally new factor.

2. Ask for someone to speak not involved in the dust up, and if all else fails...

3. Drop in a light hearted remark.'[123]

Hunt, like Trend, and indeed all their predecessors, was deeply interested in diplomatic and intelligence matters, and thrived in a new role as the Prime Minister's representative or 'Sherpa' at the regular meetings of G7 leaders. This role developed out of an official gathering in 1974 of senior financial figures from the US, the UK, West Germany, Japan and France. In 1975, President Giscard d'Estaing of France invited finance ministers and central bank figures from these five countries, plus Italy, to continue to discuss the global economic crisis at Château de Rambouillet near Paris. It morphed into the meetings of the national leaders of the six which, joined by Canada, became the 'G7'. The task drew Hunt into working closely with the US, helping facilitate the agreement between the Prime Minister and President Carter to supply Trident missiles to replace Britain's ageing Polaris missiles. Much of his time was expended working to revitalise oversight of the intelligence agencies, as Beesley writes, 'notably in the aftermath of the United States Watergate scandal'.[124] Despite his own warnings to Heath about the dangers of the Cabinet Secretary losing focus, hence the importance of divesting himself of some responsibilities, he was finding out the hard way that the job was relentless and all-consuming. And that was without the added burden of being Head of the HCS, a job done by William Armstrong until 1974, then Douglas Allen until 1978, then Ian Bancroft until 1981, none entirely satisfactorily.

Hunt, nevertheless, found the space to achieve his most enduring legacy as Cabinet Secretary: the welding of the Cabinet Office into a strong and better staffed force in Whitehall. By the time he left in 1979, he had five deputies beneath him, including the new post of 'Deputy Secretary of Economic, Industrial and Scientific Affairs'. The other four deputies were responsible for Home and Social Affairs, Defence and Overseas, Europe, and Intelligence. To Bernard Donoughue, head of the new Policy Unit at No. 10 from March 1974, Hunt was 'the single most powerful official in Whitehall or indeed the country', who succeeded in drawing power back into the office and recovering its prestige.[125] To Joe Haines, Wilson's Press Secretary (1969–76), Hunt was 'the most powerful man in Whitehall ... power flowed into the Cabinet Office during the Hunt stewardship'.[126]

Hunt later told a seminar at the Institute of Contemporary British History that Cabinet government 'is cumbersome, ... difficult [and] a bit of a shambles', but then added, 'it has got to be so far as possible, a demo-cratic and accountable shambles'.[127] Hunt's mission was precisely to ensure this: he wanted to bring structure and good order back to the centre.

Wilson's new team admired the no-nonsense, straight-backed Hunt after they picked up the reins in 1974, a welcome contrast to the austere Cabinet Secretary they remembered working with before the election of 1970. He also spoke truth to power. 'Hunt, who is very helpful in many ways, felt this Labour government read too many newspapers,' recorded Donoughue in his diary, while he thought 'the last Tory government listened to too much BBC Radio and claimed it was run by communists'.[128] Hunt was far from thrilled when Wilson told him about his intention to set up a 'Policy Unit' in No. 10, run by LSE academic Donoughue. Wilson felt he wanted more policy advice at the heart of his premiership than he had received in 1964–70; the distinctive feature of the Policy Unit being that it worked solely for the Prime Minister, unlike the CPRS, which worked for Cabinet as a whole.[129] Hunt sought to tame it and integrate it into the Whitehall machine, much as Trend had done with the CPRS. He came up with a framework document defining the Policy Unit's remit, including its access to Cabinet Committees. The Policy Unit, it said, could have limited access to Cabinet Committees, but could not communicate directly with the No. 10 Private Office, nor have access to steering briefings.

Donoughue was a savvy operator, who was not going to be outsmarted by a mandarin. He had written a biography the year before with George Jones on the wily and powerful Labour politician Herbert Morrison. Donoughue was a survivor, and as much of an operator as Hunt himself. One of Hunt's strengths was his capacity for gaining the trust of those who had his Prime Minister's trust, as Donoughue and Haines certainly did. Donoughue was intrigued by the question that lay at the heart of the Cabinet Secretary's job, did 'prime responsibility lay to the Cabinet as a collective whole, or personally to the Prime Minister, whose right hand always sits in Cabinet'. He observed how when there was a conflict, Hunt would always give his support to 'his final master and centre of power, the Prime Minister'.[130] Both Wilson and Callaghan used Hunt's guile and ability to influence issues raised at Cabinet, and which ministers sat on which committee, to advance their own agenda, and to deter those opposed to them, notably Tony Benn.[131]

The Crossman diaries were to cause a major headache for Hunt. Crossman had died in April 1974, but his literary executors and the *Sunday Times*, who wanted to serialise the diaries, pressed for publication. 'There will inevitably be problems since the diary contains a blow by blow account of many Cabinet discussions,' wrote an alarmed Hunt, fearful that publication 'could mark something of a watershed'. Donoughue and Haines counselled strongly against taking action, but Hunt insisted, and Wilson supported his line. Wilson authorised Hunt to speak to Attorney General Sam Silkin, who took an even stronger line, and unsuccessfully tried to get an injunction to stop publication, while Hunt asserted that publication would be against the public interest. Wilson, Donoughue said, 'sat back, chuckled, and was quite happy' to see his Cabinet Secretary discomforted.[132] Public sympathy and critical opinion were strongly behind Jonathan Cape, the publisher, and the *Sunday Times*, who went ahead with serialisation regardless. But if Hunt had not registered his strong protest, he felt, further breaches by ministers could not be stopped. Hunt found it a painful episode, but he moved on quickly, and 'Radcliffe Rules' on ministerial memoirs produced some sensible new guidelines, sparked by the Crossman diaries.

Hunt was not at all sure of one member of Wilson's team, Marcia Williams, who was less of a present figure than in 1964–70, but could still be a formidable and disruptive presence. After she would lay into Wilson, he would retreat into brandy. The curious hold she held over him was a matter of frequent comment in the building. She distrusted Donoughue and Haines: whenever she felt a threat of being eased out, she would pointedly tap her handbag, in which resided some secret about Wilson which she surmised, not incorrectly, no one would want to see her produce in public.[133]

Britain's entry into the European Community in January 1973 created problems for Labour, divided down the middle as it was. Wilson alighted on the expedient of holding a referendum in 1975 on whether Britain should remain a member. The detailed work was carried out in the European Secretariat in the Cabinet Office, led by senior official Patrick Nairne, which reported up to Hunt. A referendum would throw up novel problems if government ministers were to be arguing in public against one another. Hunt came up with the idea of a Cabinet 'agreement to differ' to preserve Cabinet responsibility, drawing on the 1932 precedent for the Cabinet to differ, set by Ramsay MacDonald, over tariff reform. An official who worked alongside Hunt described how dominant he was in the execution of the agreement, 'owning the document, and determining that what came out at the end would make sense'.[134]

Hunt's empathy with Labour ministers, and his wit, were seen in February 1975, when Cabinet ministers were discussing a paper by Ted Short, the Leader of the House of Commons, on the complexities of their position. Barbara Castle wondered whether ministers should have a 'referendum kit' to simplify matters. Quick as a flash, Hunt passed her a note:

Referendum Kit?

Outcome of renegotiation

Government recommendation

Case for

Case against

Map to polling station

Polling card

Opinion poll response cards

1 bottle champagne
1 bottle arsenic[135] } To be taken at choice according to result

Wilson was confident about the referendum result. Nairne later said: '[T]he Cabinet Secretary John Hunt and I [went] to have a talk with the Prime Minister the night before the referendum, and he wasn't interested, he took the view that clearly it was going to go "yes".' Hunt was nowhere near as confident. Nairne remarked: 'In spite of everybody's assumption that, quite clearly, the pressure of the media was such that the "yes" supporters were bound to win, that certainly was not the assumption at the top of the Cabinet Office.'[136] It thus spent time pondering a 'no' result. Contingency planning for a rejection of the European Community was a vastly easier exercise in 1975 than it was to prove forty years later. After just two years in, Britain was barely embedded in Europe, and as Nairne said of the politicians, 'you couldn't carry them all that far'.[137] One reason why ministers believed the vote would be to remain was that, unlike in 2016, the press was solidly behind Europe.

With the referendum successfully out of the way and a 67 per cent vote to remain in the European Community, Wilson looked forward to carrying out his secret plan of leaving two years after his return to No. 10 in March 1974. Cabinet was stunned when he announced his resignation in March 1976: it was one of the few secrets that Wilson had managed to keep. Donoughue recorded how Wilson set off for the Palace at 10 a.m.: 'I went to the front door as they drove off – there was not a single reporter or journalist nor when they returned … it was the best secret ever kept.'[138] While ministers had been gathering for Cabinet on 16 March, Wilson caught 'Ted Short, Denis Healey and me and broke the news to the three of us', as Callaghan recalled.[139] Shirley Williams suggested that a tribute be released to the press, amended by Roy Jenkins and Callaghan, who accepted Hunt's suggestion that the statement be released in the Prime Minister's absence. As Castle recorded, '[T]hese civil servants think of everything.'[140] A grand farewell dinner for Wilson was held in the large dining room upstairs in No. 10 for all twenty-three Cabinet ministers, as well as John Hunt and Burke Trend, who had been invited back. 'Trend seemed very agitated about missing his train back to Oxford and left at 9:45 before H. W. spoke,' was Donoughue's telling comment.[141]

HUNT AND JAMES CALLAGHAN, 1976–79

Callaghan became Prime Minister on 5 April 1976, ushering in a period where Hunt was at the height of his powers. He needed to be, because challenges came swiftly. Hunt immediately fell into a good working relationship with Callaghan, who admired Hunt's skill as an efficient deliverer of business. They shared a respect for the military. Callaghan loved Cabinet government, to Hunt's great pleasure. Neither possessed great imagination, but both men were extraordinarily straight. It was a happy relationship, even if, as Kenneth O. Morgan says, he never heard Callaghan express any great warmth for him.[142] The government had achieved only a fragile majority in the October 1974 election, which disappeared altogether in 1977, precipitating a Lib–Lab pact. According to Beesley, 'Hunt's great contribution was that he still managed the flow of Cabinet business' under these precarious circumstances.[143] He was undisputed master of the Cabinet Office, widely regarded as 'a senior guy, who had been around a long time, with views of his own ... he'd set his own standard'.[144] His task was not eased by some difficulty achieving Cabinet cohesion: '[T]here were far too many marsh-mallows and too few vertebrae in Jim's Cabinet,' said one.[145]

Callaghan's government was coming under pressure from all sides, includ-ing from the Chrysler Corporation, which sought '$325 million of aid from the government, threatening to close its operations in the UK'.[146] The trade unions, which had been speedily pacified by Wilson after the February 1974 election, were beginning to flex their muscles again, frustrated as the econ-omy showed no sign of revival. Scotland and Wales were pressing too for greater devolution of power. To underpin his working majority in the House of Commons, Callaghan made a deal with the SNP and Plaid Cymru, agree-ing that the government would devolve powers to them. Hunt helped pave the way, while remaining personally sceptical, and was the first to highlight the significance of the famous 'West Lothian' question, whereby Scottish and Welsh MPs could vote on issues that only concern England, whereas England's MPs lost their vote over similar matters in Scotland and Wales.[147]

The most fraught issue for the Callaghan government came early in its life with the IMF crisis in the summer of 1976. Investors became con-vinced, especially after the defeat of the government's public expenditure White Paper earlier in 1976, that the pound would lose its value. When it reached a record low in June 1976, the government applied for a stand-by loan from a consortium of banks for $5.3 billion, borrowing $1 billion from it by September under the condition that it be repaid by December. It became clear that a loan would be required from the IMF for a sum of $4 billion. As a condition, IMF officials wanted deep cuts in public spending, which was always going to be difficult for a Labour government to enact, as Ramsay MacDonald had found in 1931. Callaghan sought to keep his divided ministers together over nine Cabinet meetings, with Tony Benn recommending a siege economy, and Chancellor Denis Healey at the other end, favouring acceptance of the terms. Hunt worked by Callaghan's side at every step, advising him on handling his ministers and ensuring that collec-tive responsibility remained intact. He noted how Callaghan worked his way round to backing the Treasury's line: 'I do not think he was committed to supporting Denis Healey. To some extent he was testing the Treasury view and was looking at what other solutions could be found, [but] at the end of the [key] ... torturous meeting, he decided to come down on the side of Healey.'[148] Hunt worked closely, too, with Kenneth Berrill, Rothschild's successor as the new head of the CPRS, in preparing a 'doomsday scenario', i.e. in the event an agreement could not be reached, of which only four copies were made.

The document, signed by Hunt, entitled 'What happens if we do not get the IMF loan' was handed to Callaghan at the beginning of December 1976. It was a grim read. 'There would almost certainly be an immediate sterling crisis', Hunt wrote. 'We could take certain steps (e.g. closing the foreign exchange market) which would get us through a few days, but no more'. The paper then went through Britain's options, considering how, for example, 'abandoning our defence commitments ... would create the maximum international ill-will and loss of confidence in Britain'. It concluded:

> We cannot ignore the fact we have a £250 million monthly deficit on current and structural capital account. Our reserves, reduced by paying the stand-by, could not plug that hole for long ... This seems to suggest that the only possible course open to the Government ... would be ... to allow all concerned (our main creditors, the IMF and ourselves) to think again and to await the arrival of a (possibly) more helpful Carter Administration.[149]

Jimmy Carter did win the US presidential election in November 1976, but their help was not required. Callaghan sent Hunt as his envoy on a secret mission to Germany to see Chancellor Helmut Schmidt to see if they could offer financial help. German help equally was not needed. Ultimately, the government agreed to the budget cuts, and the IMF agreed to give Britain the loan. The economic climate in 1977 improved more quickly than anticipated, and the government did not need to draw upon the entirety of the loan. But it had been a humiliating experience, which helped prepare the country for the strong medicine that Thatcher was to give it after 1979.

With Hunt as the pre-eminent figure in Whitehall, despite his not being the Head of the HCS, tensions with the Treasury surged. A turf war with

Permanent Secretary Douglas Wass threatened to get out of control. In April 1976, Robin Butler, who returned to the Treasury in 1975 after leaving Wilson's Private Office, reported that 'there was still great tension between the Cabinet Office and Treasury'.[150] Douglas Allen, the Head of the Civil Service and Wass's predecessor as Permanent Secretary to the Treasury, offered his opinion in October 1976: '[Allen] was very critical of the Treasury.'[151] Hunt and Callaghan, who had himself been Chancellor of the Exchequer (1964–67), discussed the idea of splitting the Treasury into a Ministry of Finance and a Department for Public Expenditure. Callaghan's biographer, Kenneth O. Morgan, speaks of Callaghan's instinctive mistrust of the Treasury as Prime Minister, believing he had not asserted himself strongly enough against Treasury officials as Chancellor, especially over devaluation in 1967.[152] Hunt raised the issue of splitting it up again, as had happened in 1964, at a Parliamentary Select Committee in February 1977. Hunt had a conversation with Donoughue about it, after which the latter wrote: 'What I would like to know is whether the Prime Minister authorised Hunt to fly the kite. It is hard to believe the Cabinet Secretary would put up a proposal to carve the Treasury without higher authority.'[153] Hunt, who had spent comparatively little of his life in the Treasury for a Cabinet Secretary, was himself far from a Treasury fan. The minute he sent Callaghan about the proposals elicited Callaghan's praise in the margins ('very good').[154] The Treasury was more than flustered at this existential threat: 'What a strange man Hunt is,' Wass commented, while his political boss, Healey was considerably more belligerent: '[W]e are now embarked on the dismantling of John Hunt.'[155]

Donoughue was impressed by the way Hunt fought his corner in this boxing match between the two Whitehall big beasts: the Cabinet Secretary beat the Head of the HCS in a straight fight. He wrote that Hunt was 'certainly the fastest and most effective operator in Whitehall', that he was 'impressively efficient and tough' and 'the iron fist in the iron glove'.[156] Donoughue's close watch on the Cabinet Secretary would prove extremely useful. He was a consultant to the classic television series *Yes, Minister* (1980–84) and *Yes, Prime Minister* (1986–88). The semi-fictional Prime Minister's PPS, Bernard Wooley, possessed more than just Donoughue's first name, while his senior official, Sir Humphrey Appleby, shared many of the steely features of Hunt.

As Donoughue later commented, '[S]ome of Sir Humphrey's silky and Jesuitical skills were indeed present in Sir John. But he was in no sense a comical figure.'[157] Indeed. But the real life incidents on which Donoughue drew for his advice had their comical aspects. Donoughue was particularly amused by Hunt having to phone No. 10 whenever he wanted access via the famous green and beige internal door, connecting the Cabinet Office to it. In league with the PPS, he would periodically taunt Hunt by refusing to grant immediate access, claiming the Prime Minister was tied up. 'Access is the ammunition of Whitehall power,' he said. This vignette duly filtered into an episode of the television programme.[158]

Hunt outlived the Labour government that defined his time as Cabinet Secretary. In May 1979, the election was won by the Conservatives under Margaret Thatcher, heralding the beginning of her turbulent, pivotal and decisive premiership. When entering Downing Street, she received her lengthy briefing from Hunt about the situation that she was inheriting. It concluded: 'There is a great deal to be done in the short term on these issues ... The most immediately pressing is the shape of the Budget and associated matters like the money supply target.' Hunt emphasised the centrality of the Secretariat: 'An essential concern of the Cabinet Office is ... to ensure the work ... is tackled in an orderly fashion and in good time so ministers have a sound basis for decision-taking.'[159]

Hunt was rapidly swept up into the Thatcher maelstrom. His interventions were diverse. At one point he declined the Japanese government's offer of twenty 'karate ladies' to protect Thatcher at the Tokyo Economic Summit: 'Sir John said that Mrs Thatcher will attend the Summit as Prime Minister and *not* as a woman per se, and he was sure that she would not want these ladies.'[160] But for all his adept skills, Thatcher had little time for either of the civil servants she inherited from Labour: Hunt and PPS Ken Stowe. 'She did not trust Hunt,' said a well-placed insider, 'he was too obviously a fixture of the previous era, and there was no time for a relationship to forge. His departure was not regretted.'[161] John Campbell, who also wrote a Thatcher biography, said she found him 'too managing – brisk and business-like but too inclined to tell her what to do'.[162]

Hunt was ready to retire at the age of sixty, refashioning himself into a successful commercial figure, first as chairman of the Banque Nationale de Paris (1980–97), and then chair of the Prudential Corporation (1985–90). A devout Catholic until the end of his life, he was chairman of the trust that published the Catholic journal *The Tablet*. Following his death from cancer aged eighty-eight, a requiem mass was held for him in the Catholic Westminster Cathedral in October 2008.[163] Michael Quinlan, the leading Whitehall defence mandarin, summed him up at it: 'Both by what he did and what he was, he enriched the public life in this country.'[164]

ROBERT ARMSTRONG, ARRIVING AT
HEATHROW AIRPORT IN 1986

ROBIN BUTLER, PHOTOGRAPHED
THREE DAYS AFTER BECOMING
CABINET SECRETARY IN 1988

CHAPTER 8

Robert Armstrong and Robin Butler: The Last of the Traditionalists, 1979–98

AFTER TWO DECADES of relative difficulties and decline, Britain re-emerged on the world stage under a strong, if controversial, leader in Mrs Thatcher. Britain had just two Prime Ministers in these years, both Conservative, and two Cabinet Secretaries. Armstrong and Butler were two outstanding public servants of the postwar era. Both were so alike in their inner convictions and values, but so different outwardly: one Eton, the other Harrow; one a Rolls-Royce Silver Shadow, the other a Bentley Continental Convertible; one the Albert Hall, the other Twickenham. Britain was changing quickly, the Cold War was ending, and the government was shrinking. How would these two great traditionalists manage the state?

Robert Armstrong

Robert Armstrong could not have been better qualified for the post of Cabinet Secretary, while simultaneously appearing utterly incompatible with the Prime Minister he was to serve for his entire tenure. He was the only Cabinet Secretary in the twentieth century to serve just one figure in No. 10. He was a close friend of Ted Heath, a staunch European, establishment to his fingertips, and an Old Etonian. In some ways, it was a surprise Thatcher accepted the recommendation that she appoint him. Later on, she might have been less biddable and demanded someone more tractable. But she would have regretted it if she had not appointed him. The son of distinguished musician Thomas Armstrong, he had been a scholar at Christ Church, Oxford, where he received a second-class honours degree in Classical Mods and Greats. His golden career in Whitehall began with entry into the Treasury as an Assistant Principal in 1950, where his talents were quickly identified, entering the Private Office of Chancellor Rab Butler in 1954. Seconded to the Cabinet Office from 1964 to 1966 to work under Burke Trend, a man he greatly admired, he became PPS to Chancellor of the Exchequer Roy Jenkins. In July 1970, he was appointed PPS to new Prime Minister Edward Heath, following the early departure of Alexander 'Sandy' Isserlis who had only been in post for a few weeks. Armstrong continued to serve Wilson for his first year, before being appointed Deputy Secretary to the Home Office, and two years later Permanent Under-Secretary.

Armstrong served under Thatcher from 1979 to 1987, and became a master in understanding her. However, he never became truly 'one of us', in Thatcher's terms, as were her two key officials, Press Secretary Bernard Ingham and Foreign Affairs Private Secretary Charles Powell. Nevertheless, he and Thatcher established a singularly successful relationship in the mould of Bridges and Churchill or Brook and Attlee.[1] He thus avoided the trap of over-identifying himself with her, as Brook did with Churchill, or as Charles Powell later did with Thatcher: '[I]n a strange sense, it was quite hard to tell what was me and what was her,' Powell said of their relationship.[2] Armstrong was never haughty with her, as some officials could be.[3] He kept a distance, adamant as Robin Butler was after him 'not to become an addition to the Private Office'; it meant there was always a sense that the Cabinet Office was a rival power to No. 10.[4]

Armstrong would see Thatcher several times a day, and on Friday mornings they would have a long meeting to discuss upcoming Cabinet and Cabinet Committee business. Early on, she criticised him about a memorandum he had written, to which she took exception:

I suddenly heard myself say: 'No, Prime Minister, you're wrong.' When I said that, she stopped in her tracks and said: 'Why do you say I am wrong, Robert?' [I never called her Margaret, but always 'Prime Minister'.] So I said why I thought she was wrong, and she didn't interrupt, and when I had finished she said: 'Thank you, Robert, you are quite right, I was wrong.' I realised then that though she very much knew her mind, she was very willing to discuss, and she would listen if you knew what you were talking about. I never used to tangle with her in public, but in private we could.[5]

Armstrong sat on her right-hand side throughout Cabinet meetings, as do all the Cabinet Secretaries, and observed her interactions acutely. On one occasion, to help facilitate the conduct of business, he advised her to make a break with her usual style of announcing her own view at the outset, but instead to chair the meeting in the 'conventional way: invite the minister presenting his case to do so, and then listen to the discussion'. He proposed this because he had learnt that her opposition to the paper would put her in a minority of one. She heeded his advice: 'She sat there quietly, and it was like sitting next to a piano wire being tensed, tauter and tauter and tauter, I wondered whether it was going to snap.' After she summed up the sense of the meeting, which was unanimous support for the paper, she turned to Armstrong and said: '"Did I do all right, Robert?" And it was very endearing … I said: "Yes, Prime Minister."'[6]

Armstrong utilised all the guile that he had acquired as PPS to Jenkins and Heath. To help Heath when he had been his PPS, he had devised a blue Prime Ministerial box with a red band round it, into which he would put the most secret intelligence and personal papers. A previous 'double envelope' system, where top-secret papers were placed so that lesser officials and aides in No. 10 would not see, was becoming too laborious to service. Wilson christened his creation 'Old Stripey'. The colourful system survived Callaghan, continuing into Thatcher's premiership. If there was something he particularly wanted her to read overnight, he would craftily slip it into 'Old Stripey', 'even if it wasn't quite as secret as some of the other stuff'.[7] He knew she would always give the box her priority.

Armstrong did not travel on trips abroad with Thatcher as regularly as

Trend or Hunt had done. He accompanied her, however, along with a bevy of officials, on her visit to see the newly inaugurated President Reagan in February 1981. He was in the US again with her for the Williamsburg Summit at the end of May 1983, the week before the general election, carrying on as the British 'Sherpa' for the G7 as inherited from Hunt. The White House had not warmed to Armstrong: 'As you know, we have been having trouble with her personal representative [Robert Armstrong] in the preparatory process. Instead of supporting us in beating down unhelpful French initiatives, Armstrong has been attempting to mediate between us and the French,' complains an indignant memo from the Reagan White House.[8] He would travel less with her as time went on, not because he was instinctively more a European than an Atlanticist, but mostly as a consequence of Charles Powell's arrival in 1984, who became her go-to person on foreign policy.

Armstrong thus did not make the same impression on the Reagan administration that Trend had left on the Nixon administration. But Reagan specifically sought his advice about whether to meet 'British Labor' leader Neil Kinnock in 1984, because he thought that it would be inappropriate to make an overture to Thatcher directly.[9] Armstrong was understood to be the proper, non-partisan figure to deal with such matters. Reagan's aide Robert McFarlane thus sent a cable to Armstrong:

WHILE THE PRESIDENT IS NOT INCLINED TO MEET WITH KINNOCK, WE DO NOT WISH TO CREATE A POLITICAL CONTROVERSY IN BRITAIN. THEREFORE, IF MRS THATCHER BELIEVES THAT THE PRESIDENT SHOULD AGREE TO SEE HIM, PLEASE LET ME KNOW. I AM VERY PLEASED THAT OUR CLOSE RELATIONS MAKE IT POSSIBLE TO POSE SUCH FRANK AND DIRECT QUESTIONS.[10]

Armstrong offered no objections, and Kinnock's meeting with Reagan was subsequently arranged for February 1984. It passed without incident, but did little to boost Kinnock's credentials as a statesman-in-waiting.

Thatcher's initial sense was that Whitehall mandarins opposed her radical ideas, an instinct that grew over time, not because she thought them anti-Conservative, but because they were, she suspected, conservative.

As they went in to a dinner in 1980 with the Permanent Secretaries, she whispered to Robert Armstrong: 'They're all against me, Robert, I can feel it.'[11] Interestingly, she did not say 'you', but she deliberately used the word 'they', suggesting that she regarded him as on her side, which, by and large, he was. She had little time for the Head of the Civil Service, Ian Bancroft, and his Civil Service Department, created following the Fulton Report of 1968. So she decided to abolish it in November 1981 and divide the duties between the Cabinet Office and the Treasury, with Bancroft taking early retirement. For two years, Armstrong and Wass were joint Heads of the HCS, but when Wass retired in 1983, she decided that she did not want his successor as Permanent Secretary of the Treasury, Peter Middleton, to assume the title of joint Head of the Civil Service. 'I don't want a Pinky and Perky arrangement, Robert: you'll have to do it by yourself,' she told him.[12] The jobs had been combined first under Brook in 1956 after Bridges left, but when it was clearly too much for him, the job had been split again when he left at the end of 1962. Both Armstrong's immediate predecessors, Trend and Hunt, significantly wrote to Armstrong to congratulate him on the decision: 'They thought, as I thought, that it was the right arrangement for the times, and wish[ed] they had been able to bring it about themselves.'[13]

Thatcher was keen for the Cabinet Office's compass to be expanded 'to mesh the work of the great Whitehall departments into a coherent whole, and then to constantly progress it, revise it and keep it from dissolving into the usual government confusion'.[14] Armstrong was initially unsure about whether he wanted to take on all the extra responsibilities. He knew Brook had found it difficult. Much though he prided himself on his ability to switch from one topic to another in the bat of an eye, and then 'to come back to the topic without a change in gear',[15] his great strength was as a counsellor and guide at the centre, rather than as an overall manager of an organisation so vast as the Civil Service. But he accepted the job in part because he was worried that management of the Civil Service, which was badly needed, would 'go by the board' if it went back into the Treasury. The Cabinet Secretary was ideally placed as the 'point person' who, unlike any other Permanent Secretary in Whitehall, is in daily contact with the Prime Minister. Thatcher, moreover, unlike many Prime Ministers, wanted to know what was going on across the whole of Whitehall, and made it her business to travel around departments. She saw herself as head of the whole executive, as indeed she was, and took answering Prime Minister's Questions about it very seriously: 'That very much affected the way that No. 10 had to work, because she had to have a briefing system which enabled her to cope with questions in this way.'[16]

His already bursting role was enhanced still further when, in February 1985, he issued an official guide on the 'duties and responsibilities of civil servants' – the first codification since Bridges.[17] Its second version, published two years later, gave officials the right to appeal to him as the Head of the HCS on issues of conscience.

The CPRS was another casualty of Thatcher. She abolished it in 1983, partly because she blamed it for leaks. She also believed that the Civil Service needed to be slimmer, focusing less on strategy formation and more on managerial efficiency. John Hoskyns, her first Head of the Policy Unit from 1979, believed that in contrast, whereas the Cabinet Office did an effective job coordinating Whitehall and producing briefs for the Prime Minister, the centre was still far too weak. So he believed the CPRS could and should have fulfilled the job within Whitehall of being 'a central brain'. But he could not persuade her. The size of the Civil Service under her was cut by a fifth, in part by shifting functions to outside agencies.

Armstrong could be a feisty defender of Thatcher. In January 1981, a meeting about the economy was held with the Permanent Secretaries of the main Whitehall economic departments. Christopher Dow, minuting the discussion, noted 'the general feeling was quite clearly despairing worry at the developing recession and the growing unemployment'.[18] Treasury Permanent Secretary Douglas Wass asked: 'Was there anything that those at the meeting … should do? Should they seek to make ministers take stock of the political dangers facing them – not just a half-hour discussion in Cabinet, but a half-day at Chequers?' Armstrong intervened forcefully to say that there would be a clear 'kickback' if civil servants started trying to tell ministers about politics: 'No political stock-taking would take place unless the PM desired it, which she did not,' he said emphatically.[19] Dow recorded in a confidential note for the Governor of the Bank of England: 'Armstrong himself evidently thinks quite strongly in terms of lowering the exchange rate by any means possible, and of joining the EMS [European Monetary System].'[20]

James Callaghan and his Cabinet, March 1978.

President John Kennedy with Harold Macmillan in the White House, April 1962. Norman Brook is on Macmillan's right and the British Ambassador to the US, David Ormsby-Gore, is on his left.

'Secretaries of the Cabinet', painted in 1984 by John Stanton Ward, featuring Burke Trend, Robert Armstrong and John Hunt.

Queen Elizabeth and Pierre Trudeau sign the Canadian Constitution in April 1982. Behind the scenes, Robert Armstrong had played a vital role.

air's first Cabinet meeting in May 1997, with Robin Butler to his right.

chard Wilson as Cabinet Secretary with Tony Blair. Jonathan Powell is over Wilson's shoulder.

Gus O'Donnell welcomes David and Samantha Cameron into No. 10.

Jeremy Heywood and David Cameron in the Prime Minister's office at the end of the Cabinet Room.

One aspect of the Cabinet Secretary's job, which had been central to the work since Hankey, but was receding in importance, was liaison with the Commonwealth. Armstrong's extra responsibilities for the Civil Service meant he had even less time to give to the Cabinet Secretary's traditional overseas work. One particular Commonwealth issue, however, was to loom large for a time during Thatcher's first term (1979–83). Canada had been self-governing since the 1840s, a dominion since 1867, and de facto independent since the Statute of Westminster in 1931. However, the Canadian Constitution could only be amended by an Act of the Westminster Parliament, making Canadian institutions technically subordinate to the British and formally governed by British law. Prime Minister Pierre Trudeau, wanting to 'patriate' the Canadian Constitution, raised the issue with Thatcher at the G7 Economic Summit in Venice in June 1980. Armstrong briefed Thatcher beforehand that she should be clear with Trudeau that a unilateral request for patriation would present her with problems, as Canada's ten provincial Premiers were not all in favour.[21]

The problem intensified during the course of 1980, with Armstrong alarmed that the British government was being boxed into a corner. If the Canadian Parliament passed a unilateral resolution, Britain would be compelled to pass a similar Bill through the Westminster Parliament 'for fear of being attacked for unwarranted interference in the internal affairs of Canada: but equally, it could be attacked by some provincial governments, notably Quebec, for a breach of trust'.[22] Armstrong worked closely with his counterpart in Canada, Clerk of the Privy Council Michael Pitfield, with whom he had a close relationship – so close that Lord Moran (the son of Churchill's doctor) the British High Commissioner in Ottawa, felt left out of discussions. Moran came to see Armstrong in November 1981 to say that Armstrong's relationship with Pitfield 'affected his standing as an *"interlocuteur valable"* in the eyes of the Canadian Prime Minister'. Moreover, whereas the American Ambassador in Ottawa had made it known that he had enjoyed a full conversation with President Nixon before taking up post, he himself 'was not able to say that he had seen the Prime Minister either before taking up his appointment or any time since'.[23]

A constitutional crisis was averted, to Armstrong's relief, when Trudeau reached an agreement with nine of the ten provincial Premiers on a draft measure for patriation. Only Quebec held out, with the premier René Lévesque arguing that the measure should not be enacted, and writing to Thatcher explaining his position.[24] Pitfield phoned Armstrong to say he hoped 'British Members of Parliament who had hitherto been standing out against the constitutional proposals would not enter the lists [i.e. go into battle] in support of Quebec'.[25] They did not, and the Bill passed. The British government introduced the Canada Act into Parliament, which speedily passed in February 1982. That April, the Queen went to Canada to sign it into law in Ottawa as Queen of Canada.[26]

The same month, Armstrong was to face his biggest challenge yet under Thatcher. His career, in contrast to that of many of his predecessors, had not involved him much in either overseas or military activity. The Falklands War, nevertheless, showed him to be a man of prescience on foreign policy, as well as a calm dispatcher of business in the very eye of the storm. Armstrong had written to Thatcher in January 1980, warning her that the Argentinians were pressing for a response from Britain on the future of the Falkland Islands: might some surrender of British authority in the future be in British interests? He noted that there was little prospect of repelling an Argentinian invasion: the nearest British base was at Ascension Island over 3,000 miles away, and it would take three weeks for warships to reach Port Stanley. Moreover, to have any prospect of success, a British force would have to be 'larger in present size than the entire population of the islands'.[27]

News of long-feared aggression came on Friday 2 April 1982. Cabinet met at 9.45 a.m. and Armstrong's minutes record: 'THE PRIME MINISTER said that it appeared that an Argentine invasion of the Falkland Islands in South Georgia was imminent.'[28] Cabinet met again at 7.30 p.m. that evening: 'The Prime Minister said that although no direct information had been received from the Falkland Islands, it appeared that Argentina had invaded them. It was not known what resistance there had been, nor the extent of any damage or casualties.'[29]

Thatcher summed up that the Cabinet agreed the naval task force should be ordered to sail as soon as it was assembled, and told ministers she would have more to say in the debate in the House of Commons to be held the following day, a Saturday.[30]

A War Cabinet was convened – official name: Overseas and Defence

Committee, South Atlantic (ODSA) – with its five ministers meeting every day at No. 10 at 10.30. Armstrong attended by Thatcher's side, as he would in Cabinet. The Cabinet Office delved back into the records of the War Cabinet in both world wars and Suez to see if lessons could be learnt. After the meeting was over, Chief of Defence Staff, Terry Lewin, would go back to Armstrong's room in the Cabinet Office, where they would meet Antony Acland and Frank Cooper, Permanent Secretaries of the FCO and Ministry of Defence respectively. They told them what ministers had decided, what actions were needed, and what briefing would be needed for the War Cabinet the following day. This meeting of officials in Armstrong's room was known as the 'Armstrong group', but, the eponymous leader said: 'I didn't ever give it official status, because I didn't want the Prime Minister to think that there was an official committee second-guessing the War Cabinet.'[31]

Armstrong was able to observe Thatcher as acutely as Bridges had scrutinised Churchill during the Second World War:

[S]he lived in those weeks more fully than at any other time in her Premiership. She was conscious … of the responsibility that fell on her, to rise to it … She didn't want to have to take a decision until it actually had to be taken, but once she had taken it, she moved on. She didn't agonise.[32]

During the whole war, Armstrong was struck by Thatcher's 'constant concern to minimise loss or injury', along with her human empathy: '[S]he had much more compassion than people had given her credit for, and it showed in those weeks and … [in] her concern for … the widows and families of those who were killed. She wrote a letter to the relatives of everybody who died in the war.'[33]

It was not a side of her personality that she revealed to many people, Armstrong said. She was perfectly content 'when the real need was to be decisive and consistent, to be the Iron Lady'.[34]

With the war drawing to a close, Armstrong wrote a paper for Thatcher at the end of May. Insufficient attention to postwar planning was to be a major criticism of the Iraq operation in 2003. In contrast, Armstrong had found the time to think ahead. 'It seems to me that the Government will be faced with an acutely difficult problem of political management.

When we have repossessed [the Islands],' he wrote to her, 'British public opinion will see it as a great victory, they'll want the Governor Rex Hunt back, and the Falklands garrisoned and protected.' He cautioned of the continued vulnerability Britain would experience against an Argentina that might not accept the fait accompli, and might continue to harass the islands militarily 'in order to make our victory as pyrrhic and as expensive as possible'.[35] International and American opinion he wrote, moreover, would not be content with British colonial rule continuing in perpetuity.[36] Thatcher, however, was in no mood to compromise on a great British victory. Ultimately the islands were heavily reinforced by the military, creating a 'Fortress Falklands', and restoring an uneasy *status quo ante*.

Thatcher's second term (1983–87), bookended by two strong election victories, saw her most successful years as Prime Minister. Her ministers and the Civil Service moved into gear more fully behind her. They read the runes: the dismissal of her opponents in Cabinet in the reshuffle of September 1981, the Falklands victory in 1982, the June 1983 landslide. They realised that she was all but unstoppable. She was triumphing, too, over the Civil Service, ensuring that people of whom she approved moved into senior positions; a strategy epitomised by the pro-monetarist Peter Middleton, succeeding Douglas Wass as Permanent Secretary of the Treasury. With Armstrong's deft nudging, Cabinet government had revived too after the Falklands War; there were more meetings of Cabinet Committees, fewer decisions taken in ad hoc groups, and thus a reassertion of collective responsibility. It is no coincidence that 1982 saw the largest number of Cabinet meetings of any year of Thatcher's premiership: fifty-three, compared to forty-five in 1980, forty-one in 1981, and then between thirty-eight to forty a year from 1983 onwards.[37] It was too good to last. By 1985, she had started drifting back to her old ways of reaching decisions in informal groups outside the Cabinet Committee structure. The Westland Affair in December 1985 and January 1986 was a shock for her, and collective responsibility reasserted itself, at least for a while after.[38]

The Anglo-Irish Agreement of 1985 was very much the fruit of Armstrong's personal endeavours. It was one of several events which, when writing her memoirs, Thatcher looked back on with frustration, believing that she had succumbed to the official embrace, specifically Armstrong's, and agreed against her better judgement.[39] The supreme patriot, she was uncomfortable, as with Europe, with any moves that diluted British sovereignty. His personal input as Cabinet Secretary was never seen more artfully than over Ireland. The archives from her first two years in power heave under the weight of papers about how to find the best way forward. Armstrong wrote to her in November 1980 about developments at the Maze Prison, where a hunger strike was taking place. He wrote:

[T]he problems are going to be to keep the peace in the streets of Northern Ireland ... I think there are reasons to think that both the PIRA [Provisional IRA] and the INLA [Irish National Liberation Army] may be thinking in terms of some kind of 'spectacular' act of terrorism in support of the hunger strike at some stage.[40]

Six months later, hunger strike leader Bobby Sands starved himself to death, very significantly escalating tension.

His death increased Armstrong's determination to find a lasting way forward, working closely with his opposite number, Dermot Nally, in Dublin. Thatcher was content to give Armstrong wide rein. She did not trust the Foreign Office to deal with the Irish, deeming them insufficiently keen to protect British interests, nor did she have a high regard for the Northern Ireland Office. Negotiations continued over many months, with Armstrong leading a team of British officials drawn from the Cabinet Office, the FCO and the Northern Ireland Office. Thatcher's unwillingness to compromise made Armstrong gloomy about the chances of success, despite his striving tirelessly to convince her and British ministers. Armstrong hoped that there might be 'a means of giving the Irish Government some measure of association with the administration of Northern Ireland at the political level, in a way which would go some distance to meet Irish aspirations but would not compromise British sovereignty, and might just be saleable to the Unionists'.[41]

The Anglo-Irish Agreement was eventually signed in November 1985, giving the Irish government an 'advisory' role in the government of Northern Ireland, but agreeing that there could be no change in the constitutional position of Northern Ireland without a majority of the province's population voting in favour. Hugo Young, one of Thatcher's early biographers, described it as 'one of Armstrong's finest hours'.[42] Nigel Lawson, in his memoirs, wrote that the agreement 'had been negotiated in total secrecy, largely by the Cabinet Secretary, Robert Armstrong. Not without cause, Margaret clearly regarded the Cabinet as far too leaky to be taken into her confidence.'[43]

Thatcher agreed to sign the agreement partly because of pressure from the United States to reach a compromise with Dublin, but also as a reaction to the wave of IRA bomb attacks in the early 1980s, culminating in the Brighton bomb in October 1984.[44] Terrorist Patrick Magee had stayed in Brighton between 14–17 September, planting a bomb under the bath in his room, No. 629 in the Grand Hotel on the seafront. He anticipated that its blast would rip into the rooms it was known Thatcher would occupy at the Conservative annual conference a month later. It detonated at 2.54 a.m. on 12 October, killing five people and injuring many more. Thatcher was awake in her bedroom suite at the time, working on her conference speech for the following day. The bomb blast caused great damage in her bathroom, but neither she nor husband Denis were injured. As a civil servant, Armstrong was not present at the party event. 'The news came through … and I didn't know whether the Prime Minister was still alive,' he recalled:

> I went through what I would have to do if she were dead and what would have to be done to find a successor, and the process by which one would have to have an interim Prime Minister until the process of election took place, and who I would have to talk to, and who I would have to recommend…[45]

Robin Butler, her PPS, called Armstrong an hour after the bomb went off to tell him the vital news for the senior custodians of the British state: the Prime Minister was safe. The events of the next few hours did much to cement their relationship, and paved the way for him succeeding Armstrong as Cabinet Secretary. Butler had been helping her with those parts of her speech relating to government business. She had finished preparing her speech by 2.30 a.m., 'quite early by her standards'. Her speechwriting team left, and Butler was left alone with her for a few minutes in the sitting room. He had a minute from No. 10 regarding a reasonably parochial matter, the future of the Liverpool Garden site after the end of the 1984 festival, and she told him – this was 2.30 in the morning and she had a major speech to deliver the next day – that she would rather read the document there and give an answer immediately, before Butler left. So, Butler remained, awaiting Thatcher's judgement on the Garden site, before he could leave and go to the bed he longed for.

As he sat thinking how much longer she would take, a loud explosion rocked the room. He had heard several bombs detonate, including the one that killed Thatcher's right-hand man Airey Neave during the 1979 general election campaign: 'I knew at once what it was, so I came to rather rapidly, and thought, well now here you are ... alone with the Prime Minister, and somebody is trying to blow her up, so you had better do something sensible.'[46] Butler was afraid another bomb might detonate at any moment, and advised her to stay away from the windows, fearing the prospect of shattered glass. Oddly, he recalled, the lights in the sitting room remained on. Thatcher's first reaction was: 'I must see if Denis is all right ... I'm not leaving.'[47] A fireman burst in shortly after, who escorted her down to the No. 10 cars, where she was speedily driven to the Hove Police Station. Butler then returned alone to the Prime Minister's suite to retrieve the conference speech, the government papers and clothes.

With the casualty position at the Grand Hotel still far from clear, the Thatchers were then sped from Hove to the secure area of the Lewes Police Training College, where there were rooms available for them to sleep. Shortly after arrival at 5 a.m., Butler took a phone call from John Gummer, chairman of the party, to say that there had indeed been fatalities. Butler debated whether to wake up Thatcher, but decided against it:

[A]t eight o'clock in the morning Mrs Thatcher appeared, and I said, 'It's much worse than we had supposed. Norman Tebbit and John Wakeham are seriously injured, and Roberta Wakeham is dead. Margaret Tebbit is seriously injured, and the Macleans are dead.' She hardly hesitated for a moment, and responded: 'Well it's eight o'clock, and the Conference must begin on time at nine thirty.' I was appalled. I said, 'Surely you can't go on with the Conference? You know, some of your closest colleagues have been killed, and others are injured.' And she said, without any hesitation,

'We must show that terrorism can't defeat democracy.' And of course she was right. And so the Conference did start at nine thirty. She was on the platform, dressed in the clothes that I'd brought out of the Grand Hotel, looking like a new pin. And she said, 'Here we are, shaken but not daunted.' And it was a marvellous gesture of strength.[48]

She became still closer to Butler during the miners' strike. Butler was one of those, along with Armstrong, who saw the actions of Arthur Scargill's NUM as a threat to the British state itself: '[T]hose who had lived through the Heath government at No. 10 were especially prone to see it that way,' wrote Thatcher historian Chris Collins.[49] Starting on 6 March 1984 and finishing almost exactly a year later, it proved the most serious union unrest since the 1926 General Strike, comfortably eclipsing the strikes during Heath's premiership. Defeating the NUM significantly weakened the trade union movement and constituted a major victory for Thatcher. Armstrong helped keep her on track as she was driving policy forward on several fronts during those fraught twelve months. He and Butler were constantly by her side throughout the struggle. Armstrong wrote to Thatcher at the end of July to reassure her that oversight of the miners' strike would be adequately covered during August, suggesting she chair one meeting of 'MISC 101', the Cabinet Committee overseeing the strike, before she departed for her holiday. He reassured her that 'the Home Secretary and Lord President' were to remain in the country, with regular monitoring all month by the Department of Energy: 'The Cabinet Office would be able to service any meeting required in August ... At least one [of the two] member[s] ... of the MISC101 secretariat will be in the office.'[50] Another responsibility Armstrong fulfilled was ensuring his Prime Minister took holidays.

Insight into Armstrong's handling of Thatcher can be seen in a typical brief he prepared for her in this middle period, placed in her overnight box on 15 November 1984 to read upstairs in her flat above No. 10. 'It may be convenient to divide tomorrow's discussion into the following three parts: progress reports; timing the benefit changes affecting strikers; line to take,' he advised.[51] She could open the meeting, he said, by inviting a report on the numbers of pits and miners working from the Energy Secretary; on violence from the Home Secretary; on the likely attitude of the TUC from the Employment Secretary. The Lord Chancellor might be asked about the lack of progress in prosecuting serious offenders for picket line violence. He offered her detailed views of where all her key ministers stood, predicting that the Social Services Secretary would be likely to raise the timing of changes to benefits relating to strikes, and how she might want to respond. He concluded that she might

> wish to conclude the discussion in the usual way, by inviting proposals from the Secretary of Energy for the line to take, and in particular on: the return to work; violence; benefit changes. Finally the note reminded her that after tomorrow's Cabinet, the next meeting of MISC 101 would take place on 20 November.[52]

Thatcher was particularly alert to the propaganda value of news that Scargill and the NUM were receiving money from the Communist USSR. 'Steps had been taken to prompt journalistic enquiries into Mr Scargill as to whether he or other members of the NUM have been in contact with the Soviet or any other European Embassy to discuss or receive the provision of aid,' wrote Armstrong to Butler. 'His [Scargill's] replies are likely to be evasive if not deceitful; but the fact that they are so could well soon or later become a matter of public knowledge.'[53]

Thatcher did not see eye to eye with Armstrong on all aspects of handling trade unions. She notably fell out with him over whether employees at GCHQ, the government's intelligence and surveillance centre in Cheltenham, could belong to them. Armstrong had brokered an agreement enabling the Civil Service unions to retain membership in GCHQ, but ensuring that union members in GCHQ would never be called upon to take industrial action. Thatcher peremptorily overruled the deal in January 1984, believing unions at such a sensitive institution were contrary to the interests of national security. If staff were members of unions, she argued, they would have dual loyalty, and so she rejected Armstrong's compromise. Months of wrangling followed before the Law Lords allowed the Thatcher ban to remain. Her ban angered employees at GCHQ, as it did some top mandarins. They felt she had allowed Armstrong the space to negotiate a compromise, in which he had invested personal capital, only to decide that she was not interested in compromise. 'I think that is disreputable behaviour – though I never heard Robert complain about it,' said a Permanent Secretary, 'but a lot of other people, including some ministers, thought she had used him deplorably ... she dropped him in it.'[54]

She was to be criticised far more heavily for her treatment of Armstrong over the infamous *Spycatcher* affair. In 1985, former MI5 officer Peter Wright planned the publication of his memoir, *Spycatcher*. It was a highly contentious text, including, among other claims, the now discredited details of a joint MI5–CIA plot against Harold Wilson. Wright's most damaging charge was that Roger Hollis, Director General of MI5 (1956–65), was a Soviet spy. The allegations proved naturally controversial, and were probably unfounded. Thatcher was outraged by Wright, fearing that his book would open the floodgates to memoirs of other civil servants and members of the secret services. She immediately ordered that *Spycatcher* be banned in the UK. But because Wright was living in Tasmania, the matter would have to be pursued in courts in Australia, where the book was being published. Unfortunately for Thatcher, the Official Secrets Act, which he had breached by the publication, did not extend outside the United Kingdom. But who should go to Australia? Thatcher debated the possibilities with Armstrong: the head of MI5 was ruled out because the service did not officially exist; so too the Attorney General, because it was deemed improper for him to appear as a witness in an Australian court; while the Permanent Secretary at the Home Office was deemed to have insufficient knowledge of the case. That left Armstrong.

Thatcher discussed the matter with him, explaining that she could not go herself, but that someone would have to. 'I am not directing you to go ... if you don't want to,' she expressly told him, but then added that she thought he would be good representing the British government. Not one to shirk responsibility, Armstrong assented, reassured that he was at least well versed in the case, having been closely involved with the question of whether any British intelligence officers had been compromised by the Soviet Union. Trend had told him about the suspicions around Hollis, and that the art historian Anthony Blunt had definitely acted as a Soviet agent. The Blunt story was confirmed in November 1979 when Thatcher, acting on Armstrong's advice, named him in public as the 'fourth man' in the Cambridge Soviet spy ring. 'I had lived with it since 1972', said Armstrong, 'and I knew probably more than anybody else, outside of the Security Service, about the background. I also knew what I was supposed not to know and couldn't reveal, so I thought that it was right that I went.'[55] At the back of Armstrong's mind was the thought that

> what Peter Wright had written had outraged other members of the Security Service, and they were saying that if he was allowed to get away with it and publish the book, they would publish their own books to counter and refute what he had written ... [Spycatcher] was full, not only of breaches of security, but of misinformation, untruths and inaccuracies.[56]

It was to prove a far from happy experience for Armstrong, and he was not helped by an altercation that he had at the airport on the way out, when he 'lashed out with his briefcase at photographers and pushed one of them against the wall'.[57] The uncharacteristic behaviour by such an urbane man revealed the extent of the unusual public pressure exerted by the case. Once in Australia, he had another shock. Rather than the Chief Justice, whom he had expected to be hearing the case, he discovered it would instead be heard by Mr Justice Powell, and that the publisher would be represented by the formidable lawyer, Malcolm Turnbull, later Prime Minister of Australia (2015–present day). Turnbull was able to run circles around Armstrong, comparing him to 'Sir Humphrey Appleby' from Yes, Minister, and forcing Armstrong to admit he was being 'economical with the truth', a phrase upon which the media pounced with glee. Armstrong subsequently pondered whether he was right to have used this phrase, which passed into popular folklore, although he confessed that it 'had become quite a trademark of his since'.[58] The whole affair descended into farce, as newspapers in the UK were served with gagging orders when they tried to report the substance of the book, and were tried for contempt of court. Throughout, the book continued to be sold in Scotland, and was increasingly available in England. In mid-1987, the ban on English newspaper reportage was lifted.

After he had retired in 1987, Armstrong sought comfort in the final judgement in the House of Lords. It condemned Wright for his breach of confidence, confirming he had been in breach of the Official Secrets Act:

'[S]o I felt that at the end of the process, it had been right to pursue it,' he said from the tranquillity of retirement.[59] Thanks to all the publicity, Wright's controversial book became an international bestseller, topping the *New York Times* bestseller list, and made the author into an unlikely popular hero. With hindsight, it was an error for Armstrong to have gone, because it was too easy for both him and the government's case to be ridiculed. But equally, to have done nothing flew in the face of everything Thatcher and Armstrong believed. Wright's action in publishing the book had thrown down a gauntlet to the British government, for which there was no easy or clear response. On his return, and behind closed doors, Thatcher gave Armstrong two bottles of whisky – a recognition, perhaps, that she was at least in part responsible for the affair.[60]

Thatcher might have been at the height of her power in the middle years of her premiership, but the *Spycatcher* affair had rattled her, and now the Westland Affair was to even more. The episode arose out of a bailout deal for a company, Westland Helicopters. Thatcher favoured an American company, Sikorsky, while Defence Secretary, Michael Heseltine, favoured a European consortium. Heseltine claimed that Thatcher was riding roughshod over his case, and not allowing proper Cabinet discussion of a legitimate issue. An exasperated Heseltine took his case public, arguing outside Cabinet for the European solution for Westland. On 6 January 1986, a letter from the Solicitor General was leaked by the government accusing him of 'material inaccuracies'.[61]

On 9 January 1986, Armstrong sat down to take the minutes at the most uncomfortable Cabinet of his tenure. Thatcher told ministers that henceforth their statements on Westland had to be cleared by the Cabinet Office. The minutes recorded the Secretary of State for Defence saying: '[T]here had been no collective responsibility on the matter. There had been a breakdown in the propriety of Cabinet discussions. He could not accept the decision recorded in the Prime Minister's summing up. He must therefore leave this Cabinet.' The minutes then state that 'the Secretary of State for Defence withdrew from the meeting at this point'.[62] Heseltine walked out of the Cabinet Room door, down the long corridor of No. 10 and made a very public exit in front of the cameras. Cabinet continued sitting, and Armstrong's minutes record:

The Cabinet have reaffirmed that it is the policy of the Government that it is for the company to decide what course to follow in the best interest of Westland and its employees. Cabinet discussed how this decision should apply in practice to ensure that collective responsibility was upheld. It was agreed that during this period when sensitive commercial negotiations were in process, all statements by Government Ministers should be cleared interdepartmentally through the Cabinet Office, to ensure that all answers given by the Government were consistent with the policy decided by the Cabinet. Mr Heseltine found himself unable to accept this procedure and left the Cabinet. The Prime Minister expressed her regret at his decision.[63]

Talking twenty-five years later, Armstrong recalled the dismay among Cabinet when Heseltine walked out:

And we weren't sure whether he was just leaving that meeting or resigning his office. So he sort of stalked out of the room with his papers and we all sat there, licking our wounds, as it were, after the argument ... A couple of minutes later somebody came into the room and with great excitement said, 'Michael Heseltine is on the doorstep saying he's resigned!' ... And then the Cabinet adjourned for half an hour while the appointment of George Younger was submitted to the Queen and her agreement sought, and then it resumed with the new Secretary of State for Defence and without a Secretary of State for Scotland.[64]

Armstrong's subsequent actions came in for criticism. Michael Havers, the Attorney General, went to see him, demanding an inquiry into the leaked letter, threatening that if it did not happen within the Civil Service, the police would conduct it. Armstrong went to see Thatcher and volunteered to conduct the inquiry himself. John Campbell is critical of Armstrong's conduct: '[I]nviting Robert Armstrong to undertake [the] inquiry was a charade from the start. It could only be a cover up, and it was.'[65] He goes further, accusing him of going too far in helping Thatcher escape censure, appearing himself in front of the Parliamentary Select Committee: '[S]he blocked the Select Committee by refusing to allow [Charles Powell] and [Bernard Ingham] to give evidence; instead Robert Armstrong appeared for the Civil

Service and performed a masterly whitewash on the whole business.'[66] But, by then, Thatcher was in the clear. Home Secretary Leon Brittan resigned on 23 January after the release of the Armstrong Inquiry, taking responsibility for the leak. The debate in the House of Commons was expected to be dramatic. Thatcher feared for her survival. But Labour leader Neil Kinnock fluffed his big day, failing to rise to the occasion, and Thatcher was safe.

After the break-up of the Civil Service Department (CSD) in 1983, Armstrong recognised the need to devolve some power within the Cabinet Office. Even with the Treasury taking over the Civil Service's pay and number functions from the CSD, the Cabinet Office was left with recruitment, training and personnel, while Armstrong himself took over from 1981 the Senior Appointments Select Committee (SASC) for top Whitehall appointments, in addition to advising the Prime Minister on public appointments and suggesting honours for the 'Prime Minister's List'. So he decided that in future, Deputy Secretaries overseeing the secretariats should step up and brief Thatcher directly, copying their briefs to him so that he could provide supplementary comment if need be. They themselves would also approve minutes on his behalf for the committees that the Prime Minister was chairing. The upgrade in responsibility justified the secondments of officials of high calibre from Whitehall departments to the Cabinet Office, and made the jobs even more attractive to officials on the up.

The Cabinet Office changed its size and ambitions under Armstrong's tenure in other ways, too. Thatcher had appointed an 'Efficiency Adviser' in 1979, Derek Rayner, based physically in the Cabinet Office, but working as part of the No. 10 team. The Management and Personnel Office (MPO) was expanded when the Financial Management Initiative (FMI) started in 1982, run as a joint Treasury and Cabinet Office operation. Following the abolition of the CPRS in 1983, a new 'Science and Technology Secretariat' was set up, resulting in further expansion of Cabinet Office staff. The Secretariat quickly established itself as a powerful presence in Whitehall, encouraged by the scientifically educated Thatcher. In 1986, its authority was enriched by the appointment of John Fairclough as Head of the Secretariat, a proactive and energetic official, who had been recruited from IBM.[67] It became the fifth Secretariat operating under Armstrong, the others being: Economic, Home, European, and Overseas and Defence. Additionally, the Intelligence

Assessment Staff (IAS) oversaw its own specialist field, with its head combining the task of being chairman of the JIC with assisting Armstrong in coordinating MI5 and MI6. In 1986, the job was split between the job of coordinator and chairing the JIC.

The Economic Secretariat, responsible for the economy, energy and industry, was the one that interested Thatcher most. It had a succession of notably able deputies in charge, including Richard Wilson, the later Cabinet Secretary. The European and Science/Technology Secretariats operated in a more proactive, 'hands-on' way to the others, all of which were time-honoured, reaching back to Brook and before. The European Secretariat coordinated policy to the European Community across the board, with its head briefing Thatcher before every European Council meeting. The Fontainebleau Council in June 1984 was a particular coup, where Thatcher achieved a substantial rebate, and saw her confidence in the work of the European Secretariat surge.[68]

Thatcher held Cabinet meetings once a week on Thursdays, usually at 11 a.m. at No. 10. Her preference, which Armstrong constantly contested, was not to bring key decisions to full Cabinet, nor indeed to Cabinet Committees, but to decide them in informal meetings with officials.[69] When Trend left in the autumn of 1973, full Cabinet was still the critical decision-making forum for Britain. After Heath's departure, the usual pattern of Cabinet meeting twice weekly was terminated: Wilson and Callaghan summoned Cabinet on average a little over once a week during the Whitehall year, with increasing frequency during points of tension, such as the IMF crisis in 1976. By the time Hunt left in 1979, the principal standing committees (Home and Social Affairs, Overseas and Defence, Economic Affairs and Legislation) had replaced Cabinet as the principal forums where decisions were made:[70] '[I]t is almost a failure when a matter has to go to full Cabinet for discussion – under Margaret Thatcher it seldom happens,' said one minister.[71] Thatcher's personal style was partly responsible for the change. Her experience as Education Secretary (1970–74) had taught her that meetings of large numbers rarely achieved the conclusion she desired. It was one of Armstrong's great achievements that after the Falklands and Westland in particular, he reinstated Cabinet government and committees: but it was a constant battle for him to preserve the status quo.

Before Cabinet meetings, Thatcher would chair a thirty-minute meeting with the business managers of both Houses, and her Press Secretary Bernard Ingham, to ensure that she was thoroughly briefed and likely to achieve the outcome she wanted:

> Thatcher made it plain that she wanted decisions taken lower down … The group of twenty plus [people] in full Cabinet made it not an appropriate forum for routine decision making. Ministers, moreover, would only be willing to bring matters to full Cabinet if they were fairly confident in winning, as defeat would be humiliating.[72]

Nigel Lawson remembered Cabinet meetings as one moment during the week where he could relax, because nothing important really happened.[73]

Within Cabinet, meetings tended to discuss political business first, followed by foreign affairs. The latter topic usually finished with a discussion of European Community business. After this, there was discussion of various relevant topics and sometimes discussion of financial affairs.[74]

Thatcher's style and increasing impatience with procedure, and periodically with Armstrong himself, added to his burden. The workload was becoming unsustainably intense, leaving him an estimated twenty-one days off a year.

Armstrong fought to uphold Bridges's vision of the role of the impartial Cabinet Secretary and independent Civil Service, trying to observe the correct demarcation between the responsibility of officials and elected ministers. Thatcher's individualistic style brought it under severe strain, as did her increasing reliance for policy advice on just two advisers, Ingham and Powell, who served her loyally until the very end. Armstrong served the Prime Minister and British state with extraordinary distinction and self-sacrifice. But it was becoming almost untenable to retain the dual role as conscientiously as he lived it: something had to give.

ROBIN BUTLER AND THATCHER

For his successor Armstrong recommended a shortlist of two: Clive Whitmore and Robin Butler. Both were highly qualified, both had been Thatcher's

PPS. His first choice was Whitmore, who was by a few years the senior, and Butler was the natural candidate to be the next Permanent Secretary to the Treasury. But she chose Butler, with whom she had survived the Brighton bomb.[75] Butler had followed the typical trajectory of the elite: head boy at Harrow, double First in Greats at Oxford, before entering the Treasury in 1961 and making it to No. 10 after just a decade, serving as Private Secretary below Armstrong as PPS to Heath and Wilson, from 1972 to 1975. When Butler himself retired as Thatcher's PPS in the summer of 1985, he wrote her a six-side letter, suggesting how close they had become:

> Dear Prime Minister, your kindness – not just last week but over the last three years – has meant a great deal to me and my family. But I was touched by you giving me such a send-off from No. 10, when you must be quite exhausted by the pressures of the last few weeks.[76]

Before he left, she had given him a special leaving dinner at No. 10, inviting his parents, his wife Jill, and their three children. He concluded his letter: 'If there is one thing that I am sad about, it is leaving you at a time when people have been getting at you so much. But I console myself by thinking politics always has ups and downs.'[77] Thatcher then helped arrange his new job at the Treasury, where he became Second Permanent Secretary in charge of public expenditure in 1985–87. The relationship was helped through a rugby connection to Denis Thatcher, who had refereed several games in which Butler had played.[78] The choice of the Thatchers' personal house in Dulwich, where the Butlers lived, was in part due to him, although she came to dislike the building.[79] So he returned to her side in January 1988 alive with excitement and optimism. Both believed his tenure would be mutually rewarding. Both sides were to be disappointed.

Butler saw the appointment as the very apex of a civil servant's career: 'I always thought our Civil Service had very high standards, and I was very proud to be head of it,' he said:

> You can't avoid having a sense of history when you sit in the Cabinet Office with the Conference Room, the Treasury Board Room, just opposite, where King George III used to meet his ministers in the eighteenth

century ... The Cabinet Secretary's room is over the site of the old cockpit ... You're in a palace. And then you come into No. 10, and [are reminded of] all the things that have happened there since it became the Prime Minister's residence ... You think of Churchill at the beginning of the war meeting Chamberlain and Halifax ... You can't help having a very strong sense of history and that adds, I think, to one's pride in the post.[80]

Butler had even timed his age to perfection, always important: he was aged fifty, so had a full ten years in post until the mandatory retirement age of sixty kicked in. Butler had been mentally prepared to be Cabinet Secretary for a long time, his mentor being Robert Armstrong: 'I was his boy, I was his lad, I was his protégé. He had been my mentor over many years.'[81] It was Armstrong who, in 1972, secured Butler the job of Economic Affairs Private Secretary in No. 10, ensuring the two worked closely together for three years. Again, it was Armstrong who was keen for Butler to succeed Whitmore as Thatcher's PPS in 1982, 'so really, by 1988, I had learnt everything I could have learnt from him'.[82] Burke Trend was another influence: '[H]e struck me as lean, ascetic, devoted to the job, not looking for any thrills, no self-indulgence, very self-disciplined.'[83]

As the first Cabinet Secretary in history to be Head of the HCS for his entire time in post (Brook and Armstrong only took on the responsibility midway), he wanted to devote quality time to the headship role. He made a feature of travelling outside Whitehall to visit government offices across the country. Much of his time was consumed by implementing the 'Next Steps' initiative, overseen for him by Peter Kemp, involving a thorough-going reform of Westminster's functions, by 'hiving off the delivery functions ... into autonomous arm's-length agencies', often run by figures recruited outside of Whitehall.[84] Over his ten years, over 75 per cent of Civil Service activity was thus transferred to these agencies. He believed strongly in the philosophy of Next Steps delegation, and in the empowerment of departments and agencies. He worked very closely with Terry Burns, Peter Middleton's successor as Permanent Secretary to the Treasury (1991–98), who shared his outlook on delegation: 'We believed in a way of running the Civil Service which was much more about the creation of people who were responsible for operations, were given a budget, were expected to keep within it and deliver the targets that the government had set,' Butler

said.[85] He described his style as 'definitely first of all captain of the team …
I wanted my Permanent Secretaries to feel that … I would support them
and expected them to support me, and that we would cooperate for the
benefit of the government and for the Civil Service.'[86] Diana Goldsworthy,
who worked in the Cabinet Office at the time, captured the transitional
nature of his period in office: 'Looking back, it seems to me that Robin's
time was a change between a Civil Service of the old type … the ministers
disposed, civil servants proposed' to the modern, early 21st-century world.[87]

Butler's focus on heading the HCS was assisted by his withdrawal from
a side of the work that had preoccupied his predecessors: the Cabinet
Secretary's role as Sherpa for the G7/8 meetings, Commonwealth heads of
government, and European Councils. He delegated much to the powerful
heads of the European Secretariat within the Cabinet Office, thankful that
the battle with the Treasury had been won in 1972–73, placing European
coordination within the Cabinet Office. Achieving the right balance between
the post's responsibilities to the Prime Minister and to Cabinet as a whole
was a major concern, thereby avoiding the Cabinet Office becoming the
Prime Minister's department or speaking on behalf of the Prime Minister:
'I believed we could only effectively get the cooperation of the departments
and ministers, and let the Cabinet operate, if they thought the Cabinet
Office were honest brokers, and not just trying to manipulate things so that
the Prime Minister got their own way.'[88] Unsurprisingly, he found this task
easier when Major, rather than Thatcher or later Blair, was Prime Minister.

Butler relished the opportunities that his dual role afforded him. As
Cabinet Secretary, he regularly had the opportunity to raise Civil Service
issues with his Prime Ministers. Generally, he found they had little interest
in Civil Service issues, or time for it. The two roles demanded artful jug-
gling because of their polar-different public profiles. As Cabinet Secretary
he needed to be discreet, serving Prime Ministers and the Cabinet confiden-
tially, while as Head of the HCS, he needed a public platform to represent
the Civil Service in the media.

When Butler returned to Downing Street after two and a half years of
absence, he found Thatcher 'more tired than when I served her as PPS …
She was no less acute [but] she was a bit more abrupt in taking decisions, and
more dependent on other people in her Private Office.'[89] Butler's comments

cut to the heart of the tension that came between them. He saw her reliance on Bernard Ingham and Charles Powell as 'very dangerous'.[90] He was particularly critical of Powell, who proved a serious obstacle to Butler's successor as PPS, Nigel Wicks (1985–88). Powell was the dominant voice within his specialist remit of foreign policy, but came increasingly to be involved in domestic policy as well. 'I think [Nigel] felt that I intruded far too much,' reflected Powell many years later.[91] Indeed he did. The breakdown in relations between Butler and Powell was unforeseen as they had been friends for fifteen or more years, were close neighbours and had often travelled into work together in their younger years, when Butler was with the Treasury and Powell the Foreign Office.[92]

A sign of the Cabinet Secretary's dwindling prestige on the world stage relative to the position of Powell came when Robin Butler was denied a request to see White House Chief of Staff Howard Baker in March 1988. While noting that Armstrong had met the Defence Secretary Frank Carlucci 'several times last year', the internal White House paper advised that:

> Sir Robin Butler, as Secretary of the Cabinet, occupies a position in London similar to that held by Senator Baker here in the White House. There are major differences, however. Sir Robin Butler is a civil servant. His position in the Cabinet is that of an official who speaks for the senior civil servant to the political figures at 10 Downing Street. In this sense, Sir Robin Butler does not involve himself in general political matters.[93]

Matters came to a head three months later, when President Reagan was to visit London. Thatcher and Powell did not plan for Butler to be part of the home team. Butler told her bluntly that if he was to retain any credibility over intelligence matters regarding the United States, he would have to be present at the key meetings.[94] Robert Armstrong had earlier been concerned and thought in 1986 that, after more than three years, Powell had been in 10 Downing Street long enough, and should be resuming his diplomatic career. Armstrong negotiated and agreed with all concerned, including the Prime Minister and Powell himself, arrangements for his taking up an ambassadorial posting towards the end of 1987. After the general election in 1987 and not long before his own retirement, Thatcher changed her mind, telling

Armstrong that she could not spare Powell for the time being. So the issue was inherited by his successor.[95] Quite early in his term, Butler decided that it was high time for Powell, who had already been Private Secretary for five years, instead of the customary two or three, to move on:

> Patrick Wright [FCO Permanent Secretary] would say to her that 'it is really time that Charles moved on'. She would say, 'oh no', and they would reply: 'We want him to go, Prime Minister.' They started offering me Sweden, and she said, 'no, no'. Six months later, they came back with Switzerland and she came back with 'no, certainly not, no, no'.[96]

A final straw came when Nicholas Gordon-Lennox was persuaded to retire early from the Embassy in Madrid to make way for Powell. Thatcher had approved it, but then she and Powell changed their minds. Butler later estimated that it was the clearest single occasion when she rejected his advice.[97]

He believed he had no alternative but to take Thatcher to task over Powell. The Civil Service tradition discouraged over-long stays in the Private Office precisely to prevent officials from 'going native' and creating problems on returning to their home departments. Thirty years before, a similar problem had occurred when Macmillan had become overly dependent upon Philip de Zulueta, who served as his Foreign Affairs Private Secretary for six years, causing similar tensions with the Foreign Office and the rest of Whitehall. Beneath the surface, was jealousy about access to the Prime Minister at play? Butler later admitted: 'I certainly did not have the same standing and influence with her that I had when I had been her PPS.'[98] The more her energy waned, the more dependent she became upon Powell and Ingham for advice. Powell's admission that he was not quite certain where Thatcher's views ended and where his views began was very telling; they had become so blended in outlook and identity. Percy Cradock, a Foreign Office diplomat (latterly Ambassador to China) whom she appointed chairman of the JIC in 1985, had been an important influence on her foreign policy thinking in her second term, but he faded away thereafter, leaving the field clear for Powell. Another worry for Butler was questions being aired about top-quality officials for Thatcher's Private Office in No. 10. So great was the fear of No. 10, and of Thatcher's dysfunctional Private Office, that officials from the Treasury and the Home Office were concerned about being damaged in the crossfire.

During the period leading up to her Eurosceptic Bruges Speech on 20 September 1988, Powell kept the drafts so close to his chest that Butler had little involvement.[99] The FCO under Foreign Secretary Geoffrey Howe had been urging Thatcher to make a 'positive' speech on Europe, suggesting she use her invitation to speak at the College of Europe in Bruges as her platform. Chief among the agitators for a pro-Europe speech were two diplomats, John Kerr in charge of European affairs, and Stephen Wall, PPS to Howe. Wall cautioned 'not to sell the idea too hard', while Kerr thought 'it is worth a run I think', to see what Thatcher might produce.[100] Kerr set about making Thatcher's speech as pro-European as possible, to reassure the European capitals that were increasingly concerned about Thatcher's Euroscepticism.

Two months before it was due to be delivered, No. 10 (unusually) asked the FCO for a draft. Hackles were raised on 6 July, however, when President of the European Commission Jacques Delors told the European Parliament that, within ten years, he expected 80 per cent of economic legislation, including tax and social legislation, to be made in the European Community. A Thatcher response was inevitable. It arrived a week later on the BBC's *Jimmy Young Show*, when she said that 'Delors was wrong … he went over the top and I do not think he should have said it'.[101] The FCO draft was eventually submitted to No. 10, but Powell rewrote it, using almost nothing of the FCO's text. Butler was close to Howe personally, as well as close philosophically to him on Europe, and they talked a great deal during this period. He was not sorry to read Howe's response to Powell's draft:

> The Secretary of State's overall comment is that there are some plain and fundamental errors in the draft and that it tends to view the world as though we had not adhered to any of the treaties. Nor does the speech accommodate the diversity of visions of Europe – even in one country.[102]

Powell was spoken to by both Wall and Kerr, the latter writing a note on 6 September suggesting that Powell was not in fact unsympathetic to their concerns. But, two days later, Delors aggravated matters again when he spoke at the TUC conference in Bournemouth, urging that collective bargaining should take place at a European level, and inviting delegates to join the architects of Europe, for which he received a standing ovation. Chancellor Nigel Lawson, a Eurosceptic, believed the FCO had encouraged the TUC to invite Delors to speak, and blamed them for their own goal. Delors's words were a red flag to Thatcher and further entrenched the belief that her own speech should be a passionate declaration of her own views on Europe. She argued that the Community was strongest when accepting national traditions, and not being distracted by the 'utopian'. Famously, she said: 'We have not successfully rolled back the frontiers of the state in Britain, only to see them re-imposed at a European level with a European super-state exercising a new dominance from Brussels'.[103]

Her speech in Bruges proved highly controversial and became a pivotal historical moment, when the Conservative Party ceased to be 'the party of Europe' in British politics, and began its twenty-year journey to become the 'party of Euroscepticism'. The FCO blamed Ingham for spinning the speech, which had many positive words about Europe, in a way deliberately unhelpful to their cause. Butler believed that it was here that Thatcher laid the seeds of her future downfall. Howe agreed with this view, writing in his memoirs: 'I can now see [the Bruges Speech as] probably the moment which began to crystallise the conflict with loyalty I began to struggle with perhaps for too long.'[104]

Her fall-out with her Cabinet over Europe and over the 'poll tax' had an almost inevitable logic to it, Butler concluded. Great leaders can often be impossible with their staff and colleagues: Churchill certainly could be during the war, and many found Attlee's heroic detachment a challenge. By 1986, Thatcher was certainly becoming tense and frustrated with her Civil Service, and they with her. She blamed the Westland fiasco partly on the machine not functioning as it should. She blamed the machine for not finding her a suitable adviser after the economist Alan Walters left her in 1984. She became prone to idealising departed Private Secretaries and advisers, at the expense of new recruits. Were Powell and Ingham guilty of overprotecting her, and preventing her from adapting to able new staff who threatened their power base? Or were they themselves heroic figures, protecting a damaged and increasingly frail Prime Minister, and allowing her to continue?

The poll tax debacle ironically emerged from one of the most 'textbook' policy processes of her premiership. But ministers did not seem to have engaged with the risks of its introduction. To Lawson and many others, 'it was the most disastrous decision that the Thatcher government took. The explanation of why this happens … [is] the Prime Minister getting out of touch with her own ministers.'[105] Certainly, there were signs of declining cohesion and corporate thinking in Cabinet, as opinion polls took a downward turn over the course of 1990. Before one meeting with Butler, the preliminary briefing for Thatcher said that one Secretary of State seemed to be suffering from sagging morale, and required a 'pep talk'.[106]

Her final year was indeed her most fraught, and her behaviour its most volatile. In August 1990, Iraqi dictator Saddam Hussein invaded Kuwait. She and President Bush played a key role in galvanising the multinational coalition against Iraq. The Cabinet Office was excluded from the bureaucratic process of the War Cabinet, with Powell taking the minutes. Thatcher deliberately avoided constituting the War Cabinet as a Cabinet Committee, thereby bypassing the Cabinet Office. No Prime Minister, not in either world war, nor during Suez or the Falklands, would have dreamt of not constituting the meetings as a formal Cabinet Committee. As one insider said: '[S]he became odder over the Gulf and it was getting pretty chaotic. Bureaucratically it was getting into a tangle. It was constitutionally pretty dangerous.'[107]

Butler tried to suggest other arrangements to regain control. A brief by Andrew Turnbull (her PPS from 1988, following Wicks) for her meeting with Butler on 27 September said that the ad hoc group on the Gulf should start meeting in COBR, just in case it needed to be activated in the event of hostilities. He suggested rehearsals, for fear that word getting out about the meetings would be a sign that military action was imminent.[108]

By the time of her fall in November 1990, Butler was unable to prevent the inevitable. Their relationship was at a low ebb, as indeed it remained throughout the 1990s, although she was said to be sad about it. So too was he. 'I like good order,' remarked Butler recently. 'I do not like to see Prime Ministers moved out. I certainly did not do anything to accelerate her removal from power. I did not have much power to prevent it. Though I certainly thought, as did Denis Thatcher, that she should have gone a bit earlier then she did.'[109]

BUTLER AND MAJOR

Butler was pleased, more for the Civil Service than for himself personally, that Thatcher's replacement in November 1990 was John Major. The succession meant a return to the conventions of Cabinet government; under Major, the Cabinet Office and Cabinet system experienced the most regularised and conventional years of the entire Armstrong and Butler eras. When the door of No. 10 was opened to John and Norma Major at 11 a.m. on 28 November, Butler was the first person who greeted them and welcomed them to their new home. He immediately made a good impression on Major and his close team, Sarah Hogg (Head of Policy Unit) and Jonathan Hill (Head of Policy), impressed as they were by the quality of his briefing paper awaiting them, and his smart advice on the reshuffle. Butler knew the ministerial gene pool inside out, possessing a knowledge of capability and character far superior to their own, as they found again in the reshuffle after the 1992 general election.[110]

Major and Butler were not strangers to each other; Major had been Chief Secretary (1987–89) during Butler's time as Second Permanent Secretary to the Treasury, and the two had worked closely together on public spending. During this time, Major had learnt to trust Butler's judgement, particularly as he came to the Treasury in the midst of a public expenditure row. Butler acknowledges: '[T]o a considerable extent he looked to me for advice.'[111]

They were an odd couple. Major was state-school educated and never went to university, from a modest background. Butler was a Harrow and Oxford educated grand mandarin. Opposites attract, and they succeeded in establishing a successful relationship, with sport, particularly cricket, common ground.[112] Butler applauded Major's determination to return to Cabinet conventions. Major said:

Margaret had often introduced subjects in Cabinet by setting out her favoured solution: shameless, but effective. I, by contrast, preferred to let my views be known in private, see potential dissenters ahead of the meeting, encourage discussion, and sum up after it. A different approach; but, I believe, one that is equally effective.[113]

Butler concurs: 'He wanted to re-establish Cabinet Government. He wanted to be less dominant in the Cabinet. He wanted to encourage Cabinet discussion.'[114] Major's determination to adhere to conventions endeared him to officials across Whitehall. Even Powell, who remained as Foreign Affairs Private Secretary for the first few months, fell back into line, and proved himself loyal and valuable to the new Prime Minister. Major himself had no hesitation in placing Butler in charge of the War Cabinet minutes during the build-up to the First Gulf War (1990–91).

Aerial bombardment from the coalition began on 17 January 1991, with the ground assault following on 23 February. It fell to Butler to establish a system of support for ministers during the war. The day began early, with assessment staff meeting in the Cabinet room at 4.30 a.m., JIC at 6 a.m., the Permanent Secretaries of the relevant departments at 8 a.m., followed by ministers at 10 a.m., before the lobby briefing at 11 a.m. For Butler, it was the most intense period as Cabinet Secretary.[115] One hundred hours after the ground campaign started, President Bush declared a ceasefire on 28 February, declaring Kuwait had been liberated. Butler was very deliberately permitted under Major to travel on all the international trips he wanted to attend, including the first visit Major made to see George Bush in December 1990. On the plane home, Butler wrote to thank George and Barbara Bush 'for your extraordinary warmth and kindness in allowing me to share in the weekend at Camp David ... It was a great privilege and an unforgettable experience.'[116] He was also present on the trip to Washington DC in February 1993 to meet newly inaugurated President Clinton.[117]

Shortly before the ground war began, the new government received a violent reminder of another war. At 10 a.m. on 7 February 1991, a meeting was taking place in the Cabinet Room in No. 10. As ever, Butler was sitting on Major's right. A short distance away, in Whitehall, a white van with three mortar tubes inside was parked by the Banqueting House – its drivers fled on a motorbike. Moments later, the improvised mortars in the back fired three shells at Downing Street. One exploded in the garden about twelve metres from the Cabinet Room, shattering windows, damaging the building and leaving a crater over a metre wide.

Butler remembers what happened in vivid detail:

The last word I remember John Major uttering before the mortar bomb exploded was the word 'bomb'. And suddenly, there's this bomb. The room shakes, the windows shiver, shatter ... The French windows at the end of the Cabinet Room blow in, and what I immediately supposed ... [was] that this was a terrorist attack, and [that] people had come over the back wall, and they were going to appear at the Cabinet windows spraying sub-machine guns at us. And so, I got under the table pretty quick. I found John Major was under the table beside me.[118]

In Butler's mind, Iraqi agents were launching a terrorist attack in retaliation for the aerial bombardment. Charles Powell, who had been at the meeting, shouted: 'Put into action the drill!', reminding everyone of the procedure – if No. 10 came under attack, the Prime Minister was to be rushed into a safe area.[119] Butler joined a surprisingly calm Major in another room. They wondered whether a car bomb had been detonated nearby. When it became clear that there was no likelihood of further attacks, nor further obvious danger, they resumed the meeting elsewhere. Nobody had been killed in the attack, unlike in Brighton: the worst injury was a member of staff who suffered a cut to the back of their head from flying glass. David Hunt, the Welsh Secretary, wrote in his diary: '[I]t is probably only in the UK you get the Cabinet after a mortar attack discussing severe weather conditions in East Anglia and South East of England.'[120]

Butler took his intelligence duties very seriously. One of his early contributions was to convince Major that the responsibility for tackling the IRA on the mainland should be transferred from the Special Branch of the Metropolitan Police to MI5: 'Cold War subversion targets were shrinking; domestic counter-terrorism was welcome new work for MI5. The service performed admirably, placing pressure on the IRA and earning the Prime Minister's personal congratulations.'[121]

The rhythm of Cabinet Committee meetings for ministers and officials began to be re-established under Major: '[T]he Cabinet system has thus become far more institutionalised and more firmly embedded in the established framework of government.'[122] The establishment of the Office of Public Service (OPS) within the Cabinet Office boosted managerial efficiency during these years.

Major's team appreciated the support Butler gave before, during and after the launch of his biggest single initiative in July 1991: the Citizens Charter. Butler alongside Turnbull helped drive it through a sceptical Whitehall. At one point, there was a clash over the question of whether public servants should identify themselves by name, with some arguing that it would make staff 'vulnerable', while others responded that a name encouraged people to treat faceless bureaucrats as human beings. Butler even arrived at the Charter's No. 10 launch event wearing a name badge reading 'I'm Robin – can I help you?'[123] The initiative was to be widely criticised for claiming to improve public services while reducing their expenditure. Others saw it as an attempt by a man who had grown up outside the establishment to bring order to the state to ensure that it was accountable to the ordinary citizen, an agenda ahead of its time.

Butler found himself increasingly adopting a public stance. His highest-profile intervention came over the Scott Inquiry into the arms sales to Iraq in the 1980s. The inquiry was commissioned in 1992, overseen by Lord Justice Richard Scott, and was concluded in 1996. 'It had a very high pro-file,' recalled Butler:

I think a lot of the media thought it might be Watergate, with terrible skulduggery on the part of the government going to be revealed. And so they were always looking for that, and that went on for three years. That took up quite a lot of time and involved a certain amount of public exposure ... I was quite clear that I hadn't done anything that I had to be worried about and that gave me confidence. But nonetheless we were all under very, very, very intensive scrutiny.[124]

Butler found himself disputing accusations levelled at the government for sleaze and impropriety. Major's government was fragile, with a low majority, under constant attack from the Eurosceptic right. Against this landscape, a newly confident Labour Party emerged under John Smith from 1992, and then after Smith's death, Tony Blair from July 1994.

Sleaze was the most difficult issue that Butler confronted as Cabinet Secretary, as the job involved advising the Prime Minister about ethical breaches. When Jonathan Aitken was accused in April 1995 of breaching ministerial rules by allowing Saudi businessmen to pay a hotel bill at the Paris Ritz, he publicly denounced his accusers and declared his innocence. In private, he swore his innocence to Butler, who came out in public to say he believed his story. The subsequent trial proved Aitken had lied about the hotel bill, and he was imprisoned. 'If I think back, that was the most difficult episode for me, and most embarrassing,' admitted Butler.[125]

Given the fracturing nature of his political inheritance, perhaps Major's greatest single achievement was staying in power for seven years. Such a long premiership looked doubtful, with polls foretelling a hung Parliament after the election. In 1991, Butler wrote to the Queen's Private Secretary, Robert Fellowes, in anticipation of a hung parliament. Butler also sought advice from lawyers on issues such as at what point a Prime Minister becomes Prime Minister and, prompted by Major, what would happen if a Prime Minister sought a second dissolution immediately after an inconclusive election result. His discussions led to the conclusion that it was unheard of during the twentieth century for the monarch to refuse to dissolve Parliament so soon after an election, and the Queen should not be asked to do so.

Butler took responsibility for scenario planning, as did the Cabinet Office generally, when polls suggested the possibility of an inconclusive general election. The archives show that the Cabinet Office, for example, anticipated a situation in which the Conservatives won by just one seat, or were three short of a majority, or where Labour were twenty-two, twenty-six or eleven seats short of a majority. Butler wrote to Major on 3 March to outline how the election might play out:

If the Conservatives have the greatest number of seats but no overall majority, and you were not prepared to lead them into a pact or coalition with another party but someone in your Cabinet was, you could suggest to the Queen that she send for that someone else and she would be likely to do so. However, at that stage there would probably be no assurance either that the person concerned could do a deal with the other parties or that he would not be opposed in a contest for the leadership of the Conservative Party. The Queen would not want to appoint someone as Prime Minister who ... could not get the support of his Party. So she would likely ask the person concerned to explore whether he could form a viable government and gain the support of his party, without at that stage asking him to become Prime Minister. She would probably ask you to continue holding the fort in the meantime, as Mrs Thatcher did during the last leadership election ... It is relevant that Mr Ashdown at least would probably want some time to negotiate the terms of a coalition. Then he would want them endorsed by the Liberal Party. This could be an uncomfortable period, not least on the exchanges...[126]

Butler was taking no chances, and asked a researcher to compile a list of every election result, and every major defeat the government had suffered 'from 1835 to 1979'.[127] He wrote a memo to Turnbull, observing that, 'compared with six months before the election, the governing party gained in all elections except 1974 (October) and 1979' and that, 'compared with six months before, opinion swung to the Conservatives in every election since 1970'.[128] Butler was right. When in the early hours of 10 April 1992, the election results started to trickle in, contrary to expectation, Major emerged the winner, with a loss of forty seats since 1987, but a workable majority of twenty-one seats.

The capital Major gained through a general election victory against the odds speedily and precipitously evaporated when, on Black Wednesday in September 1992, Britain was ejected from the Exchange Rate Mechanism (ERM). It severely damaged Major's reputation and the economic credibility of the government. Butler became the steadying hand in the premiership at a very fragile time, with Major and his close team in shock. Though Butler was always careful to observe a distance at difficult moments, he never failed to respect Major, and was always ready to offer his best advice. Butler found himself increasingly in despair, not at the conduct of Major, as he had been with Thatcher, but with Cabinet ministers in general. Shortly after he stood down as Cabinet Secretary in 1998, he spoke of how 'divided the Cabinet was over Europe and [how] lacking [it was] in self-discipline or respect for convention, that what was said in Cabinet could be read accurately in later additions of the *Evening Standard*'.[129] Butler did little to appease Major's enemies on the right of the Tory Party by working so loyally for Major, and due to his evident sympathy for Europe. Though he escaped the pounding Trend received from Wilson's ministers, he did not altogether escape their ire. John Redwood, a leading critic and Eurosceptic, was dismissive of Butler's recording of Cabinet discussions: 'Very bland,' he scorned. 'They will tell historians little about the Major years.'[130] We can hear echoes of Crossman in his words.

Major appreciated Butler's wide-ranging support, not the least for his path-breaking quest to bring peace to Northern Ireland. Major's closest aide here was Rod Lyne, Foreign Affairs Private Secretary in No. 10, closely supported by John Chilcot and Quentin Thomas in the Northern Ireland Office. Butler, like Armstrong before him, also worked closely with Dermot Nally in Dublin. In June 1993, Butler made a covert trip to Ireland to receive a text from Irish Taoiseach Albert Reynolds of what would later become the Downing Street Declaration, flying in to the military airport on Baldonnel outside Dublin where he was met by Reynolds. Over a coffee, Reynolds placed the envelope in his hands, emphasising that for the first time he had managed to secure a historic IRA agreement to the 'consent principle', where only a majority decision of voters would determine whether or not Northern Ireland was to leave the United Kingdom and join the rest of Ireland.[131] Butler was back in Dublin that November, to communicate that Major saw an opportunity for peace, but he stressed the mountain that had to be climbed to overcome the suspicion of the Unionist community.

One particular occasion where Major followed Butler's advice came after a close defeat for the government on the passage of the controversial Maastricht Bill in the summer of 1993. Major, Butler and Douglas Hurd (Foreign Secretary 1989–95) held a meeting where Butler's clear advice was to hold a vote of confidence the following day, which he said would secure the victory that Major needed. 'I ventured to say that the best thing to do is to grasp the nettle and make it an issue of confidence and get it out of the way', said Butler, adding, 'I might have hesitated to give that advice to Margaret Thatcher.'[132] He was right. Eurosceptic Conservative MPs, faced with the prospect of bringing down their own government, came back into line, which meant that it passed with forty votes, and the Maastricht Treaty was ratified.

On other occasions, Major rejected Butler's advice, as with his decision in June 1995 to resign from his party's leadership and run for re-election.

Butler always thought Major apt to be oversensitive to criticism from the media, and that he spent too much time agonising over perceived maltreatment (which was constant and merciless, especially from the right). On the morning of 22 June, Major, who had not shared his plans with Butler, told him that he was going to announce his resignation as leader of the Conservative Party, and put it to his MPs to decide whether or not he had their confidence as Prime Minister. Butler recounts that 'there was no real disagreement. He told me that morning he was going to do it and I said, "I am afraid I think that is a mistake", but we never referred to it again.'[133]

In an effort to bolster Major's position, he felt the need for a Cabinet 'fixer', akin to the role William Whitelaw had played for Margaret Thatcher. Butler duly 'helped establish' the details of Michael Heseltine's new Deputy Prime Minister role in 1995.[134] Heseltine was concerned that the position would be a mere sinecure, but Butler, over the course of a two-hour meeting in July 1995, was able to convince him otherwise.[135] During their time together, Heseltine made clear that his new office accommodation should match his status:

> … when I went to see Sir Robin I was shown into his office – palatial, panelled, it is precisely what you would expect the Head of the Civil Service to achieve. After all, ministers come and go but the Civil Service remains. Over a coffee, as I sat on his elegant sofa, I told him the story of Duncan Sandys, who had years before become Minister of Housing. He had been greeted by the Permanent Secretary of that Ministry, who showed him round the offices and indicated the one that he thought would be right for the newly arrived minister. They had then retired to the Permanent Secretary's office for coffee. Duncan asked, apparently innocently: 'Whose office is this?' The Permanent Secretary replied: 'Mine, minister.' 'Good, it'll do,' Duncan had said. Robin perhaps got the message. I was awarded a very large conference room on the third floor of 70 Whitehall as my office – with a security pass for the connecting door into No. 10 itself.[136]

Despite the victory in the leadership election, and with the feisty Heseltine ensconced in his large office fighting by his side to bring order to a fissiparous government, Major was unable to regain the initiative convincingly in his two final years. A Blair victory in the coming general election was increasingly accepted as inevitable across the political world. Butler continued to work closely with Major until the end, aided by his tenacious and highly able PPS, Alex Allan (1992–97). History can judge the seven-year Butler–Major relationship as one of the most effective of the 100 years. Eighteen years of Conservative government was suddenly at an end. Would the Prime Minister/Cabinet Secretary concord survive the transition to the new guard in Downing Street?

RICHARD WILSON,
PHOTOGRAPHED IN 1997

ANDREW TURNBULL

CHAPTER 9

New Labour, New Challenges: Wilson, Turnbull and O'Donnell, 1997–2010

L ABOUR UNDER Tony Blair won a great majority in the 1997 general election, in 2001, and again in 2005. The government came to power with an ambitious plan to modernise an outdated country. In its eighty-first year, the Cabinet Office faced an unprecedented challenge: a Prime Minister with a presidential style, determined to drive his agenda forward from his own office in No. 10 rather than the Cabinet Office. He faced four very different personalities as Cabinet Secretaries, each with their own approach, all united in their determination to bring the Whitehall machine into line to help the singular Prime Minister, but equally to support the Cabinet ministers. How would the Cabinet Secretaries fare with Blair? What unfolded over the coming years came as a surprise to many.

Butler admired the fight that Major had put up in the 1997 general election, but, like Major, he knew the Conservative Party was doomed.[1] On the night of the general election, 1 May 1997, Butler held an election night party, which included two of the other most senior officials in the country – the Queen's Private Secretary Robert Fellowes, and PPS at No. 10 Alex Allan – to fine-tune arrangements for the transfer of power and ensure the Friday would run smoothly.[2] Butler was swept up in the excitement of a new, youthful government coming into power, with the prospect of a fresh approach to policy. He had a point to prove: after eighteen years of Conservative rule, 'we wanted to show that the Civil Service would serve the Labour government as it had the Conservative government'. Especially because 'we did not know them that well. I wanted to manage the transition to the new government smoothly.'[3] On a personal level, he felt comfortable with his own tenure, reassured that his retirement was due in eight months' time, 'so if we did not get on well with each other, we were not together forever'.[4] He was about to find out the answer very quickly.

BUTLER AND BLAIR

Friday 2 May 1997 seemed to many outside and within No. 10 the dawning of a new, optimistic age:

> It was a beautiful day and, of course, there were all the crowds outside waving the flags and so on. And I was standing outside the Cabinet Room. The No. 10 staff were lined up either side of the front door in the traditional way. And I think it was best summed up by the Blairs coming in, the Blair family, and Tony Blair acknowledging, clapping, and so on. And there was one of the garden room girls with tears pouring down her face, and he stopped and said, 'What's the matter?' And she said, 'Well, you're very welcome but I do so miss that nice Mr Major, so much.' And, of course, Tony Blair entirely understood. And, … I received him at the end of the corridor, shook hands with him, opened the door of the Cabinet Room, [and] went in.[5]

One of Butler's first tasks with Blair, as it had been with Major, was to explain the responsibility of a Prime Minister in the event of a nuclear war. This includes the 'letter of last resort' that Blair had to write, giving instructions to the commanders of British Trident submarines, assuming the Prime Minister was dead or incapacitated, about whether to retaliate with nuclear missiles in the event of Britain being attacked by enemy nuclear weapons. Commanders have to follow what the Prime Minister of the day decrees.

No one knows what the Prime Ministers decide: Blair 'went very quiet and pale' when learning about his new responsibilities.[6] The conversation over, they went out to the patio outside the Cabinet windows, where they sat on the wicker chairs overlooking the garden, discussing Cabinet appointments. It soon transpired that Blair and his team were not much interested in Butler's opinions on appointments. Blair was clearly exhausted from lack of sleep, but that initial meeting struck Butler as promising.

Butler and Blair were not strangers to each other: they had first begun to talk in earnest a year before, when Butler had engineered a private dinner party with his wife Jill at their home for Tony and Cherie Blair. They agreed on many things; the Blairs accepted Butler's idea that they should move from the traditional Prime Minister's flat in No. 10 to the much bigger flat above No. 11, which is much more suitable for a bigger family. The Blairs asked for a child carrier to transport the children around, to which Butler readily agreed. The one moment of awkwardness came over the appointment of Jonathan Powell, the diplomat and younger brother of Charles, who had joined his personal staff in 1995. 'I very much hope you are going to make Jonathan Powell your adviser, but not PPS,' Butler said to Blair. Blair put his mind entirely to rest: 'I have no thought of making him Principal Private Secretary.'[7] A year passed, and with a Labour victory likely and imminent, Butler went up to the Blair's house in Islington for a further conversation. A beaming Blair told him he wanted to make Jonathan Powell PPS. Butler was shocked. Never in history had a political appointee come into the post of the Prime Minister's PPS; even one who had spent much of their life in the Civil Service as Powell had. The job always goes to Whitehall's (usually the Treasury's) brightest and best. Butler and Blair had an argument about it, as a result of which Blair 'grudgingly' agreed that Alex Allan should stay on for the first three months before he chose a PPS successor to his liking.[8]

The awkwardness of the Islington discussion descended rapidly on Downing Street as Blair asserted his will. David Blunkett confided in May 1997 that 'we have had a struggle about how many special advisers we are allowed. Robin Butler has been trying to persuade Tony that there should be a very, very strict regime, but there seem to be exceptions all round for

No. 10.'[9] Butler proposed an extension of the existing Order in Council exception for a person 'appointed by a Minister of the Crown for the purpose of providing advice to any Minister, and [whose appointment] terminates at the end of an administration', so that their role was not restricted to merely giving advice to ministers but included supervising civil servants.[10] However, Powell and Campbell quickly concluded that Butler was on a completely different wavelength to them. Nicknaming him 'Old Butleshanks', they wrote him off as a Sir Humphrey-style obstructer, of no value to them in their modernisation project. Only when Powell published his book *The New Machiavelli* in 2011 did Butler begin to fully appreciate the depth of hostility towards him from the Blair team. He was surprised to learn that Powell had interpreted Butler's conversations with the fatigued Blair that first Friday morning, and his explanation of the nuclear responsibility, as a deliberate attempt to patronise and impose himself on a young and inexperienced Prime Minister. Butler thought Powell's thesis was quite ridiculous and ludicrous.[11]

Butler presented Blair with a briefing for the incoming Prime Minister, which the Cabinet Office had been busy preparing during the campaign. It covered all the main issues that a new Prime Minister might face in government, including honours, the structure of government, how to appoint ministers, 'Procedural Guidance for Ministers', 'Queen's Speech and Legislative Programme', 'Constitutional Reforms' and official residences. Butler had some precise advice on how he might want to conduct himself as head of government: he knew Blair wanted a strong central direction of government but no Prime Minister could perform all the central roles himself. There would not be time and, anyway, the Prime Minister should often hold himself back as a final court of appeal.[12]

The Cabinet Office briefing reminded Blair that Cabinet had to be kept to twenty-one members, and provided helpful advice on how to achieve this magic number. They suggested the posts of Deputy Prime Minister and Chancellor of the Duchy of Lancaster could be merged, while the Secretary of State for Transport's department could be subsumed within a Department of Environment and Transport.[13]

Butler wrote to Blair to discuss Cabinet, asking him to consider the role he wished it to play in his new government. He explained how the political environment had led to a situation in which it was little more than a talking shop, with ministers gathering to discuss recent events and let off steam. Otherwise, it was the Cabinet Committees or ad hoc groups that made decisions.[14]

Butler's underlying hope was that the new Prime Minister might restore traditional Cabinet government. The briefing reminded Blair, delicately, that he did not himself 'run' No. 10: the Cabinet Office did.[15]

The heart of the brief was the implementation of Labour's manifesto pledges, noting that reform to the Lords to remove the voting rights of hereditary peers would be short but extremely controversial, while passing a 'Freedom of Information' Act was medium-length, broadly uncontroversial.[16] Of the two measures, Blair and his successors were destined to regret the latter, as it generated a vast amount of extra work for counteracting attempts to probe government secrets. The briefing gave a thorough overview of the international situation and security threats to Britain. There were lengthy sections on the situation in Northern Ireland, to ensure that the Prime Minister was best placed to combat the threat of terrorism and to continue the efforts to end the Troubles.[17]

Butler worked well enough with the new government over its first three months until summer. But the death of Princess Diana in the early hours of 31 August 1997 illustrated how marginalised he had become by the end of his tenure. When he awoke at home at 6.30 a.m. that Sunday morning and turned on the radio, he initially thought he was listening to a historical obituary programme talking about Princess Grace of Monaco. When the reality dawned, he immediately phoned Fellowes, Diana's brother-in-law, whose distressed wife Jane picked up the phone. Butler was involved in much of the logistical work initially on the Sunday, but as the days went on, Blair's own team, of which he was clearly not a part, took over. In the middle of the week, a Whitehall colleague phoned him in the evening and said:

'You must walk across the park and see what's happening in the Mall. It's the most extraordinary event.' And so I did. I walked across St James's Park and it was amazing because there was complete silence in the Mall, complete silence. And yet, thousands of people lining up to put their tributes down, and I've never seen anything like it – I don't think there's ever been anything like it. It was the silence of the crowd that was the most extraordinary thing.[18]

Butler's exclusion from decision-making during that crucial week was symbolic of the distance that had entered his relationship with Blair. Like several of his predecessors, Butler was not sorry to leave at the normal retirement age of sixty. Butler had been at the heart of the premierships of Heath, Wilson, Thatcher and Major, and so his advice could have provided New Labour with valuable insight into how to operate the machine in their favour. Instead, they spurned his counsel as of no value to them. Blair's team thought they knew it all. The argument of the first volume of my biography, *Blair*, is that in their first term, they neither knew how to use power, nor what they wanted power for.[19] Blair, nevertheless, was determined that Butler's exit should at least be dignified. He hosted a farewell dinner for the Butler family at No. 10, gave him a generous present, together with a letter of thanks, and put him into the House of Lords. In trying to remain true to his vision of his job and the norms of Cabinet government, Butler had become distant from two Prime Ministers: Thatcher and Blair. His job was becoming difficult to transact.

RICHARD WILSON, 1998–2002

Even before the general election, Blair's team had been eager to handpick a successor to Butler upon his retirement at the end of 1997. Blair delegated the task of finding that right figure to his mentor, Lord Chancellor Derry Irvine, with a brief to find the most capable mandarin in Whitehall to galvanise the Civil Service and deliver Blair's agenda. Candidates included Richard Mottram, Permanent Secretary at Defence, Hayden Phillips, Permanent Secretary at the Department for Culture, and Andrew Turnbull, Permanent Secretary at the Department for the Environment. Richard Wilson, Permanent Secretary at the Home Office, was selected as the outstanding candidate and the one Whitehall had expected to succeed, given his great experience at the Permanent Secretary level and at the Cabinet Office.

Wilson came from a similar educational background to his two predecessors, attending Radley College, the public school near Oxford, before going on to study Law at Clare College, Cambridge. Deciding against becoming a barrister, he entered the Civil Service in 1966, albeit not via the traditional pathway of Cabinet Secretaries (which lay mainly through the Treasury or Home Office), but through the Board of Trade and subsequently the Department of Energy. Wilson's stellar reputation developed as Head of the Economic Secretariat in Thatcher's last three years, as Permanent Secretary for the Environment from 1992 to 1994, and then at the Home Office. Home Secretary Michael Howard had been at war with the department when Wilson arrived in 1995, convinced that it was pursuing its own agenda separate from government policy. Wilson helped steer a fragile relationship between minister and department into calmer waters, gaining the reputation as a can-do mandarin.

Wilson's appointment as Cabinet Secretary was announced in July 1997, leaving him five months until his succession in January 1998 to prepare for the challenge of the top job in Whitehall. He put huge energy into preparations, including a series of meetings with Butler, who outlined all the difficulties that Wilson would face. 'I would look slightly paler as each week went by with him,' he recalled.[20] He read up widely and talked to everyone he could. His eagerness to think afresh and learn from others augured well. A different personality to Butler, less patrician, younger in person and outlook, he seemed a promising choice.

He sat on the veranda of No. 10 with Blair before he took up post, where Blair spoke of his unique position as the first Prime Minister whose vision of Europe was not clouded by the Second World War and aftermath.[21] Wilson was hugely excited by the prospect of working with the new Blair government. Before he began, he saw the New Labour team as akin to the Kennedy administration when it came to power in the United States in 1961 amidst talk of a new Camelot. Here was a new generation coming into office in Britain, and he would have the chance to help them achieve their grand vision. The country was gripped by their new, easy-going, media-friendly Prime Minister. He had charisma and an energy quite unlike that of Major, too easily dismissed as grey and dull, as in the contemporary television satire, *Spitting Image*.

Wilson had a very clear conception of the job of Cabinet Secretary, and hoped it would chime with Blair's. His role models were Trend, Armstrong and Butler: 'I knew roughly how Burke Trend and Robert Armstrong did the job,' he said, while he witnessed Butler operating much closer up.[22] Butler had clashed with the Blair team and its distinctive approach for his final months, but Wilson hoped he could establish a modus operandi with them. He fought hard to preserve the system of collective Cabinet government in which he believed. In doing so, he ensured that the system survived the greatest challenge to convention since Lloyd George in 1918–22. Blair (and Brown after him) were idiosyncratic and dismissive of Cabinet government, and it took all of the skills of Wilson, one of the finest mandarins of his age, to curb their aversion and establish a working relationship. He saw it as his role to support the government, while they learnt the ropes, a learning curve that was to last much of the first Parliament. The great majority of ministers, including the Prime Minister and Chancellor, had never served in government before, nor indeed in any large private or public sector organisation.

Cabinet met slightly less than it had even under Thatcher, with just thirty-six meetings in 1998, thirty-five meetings in 1999, and thirty-six in 2000. The number of meetings reached its lowest postwar figure in 2001 with just thirty-three Cabinet meetings. However, as Blair's decade passed, the number of Cabinet meetings rose again, with thirty-nine in 2003, thirty-eight the following year, thirty-six in 2005, and thirty-seven in Blair's last full year, 2006.[23] By the time Blair came to power, few expected decisions to be made at the weekly Cabinet meetings. Blair knew that a core expectation of him as Prime Minister was to chair Cabinet, which he used as an opportunity to inform ministers about upcoming issues on the grid in the next one or two weeks, and what they could do to ensure the government's message was put across. Like many of his predecessors, Wilson felt full Cabinet became less important in his years: '[T]here were a number of other occasions when big issues were discussed, [like] Northern Ireland … or foreign affairs … So I don't want to imply that there wasn't substantive discussion. But as the supreme place where decisions are taken … the power shifted away from Cabinet over … my career.'[24] The writing had been on the wall from the first days of the new government. In August

1997, the latest version of *Questions of Procedure for Ministers* was published: 'Goodbye Cabinet government. Welcome to the Blair Presidency,' wrote journalist Peter Riddell. 'The ministerial code is … the biggest centralisation of power seen in Whitehall in peacetime. All of the familiar textbooks about the Cabinet system will have to be rewritten. The idea that heads of department have an independent standing has been torn up.'[25]

Contrary to popular image, Cabinet Committees flourished during Blair's first term, despite Blair's personal lack of involvement: thirty-eight were in existence in November 2001, compared to just nineteen under Major in 1995.[26] Wilson ran a firm regime to ensure that Cabinet Committees operated smoothly and effectively. Every Thursday he would meet with his senior secretariat and with key figures from No. 10 (particularly Jeremy Heywood, the senior domestic private secretary at No. 10 and from 1999, PPS, and David Miliband, Head of the Policy Unit), to plan Cabinet Committee business over the next three weeks and to review the handling of key issues across government. Every quarter, he had a longer-term 'forward look', based on a trawl of government departments, listing issues they anticipated would arise, indicating which Cabinet Committee each items should go to or how they might otherwise be handled. 'The collective committee system was alive and kicking and quite popular', said Wilson to the Iraq Inquiry, 'a lot of decisions took place through it in the Blair years'.[27] This included, above all, the significant body of constitutional change which was implemented in Blair's first term.

Difficulties arose because of New Labour's vision of how government should be run, articulated by Peter Mandelson even before Labour came to power, which sat uneasily alongside conventional Cabinet government.[28] To the New Labour leaders, collective government as championed by the Cabinet Office since 1916 was a sign of weakness, a view honed by watching Major, who they denigrated for behaving 'as if he is one among equals in his Cabinet'.[29] They believed Cabinet, as it had traditionally operated, had become inefficient and ineffective, and was an obstacle to radical reform. Their vision was for Blair to be like a chief executive, devising and imposing a clear strategy on the government, utilising his personal team in No. 10 to drive his policy through the system. In this brave new vision, Wilson was to act as the director of Permanent Secretaries. Wilson, in surprise, reminded

Blair that a core part of the Cabinet Secretary's job was to serve not just the Prime Minister but Cabinet as a whole. Blair replied: 'We'll deal with them'. Blair was fully committed to a command and control model of government, at variance with the modus operandi of even Lloyd George and Churchill when guiding the country through two world wars.[30] If Major was his fall guy, to the New Labour strategists the hero was Thatcher, for all their political differences. They admired her for her forceful views, even though Wilson would tell them that they misunderstood her. She had often used Cabinet Committees in orthodox ways, albeit through gritted teeth, which was part of the reason for her effectiveness. Wilson, throughout his period in office, held firmly to his beliefs:

> I support collective government and the Cabinet Committee system. I think it introduces good order and discipline into decision-making in a very complex world. It gives you the best chance of a good decision, though it doesn't guarantee it. It underpins collective responsibility. Cabinet collective decision-making binds people in. It is a check on the exercise of power by too few people at the centre.[31]

This tension between two mutually incompatible approaches to government was apparent to Wilson from very early on, and he believed it made it all the more important for him to establish a reasonable relationship with Blair. They met together at 10 a.m. every Monday morning to talk about current meetings which Heywood and Powell usually attended. Wilson and Alastair Campbell regularly had discussions about how government worked, little of which appears in Campbell's diaries. At one point Campbell told Wilson: 'I thought being in government would be just like opposition, except that things would happen'.[32] At 11 a.m., Wilson would spend an hour with Peter Mandelson or later Charlie Falconer talking over government business. On Wednesday mornings at 10 a.m., Wilson chaired the regular Permanent Secretaries meeting. Cabinet would take place on Thursday at 10.30 a.m., followed by his weekly meeting with his heads of secretariat in the Cabinet Office in the afternoon. On Fridays, he would finalise a note for Blair, listing some fifteen to twenty current issues across government, which would go into Blair's weekend box for them to discuss at their 10 a.m. meeting the following Monday.

The relationship between Wilson and Blair may not have been as close as that between Brook and Macmillan, or Armstrong and Thatcher, but it was more trusting than the portrait given in New Labour memoirs. As with Butler, their hostility to him was not apparent to him while they worked together. On Wilson's first day in office in January 1998, Blair gave him a list of tasks that he wanted, and areas on which he sought advice: the first being welfare reform. Blair explained to him that New Labour's 'inner circle' consisted of Blair, Mandelson, Campbell, Brown, and the pollster Philip Gould. Powell was not initially a member, and Blair for a while retained private doubts about whether he had selected the right chief of staff. The possibility of Powell's returning to the FCO was mooted. But a short time after Wilson's arrival, Powell proved his value to Blair over Northern Ireland, and his elevation to the inner circle followed.

During Wilson's first few months in office, he submitted a series of minutes to Blair on how to run the government to achieve his objectives, partly a response to Blair's plaintive admission to Wilson when he had been interviewed, that he felt he was 'sitting in a Rolls-Royce and I can't find the key'.[33] Wilson would explain the value and necessity for Cabinet Committees. Blair was not convinced: he would sometimes give Wilson a withering look when he suggested, if only half seriously, that he should handle an issue through a particular domestic Cabinet Committee, for which he had little appetite. He was, however, content to chair committees connected with military action, as over Kosovo, Sierra Leone, or Afghanistan.[34]

Blair's willingness to lean on Wilson was evident in his first major reshuffle in July 1998, when he sacked four failing ministers.[35] When a relationship between a Prime Minister and a Cabinet Secretary is successful, they are closely involved in Cabinet reshuffles: they provide administrative advice, ensure the numbers work, that the technical rules are followed, and the complex jigsaw of moves work out effectively. Wilson attended the pre-meetings in the inner group that took place over the preceding weekend, and when it came to the reshuffle day, which Blair executed in the Prime Minister's room in the House of Commons, he became nervous about delivering the bad news: 'I really want you to sit in on every meeting,' he told Wilson.[36] After the meetings were over, Blair sat hunched and looking totally drained.

Wilson was mindful from the outset of his parallel role as Head of the HCS. On 14 October 1998, he duly convened a large conference in Islington, designed to bring together senior civil servants with the New Labour team, and to ensure they worked harmoniously together, and to give Labour the chance to explain what they wanted of the Civil Service. Wilson drafted Blair's speech for the gathering: it was on the subject of modernising central government, on which Wilson was a progressive, albeit milder than those in the New Labour cabal. Wilson believed in evolution: New Labour in revolution – the Blair revolution – a revolution that largely failed to materialise. After the conference, Wilson worked with his permanent secretary colleagues to draw up a programme of Civil Service reform which he continued to implement steadily in the remainder of his time, although Blair's team did not fully engage with it.

Wilson, a born optimist, continued to believe a successful modus operandi with Blair was nevertheless achievable, and appreciated his strengths as a communicator, while being frustrated by his flaws and ambiguities. He saw many different figures coexisting simultaneously within him: a visionary about his own role in the world, capable of being extremely ruthless, but equally of being utterly charming. He was 'a brilliant communicator, whether to large crowds or one-to-one, very calm and affable on the surface, but complex deep down'.[37]

I think Tony Blair is driven to hurl himself at challenges which have defeated previous generations of politicians, [such as] making the Labour Party electable, or Northern Ireland, or Kosovo, a kind of Balkan Northern Ireland. Or Afghanistan, or Sierra Leone, or Iraq … His career was a whole succession of growing levels of challenge where he got growing confidence.[38]

He noted the sharp contrast in the style of Cabinet meetings under Blair to those under Thatcher:

[W]ith Tony Blair, we would have tea and coffee outside the room, the Cabinet door would be open, people would go backwards and forwards, they would put their papers on the table, and talk business in the corners of the room, and Tony Blair would be having a bilateral with John Prescott in his study and would sort of saunter in eating an apple in his shirt-sleeves. I remember watching for the first time, thinking that 'this is a different generation'.[39]

He recalls another vignette during the delicate negotiation with Sinn Féin leaders in Downing Street: 'I was looking out into the garden of No. 10 and Mr Blair's children were playing skateboarding. They had a plank on a barrel and they were going up the plank and it would tip and go down the other side. And there was Gerry Adams and Martin McGuinness watching them and then Gerry Adams saying, "let me have a go", and actually falling quite badly ... I think for my generation Northern Ireland was one of the big things.'[40] Indeed, the signing of the Good Friday Agreement in 1998, the tortuous and relentless work leading up to it, and nine years of intensive negotiations after it to lock the peace down, was Blair's, together with Powell's, greatest achievement in his first term.

Whitehall's senior officials empathised with Wilson, a popular figure. 'The NHS cannot change overnight when the Prime Minister says something,' said a mandarin. 'Whitehall cannot just agree things and then [they] happen. I don't think Blair really got that, and Richard got the flak for what Blair saw as lack of progress.'[41] Towards the end indeed, Wilson was blamed by Blair's circle for the government's failure to make more progress, with negative briefing to the press. He even found himself blamed for his inability to bring Brown into line: 'If Blair could not do it, how could Richard get Brown to behave more collectively?' asked an official.[42]

The profound fissure between Brown and Blair, and their highly partisan camps, made life much more difficult for Wilson than it already was. The 100 years since 1916 had seen no such prolonged hostility between a Prime Minister and their Chancellor. The sense of betrayal that Brown felt towards Blair was already present when Labour won the election in 1997, and the rift was fed by a powerful tribalism. When Blair and Brown cooperated together they were unstoppable.[43] But

there was a diversion of energy because of the Blair/Brown relationship, which was a considerable problem throughout my time as Cabinet

Secretary and also that of my successors. ... It was felt not only in the conduct of business within the central departments, but also in the behaviour of departments. The basic problem was that the Brownites looked to Brown for leadership, and not to the Prime Minister. How can you run and coordinate Permanent Secretaries, when a lot of their ministers are following the lead of the Chancellor, not the PM? The problem ran like letters through a stick of rock throughout my time.[44]

Wilson found himself in the middle: Blair wanted to talk to him about Brown, while Brown wanted to talk to him about how to handle Blair. Wilson confided in Campbell on his return from one such long meeting with Brown at the Treasury in January 1998. 'T. B. MUST start building other alliances,' Campbell recorded Wilson as saying. Campbell replied, '"So what you are saying to me is that spending so much time with G. B. is like marooning yourself on a desert island with someone who wants to kill you." He laughed.'[45]

The Blair/Brown split also had a profound impact on the conduct of Cabinet business. Wilson tried to ensure that it operated as smoothly as possible, with an agenda following a habitual pattern: parliamentary business, international business, domestic business, Northern Ireland and other matters. Periodically, arguments would break out between ministers over space on the legislative programme. Brown would keep his Budget very close to his chest, rattling off the details to Cabinet on the morning he was due to deliver in double speed.

Blair had absorbed a key lesson from President Clinton: that the core job of his first term was to win a second, which meant he was in constant campaigning mode during his first four years in power. As the general election approached, which he called for 7 June 2001, he began to wonder how he might enhance his position to achieve more than the relatively paltry achievements from his first term. 'Is this it? Is this all I have inherited from John Major?' he would ask. 'We are the fourth largest economy in the world and have a major role in Europe, and I don't even have the proper department to serve me?'[46] His mind increasingly turned to having a Prime Minister's department to serve him alone. He concluded this was what he needed: the absence of such a department explains why his first term was not more radical. But Wilson was very unhappy, and fought tooth and nail against the plan. He told Blair that the creation of such a department in No. 10 would be a decisive step towards his role becoming presidential, which he considered very unwise administratively and politically, making it plain he would not welcome more political appointees into No. 10 to create a department.[47]

Wilson began to devise a plan for reorganising the wider machinery of government for after the 2001 general election, to give Blair some of what he wanted without breaching conventions. From the autumn of 2000, he duly spent part of his 10 a.m. Monday meetings with Blair talking about his plans for major reorganisation, department by department. Together, they worked out an elaborate system, with notes and diagrams about how it would function. At a lengthy meeting before the general election, the plans were confirmed. Blair would not establish a Prime Minister's Department. But a core compromise in the plan was that the Heads of the European and Foreign Policy Secretariats should jointly work in the Cabinet Office and in No. 10. Their Secretariats were to remain in the Cabinet Office but their Heads would be 'double-hatted', reporting jointly to the Prime Minister and Wilson. The aim was to expand Blair's foreign policy team and capacity. John Sawers, Foreign Affairs Private Secretary (1999–2001), provided a rationale: 'it was partly because of the foreign policy issues that Tony Blair was dealing with, partly the way he liked to work, partly because of the growing need for No. 10 to match the resources of the foreign leaders with whom Blair was engaging'.[48] The European secretariat was intended to spearhead the drive for Britain's enlarged role in Europe after the anticipated joining of the euro, while the foreign policy head would be the equivalent to the National Security Adviser in the White House.

Blair duly secured his second landslide on 7 June 2001 with a majority of 167: 'You now are at the peak of your powers and may never be as strong again as you are now,' Wilson told him when he greeted the Prime Minister in No. 10 after his return from Buckingham Palace.[49] He had a surprise for his Cabinet Secretary that Friday morning: 'You are not going to be pleased with me over this,' Blair confessed to him, 'but I have decided that John Prescott should be moved into the Cabinet Office.'[50] Implanting such a potentially disruptive figure into his department came as a considerable surprise to Wilson. During their prolonged negotiations about the remodelled centre, 'there had been no "John Prescott" slot in it'.[51] Blair wanted Prescott to act as a chair for committees and enforcer of his will across Whitehall, a role not dissimilar to that played by Whitelaw under Thatcher. Officials attributed Blair's change of mind to his exhaustion and 'rebellious mood'.[52]

Wilson was preparing for his final full year in office when, on 11 September, the American passenger planes struck the Twin Towers in New York. Wilson was involved with intelligence. He had fought Brown, who had shown little interest in defence or intelligence, but who nevertheless decided that an 'internal market' for intelligence should be created, with the Foreign Office, Ministry of Defence and Cabinet Office paying for it. Wilson suggested to Brown that trying to build a customer relationship between the agencies and the departments was untenable with such a highly delicate commodity, running the risk it would spell 'the end of objective intelligence reporting'. He fought hard and, as he later said, 'I am pleased to say I won.'[53]

As events unfolded in New York, Blair was preparing to speak to the annual TUC conference in Brighton. Wilson was being driven around Parliament Square, back to 70 Whitehall, when his driver told him about the news from Manhattan. They listened to the radio and heard about the second plane being flown into the World Trade Center. 'This was not an accident. This is a horrible event that is happening,' Wilson realised.[54] He immediately got on the phone to No. 10 to speak to Heywood, the PPS, who told him that they had just heard that the White House might have to evacuate. Heywood asked: 'Should we be evacuating No. 10?' Wilson replied: 'If you evacuate, where do you go to?'[55] An image entered Wilson's head of No. 10 staff with laptops and briefcases standing outside looking for somewhere to go. Wilson had a very quick conversation with Blair in Brighton, who had decided to say a few words at the TUC before coming back to London.

Whitehall had been caught on the hop. The newly formed Civil Contingency Unit (CCU) were on a team-building exercise in Yorkshire, while the Overseas and Defence Secretariat, who oversaw COBR, were on their way to Hereford. As they drove past Heathrow on the M4, Wilson told them to turn around. A rush of phone calls followed to Parliament, Buckingham Palace and the intelligence agencies. Whether London itself was going to be a target was a prime concern for him, and an order was given to ban all aircraft over London: 'I kept looking from my office window across Horse Guards wondering if a plane was about to approach, it was a scary moment,' Wilson recalled.[56]

9/11 was to prove a great test of the effectiveness of the Overseas and Defence Secretariat. It came in the wake of a series of three episodes over the preceding twelve months, known in Whitehall as the 'Three Fs': the foot-and-mouth outbreak, wide-scale flooding, and the firemen's strike. Blair leant heavily on Wilson for advice on handling these episodes, praising him in his memoirs, *A Journey*.[57] In the early 1990s under Major, the work of the CCU had returned to the Home Office from the Cabinet Office, though the terrorism section was retained within the Overseas and Defence Secretariat. The assumption was that civil emergencies would be dealt with in the post-Cold War world by the Home Office. The three crises coming in rapid succession induced the thought in Blair: 'We need to pull this in centrally. We have got a machine, we have got people who know how to deal with a crisis, why don't we centralise this in COBR?'[58] So the CCU was set back up in 2001, repatriating various functions from the Home Office back to the Cabinet Office. The plan had in fact already been conceived by a senior official, Mike Granatt, who became its first head in association with Wilson.

9/11 and its aftermath was to prove a major distraction for Blair in achieving his ambition for a more efficient second term. His quest was not helped by any of the augmented No. 10 elements following the 2001 election, which proved a disappointment. None gave him the elusive tools he sought. Former BBC Director General John Birt was one of several experienced thinkers enlisted to stimulate thinking about how to strengthen the No. 10 operation. He and Heywood were asked to produce a plan. One early fruit of this was the creation of the No. 10 'Policy Directorate', by merging the No. 10 Private Office with the Policy Unit, took charge of Blair's day-to-day work and short-term policy advice. The brainchild of Heywood, who came closer than any civil servant in understanding how Blair worked, the Directorate glowed for a while, boosted greatly by the input of Andrew Adonis, who was promoted to acting 'Head of Policy', but did not long survive Heywood's departure at the end of 2003. Adonis was to prove the most creative force in Blair's premiership on the home front: 'I know almost telepathically what he will think on any big issue,' he said, unconsciously echoing what Charles Powell said of his relationship with Thatcher.[59] A Strategic Communications Unit was created under Campbell, separating it from the Press Office, to be run by career civil servants. Campbell was thereby taken away from day-to-day media handling, to reduce the damaging perception of 'spin'. But Campbell left No. 10 in the summer of 2003, unable to reinvent himself or to play the strategic role that he and Blair had wanted. A Government Relations Unit was set up, in part to keep Blair aide Anji Hunter in No. 10; but she had left by the end of 2001, and her successor Sally Morgan went on to have a different role. Not even the plan for Prescott to be a 'Chief Secretary to the Cabinet', operating out of the Cabinet Office and overseeing its expanded collective work, proved a success: such a role was not his *metier*.[60] An Office of Public Service Reform under Wendy Thompson was set up to stimulate change but did not survive long.

Nor did the new arrangements for the Overseas and Defence Secretariat and the European Secretariat have their intended impact or longevity. The first had David Manning at its head, brought back to fill it shortly after taking up his post as British Permanent Representative of NATO. The European Secretariat was headed by Stephen Wall, who had been running the pre-existing Secretariat in the Cabinet Office, before being moved symbolically into an office just within No. 10, close to the celebrated door that connected it to the Cabinet Office. With relations so strong between Wall, Manning and Powell, the new arrangement worked – for a while. The gain of the new arrangement was that the Prime Minister's senior representative on foreign policy could speak on equal terms with the senior foreign policy advisers to the American President, the German Chancellor and the French President. The arrangement worked well under Manning and his successor Nigel Sheinwald, who felt it very well suited to a Prime Minister like Blair.[61] But the gain was less clear on the European side: 'I was now thirty seconds away from the Prime Minister, because I had physically moved into No. 10, rather than ninety seconds away, when the European Secretariat had been in the Cabinet Office,' Wall said. 'But it made little practical difference to my job. If anything it was a disadvantage because I rarely saw the Prime Minister, and I was cut off from my own senior staff who remained in the Cabinet Office.'[62] The two secretariats succeeded neither in helping Blair achieve his ambition of Britain joining the euro, nor in preventing serious errors in the Gulf War and its aftermath.

So metamorphosis of No. 10 into a Prime Minister's mini-department did little to enhance Blair's grip on domestic policy. The chief success of the new arrangement was the Delivery Unit, an idea originating from Wilson and Heywood, to improve the Prime Minister's ability to monitor progress in critical home departments. Its head, Michael Barber, moved across to run it from the Education Department, where he had monitored targets for schools, and now brought much needed discipline and structure into Blair's supervision of the performance in the 'delivery' departments.[63]

Wilson might have been only partially successful in blunting Blair's centralising tendencies, but he did manage to bring about the most radical restructuring of Whitehall for several years. The giant Department for Environment, Transport and the Regions (DETR) was dismembered, while several new departments were created: the Department for Environment Food and Rural Affairs (DEFRA), the Department for Work and Pensions (DWP) and the Department for Education and Skills (DfES). The Home Office, which Wilson thought was overloaded since his time as Permanent Secretary, was reformed to refocus on crime and justice.[64] These were some of the fruits of Wilson's desire to give more time to his role as the Head of the HCS. He despaired of engaging Blair's interest in it. Officials complained of the 'Blair garden look', where his eyes glazed over and he looked out to the garden whenever the word 'management' was heard.[65]

In his last months, when his successor was being appointed, Wilson put it bluntly to Blair: 'Your problem is that neither you nor anybody in No. 10 has managed anything on a large scale,' he said. 'I have managed the Labour Party,' retorted Blair. 'You have never managed them, you have led them, there is a big difference,' Wilson replied defiantly. 'There is a huge difference giving orders to party officials, and managing a public service.'[66]

Wilson battled, like his predecessors, to find the balance between the two very demanding jobs of HCS and Cabinet Secretary, dividing his time roughly half and half between both. He invested great effort into leading the Civil Service, visiting its operations in London and outside, and raising morale. He found time to give attention to the 'official histories' work of the Cabinet Office, commissioning the last series of books to be written. Science was another subject that interested him. When in the Cabinet Office under Thatcher, he had been in charge of guiding the Chief Scientific Adviser, then John Fairclough (1986–90). As Cabinet Secretary, he did not seek to bring the position back into the Cabinet Office, but he was concerned to enhance the understanding of science among both ministers and senior officials. One of several initiatives was to organise visits to Cambridge twice a year, where leading figures, including astronomer Martin Rees and economist John Eatwell, would organise talks for them and they would consider the policy implications. Wilson worked closely with the two Chief Scientific Advisers during his time as Cabinet Secretary, Robert May (1995–2000) and David King (2000–08).

In Wilson's final months, a distance came between him and Blair, as well as with Campbell and Powell. Disappointment that the pace of reform had not picked up in the second term was partly responsible, which led to unfair attacks on Wilson personally. It made him even more determined to stand up for what he believed. In his final year, he gave perhaps his most important speech as Head of the HCS: 'The Portrait of a Profession Revisited' on 26 March 2002. It proved to be a passionate restatement of his views of government. Blair was not happy when Wilson submitted the text, and held a private meeting with him to talk about it. 'Look, I am not going to stop you saying it', he said, but left Wilson with the distinct impression that if he went ahead, he would be remembered as part of an outmoded vision of how to run a government rather than the future. Wilson took note of concerns but went ahead with his central argument, aware that by doing so, he would risk their disapproval. It was Wilson's vision, not Blair's, however, which was the more accurate description of how government was to develop in the years that followed.

Over the course of 2002, he was excluded from most of the discussions over policy towards Iraq, whereas he had been deeply involved in policy over Afghanistan. He surmised it may have been because Blair and his team saw that his time as Cabinet Secretary was limited. Other than the discussions in Cabinet, he attended just one meeting on Iraq, near to his last day in office, and was startled to learn how far the discussions had progressed towards invasion.

The deepest disagreement between Wilson and Blair's team, however, came about over his successor. He was due to retire on his sixtieth birthday in October 2002. Before the Christmas holidays in 2001, Wilson put a proposal to Blair about how his successor might be appointed, recommending that the post be advertised in Whitehall, with a job description being agreed in advance, and with a panel drawing up a longlist. The panel would then interview candidates, and a shortlist would go forward to Blair to make the final choice. Blair approved this formula in January 2002 but, without Wilson's knowledge, Blair's team concluded that none of the likely candidates would have the necessary radicalism nor dynamism in delivery. In secret, they sounded out a number of names from across the private sector. Matters came to a head at one of Wilson's Monday morning meetings with Blair in the second half of March.

Wilson had become concerned because nothing seemed to have happened about the names the panel had submitted, including David Normington, Permanent Secretary at Education, David Omand, Permanent Secretary at the Home Office until recently, John Gieve who had taken over from him, and Andrew Turnbull, Permanent Secretary at the Treasury since 1998. Blair told him that he wanted to short-circuit the selection process and interview Michael Bichard, Permanent Secretary at Education until his departure from Whitehall in 2001, who had impressed Blair's team greatly in driving forward school reform from 1997. Before that, Bichard had spent ten years as a chief executive in local government. Wilson told Blair forcefully that the entire Civil Service understood the appointment procedure, to which Blair himself had agreed, and that bringing in a new candidate at this late stage would discredit the entire process. He had never been tougher with Blair or his team. The meeting was inconclusive and Wilson went back to his room in the Cabinet Office, uncertain what was going to happen. Later that day, Heywood came to tell him that Blair had conceded.[67] Bichard was quietly dropped.

At the end of July 2002, Blair hosted a farewell dinner for Wilson at No. 10 for his family and some of the Private Secretaries and other key figures in his life. Campbell and Powell were present, joining in the festivities. Blair delivered a warm speech and gave him a pair of cufflinks with an image of the fanlight over the front door at No. 10. At his final Cabinet that month, Blair and his ministers presented him with a silver inkwell inscribed by the Cabinet. Whatever differences had come between them, the farewell between Wilson and Blair had all the appearance of being warm and sincere.

ANDREW TURNBULL, 2002–05

Andrew Turnbull emerged as the strongest and most acceptable candidate from the appointment process, becoming Cabinet Secretary on 1 September

2002. Turnbull was very content not to have been awarded the position first time around as it opened the way for him to serve as Permanent Secretary at the Treasury, much enhancing his experience at the top of the Civil Service for his new post. Selecting someone who had worked so closely to Brown for four years might have appeared a gamble given the state of the Blair–Brown relationship and the importance of Turnbull and Blair's mission, but he was impressed by Turnbull's determination to get the jobs he was given done. Blair above all wanted momentum in his second term: 'Don't waste it like I did,' President Clinton had warned him.[68]

Turnbull was the first Cabinet Secretary not to have attended a public school. Born in January 1945, he went to Enfield Grammar School before studying Economics at Christ's College, Cambridge, achieving a First and entering the Treasury in 1970. After a two-year secondment at the IMF in Washington from 1976 to 1978, he made his mark as Economic Private Secretary to Thatcher from 1983 to 1985. When a strong-minded replacement was needed in 1988 to succeed Nigel Wicks as her PPS, he seemed the ideal candidate. Butler had formed a high opinion of him when he himself had been PPS to Thatcher, and thought he had the required qualities for the job at such a delicate time. Promotion for Turnbull thereafter was rapid. He became Second Permanent Secretary at the Treasury in charge of expenditure from 1993 before his appointment as Permanent Secretary at Environment in 1997, and then first Permanent Secretary of the DETR after the general election in 1997, the super department created particularly for Prescott. When it became clear that Brown could not work with his Permanent Secretary, the highly able Terry Burns, the nod went in 1998 to Turnbull.

Turnbull was a very different figure to Wilson; less urbane and donnish. Turnbull described his own style as 'quite functional, getting things done, making things happen'.[69] He was the first economist to be Cabinet Secretary, and his training and experiences at the Treasury, overseeing monetary policy and public expenditure, were formative. He was told clearly by Blair that his brief was to focus on public service reform, which meant his exceptional insight into a wide range of policy areas would not be drawn upon. Turnbull believed when he came to office that 'the Prime Minister should turn to the Cabinet Secretary first and foremost': it was after all what he had seen happen with his predecessors, but he came to reluctantly accept that

'Blair was not looking towards his Cabinet Secretary to be a major policy adviser'. The reality was that 'I never achieved the kind of reflex action, go-to status that Robert Armstrong had with Mrs Thatcher'. He believed nevertheless that he could adapt himself to Blair's vision for his job: 'I could make it work,' he said.[70] So he never tried to become a member of Blair's inner team, aware that the competition for 'face time' with Blair had become far fiercer by 2002. Troubleshooting the row that occurred between Blair, Brown and Alan Milburn over foundation hospitals in 2002 might have been the first of several such occasions where his policy and problem-solving talents were sought and accepted: 'but such incidents were rare'. Significantly, it was Heywood, not Blair, who involved Turnbull, knowing him to be someone who 'understood money and was effective'.[71]

Turnbull took a clear decision early on that he could do two of the three components to the job, as he interpreted it: the Cabinet Secretary's role of coordinating policy and implementing decisions; the Head of the HCS, including the oversight of propriety and ethics; and finally, the oversight of intelligence and security. When the latter became mainstream for Blair after 9/11, he concluded, 'You can't do all three.'[72] Even in the less security-intense post-Cold War world, he had watched as his predecessors Armstrong and Butler became embroiled in a whole series of security incidents, notably *Spycatcher* and the Matrix 'Arms to Iraq' scandal, where they 'found themselves being pitch-forked into solving something that had been brewing for a long time: you should never be caught by surprise and be drafted in as a firefighter'.[73] By happy coincidence, David Omand had become available again after a serious illness, and had just the expertise required for a new post, created in 2002, of 'Intelligence and Security Coordinator'. Omand was admirably well equipped for it, but there was a big downside. The Cabinet Secretary became removed from advising the Prime Minister on security and intelligence, and the new Intelligence Coordinator did not attend Cabinet, nor was he available as part of the Cabinet Office to advise ministers on their collective responsibility for defence and overseas matters. O'Donnell eventually took the portfolio back into the Cabinet Secretary's job when he succeeded Turnbull in 2005. Turnbull, however, felt he had been vindicated when, in 2010, David Cameron created the National Security Adviser post, which Turnbull saw as being foreshadowed by his initiative in 2002.[74]

The creation of this new position, alongside the Overseas and Defence Secretariat established in 2001, meant that the Cabinet Office was less immediately involved in the Iraq War than in any other British war over the previous century. When considering the impact of these innovations, the review on Intelligence and Weapons of Mass Destruction, overseen by Robin (now Lord) Butler, reported in July 2004: 'We believe that the effect of the changes has been to weight their responsibility to the Prime Minister more heavily than their responsibility through the Cabinet Secretary to the Cabinet as a whole.'[75] 'If I had been the overseer of the intelligence ... I would have been sucked into the Iraq War at the expense of my other responsibilities,' Turnbull responded, not altogether unhappy to have been one stage removed from the whole Iraq episode.

Cabinet discussed Iraq as a specific item twenty-four times in the year leading up to the war in March 2003. The force of Blair's personality, conviction and authority, having just won his second landslide, as well as his command of the confidential detail, meant Cabinet ministers were discouraged from challenging him at these meetings. Resignations were few: notably Foreign Secretary Robin Cook in March over his lack of a fresh UN mandate, and Clare Short in May 2003. The Defence and Overseas Cabinet Committee did not meet at all, whereas there were twenty-five meetings of the small ad hoc group with Blair and key officials. The Butler Report on intelligence noted the informal and restricted nature of decision-making had a significant impact on the effectiveness of collective discussion.[76] Critically, the Cabinet Office was not asked to provide a secretariat function recording minutes of Blair's informal Iraq meetings. One can only speculate how events might have turned out differently had there been a Cabinet Secretary occupying the traditional role, and insisting that the spirit and letter of collective responsibility be applied. If they had, might they have appeased the Prime Minister, as Brook did with Eden over Suez, or stood up to them, as Brook did with Churchill, and Hunt did with Wilson?

Turnbull told the Chilcot Inquiry that by the time he took up his post in September 2002, the decision had been made:

We had agreed, not only what we wanted to do but the Prime Minister ... had agreed with the President of the United States what was going to be done next and the idea of formulating [a] single resolution, and you could almost say setting a trap for Saddam Hussein – the idea of an ultimatum, that was all formulated at around that time.

The moment for arguing the 'pros and cons' of military action, he said, had passed.[77] The Cabinet Office had provided a discussion paper in July 2002 entitled: 'Iraq: Conditions for Military Action'. The minute says 'the legal advice is, as ever, far too narrow'.[78] It was decided that the Cabinet Office should coordinate the publication of a 'public dossier' regarding Iraq and that Campbell should retain a leading role on the timing for its release.[79] Ultimately, the dossier, *Iraq's Weapons of Mass Destruction: The Assessment of the British Government*, was released in September 2002. It would, like every other aspect of the Iraq War, prove deeply controversial.

The dossier was inextricably involved in Turnbull's worst moment as Cabinet Secretary, the death of government weapons expert David Kelly, in July 2003. A distraught Blair, who was on a trip to the Far East, charged Turnbull, Hayden Phillips, David Omand and Kevin Tebbit, Permanent Secretary at Defence, to come up with terms of reference for an inquiry and identify a judge as chair before he landed three hours later in Tokyo. Kelly had become known as the unauthorised source to a BBC journalist about the reliability of aspects of the government's dossier on the weapons he believed were held by Saddam Hussein. Kelly was harshly questioned by a House of Commons Committee on 15 July: two days later, he was dead, the subsequent Hutton Inquiry finding he had taken his life.

Turnbull, like Wilson and Butler before him, found himself increasingly standing up for Cabinet conventions even if he was powerless to insist that Blair observed the correct decisions of Cabinet. To Blair and Powell, the difference between a properly constituted Cabinet Committee and an ad hoc meeting, which was not serviced by the Cabinet Office, was a technicality, which it was not. To their mind, working through the Cabinet Office 'was the death rattle of the mandarin class'.[80] Turnbull formed the view that they knew exactly what they were doing, and had worked out their modus operandi before they came to power in 1997. A verification of his thesis came when they told Turnbull that it did not matter whether or not the Cabinet Office provided the secretariat function as long as 'you have the right people in the room'. Turnbull's retort was that it mattered a very great deal because, 'with a Cabinet Committee you choose people who are the right people and relevant people; and you don't handpick your group of people, and you don't exclude the ones you don't want to be there, which is what Blair did.' Turnbull's explanation for Blair's approach is enlightening: 'I would describe [him] as someone who worked fast and made decisions quickly … he wanted to bypass problems and get on with it.' With the official structure of Cabinet government and collective responsibility, papers and agendas were circulated, meetings were minuted and conclusions were circulated: '[T]hey thought all this would get in the way, hence the creation of sofa government.'[81] It was as if Blair wanted to wind the clock back to Lloyd George's suburb, or even pre-1916, pre-Hankey.

July 2004 saw the publication of the Butler Report. The choice of Butler · was significant – the only time a Cabinet Secretary headed a public inquiry that discussed the conduct of a government he had served. In the final weeks, he came under intense pressure to make changes, though Butler maintains the 'broad conclusions were not affected'.[82] Though Butler exonerated Blair of the central charge of lying over Iraq, the report was critical of his style of 'sofa government': 'You could feel the personal animus,' said a Blair aide.[83]

Turnbull pressed Blair hard in its wake, along with senior Cabinet Office official Paul Britton, to oversee a restoration of Cabinet government with Cabinet Committees to be revived to debate the detail and take decisions. All sides recognised by 2004 that Cabinet could no longer be the key decision-making forum, but they thought it could be the place where major developments should be reported, and where ministers talked over the main political and economic issues. For a while, there was some success in getting them to do that.[84] But, as Armstrong found with Thatcher after the Falklands and Westland, the old habits soon started reasserting themselves.

One power that Blair could not take away from Turnbull was responsibility for organising his succession if he fell over Iraq, or in a coup by the Brownites. When Blair heard about Turnbull's discreet preparations, he admitted that he 'laughed a little uneasily'.[85] A caretaker administration under Prescott while the Labour Party completed its selection process was, for a while, the most likely option.

Turnbull had some success driving forward public sector reform as Blair wanted: Powell described it as a 'noble effort', which failed to achieve greater success due to opposition from his fellow Permanent Secretaries. By contrast, Turnbull believed his colleagues shared his own commitment on the need for modernisation across Whitehall, including smarter use of IT, better strategic thinking and more professional performance management across the Civil Service. These three years saw the high watermark of the Cabinet Office mostly serving and responding to the Prime Minister directly, rather than to the Cabinet collectively. Turnbull understood that there was a fine line; the Cabinet Office had to support the Cabinet, but also had to support the Prime Minister directly, otherwise it might simply embolden the argument for a separate support unit in No. 10. Nevertheless, with Blair at his most powerful, it is no coincidence that the Cabinet Office's departmental report in 2003 talked little of 'servicing the Cabinet', and that its first stated objective was 'to support the Prime Minister in leading the government.'[86] But, by the time Turnbull left in 2006, the wheel had turned again, and the phrase 'supporting the Cabinet' was beginning to reappear in the Cabinet office statement of purpose.[87]

The Cabinet Office was rarely involved in the most important decision post-Iraq: entering the single currency. Brown and his key aide, Ed Balls, were keen to exclude others from this decision bar themselves, and to roundly reject it. They were especially insistent that No. 10 had as little as possible to do with it. Discussions took place very deliberately at the Treasury, not at the Economic Cabinet Committee. The No. 10 team was composed of Wall, Powell and Jeremy Heywood. 'It was totally ludicrous because we never got the papers until a day or two before the meetings, and they were highly detailed and complicated,' they complained about the deliberate Brown/ Balls ploy.[88] Turnbull supported the Treasury position, and found himself attempting with Heywood to broker a compromise which, while allowing Brown to win the argument, let Blair claim some progress was being made towards his ultimate objective of joining the euro. Wall, the most Europhile of the three in the No. 10 team, was thoroughly disenchanted with Brown for presenting all the findings in a negative light, regardless of the evidence. Blair himself dreaded those meetings he was able to attend because the technical details went way over his head, another deliberate ploy of Brown and Balls.

He became 'utterly infuriated' by the insouciance with which Brown 'got to the punch-line as if it was the process of a deeply intellectual matter, and not one of political judgement which he could have stated at the beginning'. Blair had had enough, and told his sceptical team that he could sort out his Chancellor: 'Leave Brown to me,' he said.[89]

Relations became increasingly fraught between both teams, with Balls refusing outright to speak to Powell. But Blair was beginning to get cold feet when he weighed the risks. In the last analysis, he was worried about winning a referendum on the euro if the Chancellor was cool or negative, and he was fearful too of the consequences of sacking Brown or moving him to another department against his will. The level of threat and unpleasantness was high. Just after the election victory in 2001 was the apex of Blair's power: this was his chance to remove Brown. Campbell and Powell repeatedly urged Blair to do so. Turnbull had become worried that the Treasury was becoming a spending department with its own favoured programmes including tax credits, and needed to be cut back to its classic role as the controller of spending, treating all programmes equally. Turnbull knew: he had run it for four years as its Permanent Secretary. In No. 10, a standard joke was that the Treasury had become the biggest spending department of them all.[90] Blair would say, 'I am going to have my public service agenda and not be blocked or blackmailed any more by the bloody Treasury.'[91]

But what could he do about Brown? He, not malign mandarins, was the principal obstacle to his agenda. Blair could have sacked him. But he never found it within himself to take him on and, as a result, Brown stopped Britain joining the euro, though it proved to be the right decision for Britain, and hampered Blair's entire public sector reform programme. To Turnbull, the 'carve up' of the domestic waterfront that Blair and Brown had negotiated after John Smith died in 1994 was beginning to break down dangerously. Fights came over the Delivery Unit, over which Brown was nervous, and over the NHS.[92] Wall had concluded early on that Blair did not have it in him to say: 'I am going to get myself a new Chancellor.'[93] When Wall left No. 10 in the summer of 2003, Blair walked along the corridor to bid him farewell: 'You must feel disappointed about the way things turned out over Europe.' Wall could only agree, but does not recall saying anything in reply.[94]

Turnbull, at fifty-seven, was the oldest Cabinet Secretary on appointment, and was the shortest serving of the eleven. His tenure would have been just three years, terminating in September 2005: 'I was frustrated by a lot of it', he said recently.[95] He did, however, have the satisfaction of being the first official to have served as PPS to the Prime Minister, Permanent Secretary of the Treasury, Cabinet Secretary and Head of the HCS. The two aspects of the job he most enjoyed, significantly, were working alongside fellow high-calibre Permanent Secretaries and forging a closer relationship with local government, involving him travelling around the country meeting local officers and councillors. Modernising government, and trying to bring clarity to the soup of units in the Cabinet Office and beyond, he also found satisfying.[96] The three years had not seen him become closer to Blair. Significantly, he completely missed a significant 'wobble' in confidence Blair had in April 2004 over whether he should continue as Prime Minister: 'It was not visible to me at the time,' he said.[97]

Blair took one decision that did bring Turnbull some satisfaction, and utilised his very considerable skills. In January 2005, with his third general election four months away, Blair set up a team where Turnbull worked with John Birt to devise a third term programme. Turnbull's plan yet again envisaged a return to Cabinet government with a regularised use of Cabinet Committees: 'He had been particularly concerned that the Economic Affairs Committee had barely met, and when it did, Brown would not let it have any real information.'[98] Turnbull was able to point to the lessons of the Butler Report, and managed to make Blair partially realise that if he only used committees more, he could, through collective responsibility, lock in Cabinet ministers as well as the Treasury, as a united front would avoid many of the bitter battles fought in public. An unexpected opponent was Michael Barber, who believed the personalised style of Blair, with regular bilaterals with ministers and stock-takes by the Delivery Unit at No. 10, was much better suited to Blair's strengths.

After Blair's victory in the 2005 general election, Cabinet government came back in vogue for a while. But before long, Blair began to ask, 'What has happened to my stock-takes?' He became disenchanted with Cabinet Committees, saying 'these things don't really function for me: they don't enable me to have the discussions I want to have'.[99] Within a few months, the elaborate system of committee set up after the 2005 general election had become largely moribund. As Ivan Rogers, Blair's new PPS, admitted, 'His enthusiasm for chairing those committees declined very rapidly. He soon wanted to go back to more bilateral processes with the people he most trusted.'[100]

GUS O'DONNELL, 2005–12

The main candidates to succeed Turnbull were David Normington, Permanent Secretary at the Department for Education and Skills since 2001, John Gieve, Permanent Secretary at the Home Office since 2001, Nigel Crisp, Permanent Secretary at Health since 2000, and Gus O'Donnell, Turnbull's successor as Permanent Secretary at the Treasury since June 2002. O'Donnell was the second Roman Catholic Cabinet Secretary, and the first and only Cabinet Secretary to attend neither public school nor Oxbridge as an undergraduate. A pupil of Salesian College in Battersea, he studied Economics at Warwick before an MPhil at Oxford and some lecturing at Glasgow in Political Economy. He joined the Treasury in 1979 as an economist at a time when the prevailing ethos was still that of the generalist as featured in *Yes, Minister*, and where having a specialism could be a black mark against promotion.[101] O'Donnell had raced up the system despite his late entry to the Civil Service at age twenty-seven, becoming First Secretary at the British Embassy in Washington, where he oversaw Economics, before being appointed Press Secretary to the Chancellor in 1989. This was a happy career move, because the Chancellor was John Major, who felt comfortable with someone who shared a similar south London background and liked his unstuffy style (and love of cricket). O'Donnell had a knack, too, of explaining complex economics to Major in a way that he understood but did not make him feel patronised.[102] So, when Major became Prime Minister in November 1990, he asked O'Donnell to cross Downing Street with him. He helped steer Major's difficult premiership through its turbulences, including Black Wednesday and the allegations of sleaze, before leaving in 1994.[103] He went on to a series of high-flying economic posts, before becoming Permanent Secretary at the Treasury in June 2002.

O'Donnell was of very different ilk to all other Cabinet Secretaries, his easy charm and 'bloke-ish' manner chimed with Blair: significantly, they were the same age and shared a similar outlook on life.[104] O'Donnell was only a few a months older than Blair, born in October 1952: 'You are the first person I have had who I feel is of the same generation as me,' Blair told him when he took over.[105] Butler, in contrast, had been fifteen years older than Blair. O'Donnell was 'the first modern Cabinet Secretary in my view' wrote Jonathan Powell, adding, though, that 'it would take more than one person to make central government effective'.[106]

O'Donnell inevitably gained a reputation as a courtier, having gained the trust of such totally different characters as Major and Brown, blessed with rare skills of working for masters of very different persuasions. But he also had a street-fighting grit which allowed him to stand up more effectively to Prime Ministers. Less experienced as a policy adviser than some Cabinet Secretaries, he nevertheless proved a supreme operator as Cabinet Secretary. O'Donnell was the odd one out of the three incumbents since 1998, as Turnbull and Wilson worked for just one Prime Minister, whereas O'Donnell went on to serve three: the tail end of Blair, three highly charged years of Brown, and David Cameron, under the very unusual conditions for the Cabinet Office of coalition, not seen in Britain since Bridges had been Cabinet Secretary. O'Donnell described the secret of his success in managing such different personalities as 'down to trust, they have to trust that you will say what you think, that you are totally discreet. That you will not take sides and not be a yes man because that is useless to them.'[107]

No job can prepare one for being Cabinet Secretary, though some help. O'Donnell learnt particularly from being Permanent Secretary at the Treasury that the job is more about leadership than just management. To strengthen his leadership skills, he secured a leadership coach, Steve Radcliffe. A lesson that O'Donnell learnt from him was: 'Where do I want to get to?'[108] He leant heavily on a group of Permanent Secretaries, including Lee Lewis, Permanent Secretary at DWP, and David Normington at the Home Office. But he also relied on the cadre of the former Cabinet Secretaries, notably those who had worked in the Treasury – Armstrong, Butler and Turnbull: 'Quite often I would phone them up and say, "Well, you have done this before give me your wisdom."'[109] Armstrong's skills at compressed writing, and Butler's handling of sensitive issues like the publication of Alan Clark's diaries made a particular impression.[110] Turnbull was his main mentor, though. After all, it was Turnbull that O'Donnell succeeded at the Treasury and now the Cabinet Office.

One subject that O'Donnell had to contend with but his predecessors did not was the Freedom of Information Act, which came into force shortly before he took over. While philosophically in favour of greater openness and transparency, O'Donnell had to live with the downside also. Ministers started to say to him and his officials: 'I'm not sure I want that meeting, thank you very much' and 'What are you going to write down about this?' So he saw the irony that an Act intended to promote freedom of information was in danger of restricting candour and the quality of records. He said:

> What you want in Cabinet is those people who disagree with policy to actually argue their case as clearly and openly as possible and, as Cabinet Secretary, I always wanted the Cabinet minutes to reflect that discussion accurately, and they did during my time, which is why I was quite passionate about trying to keep Cabinet minutes confidential.[111]

O'Donnell joined a Tony Blair bristling with confidence, having won a third election. The clock was ticking louder, though, than Blair realised – the hands on the clock face being forced round by Brown. Blair knew he had wasted too much time early in his premiership, when he had the greatest political capital, and he needed to work purposefully. O'Donnell, after Blair's unsatisfactory relationships with his first three Cabinet Secretaries, would be key to his third term. O'Donnell had observed Blair closely for several years, summing up the position on his taking over as he saw it:

> I think eight years on, he wasn't going to fundamentally change the way he worked. And he was also, of course, a very passionate moderniser, and he wanted to move on, and he wanted public services to be better and more citizen-focused, so you needed to find ways of working with him. He was very much into stock takes to determine delivery, always asking, were we on track? Had we hit the milestones? All of that. So he had that style of rolling up his sleeves, getting down [to it] and saying: 'I want to know the street crime numbers for these streets, and come back in a week and tell me precisely the figures.' You know, he got very much into

detail and was I think somewhat exasperated by the machine, believing 'if I don't do it myself, it doesn't happen'.[112]

Despite his frantic pace in his final two years, Blair's domestic agenda was far from complete when he left office, while his policy in Afghanistan and Iraq was disintegrating around him. It became commonplace, even fashionable, to criticise Blair's premiership, particularly in the wake of Iraq. We should not overlook how much he achieved, however: not the least three general election victories, public sector reforms to the NHS and schools, constitutional changes including devolution, and a series of reforms to help the most disadvantaged and marginalised in society. The question, though, is could he have achieved more if he had worked with the norms of the Cabinet Office and the traditions of collective responsibility, rather than against it? No Prime Minister in the last 100 years of the Cabinet Office's existence had so many advantages: a strong economy, large majorities in the Commons, a (mainly) united party, and a weak opposition. Might he have achieved more, and might the misjudgements of the Iraq War have been avoided, had more respect been shown for civil servants, and decisions been more collegiate?

O'Donnell proved himself to be his own man under Blair, standing up against him on the side of the Treasury in early 2006 in a bitter row over pension reform, which built on their earlier falling out over the euro. At its high point, a meeting was held in the garden of No. 10 in early May; O'Donnell weighed in on the side of Brown, arguing a proposed link to earnings should not be restored, but phased in over fifteen years.[113] O'Donnell, unsurprisingly, was never invited to join Blair's inner circle, and watched as the remaining life drained weekly out of the premiership.

O'DONNELL AND BROWN (2007–10)

In Blair's final weeks in May and June 2007, the two Treasury-bred officials at the centre, O'Donnell and Oliver Robbins (Blair's PPS 2006–07), helped ensure a smooth transition to Brown's team. Given the history of bitterness, the reluctance of key figures in both camps to speak to each other, and the suspicion in the Blair camp that Brown had forced their man out, it was no mean achievement.[114] A new era seemed to have arrived when, on 27 June, after ten years of waiting, Brown walked through the door of No. 10 as Prime Minister, with Sarah at his side. O'Donnell was there to greet them, and give Sarah a hug.[115] Rarely had a new Prime Minister–Cabinet Secretary relationship begun so promisingly. Brown gave signals too that he wanted to sweep away not only some of Blair's policies, but his presidential style. Cabinet government was back in business, he said, and he wanted to listen to ministers' views. Brown was equally clear that the marginalisation of the Cabinet Office had to end. To Ed Balls, he entrusted a plan for revamping the Cabinet Office under O'Donnell: 'We wanted to build up the Cabinet Office to enhance the Prime Minister's reach,' said Balls.[116] Brown and Balls liked and trusted O'Donnell, having worked with him for three years when he was Permanent Secretary at the Treasury until 2005. They were sympathetic to O'Donnell's aim of establishing the close relationship his three predecessors had failed to achieve with Blair, and of achieving a traditionally run Whitehall with the Cabinet Office at the centre, with officials returning to their correct constitutional position.[117] So far, so good.

Jon Cunliffe, Heywood and Simon McDonald, spearheading the new centre, were known as the 'three amigos'.[118] 'We were seeking to move away from the spin and the actor Blair towards a genuine, straight-talking guy,' said a Brown aide,[119] summing up how they regarded Blair, and their intent, shared by many incoming Prime Ministers, to differentiate themselves from their predecessors. In these halcyon days, everything seemed possible. Brown even said policy announcements would be made first by ministers in the House of Commons rather than on BBC Radio 4's *Today* programme, and that Cabinet meetings would be longer and involve more discussion. Quite how long they would last was to take Cabinet members initially by surprise.

At his first Cabinet in late June, Brown asked for comments on a variety of constitutional changes he wanted to introduce, and he went around the table asking for ministers' opinions. The genial atmosphere soon gave way to long speeches, many of them critical of the proposals. O'Donnell was getting nervous. He passed Brown a discreet note to say: 'Look, at this rate Prime Minister, we are going to be here until midnight'. Brown promptly read out O'Donnell's note to the entire Cabinet – not what he intended, and the cause of general bemusement.[120]

Brown did not think much of the Prime Minister's Private Office apparatus bequeathed to him by Blair. In place of an outsider like Jonathan Powell as his Chief of Staff, he wanted a Treasury official playing more of the conventional PPS role. His first choice was Tom Scholar, his intellectually brilliant PPS as Chancellor from 1997 to 2001, who had gone on to Washington to work for the IMF. 'It had been axiomatic that Tom would become Chief of Staff in charge of No. 10 when Gordon became Prime Minister,' said one official.[121] Gordon liked him. 'Tom was unstuffy, popular, and extraordinarily able,' said a colleague.[122] Scholar moved in but, to the surprise of many, it did not prove a success. Scholar left No. 10 in January 2008. Many thought he had been shabbily treated by Brown, though he returned to the Treasury as Second Permanent Secretary, and went on to become Macpherson's successor as Permanent Secretary in 2016. His abrupt departure left a vacuum, an embarrassment, and a question inconveniently hanging over the Prime Minister.

For foreign policy advice, he returned to the traditional model of a Private Secretary, selecting Tom Fletcher. This raised eyebrows on account of his comparative youth and inexperience for a job at the Prime Minister's side, traditionally occupied by the FCO's highfliers, carefully chosen by the FCO to try to ensure they did not 'go native'. It was still a deliberate return to convention. As Balls said: 'The thinking was to establish a structured relationship between the Prime Minister and the Civil Service machine, with traditional political and ministerial input, which had worked so well for Gordon at the Treasury.'[123] Within months, however, all Brown's highminded aspirations began to evaporate. He decided he could not trust Cabinet not to leak, and he became disenchanted with Cabinet Committees, which he found as laborious and unhelpful for his purpose as had several of his predecessors. Nevertheless, the number of Cabinet meetings did rise during the Brown years, to forty-one in 2008 and forty-four in 2009, far higher than under his predecessor, or successor.[124]

Brown's political stock, so high in the first weeks after Blair's departure, was on the wane. Nothing did more to end the honeymoon than his withdrawing from an early general election, which would have given him a personal mandate in September 2007. After this, as difficulties mounted, he retreated week by week into the tight circle of trusted allies that he had been comfortable with at the Treasury. He had expected to work closely with his successor, Alistair Darling, the new Chancellor, imagining he would be a biddable colleague, as would Nick Macpherson, the Permanent Secretary. A bust-up with the Treasury, which he had ruled for ten years, had never been part of his game plan. But he became deeply angry when the Treasury prevented him from increasing expenditure and borrowing further, which his former officials believe he would have done had he not been blocked. The decline in his confidence in Darling and Macpherson was precipitous.

The crisis built up in the weeks before Christmas 2007. Brown berated his team angrily: 'You are not delivering.' 'You are not defining what you want,' they responded.[125] 'Gordon is finding it much harder than he thought it would be,' admitted Sarah Brown.[126] His aides were soon complaining, as had Blair's: 'Gordon has no concept of management. He is incapable of it, he is a hopeless team manager.'[127] 'Gordon is incapable of organising himself out of a box,' one of his team told me back in 2003. He did not appear to have learnt much about leadership since. Perhaps they were reluctant to tell him.[128] The No. 10 Private Office was becoming a very unhappy place: 'A real weakness of Gordon's was that he took advice from a wide range of informal advisers, which often cut across what we were doing in No. 10 and creating confusion,' said one. 'It was a total nightmare as no one ever knew what was going on,' said another.[129]

O'Donnell found himself catapulted into the heart of the most anarchic premiership of the last 100 years. None of the top-flight civil servants in the No. 10 Private Office were able to bring order to the chaos. Who could fill their place? Brown's mind turned increasingly towards Heywood, who returned to the Cabinet Office in June 2007 from the investment bank, Morgan Stanley, which he had joined after leaving No. 10 in December 2003. Might he be the person to replace Tom Scholar at the heart of the No. 10 operation? Heywood had left with a status already above that of the usual PPS. A new post of 'Permanent Secretary' at No. 10 was negotiated between Brown and O'Donnell, and dangled before him. After continued requests, he finally relented. Heywood had known O'Donnell for many years, and they were good friends: together they battled, over the next two and a half years, to bring back order to Downing Street. The three Cabinet Office directorates to assist Brown at the centre were key in achieving this:

a Foreign Directorate, led by diplomat Simon McDonald; a European and International Finance Directorate, run by ex-Treasury Jon Cunliffe; and a Domestic Policy Directorate under Heywood himself.

Ironically, it was the banking crisis which saw a return, for a while, of a semblance of Cabinet Committee governance. To manage the British response, Brown created a new body, the National Economic Council (NEC), in October 2008, made up of key ministers and officials most closely concerned with economic policy, which met in COBR. It became Brown's 'War Cabinet' for tackling the crisis and mitigating the subsequent recession, and would prove the most successful of his rare institutional innovations as Prime Minister, before it was merged with the Economic and Domestic Secretariat.[130] 'I realised quite early on how dramatic an impact the crisis would have on the economy,' said O'Donnell. 'I was fortunate to have Gordon Brown as the Prime Minister at the time: he was very interested in the economy, and he was a good leader for that period.'[131]

The NEC became the battleground for Brown's increasingly intemperate disagreements with the Treasury. Its mandarins thought he was living in a 'la-la' land, unable, apparently, to recognise either the gravity of the debt figures or his share of responsibility, when Chancellor, for the structural deficit. They worried that he was becoming dangerously influenced by a misreading of the writing of the great economist John Maynard Keynes, with much of their suspicion falling on Ed Balls, who they thought recklessly in favour of expenditure.[132] Brown was becoming increasingly embattled, and would lash out at those around him. 'He would often become very aggressive indeed: on small issues, on big issues, and behind closed doors with a number of us he would then apologise and say "I am angry with myself" and turn in on himself,' reported one of his team.[133]

Brown's biggest triumph was the G20 Conference, which he chaired at the ExCeL Centre in East London in April 2009. It helped rekindle optimism in the international community that the world would not descend into a 1930s-style depression, and that emerging economies in Eastern Europe and elsewhere would not fail. When Brown and his team returned from the conference to No. 10, there was a rare moment of joy in his premiership. Staff gathered to offer their congratulations and clap him back into his office in No. 12, where Brown had chosen to set up his new camp.

As staff sat at chairs around the horseshoe pattern of desks, a pattern he had borrowed from Mayor Bloomberg of New York, the relief was palpable. O'Donnell had organised some champagne and spoke generously in praise of Brown's great achievement.[134] He regarded the crisis as the most serious of his entire period as Cabinet Secretary: 'The G20 in London could easily have fallen apart in acrimony,' he said.[135]

The good humour was never going to last. O'Donnell found himself often in the position of having to say 'no' to Brown. Damian McBride was a particular worry, a former Treasury civil servant and close ally of Brown and Balls, who was appointed by them as Head of Political Communications at No. 10. Disquiet about him had reached a high point in the summer of 2008, above all with his briefing against David Miliband, the Foreign Secretary and Alistair Darling. O'Donnell had known McBride at the Treasury and had witnessed first-hand how he operated there. As a result, he had cautioned Brown about appointing him to No. 10.[136] His premonitions were not misplaced, so O'Donnell told Brown that he thought McBride unsuitable for Downing Street and that he needed to move on. Brown told Cabinet that he would move him away from frontline duty. But he refused to release him from No. 10.[137]

O'Donnell became increasingly dismayed in the months that followed about Brown's inability to run a stable Cabinet team, a core responsibility of the Cabinet Secretary. In the spring of 2009, he proposed to him that Brown appoint an experienced Deputy Prime Minister to provide cohesion at the centre of government. Peter Mandelson emerged as a suitable figure.[138] Brown accepted the counter-intuitive idea. When the appointment was announced in June 2009, it caused a sensation, given Brown and Mandelson's long history of bitter rivalry. But Mandelson was an experienced operator and respected by his civil servants: he knew how to make the Cabinet Office and Whitehall work for a Prime Minister. The improbable marriage strengthened Brown for a while, and Mandelson served him loyally: but it was clearly only an interim solution.

Brown's aggressive and erratic behaviour to his staff became a matter of public discussion, into which O'Donnell was dragged, when, in early 2010, the journalist Andrew Rawnsley published his book *The End of the Party: The Rise and Fall of New Labour*. When serialisation began in *The Observer*, all hell was let loose. To their discomfort, Rawnsley included among his named sources both O'Donnell and Heywood. Gordon and Sarah Brown felt betrayed by O'Donnell, whom they believed had been one of the sources behind Rawnsley's claims that Brown had bullied staff and that he had warned Brown about mistreatment. 'Surprising, to say the least,' was how Sarah Brown described O'Donnell's allegations.[139]

Brown's flat denial that O'Donnell had given him a warning about his conduct to staff placed the Cabinet Office in a dilemma: it could deny what had happened, or it could admit O'Donnell had spoken to Brown. But doing so would, as Rawnsley said, be to 'call the Prime Minister a liar', risking 'igniting a constitutional crisis'.[140] The Cabinet Office came up with a formulation: O'Donnell, it said, had held a conversation with Brown about how to achieve the 'best from his staff'. So close to the general election, the episode led to a deterioration of O'Donnell's relationship with Brown, from which it never recovered. The final breach came during the talks, following the general election on 6 May 2010, over a coalition. Brown believed that O'Donnell betrayed him, and that he conspired to ensure the talks would result in Cameron becoming Prime Minister in partnership with Nick Clegg's Liberal Democrats.[141]

CABINET OFFICE: LOWEST EBB, 1997–2010

What had gone wrong? Labour governments in 1924, 1929, 1945, 1964 and 1974 had arrived suspicious of the Civil Service, including the Cabinet Office, which they believed full of Tory-appointed and sympathising officials. Generally, though, Labour had eventually come to accommodate itself to the Civil Service, and to value its work and advice. But this was New Labour, and its key figures – Blair, Brown, Mandelson, Campbell, Gould and Powell – all saw themselves as leading a modernising 'project' to transform both the country and the Labour Party when Blair became leader in 1994. They were going to apply the same approach to running government, and were not going to bow to, or respect, the experience of Whitehall. The core New Labour text on leadership, Peter Mandelson and Roger Liddle's book *The Blair Revolution* (1996), continued to inspire and inform their thinking long after it was clear that its prescriptions were flawed. Like all fundamentalists, they remained true to their text.[142] Campbell's less-than-flattering running commentaries on the Cabinet Office are scattered throughout his diaries, while Powell still clung to the same belief and views in the book he wrote after it was all over, *The New Machiavelli* (2010).

The New Labour masterminds had little more than contempt for the principal raison d'être of the Cabinet Office, to be the guardian of collective responsibility and Cabinet government. To Powell, 'Cabinet government … if it ever existed, died before Tony Blair went into politics, and it was finally buried under Mrs Thatcher, to whom, ironically, Robin Butler, leader of the mandarin tendency, was both Private Secretary and then Cabinet Secretary.'[143] Thatcher inherited from Callaghan in 1979 a model where collective decision-making was still deeply entrenched. Cabinet government and its conventions remained very much still alive under her, for all her periodic frustrations and attempts to circumvent.[144]

When Blair became Prime Minister in 1997, Cabinet government and collective responsibility took its biggest hit since Lloyd George's coalition government (1918–22). He was not comfortable using Cabinet or committees as decision-making forums, and this knowledge sent shockwaves through the system. Although Cabinet Committees continued to operate and to be valued by ministers, and individual Cabinet Office officials came to be appreciated for their expertise and hard work, Blair's approach meant that, according to Paul Britton, a senior official in the Cabinet Office:

for some years after 1997, the Cabinet Committee system counted for nothing, and that sent a very strong message to the rest of Whitehall. Whitehall took no interest in them, and it made life very difficult for the secretariats in carrying out what ought to be one of their key functions, which is trying to solve inter-departmental disputes, because the secretariats had had little traction.[145]

Blair did not have easy relations with Butler, Wilson or Turnbull, nor did he make full use of O'Donnell, while with Brown, relations hit rock bottom. Blair was frustrated by the lack of power at the centre, and ended up being disappointed (as he was apt to be with people) by the lack of reforming zeal of many of those officials he encountered, with the notable exception of his No. 10 official Jeremy Heywood. Powell, the only other one in the inner circle who had himself been a civil servant, and whose brother Charles also left it prematurely in 1991, was the biggest sceptic of the traditional Civil Service of them all. He later said: 'We wanted successive Cabinet Secretaries to focus on the task of reform, but they kept slipping back into policy-making and crisis management because that is what they had been trained to do and what they found interesting.'[146] The blaming by the Blair team increased steadily over their years in power. But the failure was theirs in not using a system that had worked so well for predecessor regimes in No. 10, as it did again for those that followed after 2010.

The cold war between Blair and Brown damaged the operation of the Cabinet Office in these years. The Treasury, under Brown, was simply not prepared to subject itself to the normal rules of collective discussion and agreement; and Blair always preferred to resolve disputes one to one with Brown rather than using the Cabinet Office machinery. Brown became overlord of much domestic policy in what Hennessy described as 'a bi-stellar administration with policy constellations revolving around the two stars'.[147] Whitehall mandarins realised early on that the intense rivalry between Blair and Brown, that began soon after the 1997 general election, was driving much of how the decision-making was transacted. A reason Blair did not want decisions taken in Cabinet or Cabinet Committees was because the Brownites would oppose his policies on principle, trumpeting any reversal in the press as a defeat for the Prime Minister. On occasions when he was prevailed upon to take weighty decisions to Cabinet, he risked losing, as over joining the single currency.[148] Other times, as in the debate that took place under Prescott's chairing of a Cabinet Committee, Prescott sided with Blair against Brown to allow student fees to go ahead.[149] Blair's team regarded Brown's empire, ruled from the Treasury, as the effective opposition, rather than the Tories under William Hague (1997–2001), Iain Duncan Smith (2001–03) and Michael Howard (2003–05). A culture of briefing and counter-briefing of both camps, imported into Whitehall from the opposition leader's and shadow Chancellor's offices in May 1997, similarly denigrated the work of the Cabinet Office, promoting an atmosphere of mistrust. Targeting of officials, including Butler and Wilson, who were unable to answer back, was all part of the culture, and demeaned the integrity of government and the morale of the Civil Service.

The Blair–Brown war further damaged the Cabinet Office because it resulted in Blair depositing a series of units within the Cabinet Office to avoid them being placed in the Treasury, often their natural locus, to stop them aggrandising Brown's empire. The Delivery Unit might thus have been more naturally placed in the Treasury, rather than, as it was, within the Cabinet Office. Blair's instinctive response to blocks in his drive for modernisation was to create a new unit: never before in its history had the Cabinet Office become the depository for so many new outfits. Besides the Delivery Unit, the most successful was the Constitution Secretariat, set up in 1997 under Irvine to drive forward the agenda, including devolution, human rights, and House of Lords reform. A Performance and Innovation Unit under Suma Chakrabarti, which evolved into the Strategy Unit in 2002 to look at future policies and challenges on similar lines to the CPRS, had some value. After the 2001 general election, Blair set up the Office of Public Sector Reform as he had lost confidence in the Cabinet Office to drive reform in the Civil Service. Like so many of the units, directorates and initiatives piled onto the centre, with insufficient thought, and born of a lack of trust for existing Whitehall procedures, it achieved little or nothing. The staff who worked in these operations were often dedicated and capable. But they owed little allegiance to their temporary landlord, the Cabinet Office, whose cohesion and coherence were in danger of being lost in these thirteen years.

The Delivery Unit was very much Blair's baby. Blair had been impressed by the work of Michael Barber, who had worked with Blunkett in education since 1997, and decided to import his delivery-focused methodology wholesale, but broadening its application to health and crime, asylum, transport and a small number of other areas. Barber came across to head up the new unit. Blair told him he wanted reform to be more radical, more comprehensive, employing Barber's catchphrase 'a week is a long time in politics, but four years is a very short time'.[150] The unit organised 'stock-takes' at No. 10, usually on Tuesday mornings so the four departments (Home Office, Education, Health, and Transport) could have Blair's personal attention, focusing on achievement of policy objectives. In July 2001, Blair invited the heads of all four departments to a special lunch at No. 10, telling them: 'You guys will stay in these departments for the rest of this Parliament. You have got my assurance because I want you to be there.'[151] But within two years, all had gone, for different reasons.

Blair and Brown's government achieved more than their detractors maintain, with progress in Northern Ireland, to which both Prime Ministers made seminal contributions, their most important contribution. Dismissing them out of hand, and the three major landslides they achieved, is too easy. The real question is to ask how much more could have been achieved if they had come to power in 1997 not with hostility, but respect for the Cabinet Office and the conventions it upheld for eighty years? The advantages the governments possessed, including massive majorities and a strong economy, were greater than for any other in the 100 years studied in this book. How many mistakes would have been avoided, how much bitterness avoided, how much money saved, and how many lives spared?

The Cabinet Office was bloodied and more than a little bowed by the time the New Labour storm subsided. The inconclusive general election in May 2010 threw a new challenge at it: coalition. Would it cope? Could it cope?

GUS O'DONNELL,
PHOTOGRAPHED IN 2005

JEREMY HEYWOOD, ENTERING
DOWNING STREET IN 2015

CHAPTER 10

Coalition and Beyond, 2010–16

T HE SIX YEARS leading up to the centenary in December 2016 saw an unusually high number of challenges for the Cabinet Office: the first peacetime coalition government since the inter-war years; no less than three referendums to oversee, in 2012, 2014 and 2016; a swift and unexpected change of Prime Minister in summer 2016; the planning for Britain's exit from the EU (mirroring its role in preparing for entry forty-five years before); the breakaway of the headship of the Civil Service from the post of Cabinet Secretary in 2012 (for the first time in thirty-one years) and the reinstitution of the joint command in 2014; and a historically significant drive for modernisation across the Civil Service, driven strongly by the Cabinet Office, with a new focus on digitalisation, commercial skills, efficiency and transparency; and the creation of the National Security Council (NSC). The NSC is one of the most significant administrative innovations of the last 100 years, echoing the Committee of Imperial Defence, out of which the War Cabinet grew. These very years were significant for another reason too: they saw a resurgence of the Cabinet Office and a sense of cohesion and collective purpose for the Civil Service under Gus O'Donnell and then Jeremy Heywood.

O'DONNELL AND THE COALITION GOVERNMENT

Rarely had any of the eleven Cabinet Secretaries faced a more delicate task over the 100 years than that presented to O'Donnell on the morning following the inconclusive general election on 7 May 2010. In the preceding months, O'Donnell sought the advice of Britain's leading constitutional authorities, including Vernon Bogdanor, Robert Hazell and Peter Riddell, concluding that, if there was no majority in the general election, the Prime Minister should not resign immediately, but was entitled to stay to see if he could form an administration.[1] During the weeks of the campaign, O'Donnell worked with his team in the Cabinet Office preparing for various scenarios after the election. The outcome that emerged – the Conservatives short of a majority and Labour second – meant neither was able to form a government on their own without the Liberal Democrats. To ensure workable parliamentary arithmetic, Labour needed some sort of arrangement with the other parties, while the Conservatives had the simpler task of a pact with just the Liberal Democrats. The focus turned to this latter option which had been number four of the scenarios played out pre-election. With gallows' humour, O'Donnell recounted how 'the good news is that we had therefore role-played it. The bad news is that we did not actually succeed in coming to a conclusion.'[2]

Acutely aware of the precarious state of the nation's finances and economic and financial turmoil in the Eurozone that coincided with the weekend after the UK election, O'Donnell was keen for the period of uncertainty to be kept as short as possible: the average time for European countries to form a coalition was over forty days, and anything this protracted risked uncertainty in the financial markets. O'Donnell assigned a top official to each of the parties. Heywood was chosen for Brown as he could manage Brown's dual roles as Prime Minister and leader of one of the parties trying to establish a coalition. O'Donnell stayed above this process so he could be ready to work with whichever coalition emerged.[3] O'Donnell wanted to ensure that the Conservative–Lib Dem and Labour–Lib Dem talks had equal access to key facts, so he offered them briefings from the Joint Intelligence Committee (JIC) and the Governor of the Bank of England, Mervyn King.

A trio of top officials – Christopher Geidt, the Queen's Private Secretary, Heywood at No. 10, and O'Donnell – were in constant conversation as the discussions between the political parties continued. O'Donnell reminded the parties in the talks at the Cabinet Office of 'the seriousness of the economic environment' and the fragile state of the markets.[4] When it became clear the Lib Dems were not going to form a coalition with Labour, some still feared Brown might unilaterally resign as Prime Minister before the Conservatives and Lib Dems had actually agreed to form a new government. 'How long is this all going to take?' he asked, urging them on. 'I've got a very unhappy Prime Minister in Downing Street who is desperate to resign.' He told the Lib Dem team: 'I really don't think I can hold onto [Brown] any longer, but I don't want him going until I know we can advise the Queen that we have got an alternative government!'[5] Lib Dem leader Nick Clegg understood the pressures: 'There has to be an agreement today,' he told his team at midday on Tuesday 11 May, reminding them: 'As soon as I tell Brown that a deal with Labour is off, he may go to the Palace to resign.'[6]

O'Donnell later reflected how 'ex post, everyone kind of takes [the coalition formation] for granted, but during those five days it was very unclear how it would work'.[7] During those see-saw days, O'Donnell and his fellow officials were constantly aware of their primary job, to ensure Britain had a government capable of functioning. Relief was great when, by 7.30 p.m., after 'another marathon five and a half hours of negotiations', a preliminary agreement was struck. Cameron left to see the Queen to accept her invitation to form a government, returning to Downing Street at 8.40 p.m.[8] When, much later that evening, an exhausted Cabinet Secretary eventually left for his home, O'Donnell felt he was the most relieved man in Britain.

O'Donnell knew, though, that Cameron and Clegg had now to crunch through a host of detailed decisions that might take several weeks of bartering. 'I was really amazed by how mature both sides were, and there were no real bust ups … government formation was a lot less problematic than I had imagined,' he said.[9] From the outset, he understood the factor that would become the key to the coalition's success over the following five years: 'I thought there would only be one thing that would help the coalition, and there would only be one thing that would break it up, and that would be the closeness of the Cameron–Clegg relationship.'[10] The shared determination of the two leaders to arrive at solutions produced speedy decisions on a whole range of fraught matters, such as which shadow ministers Cameron was to disappoint when their expected Cabinet posts went, in lieu, to Lib Dem ministers. The chairs of the key Cabinet Committees equally were decided at pace, as were the policies that were to go into the 'Coalition Agreement', including some radical initiatives, giving the lie to those who predicted the coalition government would be cautious. The flip side was that various policies went into the agreement, including reforms to the NHS, which had been less thoroughly considered, and which were to cause considerable difficulties down the line.

O'Donnell noticed how both party leaders were secretly relieved by the opportunity coalition provided for them to drop policies they disliked.[11] O'Donnell crunched through swathes of decisions with Clegg and his senior colleagues, including where the new DPM should be based (in the Cabinet Office), and how many staff they should have now they were in government. Not many, if you were a Lib Dem. In Nick Clegg's new memoirs, he says:

> My mistake ... was to accept the model presented to me ... I simply didn't see the need to surround myself with teams of officials ... The most unforgiving consequence was the tsunami of paperwork ... I was asked my opinion on things I didn't have the remotest clue about – dense, technical issues.[12]

However, Clegg worked well with his Civil Service support and found it fair-handed. Anticipating the honeymoon between the Conservatives and Lib Dems would not last into the months ahead, working closely with Oliver Letwin, Cameron's political 'fixer', O'Donnell helped devise a 'Coalition Committee' to meet weekly and more, as needed, to resolve disputes. As it transpired, it rarely met.[13] Cameron impressed O'Donnell from the start, as he did other civil servants, with his calm, decisiveness and charm: 'You could see that David Cameron was someone used to managing,' O'Donnell said.[14]

Cabinet under the coalition naturally operated differently, with Conservative and Liberal Democrat ministers around the table. The rhythm was largely unchanged, though, with meetings lasting about ninety minutes, discussing parliamentary affairs, two or three domestic topics and then a foreign policy topic. It met slightly less often than it had under Brown, though roughly in line with the precedent set by Blair. There were thirty-eight meetings of Cabinet in 2011, thirty-four in 2013 and thirty-eight in 2014. Cameron's final full year as Prime Minister – 2015 – would see the Conservatives win the general election and become a single-party government. There were thirty-four Cabinet meetings that year. [15]

Even under the unusual circumstances of coalition, difficult issues were almost never brought to Cabinet. Decisions were more usually made at the weekly PM/DPM bilateral or in the 'Quad'. The main purpose of Cabinet was to keep the members of the government informed about major decisions and announcements. Sometimes, the stresses of coalition created tension in Cabinet itself, as during the referendum campaign over the voting system in May 2011, when the two parties found themselves largely on opposing sides, with sharp exchanges in the Cabinet Room. This culminated in a Cabinet meeting on 3 May when Lib Dem Energy Secretary Chris Huhne reportedly shouted at Cameron: 'I wanted to know if you disassociate yourself from these leaflets smearing Nick [Clegg].' Osborne, who was mostly in Huhne's sights, replied: 'I am not going to be challenged by a Cabinet colleague acting like he is Jeremy Paxman on *Newsnight*.'[16] But such incidents were rare.

Heywood had been half expecting to go to the Treasury after the general election as Permanent Secretary to replace Nicholas Macpherson. Eager to bring in fresh blood, the new Chancellor George Osborne indicated that this was his intention. O'Donnell recognised that Heywood, as someone clearly destined for the top, had yet to gain experience as a Permanent Secretary outside the rarefied environment of No. 10, and saw the sense in his returning to run the Treasury, if there were to be a vacancy, sharing the same trajectory as Turnbull from Treasury Permanent Secretary to Cabinet Secretary. Shortly after becoming Chancellor, Osborne and his influential Chief of Staff Rupert Harrison, however, saw Macpherson's worth and decided to keep him on. Cameron also rapidly realised that Heywood was not the kind of official he should be losing, and asked him to stay.[17] The plan was quietly shelved.

O'Donnell worked closely with Heywood on his first major policy of the new government. The Treasury was focused on correcting the deficit quickly. 'There might well have been an element of reassertion of Treasury orthodoxy,' pondered O'Donnell. 'They were desperate to cut the deficit and frankly they needed to be restrained. A number of us took the view they needed to cut on a much slower path.'[18] O'Donnell was thus pleased that Osborne's emergency Budget of 22 June struck a less severe balance between austerity and continuity than once contemplated.

However, within a few months O'Donnell was worrying again about whether the pace of deficit reduction was too quick. He took some flak for a paper written by the Cabinet Office's Chief Economist, Jonathan Portes, shortly before he departed in February 2011, suggesting that the government move to 'Plan B', i.e. from austerity to a more gradualist approach to stimulate the economy, which was reported in the press.[19] 'Gus was ... wobbly on [sticking with Plan A alone] ... though he was nothing like such a massive advocate of change as Jonathan,' recalled a senior Treasury official. 'It really wasn't a good thing for Gus to propose at the time. It implied that he was not wholly signed up to the government's strategy,' said one of Cameron's team.[20] O'Donnell was all too easily painted by Conservative economic hardliners as anti-austerity, and as sympathetic to Labour's policies. Steve Hilton, strongly Thatcherite on economic policy, was a particular adviser in No. 10 with whom he differed. O'Donnell also became concerned that the ambitious programme on which the government had embarked lacked the staff with the experience to drive it through, so pared back had Downing Street become.[21] He regularly asked Cameron whether he was fully aware of the implications of the proposed NHS and welfare policies. Having asked them to consider the consequences, he saw it as his job to ensure that the government's manifesto commitments were then delivered, 'because that's the way it should be in a democracy', he said.[22] It was a mark of O'Donnell's ability that he retained the trust of Conservatives throughout his period in office, alongside the trust and respect he had gained from the Lib Dems. Without this core quality of trust and goodwill, the operation of the coalition would have been more fraught.

O'Donnell never questioned that, even with the pressures and novelties of the new coalition arrangement, he would continue to bestride both the Cabinet Secretary and Civil Service Headship roles. In 2010, the word 'Home' was dropped from his title: he was now 'Head of the Civil Service', in part to emphasise that the government served all quarters of the UK, though the FCO retained its separate jurisdiction. To O'Donnell's mind, close advice on policy to both the Prime Minister and now the Deputy

Prime Minister lay at the heart of the Cabinet Secretary job. Beyond that, he believed in the necessity of serving the Cabinet at large, ensuring effective coordination and planning across ministers and departments. The job of coordinating the government's preparations for military conflict remained key to the Cabinet Office, though the creation of the National Security Adviser post in 2010 relieved him personally of direct day-to-day responsibility. Crisis management remained a core preoccupation of the job, with the riots in London and other cities in the summer of 2011 the most serious concern in his years. He recounted voices being raised, prophesying: '"The whole of society is going to break down", and demanding dramatic changes that I didn't think were necessary.'[23] One of the qualities he most admired in Cameron was his sangfroid and his ability to take decisions, even in the most trying circumstances: 'he didn't take the kneejerk response. He settled back [and] looked at the facts.'[24]

The NSC, which first met on the day after David Cameron became Prime Minister, was in fact the second main organisational innovation of the O'Donnell years. It drew on the experience of the other main innovation of his time, the National Economic Council (NEC), also made up unusually of ministers and officials, which Brown had used to steer economic policy after the financial crisis, providing him with a lever he no longer had after he ceased being Chancellor.[25] The NSC itself had a long pedigree. In 1963, the Defence and Overseas Policy Committee of Cabinet took over the work of the old CID and, in 2007, Brown replaced it with the 'Ministerial Committee on National Security, International Relations and Development' (NSID), absorbing the committee additionally that Blair had set up on security and terrorism.[26] Pressure to create the NSC had come from a number of quarters, including the Conservative Party – which had produced a policy paper about it in 2006, written by former JIC chair Pauline Neville-Jones.[27]

The NSC was a fresh departure, not only because it had its own sophisticated bureaucracy in the Cabinet Office, but also, as O'Donnell put it, 'around that table are not only the senior ministers and officials, but the experts – the heads of the agencies, heads of the armed forces'. He was struck by how quickly Cameron came to rely upon the arrangement: 'He used to say what he really liked was having all the experts lay out what they knew, the evidence, and be cross-questioned, and then the politicians have the discussion about, "OK, in the light of all of that, we've heard all this advice, what are we going to decide? ... How do we present it? ... Where do we go next? What are the things we want these officials to go off and find out more about?"[28] Another novelty was the creation of a National Security Adviser (NSA) post, initially filled by Peter Ricketts (2010–12) and then by Kim Darroch (2012–15). The traditional responsibility for overseeing war, defence and intelligence was transferred from the Cabinet Secretary to the NSA, who became one of the highest-ranking diplomats in Whitehall. The arrangement was akin to that of 1938–45, with Ismay in charge of the defence and foreign side of the Cabinet Office's work, and Bridges in overall charge, directly overseeing the civil side, albeit that the NSA worked to the Cabinet Secretary.

O'Donnell strove to devote quality time to the Civil Service, trying to ensure government was more than just the sum of its parts: 'It was very much about getting the top officials together,' he said.[29] He was swayed by the arguments of two of his officials, Gill Rider, whom he had appointed from Accenture, and Siobhan Benita, whom he brought into the Cabinet Office to enhance strategy and communications, to do more to break down barriers between departments. He thus established the 'Top 200' group (in reality, consisting of about 150 officials), with regular meetings away from departments to forge closer understandings and relationships.[30] Against a background of negative briefing about civil servants, and popular television satires like *The Thick of It* (2007–12), which gave a jaundiced view of officials and politicians, he wanted to move onto the front foot. Fellow officials, too, were anxious to show that civil servants were not all white, male and Oxbridge (which, as he admitted, could be a challenge, as he was guilty on all three counts). Under Brown, he had given the first live broadcast by a Cabinet Secretary on the BBC's *Politics Show* in July 2009, following it up with a number of public appearances, where recurrent themes were that officials should not be scared to be passionate about delivering good public services, in particular the duty of caring for the disadvantaged.

In October 2010, O'Donnell launched the Cabinet Manual, laying out the laws, rules and conventions for government in the UK. He also oversaw the establishment in the Cabinet Office of the Behavioural Insights Team under David Halpern, popularly known as the 'Nudge Unit', using insights from behavioural science, political theory and economics to try to influence decisions made by individuals or groups, to help achieve government policy objectives.[31] Another innovation proposed by the Cameron government to which O'Donnell lent his personal support was the measurement of 'well-being', at that time a far more contested topic than it became. He agrees with Aristotle that the proper aim of government is maximising the extent to which citizens flourish, and not just by monetary measures of success. From 2010, the Office of National Statistics (ONS) began to measure the nation's hedonic well-being: 'Surely in a democratic society,' he said, part of what government should be concerned about is 'how do people feel? Do they feel overall that their life is worthwhile, do they feel satisfied, are they happy?'[32]

Another task O'Donnell reaffirmed was the responsibility for the Cabinet Office for intelligence and security. The Butler Report in July 2004 had been clear that it needed to come back fully under the Prime Minister's and Cabinet's jurisdiction. Blair, sensitive to the implied criticism, had acted on the recommendation only in part; from 2007, Brown, keen to distance himself from Blair, was only too keen to embrace it. O'Donnell chose Alex Allan, Major's PPS, to take over the post as Chair of the JIC. Allan held the post until he retired at the same time as O'Donnell at the end of 2011, by which time much of the oversight of intelligence had been taken over by the NSA.

O'Donnell intended to go on his sixtieth birthday. David Bell at the Department for Education had fallen foul of Michael Gove and left to become Vice-Chancellor at Reading University. Another, Suna Chakrabarti, at the Ministry of Justice, had little opportunity to impress. That left Heywood as the pre-eminent civil servant in Whitehall; but the fact that he had never run a Whitehall department posed a problem. Cameron and Francis Maude, the minister responsible for the Civil Service, wanted Heywood to become Cabinet Secretary, and for a businessman to come in to run the Civil Service. O'Donnell thought that Heywood, his lack of experience of senior command notwithstanding, should combine both jobs. He believed strongly that the job should not be split, as the constant contact between Cabinet Secretary and Prime Minister allowed them to talk about the running of the executive, including appointments, and the pay and conditions for civil servants. But they overruled him.[33] The headship job thus went to Bob Kerslake, not a businessman, but an experienced manager who had risen to be the leading local government chief executive of his generation before being appointed Permanent Secretary of the

Department for Communities and Local Government in 2010. In addition to becoming Head of the Civil Service, he wanted to continue as Permanent Secretary, which made for difficulties from the outset. Kerslake, as predicted, found access to Cameron difficult and soon, problems mounted.

JEREMY HEYWOOD (2012 – PRESENT)

Jeremy Heywood was born on the last day of 1961, and was brought up in York. His father, Peter, a school teacher of English, was renowned for his dedication, humility and ability to inspire a love of literature in his pupils.[34] Heywood was educated at Bootham, a Quaker independent school in York, where his father taught, before gaining a place at Hertford College, Oxford to read History and Economics, where he took a First. He joined the Civil Service at the age of twenty-one, starting at the Health and Safety Executive before moving quickly to the Treasury, where his first boss was none other than Gus O'Donnell. After a stellar decade, he was appointed at the age of thirty as Principal Private Secretary (1991–94) to Chancellor Norman Lamont. He made an immediate impression as the possessor of a brilliant and creative mind. As well as leading a significant review of the struture of the Treasury, in the spring of 1992, he proposed a new 20p income tax band for the first £2,000 of taxable income to benefit four million people on low incomes – a plan willingly embraced by Major as Prime Minister.[35] Heywood was to be a vital source of strength to Lamont as he reconfigured economic policy in the wake of Black Wednesday, remaining as PPS to Kenneth Clarke, who succeeded Lamont after he was dismissed by Major in May 1993.

So quickly did he impress the new Labour masters after the May 1997 election that, just two years later, he was appointed PPS to Blair in June 1999, a position where he gained the full trust of an official-wary Prime Minister's team, and in which he served an unusually long time, until December 2003. Like some incumbents of the PPS job before him, including Jock Colville (1951–55) and Tim Bligh (1959–64), he opted to leave the Civil Service for the private sector, joining investment bank Morgan Stanley in March 2004 as Managing Director of their Investment Banking Division. Ed Balls and Gordon Brown persuaded him to return to the Civil Service, becoming Permanent Secretary for Domestic Policy in the Cabinet Office in mid-2007 and then Permanent

Secretary of No. 10 in January 2008. From that position he supported Gordon
Brown through the worst financial and economics crisis since the war, using
the full range of skills and knowledge he had aquired in a career spanning the
Treasury, the IMF and the banking sector. Heywood nominated as his successor another brilliant Treasury official in his own mould, Chris Martin, who
reverted to a more traditional PPS role. Martin died of cancer in November
2015, at the age of forty-two, a heavy loss that was felt keenly by colleagues in
No. 10, the Cabinet Office and all across Whitehall.

Few civil servants since Brook so skilfully managed the transition in
October 1951 from Labour to the Conservatives, have been as much relied
upon by Labour and Conservative administrations as Heywood. Labour
insider Andrew Adonis captured the essence of Heywood's skill:

> He is by some margin the most talented and effective civil servant I have
> worked with … He makes change happen, while giving good and frank
> advice on how best to do it and indeed whether to do it all. He defines the
> concept of the professional civil servant – free of political bias yet utterly
> dedicated to helping the elected government implement its programme.
> Without Jeremy Heywood, Tony Blair's No. 10 operation would have been
> severely weakened and Gordon Brown's would have been highly precarious.[36]

Two of his attributes, shared by many of his predecessors, are formidable
hard work, which means he comes to every meeting briefed to his fingertips,
and his ability to provide creative solutions to the myriad of problems crossing his desk. The Cabinet Secretary job was the one Heywood was made for:

> I was very clear, however, that I didn't regard myself as qualified to be
> Head of the Civil Service. I had no experience running a large depart-
> ment, no operational record beyond running a small No. 10 and a division
> at Morgan Stanley … I felt whilst I could plausibly take the role of being
> Cabinet Secretary, I didn't believe I could take up the role of being Cab-
> inet secretary and Head of the Civil Service.[37]

He relayed these views when he talked succession arrangements over with
O'Donnell in 2011:

I was very keen, if I was to be considered for that role [Cabinet Secretary], to leave enough bandwidth to do it, and in my mind that involves being very close to the Prime Minister, the Prime Minister's team, having sufficient time to be on top of the issues, to be able to make a genuine, value-adding contribution to the policy advice. If you are going to do all that it's very difficult to be Head of the Civil Service as well.[38]

Central to the role of Cabinet Secretary, as Heywood has performed it, is to be the Prime Minister's chief Civil Service policy adviser and fixer, while balancing that with being the adviser to the Cabinet as a whole, and the custodian of the Cabinet system: this is what he describes as 'the core of the job'.[39] As all his predecessors, he sits at the right hand of the Prime Minister at Cabinet meetings, recording the minutes much as Hankey did 100 years before: 'Every now and again the Prime Minister wags his finger and says, "That should be in the minutes, Cabinet Secretary," so we take particular notice at that point, and make sure that then this is followed through.'[40] Heywood's work was helped considerably by Chris Martin being only too happy to allow him to have his continuing close role inside No. 10. The relationship between the two was close, secure and trusting: chemistry and goodwill, as ever, are all important at the centre of government, as we have seen throughout these pages.

Having successfully served a Prime Minister as their PPS (or indeed Permanent Secretary) does not always guarantee a harmonious relationship if the incumbent is promoted to their Cabinet Secretary, as Butler found with Thatcher. But with Heywood and Cameron, the formula worked. The eighteen months working with Cameron from May 2010 to December 2011 allowed him valuable insight into personalities and issues. Indeed, Cameron 'never stopped regarding me as his senior Civil Service adviser' as he said.[41] That was what he wanted from his Cabinet Secretary.

Like O'Donnell, Heywood regarded Cameron as a highly proficient Prime Minister, effective in chairing meetings and explaining policy to the media and in Parliament. Calm in a crisis, Cameron focused on the big issues where he could nail his own colours to the mast, notably investing great effort in ensuring the coalition with the Lib Dems worked. While Heywood strongly recognised the vital importance of maintaining close relations between No. 10

and No. 11, and the importance of sticking with 'Plan A' on the fiscal defecit plan, both he and Cameron agreed that more could be done to stimulate credit, out of which came the 'Help to Buy Scheme', an early version of which started life in the No. 10 Policy Unit.[42]

Heywood also focused on ensuring Civil Service support to the whole ministerial team, working across Whitehall on issues from immigration and defence to education and healthcare reform. Examples would be the close interest he took in defence efficiency reviews, which were a critical part of the government's fiscal as well as military planning, or his role in driving policy on extremism.

Overseeing crises continued to be a major preoccupation of Heywood's job, as it had for his predecessors as Cabinet Secretary. He defined the difference between a peripheral and a major crisis thus: '[A major crisis] survives more than one news cycle … You gain a sense over time as to whether an issue is developing into an even bigger problem or can be managed down. It's a team effort,' he said.[43] Heywood's first five years found him having to pick a way through a number of delicate issues involving ministers, few more fraught than Andrew Mitchell and the 'Plebgate affair' in September 2012, which was sparked by an altercation at the gates of Downing Street. Heywood's term also coincided with the completion of the seven-year inquiry under John Chilcot into the Iraq War. Periodically accused in the media of obfuscation or even 'cover-up', Heywood rather gave instructions for the declassification of a significant number of documents to try to uncover the truth, including JIC papers, full records of Cabinet meetings and conversations between Blair and President George W. Bush, and thirty-one personal memos between them.

The creation of the NSC in 2010 meant he managed foreign or defence issues in a different way than any of his ten predecessors, while intelligence had long ceased to be a major executive function of the Cabinet Secretary, a change he dated back to Robert Armstrong.[44] Europe was another major area where he, in common with his predecessors, could delegate to the Cabinet Office's European and Global Issues Secretariat. However, in the run-up to the EU referendum in June 2016 and, even more so, after the result, EU issues inevitably took up more and more of his time.

By 2013, the second year of the split of the jobs between Heywood and

Kerslake, it was becoming apparent that the arrangement was not fulfilling initial aspirations. Kerslake was finding it difficult to run his major department (Communities and Local Government) as Permanent Secretary away from the centre while also taking charge of twenty-seven Permanent Secretaries and three Directors-General. A new urgency and hunger for reforming the Civil Service was also manifesting itself from the government. Francis Maude, in his capacity as Minister for the Cabinet Office responsible for Civil Service efficiency, reform, and transparency, had worked up a powerful efficiency agenda, which he thought was being insufficiently driven forward from the top, i.e. from Kerslake. Maude presented to Cabinet the Civil Service Reform Plan that Kerslake and Heywood had worked up in June 2012, which included a new performance management system, enhanced ICT across departments, and a new regime for delivering major projects. In mid-2013, he produced his 'One Year On' document, setting out the successes and failures so far, making it clear that the pace needed to be quickened. He was also coming under pressure from Cabinet colleagues to drive the reform agenda more quickly. A realisation grew among ministers, as well as Permanent Secretaries, that the reforms needed a figure leading the drive at the centre who had the ear of the Prime Minister, and who was not running a department, if they were to be successful. Heywood held out for several months against a change at the top, but by mid-2014 had come to see that the arrangement was not sustainable. He had grown in confidence and experience, too, over his two years as Cabinet Secretary, and the body of Permanent Secretaries had come to know him, and to grow increasingly comfortable with the prospect of being managed by him.

Cameron took the decision that the headship position should be reconstituted from July 2014, with Heywood remaining as Cabinet Secretary but becoming Head of the Civil Service, Kerslake to quit and a new central figure coming in from outside. This post was to be known as 'chief executive', responsible for improving the effectiveness and efficiency of the Civil Service, and working alongside Permanent Secretaries across government to institute reform. Potential concern from mandarins across Whitehall about the idea of bringing in a chief executive, albeit subordinate to the Head of the Civil Service, quietly dissipated as Heywood swung behind the proposition, and a major external competition was held in 2014 for heavyweight executives from across the private and public sectors. The position was awarded to John Manzoni, an executive at BP until he joined an oil and gas company, Talisman Energy, as chief executive in 2007. In February 2014, Manzoni had joined the Civil Service as chief executive for the Major Projects Authority, under the remit of the Cabinet Office. The fact that Manzoni was already known within Whitehall, combined with his experience of leadership in large organisations, made him the stand-out candidate. In July, Kerslake stood down and Heywood replaced him as Head of the Civil Service, with Manzoni joining as chief executive that October.

The new title took Heywood more into the public eye. The job of Cabinet Secretary, as he saw it, was one that 'faces inwards to the politicians and Cabinet',[45] whereas the Head of the Civil Service had to lead and inspire officials at the centre and across the country, and to look after their interests, which demanded more of a public-facing role. Following O'Donnell's lead, Heywood gave a talk in September 2015 at the Institute for Government, in which he sought to demystify his new joint job of Cabinet Secretary and Head of the Civil Service, arguing that the evolution of the role had depended much more upon circumstances, and the tastes and preferences of the Prime Minister of the day, than on the personality of the Cabinet Secretary himself. He described being Secretary to Cabinet as 'the one irreducible task': he prepares the agenda each week, oversees the production of minutes, as well as the eighteen Cabinet Committees.[46] Advising the Prime Minister, he explained, involves 'everything that is important, that is on the Prime Minister's mind and is No. 10's concern, where a senior Civil Service voice is needed', ranging from changes to the machinery of government, to cross-cutting policy areas such as immigration.[47] Propriety and ethics, i.e. the conduct of both ministers and officials, has always been a central preoccupation of the role, as is examining complaints about ministers and conducting enquiries into leaks. One particularly sensitive investigation required Heywood to look into the leak of a memorandum purporting to reflect the views of the Scottish First Minister about the 2015 election outcome. Running an inquiry into the conduct of the Secretary of State for Scotland and his advisers during a fiercely contested election campaign was a particularly delicate task even for the Cabinet Secretary.

Overseeing the implementation of government policies and manifesto commitments, Heywood said, is clearly a core task for the Cabinet Secretary and Head of the Civil Service. The latter is leading a team of 440,000 people (in 2016). Recruitment and management for his team of Permanent Secretaries, delivering their feedback and appraisals, which Heywood has prioritised and strengthened, is a major part of his time. He reflected on how 'I spend a lot of my time on people management: recruiting people, motivating people, hearing their feedback, giving them feedback … making sure they're happy, making sure they understand how their performance could be improved': indeed, he estimated up to a third of his time at certain times of the year could be taken on personnel management.[48] Heywood also built on his predecessor's establishment of a Civil Service Board, focusing it on a small number of top-priority issues: diversity in the organisation, talent management, as well as growing commercial and digital capacity. The modern role of Head of the Civil Service inolves much more than senior appointments and chairing meetings: suporting 'Civil Service Live', an annual series of gatherings of civil servants, and promoting Civil Service awards and work acriss the country are cental tasks. The final two areas he listed were to help make the Civil Service officials 'the most innovative thinkers about public policy anywhere in the world' – with more use of the 'nudge' team and a focus on better use of data – and representing the Civil Service externally – 'a much bigger part of the job than I realised, but it is an important part'.[49] A chart accompanied his talk, which summarises the approximate time he spends on each of his various functions, policy taking the most time with 28 per cent, followed by 25 per cent on managing the Civil Service, down to just 1 per cent appearing before Parliamentary Select Committees.[50]

Only someone capable of immensely hard and relentless work could oversee such an Everest of a job. Heywood's day begins at 6.30 a.m., clearing overnight messages on his two BlackBerries, before leaving home at 7.30 a.m. and arriving at Downing Street or 70 Whitehall by 8 a.m. By this time, he will be on top of the news agenda and pressing issues for the day. He then usually attends a morning meeting with the Prime Minister. Heywood's week has a regular rhythm, with Cabinet at No. 10 on Tuesday morning, lasting an hour and a half, and with that evening devoted to the minutes. On Wednesdays, the Permanent Secretaries come for a meeting at the Cabinet Office, while the Prime Minister is preparing next door for Prime Minister's Questions.

Heywood has been struck by how much variety he experienced in his first five years as Cabinet Secretary. Initially, he was very focused on delivering coalition policy and helping the coalition resolve its difficulties.

O'Donnell deserves credit for helping set up the coalition and guiding it through its first eighteen months, and Heywood was critical thereafter in ensuring the coalition held together, not a foregone conclusion, for the following forty-two months. He regularly attended the Monday morning bilateral meetings between Cameron and Clegg, with no formal agenda, which was the crucial nexus, brokering difficult issues within the coalition. Heywood's particular role was to help provide creative solutions to seemingly intractable problems acceptable to both sides, such as over the Leveson Inquiry, counter-terrorism legislation or energy policy.

Heywood was a regular attendee too at the 'Quad', the body that emerged in mid-2010 consisting of the four most senior coalition government figures, Cameron, Clegg, Osborne and Chief Secretary to the Treasury, Danny Alexander. This was the key group deliberating over the major financial events, notably the Budgets and Autumn Statements, but which also sometimes met to hammer out agreed ways forward on other thorny issues, including, for example, the Scottish referendum. 'Heywood helped to create the conditions that allowed the government to last five years when the general belief was it wouldn't last the course,' said Philip Rycroft, who served as Director-General of the DPM's office from 2012 to 2015.[51]

The Cabinet Secretary is the custodian of collective responsibility. In 2010, O'Donnell had suggested an agreement in the new 'Ministerial Code' that allowed for the doctrine to be laid aside in exceptional circumstances, to allow either Lib Dem or Conservative ministers to express their disagreement with government policy in public. This allowed government to continue, but required very sensitive application. Ministers of course would disagree, which required very close handling of relations between No. 10 and the Deputy Prime Minister's Office, and with the departments. Differences could generally be resolved and formal suspensions of collective responsibility were rare. Never was the oversight of both parties in the coalition more difficult than in the run-up to the 2015 general election, when the Lib Dems were struggling to get their message across, and with Osborne and Clegg becoming increasingly antagonistic from September 2014.[52] Heywood had to be particularly adept at managing the claims by both coalition parties to Civil Service time and expertise in the run-up to the 2015 general election.

The coalition period saw three referendums, on extending the powers of the Welsh Assembly Government in March 2011, on the Alternative Vote on 5 May 2011, and on whether Scotland should remain within the Union on 18 September 2014. For the latter, the Cabinet Office was told categorically by Cameron to do no anticipatory work on the break-up of the United Kingdom, an instruction they observed to the letter, even when, towards the end, the result looked uncertain. The Cabinet Office had to ensure that it was trusted by all in government across the UK, supporting ministers right up until the 28-day purdah period began. Feelings north and south of the border ran very high, and the civil servants came under great pressure. But as a result of the Cabinet Office's efforts, led by Philip Rycroft, Heywood's right-hand man on all matters constitutional, the Civil Service emerged from the very real existential threat to the UK with its reputation for impartiality substantially intact. In the run-up to the 2015 general election, the Cabinet Office engaged in preparatory work in the event of a hung parliament, as in 2010. After the election threw up a clear Conservative majority, Heywood worked for several months with a Conservative-only government, helping it get off to a running start implementing its manifesto commitments and Cameron's 'life chances' agenda, before being swept up in the EU referendum in June 2016, and its aftermath.[53] Planning by the Treasury and Bank of England anticipated the market reaction to the result of the referendum, and the Cabinet Secretary oversaw the publication of a series of papers before the referendum 'purdah' period examining the relationships that non-EU countries had developed with the EU, as well as exploring alternative models, such as the Canadian and the WTO models.

Five years into the job, Heywood is still full of ideas for improving the capability of the Civil Service, including greater capacity to do long-term strategic thinking and horizon-scanning, a role that the Cabinet Office has periodically fulfilled over the years, notably with the CPRS (1971–83). Equally, he wants to be able to test and reassure on how the UK Civil Service compares to its counterparts abroad. A personal priority is also to press ahead to make the Civil Service one of the most diverse and inclusive employers in the country, including at the top level, so that it better represents the modern society it is here to serve.

Theresa May, the nineteenth Prime Minister to be served by the Cabinet Office since December 1916, began her premiership in a blaze of activity, with the Cabinet Office responding to the new challenges of exiting the European Union and changes to the machinery at the centre. A European Union Trade and Exit Committee were established, as well as a Social Reform Committee, covering housing and race, and an Economy and Industrial Strategy Committee to coordinate policy on the economy. These main committees complemented the NSC and the legislation comittees. Hankey would have approved.

* * *

There the story of the first 100 years of the Cabinet Office ends with the 100th anniversary of the first Cabinet meeting on 9 December 2016. If Maurice Hankey was to walk into the Cabinet Office and No. 10 today, he would recognise much – not just the physical spaces, but the tasks being carried out too. Much that fills Jeremy Heywood's day overseeing the running of Cabinet and its committees, taking longhand notes at all Cabinet meetings, advising the Prime Minister and Cabinet ministers, helping to keep the government secure and the country safe, and the rest, would be familiar to him.

The guardians of the constitution have strong constitutions; over half the eleven Cabinet Secretaries are alive to witness the centenary, from Robert Armstrong onwards. Heywood, born on New Year's Eve 1961, has no recollection of seeing his two predecessors, Edward Bridges and Norman Brook, acting as honorary pallbearers at Churchill's funeral on 30 January 1965. But, by a curious quirk, Heywood, the eleventh Cabinet Secretary, was alive for a year before the first Cabinet Secretary, Maurice Hankey, died in January 1963. That means that throughout the whole of 1962, all eleven Cabinet Secretaries were alive at the same point in history.

The book opened with a discussion of Whitehall Palace and the accumulation of government power under the Hanoverians. It ends with a vision of Whitehall Palace, in the Cockpit Theatre nearby, 400 years before 1962. Shakespeare's *As You Like It* was performed there, with its 'seven ages of man' speech. We can imagine a collective portrait of the eleven Cabinet Secretaries, from infant to old age, who have done so much to guide British history over the last century.

Endnotes

INTRODUCTION

1. See Anthony Seldon, 'Ideas Are Not Enough', in David Marquand and Anthony Seldon (eds.), *The Ideas that Shaped Post-War Britain* (London, 1996), pp. 257–89.

CHAPTER 1 (PP. 1–23)

1. R. K. Mosley, *The Story of the Cabinet Office* (London, 1969), p. 1.
2. With thanks to Jeremy Black, No. 10 History Talk, 16 May 2016.
3. Paul Haupt, 'The Etymology of Cabinet', *Journal of the American Oriental Society* 28 (1907), pp. 108–11. See also Douglas Harper, 'Cabinet', 2016 <http://www. etymonline.com/index.php?term=cabinet> [accessed 21 August 2016].
4. Earl of Warrington, *The Works of the Right Honourable Henry Late L. Delamar, and Earl of Warrington* (1694) <https://books.google.co.uk/books?id=_ MIIuvu8vAMC&pg> [accessed 21 August 2016], p. 40.
5. 'Minutes of Cabinet', 17 April 1746, SP 36/83/1/68, National Archives, Kew [hereafter NA].
6. 'Minutes of Cabinet', 24 November 1746, NA SP 36/89/3/45.
7. 'Minutes of Cabinet', 31 March 1747, NA SP 36/95/1/124.
8. Trevor Williams, 'The Cabinet in the Eighteenth Century', *History* 22 (1937), pp. 240–52.
9. Daniel Baugh, *The Global Seven Years War* (London, 2011), pp. 240–41.
10. Williams, 'The Cabinet in the Eighteenth Century', pp. 240–52.
11. Historic Manuscripts Commission, *The Manuscripts of the Earl of Dartmouth* (London, 1887), pp. 372–3. See also Peter Thomas, *Tea Party to Independence: The Third Phase of the American Revolution, 1773–1776* (Oxford, 1991), pp. 178–80.
12. Piers Mackesy, *The War for America, 1775–1783* (Harvard, 1993), p. 13.
13. 'Cabinet Minute', 8 December 1781, GEO/MAIN/4362, Royal Archives, Windsor.
14. 'Cabinet Minute', 30 August 1781, GEO/MAIN/4293, Royal Archives, Windsor.

15. Lord Chancellor Eldon, 'On the State of the Government', GEO/MAIN/19632, Royal Archives, Windsor.

16. Robert Blake, *The Office of Prime Minister* (London, 1975), p. 34.

17. Walter Bagehot, *The English Constitution: New and Revised Edition* (Boston, 1873), p. 35.

18. 'Cabinet Minute', no date, c. June 1812, RA GEO/MAIN/19734, Royal Archives, Windsor.

19. Mosley, *Cabinet Office*, p. 1.

20. Robert Tombs, *The English and their History* (London, 2014), p. 493.

21. 'Government Expenditure, 2016' <http://www.ukpublicspending.co.uk/past_spending> [accessed 21 August 2016].

22. Terence Andrew Jenkins, *Parliament, Party and Politics in Victorian Britain* (London, 1996), p. 37.

23. Plamerston to Gladstone, 14 June 1864, P. Guedalla (ed.) *Gladstone and Palmerston: Being the Correspondence of Lord Palmerston with Mr Gladstone, 1851–1865* (London, 1928), p. 288.

24. Correspondence with DS Brown, 13 September 2016.

25. 'Suez Canal Shares', 18 November 1875, NA CAB 41/6/33.

26. 'Suez Canal Shares', 24 November 1875, NA CAB 41/6/36.

27. 'Defence of Natal', 8 September 1899, NA CAB 41/25/18.

28. 'Transvaal', 29 September 1899, NA CAB 41/25/20

29. Interview with Andrew Roberts, 11 September 2016.

30. Lady Gwendolen Cecil, *Life of Robert Marquis of Salisbury, Vol. 2, 1868–1880* (London, 1921), pp. 223–4, cited in Giles Edwards (ed.), *The Gresham Reader on Cabinet Government* (London, 2004), p. 14.

31. Anthony Seldon, 'The Cabinet System', in Vernon Bogdanor (ed.), *The British Constitution in the Twentieth Century* (London, 2004), pp. 100–105.

32. Ibid., pp. 100–102.

33. Robert Peel, Charles Stuart Parker (ed.), *Sir Robert Peel: From his Private Papers, Vol. 3* (London, 1899), pp. 228–9.

34. H. C. G. Matthew, *Gladstone, 1809–1898* (Oxford, 1997), pp. 235–6.

35. Beatrice Webb, *Our Partnership* (London, 1948), cited in W. H. Greenleaf, *Much Governed Nation: The British Political Tradition, Part Two, Vol. 3* (London, 2003), pp. 697–8.

36. Cited in Greenleaf, *Much Governed Nation*, p. 697.

37. Seldon, 'The Cabinet System', p. 104.

38. Quoted in Cd. 8490, Dardanelles Commission, *First Report*, HMSO (London, 1917), p. 4, cited in Edwards, *Gresham Reader*, p. 17.

39. Maurice Hankey, *Government Control in War* (Cambridge, 1945), p. 32.

40. Thanks to Andrew Roberts for this information. Interview with Andrew Roberts, 30 September 2016.

41. 'Conversation with French Ambassador', 2 August 1914, NA CAB 41/35/23.

42. 'Statement in the House of Commons', 3 August 1914, NA CAB 41/35/24.

43. 'Government Expenditure, 2016' <http://www.ukpublicspending.co.uk/past_spending> accessed [accessed 21 August 2016].

44. Thomas Jones, 'Memorandum: Staffs in Government Departments', 30 August 1919, NA CAB 24/87/65.

45. Edwards, *Gresham Reader*, p. 24.

46. Earl of Oxford and Asquith, *Memories and Reflections 1852–1927, Vol. 2* (London, 1928), pp. 23–4, cited in Edwards, *Gresham Reader*, p. 22.

47. George Cassar, *Asquith as War Leader* (London, 1994), p. 235.

48. Letter, 6 August 1914, in Michael and Eleanor Brock (eds.), *H. H. Asquith, Letters to Venetia Stanley* (Oxford, 1985), p. 158.

49. Letter, 26 February 1915, in *Letters to Venetia Stanley*, p. 449.

50. Winston Churchill, *The World Crisis, 1911–1918* (New York, 2005 [1931]), p. 464.

51. Earl of Ronaldshay, *The Life of Lord Curzon, Vol. 3* (London, 1928), pp. 316–17.

52. See Stephen Roskill, *Hankey: Man of Secrets, Vol. 1, 1877–1918* (Annapolis, 1970), p. 227. Roskill omits the final sentence, which can be found in Hankey's diary in HNKY 1/2, Archives of Lord Hankey, Churchill Archives Centre, Cambridge.

53. Maurice Hankey, *The Supreme Command, 1914–1918* (London, 1961), p. 580.

54. Quoted in Robert K. Massie, *Castles of Steel: Britain, Germany and the Winning of the Great War at Sea* (London, 2005), p. 437.

55. Tim Travers, *Gallipoli* (Stroud, 2003), pp. 30–34.

56. Ibid., p. 42.

57. Ibid.

58. Ibid., p. 46.

59. Hankey, *Government Control in War*, p. 40.

60. Ibid., p. 42.

61. Roskill, *Man of Secrets, Vol. 1*, p. 308.

62. Margot Asquith, *Margot Asquith's Great War Diary 1914–1916: The View from Downing Street* (Oxford, 2014), p. 288.

CHAPTER 2 (PP. 25–39)

1. Cited in John Naylor, *A Man and an Institution: Sir Maurice Hankey, the Cabinet Secretariat and the Custody of the Cabinet Secretary* (Cambridge, 1984), p. 9.

2. Stephen Wentworth Roskill, *Hankey: Man of Secrets, Vol. 1* (Maryland, 1970), p. 329.

3. Edwards, *Gresham Reader*, p. 39.

4. Hankey, *Supreme Command*, p. 589.

5. Ibid., p. 580.

6. Thomas Jones to Eirene Theodora Jones, 12 December 1916, cited in Keith Middlemas (ed.), *Thomas Jones Whitehall Diary, Vol. 1, 1916–1925* (London, 1969), p. 15.

7. Roskill, *Man of Secrets*, p. 329.

8. Andrew Blick and George Jones, *At Power's Elbow* (London, 2013), pp. 125–41.

9. A. J. P. Taylor, *English History, 1914–1945* (Oxford, 1965), p. 74.

10. Interview with Lord Morgan, 1 October 2016.

11. Edwards, *Gresham Reader*, p. 30.

12. 'Principles of the Cabinet system and the work of the Cabinet Secretariat': Broadcast by Lord Hankey, 1946, NA, LCO 2/3215.

13. Famously, the Suffragettes set it on fire in 1913.

14. Roskill, *Man of Secrets*, p. 355.

15. Robert Massie, *Castles of Steel: Britain, Germany and the Winning of the Great War at Sea* (London, 2005), pp. 729–31.

16. 'Immediate measures to be taken regarding the food and shipping problems', 29 March 1917, NA CAB 21/95.

17. Interview with Andrew Roberts, 11 September 2016.

18. Roskill, *Man of Secrets, Vol. 1*, pp. 512–13.

19. Ibid., pp. 370–71

20. Ibid., p. 513. See also Hankey's diary for 1 April 1917 in HNKY 1/3, Archives of Lord Hankey, Churchill Archives Centre, Cambridge.

21. Roskill, *Man of Secrets, Vol. 1*, p. 553

22. Hansard, HL Debs, 19 June 1918, Vol. 30, cc263–6

23. Hansard, HL Debs, 19 June 1918, Vol. 30, cc281–2

24. Hansard, HL Debs, 19 June 1918, Vol. 30, cc282

25. Travis L. Crosby, *The Unknown Lloyd George* (New York, 2014), p. 229.

26. Ibid.

27. 'Cabinet Conclusion', 11 November 1918, NA CAB 23/14/46.

28. 'Sir Maurice Hankey's Speech to the Secretariat of the War Cabinet', 19 November 1918, NA CAB 21/128.

29. Ibid.

30. Roskill, *Man of Secrets, Vol. 1*, pp. 633–4.

31. Hankey, *The Supreme Command*, p. 872.

32. David Lloyd George, Letter, 30 May 1919, NA CAB 63/33, Memoranda etc. prepared for Cabinet.

CHAPTER 3 (PP. 41–71)

1. Ronan Fanning, *Fatal Path: British Government and Irish Revolution 1910–1922* (London, 2013), pp. 171–2.

2. 'Instructions to the Secretary of the Cabinet', 4 November 1919, NA CAB 24/92.

3. Seldon, 'The Cabinet System', pp. 105–6.

4. Ibid., pp. 105–11.

5. Ibid., pp. 107–8.

6. Ibid., p. 108.
7. Letter from Maurice Hankey to Thomas Jones, 11 February 1919, cited in Thomas Jones, *Whitehall Diary*, p. 76.
8. Maurice Hankey, 'Towards a National Policy', July 1919, NA CAB 21/159.
9. Ibid.
10. Letter to Lady Hankey, 25 April 1919, cited in Roskill, *Man of Secrets, Vol. 2*, p. 83.
11. Stephen Roskill, *Hankey: Man of Secrets, Vol. 2, 1919–1931* (Annapolis, 1972), pp. 238–58.
12. Letter to Lady Hankey, 17 November 1921, cited in Roskill, *Man of Secrets, Vol. 2*, p. 242.
13. Letter to Lloyd George, 24 November 1921, cited in Roskill, *Man of Secrets, Vol. 2*, p. 245.
14. Fanning, *Fatal Path*, p. 263.
15. Rodney Lowe, '*Jones, Thomas: Civil Servant and Benefactor*', Irish Archives, 2011 <http://treaty.nationalarchives.ie/the-delegates/> [accessed 22 August 2016].
16. Fanning, *Fatal Path*, p. 310.
17. Ibid., p. 234.
18. Letter to Lady Hankey, 22 June 1922, cited in Roskill, *Man of Secrets, Vol. 2*, p. 265.
19. Roskill, *Man of Secrets, Vol. 2*, pp. 301–2. See also Fanning, *Fatal Path*, pp. 334–5.
20. 'Functions of the Cabinet Secretariat including a Historical Note', 10 September 1944, NA T199/65.
21. Edwards, *Gresham Reader*, pp. 38–40.
22. Earl of Ronaldshay, *The Life of Lord Curzon, Vol. 3* (London, 1928), pp. 316–17, cited in Edwards, *Gresham Reader*, pp. 38–40.
23. 'Cabinet Secretariat: Representation of the Treasury', January 1920, NA CAB 150/3.
24. 'Cabinet Secretariat: Representation of the Treasury', July 1920, NA CAB 150/4.
25. 'Cabinet Meetings: Minutes and Procedure', 1920, NA T 172/1112.
26. Hansard, HC Debs, 5 Series, Vol. 155, 13 June 1922, col. 229.
27. Ibid., col. 225.
28. 'The Secretariat', *The Times*, 30 March 1921.
29. 'The Cabinet Secretariat', *The Times*, 13 June 1922.
30. Roskill, *Man of Secrets, Vol. 2*, p. 304.
31. Hugh Purcell, *Lloyd George* (London, 2006), pp. 94–7.
32. Roskill, *Man of Secrets, Vol. 2*, p. 304.
33. Ibid., p. 305.
34. Ibid., p. 306.
35. Quoted in Roskill, *Man of Secrets, Vol. 2*, p. 306.
36. Thomas Jones, *Whitehall Diary, Vol. 1*, p. 214.
37. Quoted in Roskill, *Man of Secrets, Vol. 2*, p. 306.
38. Ibid.
39. Roskill, *Man of Secrets, Vol. 2*, p. 310.

40. Quoted in Roskill, *Man of Secrets, Vol. 2*, p. 306.

41. Ibid.

42. Thomas Jones, *Whitehall Diary, Vol. 1*, p. 218.

43. Stephen Shipley Wilson, *The Cabinet Office to 1945* (London, 1975), p. 47.

44. Quoted in Roskill, *Man of Secrets, Vol. 2*, p. 306.

45. Roskill, *Man of Secrets, Vol. 2*, p. 311.

46. Quoted in Roskill, *Man of Secrets, Vol. 2*, p. 306.

47. Roskill, *Man of Secrets, Vol. 2*, pp. 311–12.

48. Ibid., p. 315.

49. Ibid., p. 316.

50. Ibid., p. 321.

51. Ibid., p. 325.

52. Ibid.

53. 'Cabinet Conclusions', 23 January 1924, NA CAB 23/47/1.

54. Roskill, *Man of Secrets, Vol. 2*, pp. 356–7.

55. Mosley, *Story of the Cabinet Office*, pp. 31–3.

56. Ibid.

57. John Shepherd and Keith Laybourn, *Britain's First Labour Government* (London, 2013), p. 168.

58. 'Cabinet Conclusions', 6 August 1924, NA CAB 23/48.

59. Ibid.

60. Thomas Jones, *Whitehall Diary, Vol. 1, 1926–1930* (London, 1969), pp. 308–9.

61. 'Cabinet Conclusion', 5 May 1926, NA CAB 23/52/24.

62. 'Cabinet Conclusion', 11 a.m., 7 May 1926, NA CAB 23/52/25.

63. Philip Williamson, *Stanley Baldwin: Conservative Leadership and National Values* (Cambridge, 1999), pp. 159–65. Also, personal correspondence with Philip Williamson, 9 September 2016.

64. Many thanks to Philip Williamson for this information. Personal correspondence with Philip Williamson, 9 September 2016.

65. See Jones, *Whitehall Diary, Vol. 2*, p. 108. Also, personal correspondence with Philip Williamson, 9 September 2016.

66. Many thanks to Philip Williamson for this information. Personal correspondence with Philip Williamson, 9 September 2016.

67. Interview with David Lloyd George, 'Nazi Regime: Lloyd George's Visit', *The Post's* representative, September 23 1936.

68. George W. Egerton, 'A Study in the Politics of Memory', *Journal of Modern History*, 60 (1988).

69. Andrew Green, *Writing the Great War: Sir James Edmonds and the Official Histories: 1915–1948* (London, 2003), p. 6.

70. Ibid., p. 200.

71. Ibid., p. 16.
72. 'Engagement Diaries', NA CAB 63/57.
73. Roskill, *Man of Secrets, Vol. 2*, pp. 543–8.
74. Ibid.
75. Ibid., p. 548.
76. Naylor, *A Man and an Institution*, p. 200.
77. Ibid., p. 238.
78. Maurice Hankey to Herbert Stanley, 5 July 1934, NA DO 1/9/1046.
79. High Commissioner's Office letter, 14 August 1934, NA DO 1/9/1046.
80. Hansard, HC Debs, 22 November 1934, Vol. 295, col. 236–9.
81. Roskill, *Man of Secrets, Vol. 3*, p. 253.
82. Ibid., p. 215.
83. Ibid., pp. 216–17.
84. 'Confidential Annex to Cabinet Minutes', 2 December 1936, NA CAB 23/86/12.
85. 'Confidential Conclusions', 6 December 1936, NA CAB 23/86/15.
86. See David Dilks, Norman Gash, Donald Southgate, John Ramsden, Lord Butler (eds.), *The Conservatives: A History from Their Origins to 1965* (London, 1977).
87. Interview with John Barnes, 12 September 2016.
88. Interview with David Dilks, 23 September 2016 and correspondence with David Dilks, 10 October 2016.
89. Ibid.
90. Roskill, *Man of Secrets, Vol. 3*, p. 259.
91. Hankey to Inskip, 14 October 1937, NA CAB 21/626, cited in Roskill, p. 262.
92. Roskill, *Man of Secrets, Vol. 3*, p. 262.
93. Ibid., pp. 260–61.
94. 'Cabinet Conclusions', 26 July 1938, NA CAB 23/94.
95. Ibid.
96. 'Functions of the Cabinet Secretariat including a Historical Note', 10 September 1944, NA T199/65.
97. Seldon, 'The Cabinet System', pp. 111–14.
98. Ibid., p. 113.
99. See S. S. Wilson, *The Cabinet Office to 1945*, pp. 182–219.
100. Interview with David Dilks, 23 September 2016.
101. Maurice Hankey, *Politics, Trials and Errors* (Oxford, 1950).
102. Christopher Andrew, *The English Historical Review*, Vol. 90, No. 357, October 1975, pp. 863–6.
103. John F. Naylor, A Man and an Institution: Sir Maurice Hankey, the Caiblet Secretariat and the Custody of Cabinet Secretary (Cambridge, 1984), p. 271. Correspondence with Vernon Bogdanor, 27 October 2016.

CHAPTER 4 (PP. 73–103)

1. John Winnifrith, 'Edward Ettingdean Bridges – Baron Bridges, 1892–1969', *Biographical Memoirs of Fellows of the Royal Society, Vol. 16* (1970), pp. 38–56.

2. Richard Chapman, 'Bridges, Edward Ettingdene, first Baron Bridges (1892–1969)', *Oxford Dictionary of National Biography* (Oxford University Press, 2004; online edn, January 2011) < http://www.oxforddnb.com/index/101032063> [accessed 29 August 2016].

3. Winnifrith, 'Edward Ettingdean Bridges – Baron Bridges, 1892–1969', pp. 38–40.

4. Ibid.

5. George Bridges, personal correspondence, 16 July 2016.

6. Ibid.

7. Ibid.

8. Winnifrith, 'Edward Ettingdean Bridges – Baron Bridges, 1892–1969', p. 40.

9. Ibid., pp. 40–41.

10. Interview with Robert Armstrong, 3 March 2016.

11. John Colville, *Footprints in Time: Memories* (London, 1976), p. 92.

12. Mark Bridges, personal correspondence, 16 July 2016.

13. Cited in Richard A. Chapman, *Ethics in the British Civil Service* (London, 1988), p. 38.

14. Interview with David Dilks, 23 September 2016.

15. John Colville, *Footprints in Time*, p. 92.

16. Winnifrith, 'Edward Ettingdean Bridges – Baron Bridges, 1892–1969', p. 45.

17. Ibid.

18. Chapman, *Ethics in the Civil Service*, p. 8.

19. Ibid., p. 9.

20. '[Cabinet] Conclusion', 30 September 1938, NA CAB 23/95/11.

21. Ibid.

22. Bridges to Wilson, 'Supreme Control in War', 5 November 1938, NA CAB 104/124; Chamberlain's approval is in 'Minute by the Prime Minister', 7 December 1938. Cited in Edwards, *Gresham Reader*, pp. 59–60.

23. PRO CAB 104/124, cited in Edwards, *Gresham Reader*, pp. 59–60.

24. Edwards, *Gresham Reader*, pp. 59–60.

25. S. S. Wilson, *The Cabinet Office to 1945* (London, 1975), p. 45.

26. Interview with Margaret Walker, 2012, Imperial War Museum Collections (henceforth IWM) <http://www.iwm.org.uk/collections/item/object/80033495> [accessed 1 September 2016].

27. Interview with Margaret Walker, IWM.

28. Interview with Edward Ian Claude Jacob, 26 September 1979, IWM <http://www.iwm.org.uk/collections/item/object/80004439> [accessed 1 September 2016].

29. Edward Bridges, 'Institution of the War Cabinet: consequential changes in organisation and procedure of the Cabinet Offices', 5 September 1939, NA CAB 21/1341.

30. Edward Bridges, 'Institution of the War Cabinet: consequential changes in organisation and procedure of the Cabinet Offices', 5 September 1939, NA CAB 21/1341.

31. Lord Normanbrook in John Wheeler-Bennett (ed.), *Action this Day* (London, 1968), p. 17.

32. Edward Bridges, 'Edward Bridges', in John Wheeler-Bennett (ed.), *Action this Day* (London, 1968), p. 218.

33. Ibid.

34. Andrew Roberts, *Masters and Commanders: How Roosevelt, Churchill, Marshall and Alanbrooke Won the War in the West* (London, 2008), p. xxxiv.

35. Edward Bridges, Letter to Captain Clarke and Mr Hopkinson, 28 April 1940, NA CAB 21/1281.

36. Winnifrith, 'Edward Ettingdean Bridges – Baron Bridges, 1892–1969', p. 45.

37. Bridges in Wheeler-Bennett (ed.), *Action this Day*, p. 219.

38. Ibid., p. 226.

39. Lord Ismay, *The Memoirs of General The Lord Ismay* (London, 1960), p. 159.

40. Interview with Alfred John Digby Winnifrith, 1982, IWM <http://www.iwm.org.uk/collections/item/object/80006177> [accessed 1 September 2016].

41. Richard Kenneth Mosley, *The Story of the Cabinet Office*, p. 60.

42. Bridges in Wheeler-Bennett (ed.), *Action this Day*, pp. 221–2.

43. Ibid., p. 220.

44. Norman Brook, 'Lord Normanbrook', in John Wheeler-Bennett (ed.), *Action this Day* (London, 1968), p. 20.

45. Mosley, *The Story of the Cabinet Office*, p. 21.

46. Interview with Edward Ian Claude Jacob, IWM.

47. Edward Bridges, Letter to Amery, 'Number of War Cabinet Meetings held during periods 1914–19 and 1939–45', NA CAB 21/2288.

48. Roberts, *Masters and Commanders*, p. 108.

49. Hansard, HC Debs, 5 Series, 24 February 1942, Vol. 378, col. 38.

50. Quoted in Dick Leonard, *A History of British Prime Ministers: Walpole to Cameron* (London, 2015), p. 636.

51. Colville, *Footprints in Time*, pp. 172–3.

52. Bridges in Wheeler-Bennett (ed.), *Action this Day*, p. 231.

53. WM 145, '[Cabinet] Conclusions', 28 May 1940, NA CAB 65/13/24.

54. Ibid.

55. Tombs, *The English and Their History*, p. 694.

56. WM 145, '[Cabinet] Conclusions', 28 May 1940, NA CAB 65/13/24.

57. Ibid., 3 July 1940, NA CAB 65/14/3.

58. 'Revised Draft Leaflet', 24 July 1940, NA CAB 67/7/47.

59. 'Notebook', 15 June 1942, NA CAB 195/1.

60. S. S. Wilson, *The Cabinet Office to 1945*, pp. 94–5.

61. Edward Bridges, 'Institution of the War Cabinet: consequential changes in organisation and procedure of the Cabinet Offices', 5 September 1939, NA CAB 21/1341.

62. Wilson, *The Cabinet Office to 1945*, p. 98.

63. Ibid., pp. 95–6.

64. Richard Overy, *Why the Allies Won* (London, 2006), pp. 329–30.

65. Robert Tombs, *The English and their History* (London, 2015), p. 753.

66. Alex Danchev and Daniel Todman (ed.), *War Diaries 1939–1945: Field Marshal Lord Alanbrooke* (London, 2001), p. 207.

67. Roberts, *Masters and Commanders*, p. 43.

68. Ibid.

69. Winston Churchill, *The Second World War, Vol. 2: Their Finest Hour* (London, 1939), pp. 15–16.

70. Interview with Alfred John Digby Winnifrith, IWM.

71. Interview with Edward Ian Claude Jacob, IWM.

72. Ibid., p. 45.

73. Wilson, *The Cabinet Office to 1945*, p. 113.

74. Interview with Alfred John Digby Winnifrith, IWM.

75. Interview with Margaret Walker, IWM.

76. Ibid.

77. Interview with Alfred John Digby Winnifrith, IWM.

78. Bridges in Wheeler-Bennett (ed.), *Action this Day*, p. 238.

79. Colville, *Footprints in Time*, p. 78.

80. 'Functions of the Cabinet Secretariat: Memorandum by the Secretary of the War Cabinet', 14 September 1944, NA T199/65.

81. Ibid.

82. Winnifrith, 'Edward Ettingdean Bridges – Baron Bridges, 1892–1969', pp. 38–40, 45.

83. Quoted in Wilson, *The Cabinet Office to 1945*, pp. 155–8.

84. Harold Wilson, *The Governance of Britain* (London, 1976), p. 53.

85. Edward Bridges, 'Horrid thoughts', 1 November 1944, NA CAB 127/272.

86. Ismay, *Memoirs of General the Lord Ismay*, p. 395.

87. S. S. Wilson, *The Cabinet Office to 1945*, p. 45.

88. Interview with Lord Morgan, 1 October 2016.

89. 'Notebook', 14 August 1945, NA CAB 195/3.

90. Clement Attlee, 'We should declare', 28 August 1945, NA CAB 130/3.

91. Correspondence with John Bew, 30 September 2016.

92. Donald Edward Moggridge, *Maynard Keynes: An Economists Biography* (London, 1992), pp. 813–14.

93. Edward Bridges, 'Edward Bridges', in John Wheeler-Bennett (ed.), *Action this Day*, pp. 218–41.

CHAPTER 5 (PP. 105–39)

1. Norman Brook's pithy rewriting of the doggerel at the beginning of Chapter 1. With thanks to Lord Armstrong of Ilminster for this quotation.

2. Thanks to Katie Guest of Wolverhampton Grammar School for this information.

3. Cited in Kevin Theakston, *The Civil Service Since 1945* (London, 2009), p. 48.

4. Interview with Lord Armstrong, 3 March 2016.

5. Kevin Theakston, 'Brook, Norman Craven, Baron Normanbrook (1902–67)', *Oxford Dictionary of National Biography* (Oxford University Press, 2004; online edn, January 2011) <http://www.oxforddnb.com/view/article/32089> [accessed 29 August 2016].

6. Interview with Lord Sherfield, British Oral Archive of Political and Administrative History (BOAPAH), 1980.

7. Harold Evans, *Downing Street Diary: The Macmillan Years, 1957–1963* (London, 1981), pp. 16–17.

8. Lord Moran, *Churchill: The Struggle for Survival, 1945–60* (London, 2006), p. 389.

9. Peter Hennessy, *The Prime Minister: The Office and its Holders Since 1945* (London, 2000), p. 157.

10. Theakston, 'Brook, Norman', *ODNB*.

11. Blick and Jones, *At Power's Elbow*, pp. 205–6.

12. David Marquand, 'Labour's Own Captain Mainwaring', *The New Statesman*, 2–8 September 2016.

13. Kenneth Harris, *Attlee* (London, 1995), p. 403, cited in *Gresham Reader*, p. 70.

14. George Mallaby, *From My Level: Unwritten Minutes* (London, 1965), p. 57.

15. Mallaby, *From My Level*, pp. 56–7.

16. Norman Brook, 'Cabinet Government', NA CAB 21/4959.

17. Nicklaus Thomas-Symonds, *Attlee: A Life in Politics* (London, 2010), p. 209.

18. Brook to Attlee, 'National Health Service', 1 April 1950, NA PREM 8/1486.

19. Sir Norman Brook to Aneurin Bevan, 'Cabinet Government: Principle of Collective Responsibility', 19 August 1950, NA PRO CAB 21/4324.

20. '[Cabinet Secretary's] Notebook', 19 April 1951, NA CAB 195/9/7.

21. Norman Brook, 'Cabinet Government', 'Sir Norman Brook: miscellaneous engagements and personal correspondence', 26 June 1959, NA CAB 21/4959.

22. Norman Brook, 'Lord Normanbrook', in John Wheeler-Bennett (ed.), *Action this Day* (London, 1968), pp. 15–47.

23. Anthony Seldon, *Churchill's Indian Summer: The Conservative Government, 1951–1955* (London, 1981), p. 108.

24. Ibid., p. 109.

25. Rodney Lowe, *The Official History of the British Civil Service: Reforming the Civil Service, Vol. 1: The Fulton Years, 1966–81* (London, 2011), p. 67.

26. Seldon, *Churchill's Indian Summer*, pp. 108–11.

27. John Colville, *Footprints in Time: Memories* (London, 1976), p. 635.

28. Brook, 'Lord Normanbrook', *Action this Day*, pp. 15–47.

29. Moran, *The Struggle for Survival*, p. 61.

30. Seldon, *Churchill's Indian Summer*, p. 118.

31. Hennessy, *The Prime Minister*, p. 187.

32. Ibid.

33. Seldon, *Churchill's Indian Summer*, pp. 116–17.

34. Ibid., p. 117.

35. Ibid.

36. Ibid.

37. Hennessy, *The Prime Minister*, p. 191.

38. Ibid.

39. Memorandum Brook to Churchill, 21 April 1953, 'Volume of Cabinet business between 1948 and 1953, and 1957 and 1958: Cabinet Secretary provided information for Prime Minister', NA PREM 11/3223.

40. Memorandum, Brook to Churchill, 27 January 1954, NA PREM 11/3223.

41. Brook to Churchill, 15 November 1951, NA PREM 11/1734.

42. 'Brevity', 20 November 1951, NA PREM 11/1734.

43. George Mallaby, *From My Level: Unwritten Minutes* (London, 1965) and George Mallaby, *Each in his Office* (London, 1972). Mallaby had been Headmaster of St Bee's School in Cumberland, before joining Whitehall in 1940.

44. Seldon, *Churchill's Indian Summer*, pp. 116–117.

45. George Mallaby, *From My Level*, pp. 16–17.

46. Ibid.

47. Seldon, *Churchill's Indian Summer*, pp. 116–117.

48. George Mallaby, *From My Level*, p. 45.

49. Churchill to Brook Memo, 27 March 1953, 'Suggestion by Prime Minister to Sir Norman Brook that the expression "Most Secret" should be adopted in place of the American expression "Top Secret"', NA PREM 11/268.

50. Seldon, *Churchill's Indian Summer*, p. 381.

51. Moran, *The Struggle for Survival*, p. 171.

52. Ibid., pp. 177–8.

53. Seldon, *Churchill's Indian Summer*, p. 45.

54. Brook, 'Lord Normanbrook', *Action this Day*, pp. 15–47.

55. Moran, *The Struggle for Survival*, p. 226.

56. John Wheeler-Bennett, *King George VI*, p. 797.

57. Moran, *The Struggle for Survival*, p. 226.

58. John Grigg, 'Churchill, the Crippled Giant: His Last Two Years of Power', in *Encounter* (April 1977), pp. 9–15.

59. '[Cabinet Secretary's] Notebook', 8 July 1954, NA CAB 195/12/37.

60. Ibid.

61. Ibid.

62. Moran, *The Struggle for Survival*, p. 371.

63. Personal correspondence with D. R. Thorpe, 11 August 2016.

64. 'Prime Minister: Middle East', 15 March 1954, British Policy in the Middle East, NA CAB 301/141.

65. 'Prime Minister: Middle East', 14 April 1954, Report by Cabinet Secretary on UK aims for Middle East, NA PREM 11/1457.

66. Hennessy, *The Prime Minister*, pp. 233–4. The letter in question is Brook to Eden, 25 August 1956, NA PREM 11/1152.

67. Brook to Eden, 25 August 1956, NA PREM 11/1152.

68. Ian Beesley, 'Hunt, John Joseph Benedict, Baron Hunt of Tanworth (1919–2008)', *ODNB*, (Oxford University Press, Jan 2012; online edn, September 2012) <http://www.oxforddnb.com/view/article/99950> [accessed 29 August 2016].

69. 'Cabinet Conclusions', 23 October 1956, NA CAB 128/30/72.

70. '[Cabinet Secretary's] Notebook', 30 October 1956, NA CAB 195/15.

71. Hansard, HC Debs, 31 October 1956, Vol. 558, col. 1454.

72. Edward Heath, *The Course of My Life* (London, 1998), p. 172.

73. Robert Armstrong letter, 30 June 1986, 'Review of Suez records: release of records (in 1987) under the 30-year rule', NA PREM 19/1/69.

74. D. R. Thorpe, *Eden: The Life and Times of Anthony Eden First Earl of Avon, 1897–1977* (London, 2004), p. 66.

75. Interview with Lord Armstrong, 3 March 2016.

76. 'The Secret World of Whitehall: The Real Sir Humphrey', BBC, 16 March 2011.

77. Brook to Macmillan, 14 March 1958, NA CAB 301/163.

78. Anthony Eden, *The Memoirs of Sir Anthony Eden: Full Circle* (London, 1960), p. 345.

79. D. R. Thorpe, *Eden*, pp. 563–4. With thanks to D. R. Thorpe for this information.

80. See Anthony Seldon, 'Prime Minister's Office, Private, from John Martin to Chris Martin, 1945–2015', in Andrew Holt, Warren Dockter (eds), *Foreign Affairs Private Secretaries* (London, 2017).

81. Blick and Jones, *At Power's Elbow*, p. 205.

82. Harold Macmillan, *Riding the Storm: 1956–1959* (London, 1971), p. 193.

83. Harold Macmillan, Peter Catterall (ed.), *The Macmillan Diaries, Vol. 2: Prime Minister and After, 1957–1966* (London, 2011), p. 198.

84. Interview with Lord Muirshiel, BOAPAH, 1980.

85. Lord Home, *The Way the Wind Blows* (London, 1976), p. 192.

86. Brook to Macmillan, 4 January 1961, 'Volume of Cabinet business between 1948 and 1953, and 1957 and 1958: Cabinet Secretary provided information for Prime Minister', NA PREM 11/3223.

87. Ibid.

88. Seldon, 'The Cabinet System', pp. 116–18.

89. Ibid., p. 119.

90. Ibid., pp. 116–21.

91. 'Cabinet: Most Confidential Record', 'Ministerial discussions on the political situation in the UK', 11 March 1958, NA PREM 301/166.

92. Norman Brook, 'Prime Minister', 14 March 1958, NA CAB 301/166.

93. Ibid.

94. Ibid.

95. D. R. Thorpe, *Supermac: The Life of Harold Macmillan* (London, 2010), p. 387.

96. Evans, *Downing Street Diary*, p. 149.

97. 'UK: Security Nassau Meeting, 1962–63 (1 of 2), Country Files', President's Office Files, Kennedy Library.

98. Peter Hennessy, *Having it So Good: Britain in the Fifties* (London, 2007), p. 472.

99. Macmillan, Catterall (ed.), *The Macmillan Diaries, Vol. 2*, pp. 135–6.

100. D. R. Thorpe, *Supermac*, pp. 454–7.

101. Ibid.

102. Alistair Horne, *Macmillan: The Official Biography, Vol. 2* (London, 2008), p. 199.

103. Norman Brook, 23 August 1948, 'My dear Lascelles, Sir Norman Brook's trip to Canada, Australia and New Zealand', NA CAB 301/106.

104. Robert Pearce, *Attlee's Labour Governments 1945–51* (London, 1993), p. 42.

105. Hennessy, *Having it So Good*, p. 326.

106. '[Cabinet Secretary's] Notebook', 7 July 1954, CAB 195/12/36.

107. Ibid., 8 July 1954, NA CAB 195/12/37.

108. Peter Hennessy, *The Secret State: Preparing for the Worst, 1945–50* (London, 2010), p. 45.

109. Ibid.

110. Ibid.

111. Interview with David Edgerton, 29 September 2016.

112. Brook to Eden, 'Burgess and Maclean', 19 October 1955, NA PREM 11/1578.

113. Ben Macintyre, *A Spy Amongst Friends: Kim Philby and the Great Betrayal* (London, 2014), p. 189.

114. Theakston, *Leadership in Whitehall*, p. 6.

115. 'Record of Decision Reached by Sir Norman Brook and Sir Patrick Dean on 25th September 1957', 25 September 1957, NA CAB 163/9.

116. 'Joint Intelligence Organisation Chart', 'Joint Intelligence Committee: administration, structure, and functions of the committee; papers relating to the transmission of intelligence reports', c. 1957, NA CAB 163/8.

117. Hennessy, *Having it So Good*, pp. 487–9.

118. Blick and Jones, *At Power's Elbow*, p. 204.

119. Theakston, *Leadership in Whitehall*, p. 123.

120. Thorpe, *Supermac*, p. 526.

121. Macmillan, Catterall (ed.), *The Macmillan Diaries, Vol. 2*, p. 501.

122. Theakston, *Leadership in Whitehall*, p. 5.

123. 'Lord Normanbrook', 16 June 1967, *The Times*.

124. Personal correspondence, Robert Armstrong, 15 August 2016.

125. 'Reception for Lord Normanbrook', *The Times*, 13 February 1963.

CHAPTER 6 (PP. 141–51)

1. 'Former Houses Between the Sites of Pembroke House and Montague House', in Montagu H. Cox and Philip Norman (eds.), *Survey of London, Vol. 13, St Margaret, Westminster, Part II: Whitehall I* (London, 1930), pp. 180–92. Available from *British History Online* <http://www.british-history.ac.uk/survey-london/vol13/pt2/pp180-192> [accessed 17 August 2016].

2. Robert Blake, *Disraeli* (London, 1969), p. 538.

3. Hankey, *Supreme Command*, p. 589.

4. Maurice Hankey, 'Speech to Cabinet Office Staff', November 1918, NA CAB 21/128.

5. Ibid.

6. Hankey to Warren Fisher, November 1922, NA CAB 63/33.

7. Interview with Margaret Walker, 2012, IWM <http://www.iwm.org.uk/collections/item/object/80033495> [accessed 1 September 2016].

8. 'Whitehall Gardens (Montagu House) site. Memorandum by the First Commissioner of Works', 28 February 1930, NA CAB 24/210/17.

9. Ibid.

10. Treasury Letter, 7 December 1937, NA T162/589.

11. Ibid.

12. Ibid.

13. First Commissioner of Works Letter, 16 May 1938, NA T162/589.

14. 'Houses in the Bowling Green', in Cox and Norman (eds.), *Survey of London, Vol. 13, St Margaret, Westminster, Part II: Whitehall I*, pp. 236–48. Available at *British History Online* <http://www.british-history.ac.uk/survey-london/vol13/pt2/pp236-248> [accessed 19 September 2016].

15. 'Richmond Terrace', in Cox and Norman (eds.), *Survey of London, Vol. 13, St Margaret, Westminster, Part II: Whitehall I*, pp. 249–56. Available at *British History Online* <http://www.british-history.ac.uk/survey-london/vol13/pt2/pp249-256> [accessed 16 September 2016].

16. Treasury Letter, 7 December 1937, NA T162/589.

17. Interview with Edward Ian Claude Jacob, IWM.

18. *History of Government*, '1 Horse Guards Road' <https://www.gov.uk/government/history/1-horse-guards-road> [accessed 21 September 2016].

19. 'Application for Treasury Sanctions', 2 March 1941, NA T162/589.

20. Minute from the Prime Minister to Minister of Works, 7 July 1958, NA PREM 11/2355.

21. 'Downing Street and the Old Treasury', 23 July 1958, NA PREM 11/2355.

22. 'Plans for the use of 10 Downing Street, and the old Treasury', July 1958, NA PREM 11/2355.

23. Ibid.

24. Letter from G. Ford to Jon Charlton, 14 October 1960, NA Work 12/682.

25. Letter from Jon Charlton to G. Ford, 17 October 1960, NA Work 12/682.

26. Letter from F. A. Bishop to Tim Bligh, 22 November 1961, NA CAB 21/4768.

27. Interview with Lord Armstrong, February 2016.

28. Harold Evans, *Downing Street Diary: The Macmillan Years 1957–1963* (London, 1981), p. 24.

29. Blick and Jones, *Powers Behind the Prime Minister,* pp. 255–6.

30. Interview with Lord Wilson, 2 November 2012 <http://www.cabinetsecretaries.com> [accessed 21 September 2016].

CHAPTER 7 (PP. 153–93)

1. Edward Heath, 'Burke Trend', *Dictionary of National Biography* (rev. first published 2004) <http://dx.doi.org/10.1093/ref:odnb/39887> [accessed 13 September 2016].

2. Interview with Lord Roberthall, 1980, BOAPAH.

3. Ibid.

4. Interview with Lord Croham (the name adopted by Sir Douglas Allen after receiving his peerage), 1980, BOAPAH.

5. Robert Armstrong, email to author, 15 August 2016.

6. Richard I. Aldrich and Rory Cormac, *The Black Door* (London, 2016), p. 283.

7. Interview with Lord Armstrong, 3 April 2016.

8. Edward Heath, 'Burke Trend', *Dictionary of National Biography.*

9. Hennessy, *The Prime Minister,* p. 20.

10. Robert Armstrong, email to author, 15 August 2016.

11. Interview with John Chilcot, 21 August 2016.

12. Interview with Henry Kissinger, 29 September 2016.

13. Interview with Richard Thorpe, 16 August 2016.

14. Peter Catterall, email to author, 17 August 2016. Many thanks to Peter Catterall for pointing this information out.

15. Peter Catterall, *The Macmillan Diaries Vol II: Prime Minister and After: 1957–1966* (London, 2011), pp. 26–8.

16. D. R. Thorpe, *Supermac* (London, 2010), p. 613.

17. Richard Thorpe, email to author, 12 August 2016.

18. D. R. Thorpe, *Alec Douglas-Home* (London, 2007), p. 324.

19. See Anthony Seldon, *Number 10: An Illustrated History,* p. 181.

20. Interview with Lord Home of the Hirsel, 1980, BOAPAH.

21. Ibid.

22. Thorpe, *Alec Douglas-Home*, p. 341.

23. Ibid., p. 342.

24. Ibid.

25. Ben Pimlott, *Harold Wilson* (London, 1992), p. 326.

26. Norman Hunt, 'Harold Wilson: Pre-experience: Harold Wilson Interviewed by Norman Hunt', in Anthony King (ed.), *The British Prime Minister: A Reader* (London, 1969), pp. 86, 90–91. Cited in *Gresham Reader*, pp. 127–8.

27. Harold Wilson, 'Pound in your Pocket', *BBC*, 6 April 1967, cited in R. K. Mosley, *The Story of the Cabinet Office*, p. 78.

28. Kevin Theakston, *The Civil Service since 1945* (London, 2009), p. 49.

29. Interview with Philip Ziegler, 1 October 2016.

30. A letter from Trend to Harold Wilson for his first Cabinet Meeting, October 1964, NA PREM 13/6.

31. Hennessy, *The Prime Minister*, p. 306.

32. Aldrich and Cormac, *The Black Door*, p. 260.

33. Peter Hennessy, *The Secret State: Whitehall and the Cold War* (London, 2003), p. 14.

34. Ibid., p. 286.

35. Ibid., pp. 322–3.

36. Ibid.

37. Ibid., pp. 302–3.

38. Aldrich and Cormac, *The Black Door*, p. 265.

39. Burke Trend, 'Note by Cabinet Secretary on Post-Election Strategy', 1966, SaP1180a, Unreleased Document, Cabinet Office.

40. Ibid.

41. Ibid.

42. Hennessy, *The Prime Minister*, p. 289.

43. Interview with Lord Shackleton, 1980, BOAPAH.

44. Theakston, *The Civil Service since 1945*, p. 45.

45. Richard Crossman, *The Diaries of a Cabinet Minister, Vol. 1: Minister of Housing, 1964–66* (London, 1976), pp. 198–99. Cited in Edwards, *Gresham Reader*, pp. 139–40.

46. Richard Crossman, *The Diaries of a Cabinet Minister, Vol. 2: Lord President of the Council and Leader of the House of Commons, 1966–68* (London, 1976), p. 129.

47. A. Howard (ed.), Richard Crossman, *The Crossman Diaries: Selections from the Diaries of a Cabinet Minister* (London, 1979), p. 365.

48. Peter Hennessy, *The Prime Minister*, p. 45.

49. Tom Dalyell, *Dick Crossman: A Portrait* (London, 1989), pp. 235–36.

50. Chapman Pincher, 'Cable vetting sensation', *Daily Express*, 29 February 1967.

51. David Wood, '"Sensationalized" Story on State Secrets', *The Times*, 22 February 1967, p. 1.

52. Harold Wilson, *The Labour Government 1964–70: A Personal Record* (London, 1971), pp. 144–8.

53. Crossman, *Selections from the Diaries of a Cabinet Minister, Vol. 1*, pp. 702–3.

54. Ibid.

55. Hennessy, *The Prime Minister*, p. 308.

56. Interview with Lord Shackleton, 1980, BOAPAH.

57. Interview with Joe Haines, 9 October 2016.

58. Ibid. The book was Sir Harold Wilson, *The Labour Government, 1964–70: A Personal Record* (London, 1971).

59. Lewis Baston and Anthony Seldon, 'No. 10 Under Edward Heath', in Stuart Ball and Anthony Seldon (eds.), *The Heath Government 1970–74* (London, 1996), pp. 47–74.

60. Cited in Hennessy, *The Prime Minister*, p. 337.

61. Jon Davis, *Prime Ministers and Whitehall 1960–74* (London, 2007), p. 102.

62. Ibid.

63. Ibid., pp. xiii-xiv.

64. John Campbell, *Edward Heath: A Biography* (London, 1994), p. 317.

65. Peter Hennessy, *Cabinet* (London, 1986), p. 19.

66. Cited in Jon Davis, *Prime Ministers and Whitehall, 1960–74*, p. 102.

67. Edward Heath, *The Course of My Life: The Autobiography of Edward Heath* (London, 1998), p. 316.

68. Its story is told in Tessa Blackstone and William Plowden's *Inside the Think-Tank: Advising the Cabinet, 1971–1983* (London, 1990) and Victor Rothchild's *Meditations of a Broomstick* (London, 1977).

69. Burke Trend, 'Review of future business', August 1970, NA PREM 15/81.

70. Ibid.

71. Trend to Wilson, 'Crisis management', 27 July 1969, NA PREM 19/3124.

72. Ibid.

73. Chris Mason, 'London 2012: What exactly is a Cobra meeting?' <http://www.bbc.co.uk/news/uk-politics-18958032> [accessed 14 September 2016].

74. Interview with Bruce Mann, 23 August 2016.

75. Dominic Sandbrook, *State of Emergency: The Way We Were: Britain 1970–74* (London, 2010), p. 226.

76. Hennessy, *The Prime Minister*, pp. 346–7.

77. Aldrich, *The Black Door*, pp. 301–5.

78. Campbell, *Edward Heath*, p. 345.

79. All quotations from Trend to Heath, Memo, 24 April 1973, NA PREM 14/2013.

80. Interview with Henry Kissinger, 29 September 2016.

81. 'Social Plans with Douglas Fairbanks Jr', Memorandum of Telephone Conversation, 25 July 1972, in DNSA collection: Kissinger Telephone Conversations, 1969–1977, National Security Archive, George Washington University, Washington DC.

82. 'Social Plans with Katherine Graham', Memorandum of Telephone Conversation, 25 July 1972, in DNSA collection.

83. 'Vietnam Peace Talks and Ceasefire Agreement; United Kingdom–US Relations; Meeting with Yitzhak Rabin', Memorandum of Telephone Conversation, 16 January 1973, in DNSA.

84. Ibid.

85. '[Bombing Missile Sites in North Vietnam and Other Matters]', Memorandum of Telephone Conversations, 1969–1977, National Security Archive, George Washington University, Washington DC.

86. '[Dinner Arrangements with President Nixon]', Memorandum of Telephone Conversation (30.07.73), DNSA Collection: Kissinger Telephone Conversations, 1969–1977, National Security Archive, George Washington University, Washington DC.

87. Interview with Henry Kissinger, 29 September 2016.

88. Ibid.

89. '[United Kingdom–US Relations]', Memorandum of Telephone Conversation, 30 July 1973, in DNSA.

90. Witness Seminar: Britain and Brussels, Britain and Strasbourg, 23 February 1995, British Oral Archive of Political and Administrative History, LSE.

91. Simon Bulmer and Martin Burch, 'Adaptation of UK central government 1951–99' (University of Manchester, Manchester, 2000), Queen's Papers on Europeanisation, No. 9/2000.

92. Theakston, *The Civil Service since 1945*, p. 27.

93. Sir Antony Part, 1980, BOAPAH.

94. Jon Davis, *Prime Ministers and Whitehall*, p. 147.

95. Rodney Lowe, *The Official History of the British Civil Service, Vol. 1* (London, 2011), pp. 162–3.

96. Campbell, *Edward Heath*, p. 490.

97. Cited in Peter Hennessy, *Cabinet* (London, 1986), pp. 20–21.

98. Lord Armstrong correspondence, 20 September 2016.

99. Kissinger to Trend, 26 September 1973, Central Foreign Policy Files, 1973–79, US Department of State, National Archives and Records Administration.

100. Ian Beesley, 'John Hunt', *Dictionary of National Biography* (January 2012) <http://dx.doi.org/10.1093/ref:odnb/99950> [accessed 14 September 2016].

101. Quoted in the *Daily Telegraph*, 18 July 2008.

102. Ian Beesley, 'John Hunt', *Dictionary of National Biography*.

103. Memo from Hunt to Heath, 7 September 1973, NA PREM 14/20.

104. Hunt on the Cabinet Committee system, 1973, NA PREM 15/2015.

105. Ibid.

106. All quotations above from Hunt, NA PREM 15/2015.

107. Personal note from Hunt to Heath, 3 June 1973, NA PREM 15/2014.

108. Letter from Armstrong to Hunt, 7 July 1974, NA PREM 15/2014.

109. Memo from Hunt to Armstrong, 14 January 1974, NA PREM 15/2014.

110. Memo from Armstrong to Hunt, 16 January 1974, NA PREM 15/2014.

111. Theakston, *The Civil Service since 1945*, pp. 45–50.

112. Hennessy, *Cabinet*, p. 337.

113. Email from John Campbell to author, 14 September 2016.

114. One of the greatest sadnesses of my life as a researcher was planning a long interview with WIlliam Armstrong on his life, on 16 July 1980, as part of the BOAPAH series, but he died four days before.

115. See Chris Ballinger and Anthony Seldon, 'Prime Ministers and Cabinet', in Anthony Seldon and Kevin Hickson (eds.), *The Wilson and Callaghan Governments, 1974–79* (London, 2004), pp. 173–89.

116. Interview with Joe Haines, 9 October 2016.

117. Interview with Kenneth Stowe, 1999, for *Powers behind the Prime Minister: The Hidden Influence of Number Ten* (London, 2008 [1999]).

118. Interview with Lord Donoughue, 7 October 2016.

119. Barbara Castle, *The Castle Diaries, 1964–70* (London, 1984), p. 46.

120. Interview with Henry Kissinger, 29 September 2016.

121. Ian Beesley, 'John Hunt', *DNB*.

122. Interview with Lord Donoughue, 7 October 2016.

123. Ibid.

124. Ibid.

125. Theakston, *The Civil Service since 1945*, p. 49.

126. Hennessy, *The Cabinet*, p. 21.

127. Peter Hennessy, 'Cabinet Government: A Commentary' in *Contemporary Record*, Vol. 8, Issue 3 (1994), p. 484.

128. Bernard Donoughue, *Downing Street Diary: With James Callaghan at No. 10* (London, 2009), p. 26.

129. Ibid.

130. Bernard Donoughue, *Prime Minister: The Conduct of Policy under Harold Wilson and James Callaghan* (London, 1987), pp. 21–2.

131. Ibid.

132. Interviews with Lord Donoughue and Joe Haines, 7 October 2016.

133. Interviews with Lord Donoughue and Joe Haines, 7 October 2016.

134. Interview with Chris Brearley, 23 August 2016.

135. Castle, *The Castle Diaries*, p. 314.

136. Witness Seminar: 1975 EU Referendum, 5 June 1995, British Oral Archive of Political and Administrative History, LSE.

137. Ibid.

138. Donoughue, *Downing Street Diary*, p. 698.

139. James Callaghan, *Time and Chance* (London, 2006), p. 31.

140. Castle, *The Castle Diaries*, p. 389.

141. Donoughue, *Downing Street Diary*, pp. 700–708.

142. Interview with Lord Morgan, 1 October 2016.

143. Ian Beesley, 'John Hunt', *Dictionary of National Biography*.

144. Interview with Chris Brearley, 23 August 2016.

145. Bernard Donoughue, cited in Chris Ballinger and Anthony Seldon, 'Prime Ministers and Cabinet', in Seldon and Theakston.

146. Ibid.

147. Ibid.

148. Edmund Dell and Lord Hunt of Tanworth, 'The Failings of Cabinet Government in Mid to Late 1970s', *Contemporary Record*, Vol. 8, No. 3 (winter 1994), pp. 467–8, cited in *Gresham Reader*, p. 199.

149. Jimmy Carter had been elected American President the previous November, and would take over in January. John Hunt, 'What happens if we do not get the IMF loan', 1 December 1976, NA PREM 16/804.

150. Donoughue, *Downing Street Diary*, p. 9.

151. Ibid., p. 87.

152. Interview with Lord Morgan, 1 October 2016.

153. Ibid., p. 149.

154. Ibid., p. 154.

155. Cited in Donoughue, *Downing Street Diary*, p. 154.

156. Donoughue, *Downing Street Diary*, p. 178.

157. Bernard Donoughue, *The Heat of the Kitchen* (London, 2003), pp. 131–2.

158. Interview with Lord Donoughue, 7 October 2016.

159. Hunt to Margaret Thatcher, Letter, 5 April 1979, NA PREM 19/24.

160. 'Tokyo Summit', 21 May 1979, NA PREM 19/27. See also Thatcher Foundation Archive < http://www.margaretthatcher.org/document/112036> [accessed 14 September 2016].

161. Private information to author, 20 August 2016.

162. Email from John Campbell to author, 14 September 2016.

163. Ian Beesley, 'John Hunt', *DNB*.

164. 'Requiem Mass Celebrated for Lord Hunt', *Diocese of Westminster*, 29 October 2008 <http://www.rcdow.org.uk/cardinal/default.asp?library_ref=1&content_ref=2036> [accessed 11 October 2016].

CHAPTER 8 (PP. 195–233)

1. Theakston, *Leadership in Whitehall* (London, 1999), pp. 204–21.

2. Charles Moore, *Margaret Thatcher: The Authorized Biography, Vol. 2: Not for Turning* (London, 2013), p. 488.

3. Private information, 10 August 2016.

4. Interview with Lord Butler, 27 October 1998.

5. Interview with Lord Armstrong, 6 November 2012 <http://www.cabinetsecretaries. com> [accessed 17 September 2016], p. 5.

6. Ibid., p. 6.

7. Ibid., p. 8.

8. John Campbell, *Margaret Thatcher, Vol. 2: The Iron Lady* (London, 2007), p. 265.

9. 'Memorandum For the President', January 1984, 9173, Exec Sec, NSC: Country File, United Kingdom, Box 91331, Reagan Library, Simi Valley, California.

10. McFarlane to Armstrong, 16 January 1984, Exec Sec, NSC.

11. Moore, *Margaret Thatcher: The Authorized Biography, Vol. 1*, p. 521.

12. Lord Armstrong, email to author, 15 August 2016.

13. Ibid.

14. John Hoskyns, *Just in Time: Inside the Thatcher Revolution* (London, 2000), p. 356.

15. Interview with Lord Armstrong, 6 November 2012, p. 2.

16. Ibid., p. 10.

17. Anthony Seldon, 'The Cabinet Office and Coordination, 1979–87', *Public Administration*, Vol. 68, Issue 1 (March 1990), p. 105.

18. J. C. R. Dow, 'Short term economic policy group (STEP)', 15 January 1981, Bank of England, 7A173/8, MTFW 128043.

19. Ibid.

20. J. C. R. Dow, 'Minute for Governor of the Bank of England', 14 January 1981, Bank of England Archives.

21. Letter from Robert Armstrong to Michael Coles, 29 September 1980, NA PREM 19/191.

22. Letter from Robert Armstrong to Michael Alexander, 9 October 1980, NA PREM 19/179.

23. Letter from Robert Armstrong to Michael Alexander, 10 November 1981, NA PREM 19/669 (courtesy of the Margaret Thatcher Foundation online archive).

24. René Lévesque to Margaret Thatcher, 'On Behalf of the Government of Quebec', 17 December 1981, NA PREM 19/669.

25. Memo from Robert Armstrong to Thatcher, 5 November 1981, NA PREM 19/699.

26. Frederick Bastion, *The Battle of London: Trudeau and Thatcher and the Fight for Canada's Constitution* (Toronto, 2014), pp. 274–5.

27. Memo from Robert Armstrong to Thatcher, 5 November 1981, NA PREM 19/699.

28. Robert Armstrong, 'Falklands Invasion Minutes, 9.30 a.m.', 2 April 1982, NA CAB 128/73.

29. Robert Armstrong, 'Falklands Invasion Minutes, 7.30 p.m.', 2 April 1982, NA CAB 128/73.

30. Ibid.

31. Interview with Lord Armstrong, 6 November 2012, p. 15.

32. Ibid.

33. Ibid., p. 16.

34. Ibid.

35. Minute from Robert Armstrong to Thatcher, 25 May 1982, NA PREM 19/649.

36. Ibid.

37. Seldon, 'The Cabinet System', p. 127.

38. Nigel Lawson and Lord Armstrong of Ilminster, 'Cabinet Government in the Thatcher Years', *Contemporary Record*, Vol. 8, No. 3 (1994), cited in Edwards, *Gresham Reader*, pp. 241–2.

39. Private interview, 20 August 2016.

40. Memo from Armstrong to Thatcher, 7 November 1980, NA PREM 19/282.

41. Memo from Armstrong to Thatcher, 5 June 1984, NA PREM 194/1286.

42. Cited in Theakston, *Leadership in Whitehall*, p. 210.

43. Nigel Lawson, *The View from No. 11: Memoirs of a Tory Radical* (London, 1992), p. 669.

44. Simon Heffer, Lecture on Margaret Thatcher, Buckingham University, 22 August 2016.

45. Interview with Lord Armstrong, 6 November 2012, p. 16.

46. Interview with Lord Butler, 27 July 2016.

47. Ibid.

48. Interview with Lord Butler, 16 November 2012.

49. Chris Collins, email to author, 20 August 2016.

50. Armstrong to Thatcher, 'Organisation to Cover the Coal Strike in August', 26 July 1984, NA PREM 194/1332.

51. Armstrong to Thatcher, 'Cabinet: Industrial Affairs: Coal', 14 November 1984, NA PREM 19/1335.

52. Ibid.

53. Armstrong to Butler, 'Thank you for your minute…', 5 November 1984, NA PREM 19/1335 (courtesy of the Thatcher Foundation online archive).

54. Theakston, *Leadership in Whitehall*, p. 209.

55. Interview with Lord Armstrong, 26 October 1998.

56. Ibid.

57. Aldrich and Cormac, *The Black Door*, p. 567.

58. Interview with Lord Armstrong, 26 October 1998.

59. Interview with Lord Armstrong, 6 November 2012, p. 8.

60. Private information, 20 August 2016.

61. John Campbell, *Margaret Thatcher, Vol. 2: The Iron Lady* p. 487.

62. Armstrong, Cabinet Minutes, 9 January 1986, NA CAB 128/83/1.

63. Ibid.

64. Interview with Lord Armstrong, 6 November 2012, p. 17.

65. John Campbell, *Margaret Thatcher, Vol. 2: The Iron Lady*, pp. 489–95.

66. Ibid.

67. Anthony Seldon, 'The Cabinet Office and Coordination, 1979–87', p. 107.

68. Ibid., pp. 107–9.

69. Hennessy, *Cabinet*, pp. 90–94.

70. Anthony Seldon, 'The Cabinet System', pp. 122–3.

71. Anthony Seldon, 'The Cabinet Office and Coordination, 1979–87', p. 111

72. Anthony Seldon, 'Cabinet Office and Coordination', in *Public Administration*, Vol. 68, Issue 1 (March 1990), pp. 103–21.

73. Cited in Edwards, *Gresham Reader*, p. 213.

74. Seldon, 'The Cabinet System', p. 123.

75. Dennis Kavanagh and Anthony Seldon, *Powers Behind the Prime Minister: The Hidden Influence of Number Ten* (London, 2008 [1999]), p. 180.

76. Personal letter from Butler to Thatcher, 4 August 1985, Thatcher Archive.

77. Ibid.

78. Interview with Lord Butler, 27 September 2016.

79. Private email, 20 August 2016.

80. Interview with Lord Butler, 16 November 2012 <http://www.cabinetsecretaries.com> [accessed 17 September 2016].

81. Ibid.

82. Ibid.

83. Ibid.

84. Nehal Panchamia and Peter Thomas, 'The Next Steps Initiative' <http://www.instituteforgovernment.org.uk/sites/default/files/case%20study%20next%20steps.pdf> [accessed 18 September 2016], p. 1.

85. Interview with Lord Butler, 27 July 2016.

86. Ibid.

87. Interview with Diana Goldsworthy, 19 August 2016.

88. Interview with Lord Butler, 27 July 2016.

89. Ibid.

90. Ibid.

91. Interview with Sir Charles Powell, 15 May 2016.

92. Ibid.

93. 'Sir Robin Butler's Request to See Senator Baker on March 21, 1988', Nelson Ledsky Papers, Reagan Library, Simi Valley, California.

94. Interview with Lord Butler, 27 October 1998.

95. Correspondence with Lord Armstrong, 20 September 2016.

96. Interview with Sir Charles Powell, 15 May 2016.

97. Interview with Lord Butler, 27 July 2016.

98. Ibid.

99. Interview with Lord Butler, 27 September 2016.

100. Thanks to Chris Collins of the Margaret Thatcher Archives for this information.

101. Margaret Thatcher, Radio Interview, BBC Radio 2, *Jimmy Young Programme*, 27 July 1988, Thatcher Archive: COI transcript <http://www.margaretthatcher.org/document/107075> [accessed 18 September 2016].

102. Stephen Wall, Minute, 'Plain and Fundamental Errors', 1 September 1988, FOI 0242-09, FCO release <http://www.margaretthatcher.org/document/111785> [accessed 18 September 2016].

103. 'Speech to the College of Europe', 20 September 1988 <http://www.margaretthatcher.org/document/107332> [accessed 3 October 2016].

104. Cited in Margaret Thatcher, 'The Bruges Speech', 20 September 1988, Thatcher Archive: COI transcript <http://www.margaretthatcher.org/document/107332> [accessed 18 September 2016]. Thanks to Chris Collins for his memo, and for distilling the papers in the Thatcher Archive, 20 September 2016.

105. Nigel Lawson, in Lawson and Armstrong, 'Cabinet Government in the Thatcher Years', p. 443, cited in Edwards, *Gresham Reader*, p. 221.

106. Andrew Turnbull, 'Prime Minister's meeting with Sir Robin Butler', 12 September 1990, Cabinet Office documents.

107. John Campbell, *Margaret Thatcher Vol. 2: The Iron Lady* (London, 2003), p. 667.

108. Andrew Turnbull, 'Prime Minister's meeting with Sir Robin Butler', 27 September 1990, Cabinet Office documents.

109. Interview with Lord Butler, 27 July 2016.

110. Andrew Blick and George Jones, *Premiership: The Development, Nature and Power of the Office of the British Prime Minister* (Exeter, 2010), p. 214.

111. Interview with Lord Butler, 27 July 2016.

112. Anthony Seldon, *Major: A Political Life* (London, 1998), pp. 208–9.

113. Ibid.

114. Interview with Lord Butler, 16 November 2012.

115. Ibid.

116. Butler, Letter to George and Barbara Bush, December 1990, PP005-01 #220897, WHORM Subject Files, Bush Library, College Station, Texas.

117. Seldon, *Major: A Political Life*, pp. 208–9.

118. Interview with Lord Butler, 16 November 2012.

119. Ibid.

120. Anthony Seldon, *10 Downing Street: The Illustrated History* (London, 1999), p. 92.

121. Aldrich and Cormac, *The Black Door*, pp. 397–8.

122. Martin Burch and Ian Holliday, *The British Cabinet System* (London, 1995), pp. 46, 280–81.

123. Sarah Hogg and Jonathan Hill, *Too Close to Call: Power and Politics – John Major in No. 10* (London, 1995), p. 98.

124. Interview with Lord Butler, 16 November 2012.

125. Ibid.

126. Butler to Major, 3 March 1992, A092/625, Cabinet Office documents.

127. J. C. Grauberg to Butler, 'Hung Parliaments', 3 April 1992, Cabinet Office documents.

128. Butler to Andrew Turnbull, 'Movement of opinion during Election Campaigns', 2 March 1992, Cabinet Office documents.

129. Kavanagh and Seldon, *Powers Behind the Prime Minister*, p. 225.

130. Seldon, *Major: A Political Life*, pp. 208–9.

131. Ibid., p. 419.

132. Interview with Lord Butler, 27 July 2016.

133. Ibid.

134. Blick and Jones, *At Power's Elbow*, p. 248.

135. Seldon, *Major: A Political Life*, p. 584.

136. Michael Heseltine, *Life in the Jungle: My Autobiography* (London, 2000), pp. 483–4.

CHAPTER 9 (PP. 235–77)

1. Interview with Lord Butler, 27 July 2016.

2. Seldon, *Major: A Political Life*, p. 2.

3. Interview with Lord Butler, 27 July 2016.

4. Ibid.

5. Blick and Jones, *At Power's Elbow*, p. 218.

6. 'Letter of Last Resort', ITV Report, 13 July 2016 <http://www.itv.com/news/2016-07-13/letter-of-last-resort-theresa-mays-first-task-as-prime-minister-will-be-to-decide-on-uks-response-to-nuclear-attack/> [accessed 27 September 2016].

7. Interview with Lord Butler, 27 July 2016.

8. Ibid.

9. David Blunkett, *The Blunkett Tapes: My Life in the Bear Pit* (London, 2006), p. 9.

10. Private information.

11. Tom Bower, *Broken Vows: Tony Blair, the Tragedy of Power* (London, 2016).

12. Private information.

13. Ibid.

14. Private information.

15. Private information.

16. Private information.

17. Private information.

18. Interview with Lord Butler, 16 November 2012.

19. Anthony Seldon, *Blair* (London, 2005).

20. Ibid.

21. Ibid.

22. Interview with Lord Wilson, 2 November 2012.

23. Cabinet Office figures.

24. Interview with Lord Wilson, 2 November 2012.

25. Cited in Edwards, *Gresham Reader*, pp. 257–8.

26. Lord Wilson of Dinton, 'Evidence to the Iraq Inquiry', *Iraq Inquiry*, 25 January 2011 <http://www.iraqinquiry.org.uk/media/95446/2011-01-25-Transcript-Wilson-S1.pdf> [accessed 1 October 2016].

27. Lord Wilson of Dinton, 'Evidence to the Iraq Inquiry', 25 January 2011, p. 4.

28. Peter Mandelson and Roger Liddle, *The Blair Revolution* (London, 1996).

29. Ibid., p. 238.

30. Interview with Lord Wilson, 29 September 2016.

31. Lord Wilson of Dinton, 'Evidence to the Iraq Inquiry', 25 January 2011.

32. Interview with Lord Wilson, 29 September 2016.

33. Ibid.

34. Ibid.

35. Seldon, *Blair*, p. 426–8.

36. Interview with Lord Wilson, 29 September 2016.

37. Ibid.

38. Interview with Lord Wilson, 2 November 2012.

39. Ibid.

40. Ibid.

41. Private interview.

42. Ibid.

43. Interview with Lord Wilson, 29 September 2016.

44. Ibid.

45. Alastair Campbell, *Diaries, Vol. 2: Power and the People, 1997–1999* (London, 2011), p. 264.

46. Interview with Lord Turnbull, 23 May 2006.

47. Seldon, *Blair Unbound*, p. 37.

48. Interview with John Sawers, 1 May 2016.

49. Seldon, *Blair Unbound*, p. 32.

50. Ibid., p. 35.

51. Ibid.

52. Ibid.

53. Aldrich and Cormac, *The Black Door*, p. 411.

54. Interview with Lord Wilson, 2 November 2012.

55. Ibid.

56. Ibid.

57. Blair, *A Journey*, p. 312.

58. Interview with Bruce Mann, 23 August 2016.

59. Seldon, *Blair Unbound*, p. 40.
60. Ibid., p. 630.
61. Interview with Sir Nigel Sheinwald, 24 April 2015.
62. Interview with Stephen Wall, 25 June 2015.
63. Seldon, *Blair*, pp. 629–30.
64. Ibid., p. 41.
65. Seldon, *Blair*, p. 629.
66. Seldon, *Blair Unbound*, p. 41.
67. Powell, *The New Machiavelli*, pp. 77–8.
68. Seldon, *Blair Unbound*, p. 629.
69. Interview with Lord Turnbull, 14 January 2013 <http://www.cabinetsecretaries.com> [accessed 19 September 2016].
70. Ibid.
71. Anthony Seldon, *Blair Unbound*, p. 243
72. Interview with Lord Turnbull, 3 August 2016.
73. Ibid.
74. Ibid.
75. Lord Butler et al., *Review of Intelligence on Weapons of Mass Destruction*, House of Commons, 14 July 2004, pp. 147–8.
76. Ibid.
77. 'Lord Turnbull evidence to the Iraq Inquiry', 13 January 2010 <http://www.iraqinquiry.org.uk/the-evidence/witnesses/t/the-lord-turnbull/> [accessed 19 September 2016], p. 22.
78. 'Iraq: Conditions for Military Action', 19 July 2002, Cabinet Office <http://www.iraqinquiry.org.uk/media/211007/2002-07-19-note-manning-to-prime-minister-attaching-paper-cabinet-office-iraq-conditions-for-military-action.pdf> [accessed 19 September 2016].
79. John Chilcot et al., *The Report of the Iraq Inquiry*, Section 4.1 (London, 2016), p. 84.
80. Ibid.
81. Ibid.
82. Seldon, *Blair Unbound*, p. 286.
83. Ibid., p. 287.
84. Interview with Paul Britton, 14 January 2013.
85. Tony Blair, *A Journey* (London, 2011), p. 429.
86. Blick and Jones, *At Power's Elbow*, p. 293.
87. Ibid., pp. 293–5.
88. Seldon, *Blair Unbound*, p. 209.
89. Ibid.
90. Ibid., p. 330

91. Ibid., p. 214.

92. Interview with Lord Turnbull, 3 August 2016.

93. Seldon, *Blair Unbound*, p. 214.

94. Ibid.

95. Interview with Lord Turnbull, 3 August 2016.

96. Ibid.

97. Seldon, *Blair Unbound*, p. 274.

98. Ibid., p. 328.

99. Ibid., p. 329.

100. Interview with Ivan Rogers, 7 July 2016.

101. Interview with Lord O'Donnell, 30 February 2016, available at <http://www.cabinetsecretaries.com> [accessed 23 September 2016].

102. Seldon, *Major,* p. 103.

103. Ibid., pp. 140–41.

104. Seldon, *Blair Unbound*, p. 383.

105. Andrew Rawnsley, *The End of the Party* (London, 2010), p. 292.

106. Powell, *The New Machiavelli*, p. 277.

107. Interview with Lord O'Donnell, 27 July 2016.

108. Ibid.

109. Ibid.

110. Interview with Lord O'Donnell, No. 10 History Series, February 2013.

111. Ibid.

112. Interview with Lord O'Donnell, 27 July 2016.

113. Seldon, *Blair Unbound*, pp. 464–5.

114. Ibid., p. 373.

115. Sarah Brown, *Behind the Black Door* (London, 2002), p. 6.

116. Anthony Seldon and Guy Lodge, *Brown at 10* (London, 2010), p. 13.

117. Ibid.

118. Simon McDonald had been Head of the Overseas and Defence Secretariat from 2007 to 2010, and become Permanent Under Secretary at the FCO in 2015. Jon Cunliffe had been Second Permanent Secretary at the Treasury, overseeing international finance. He became UK Permanent Representative to the EU in 2012.

119. Seldon and Lodge, *Brown at 10*, p. 18

120. Interview with Lord O'Donnell, 30 February 2013.

121. Private interview.

122. Seldon and Lodge, *Brown at 10*, p. 12.

123. Ibid., p. 14.

124. Cabinet Office figures.

125. Seldon and Lodge, *Brown at 10*, p. 72.

126. Ibid.

127. Ibid.

128. Seldon, *Blair Unbound*, p. 720.

129. Seldon and Lodge, *Brown at 10*, p. 71.

130. Interview with Paul Britton, 24 August 2016.

131. Interview with Lord O'Donnell, 27 July 2016.

132. Seldon and Lodge, *Brown at 10*, pp. 254–5.

133. Ibid., p. 432.

134. Ibid., p. 234–43.

135. Interview with Lord O'Donnell, 27 July 2016.

136. Andrew Rawnsley, *The End of the Party*, p. 468.

137. Seldon and Lodge, *Brown at 10*, p. 249.

138. Peter Mandelson, *The Third Man: Life at the Heart of New Labour* (London, 2010), p. 473.

139. Sarah Brown, *Behind the Black Door*, p. 402.

140. Andrew Rawnsley, *The End of the Party*, second edition (London, 2010), p. 703.

141. Anthony Seldon and Guy Lodge, *Brown at 10*, second edition (London, 2011), p. 470.

142. Peter Mandelson and Roger Liddle, *The Blair Revolution: Can New Labour Deliver?* (London, 1996).

143. Powell, *The New Machiavelli*, pp. 59–60.

144. Seldon, 'The Cabinet Office and Coordination, 1979–87'.

145. Ibid.

146. Powell, *The New Machiavelli*, pp. 76–7.

147. Quoted in Edwards, *Gresham Reader*, p. 267.

148. Seldon, *Blair Unbound*, pp. 204–5.

149. Seldon, *Blair*, pp. 644–8.

150. Interview with Michael Barber, 6 July 2006.

151. Seldon, *Blair Unbound*, p. 43.

CHAPTER 10 (PP. 279–97)

1. Seldon and Lodge, *Brown at 10*, p. 454.

2. Interview with Lord O'Donnell, *Five Days that Changed Britain*, BBC Parliament, 10 January 2011 [accessed 26 September 2016].

3. Seldon and Lodge, *Brown at 10*, p. 454.

4. David Laws, *22 Days in May: The Birth of the Lib Dem–Conservative Coalition* (London, 2010), p. 95.

5. Ibid., p. 186.

6. Ibid., p. 179.

7. Interview with Lord O'Donnell, 27 July 2016.

8. Laws, *22 Days in May*, p. 192.

9. Interview with Lord O'Donnell, 28 July 2014.

10. Ibid.

11. Ibid.

12. Nick Clegg, 'No wonder there was a Nick Clegg Looking Sad website', *The Guardian*, 5 September 2016 <https://www.theguardian.com/politics/2016/sep/05/nick-clegg-book-extract-no-wonder-there-was-a-nick-clegg-looking-sad-website> [accessed 28 September 2016].

13. Interview with Lord O'Donnell, 27 July 2016.

14. Interview with Lord O'Donnell, 30 February 2013 <http://www.cabinetsecretaries.com> [accessed 26 September 2016].

15. Cabinet Office figures.

16. Seldon, *Cameron at 10*, pp. 120–22.

17. Interview with Jeremy Heywood, 18 December 2014.

18. Interview with Lord O'Donnell, 28 July 2014.

19. Seldon, *Cameron at 10*, pp. 208–9.

20. Ibid.

21. Ibid., p. 151.

22. Interview with Lord O'Donnell, 30 February 2013.

23. Interview with Lord O'Donnell, 27 July 2016.

24. Ibid.

25. Ibid.

26. Julian Richards, *A Guide to National Security: Threats, Responses and Strategies* (Oxford, 2012), p. 102.

27. Joe Devanny and Josh Harris, 'The National Security Council', in *Contemporary History of Whitehall* (November 2014), pp. 17–21.

28. Interview with Lord O'Donnell, 30 February 2013.

29. Interview with Lord O'Donnell, 27 July 2016.

30. Ibid.

31. See David Halpern, *Inside the Nudge Unit: How Small Changes can Make a Big Difference* (London, 2015).

32. Jules Evans, 'Sir Gus O'Donnell on the Politics of Wellbeing', The History of Emotions Blog, 16 March 2015 <https://emotionsblog.history.qmul.ac.uk/2015/03/sir-gus-odonnell-on-the-politics-of-well-being/> [accessed 29 September 2016].

33. Interview with Lord O'Donnell, 28 July 2014.

34. Interview with Jonathan M. Hales, 27 September 2016.

35. Seldon, *Major: A Political Life*, p. 270.

36. Andrew Adonis, cited in Amelia Gentleman, 'Sir Jeremy Heywood: the civil servant propping up the government', *The Guardian*, 6 December 2012 <http://www.theguardian.com/politics/2012/dec/06/sir-jeremy-heywood-civil-servant-profile> [accessed 27 September 2016].

37. Interview with Jeremy Heywood, 3 September 2016.
38. Ibid.
39. Interview with Jeremy Heywood, 22 March 2013 <http://www.cabinetsecretaries.com> [accessed 27 September 2016].
40. Ibid.
41. Interview with Jeremy Heywood, 3 September 2016.
42. Interview with Jeremy Heywood, 18 March 2014.
43. Interview with Jeremy Heywood, 22 March 2013.
44. Interview with Jeremy Heywood, 3 September 2016.
45. Interview with Jeremy Heywood, 22 March 2013.
46. Ashley Hibben, 'The role of the modern Cabinet Secretary: a conversation with Sir Jeremy Heywood', *Institute for Government*, 23 September 2015 <http://www. instituteforgovernment.org.uk/blog/12459/the-role-of-the-modern-cabinet-secretary-a-conversation-with-sir-jeremy-heywood/> [accessed 27 September 2016].
47. Ibid.
48. Jess Bowie, 'Jeremy Heywood Interview', *Civil Service World*, 19 October 2015 <http://www.civilserviceworld.com/articles/interview/jeremy-heywood-interview-cabinet-secretary-and-head-civil-service-life-top> [accessed 28 September 2016].
49. Ashley Hibben, 'The role of the modern Cabinet Secretary', *Institute for Government*, 23 September 2015.
50. Ibid.
51. Interview with Philip Rycroft, 7 October 2016.
52. Ibid.
53. See ibid., pp. 535–45.

Bibliography

Archival Sources

The Churchill Archives Centre, Cambridge

Archives of Lord Hankey of the Chart (Maurice Hankey) (1877–1963)
HNKY 1/1 Diaries.
HNKY 1/2 Diary Loose diary pages for 26 Mar – 5 Apr; 2–9 Jan 1917.
HNKY 1/3 Diary Vol. 2.
HNKY 1/4 Diary Loose diary pages for 31 October–17 November, 26 November–
    2 December 1917; 21 January–4 February, 22 March–3 April, 31 May–4 June,
    1–5 July 1918.
HNKY 2/1 Letters, photographs, newspaper cuttings, etc.
HNKY 2/2 Letters, photographs, newspaper cuttings, etc.
HNKY 2/3 Letters, photographs, newspaper cuttings, etc.

Royal Archives, Windsor

By permission of Her Majesty Queen Elizabeth II
Correspondence of George III (RA GEO/MAIN).
Correspondence of Lord Melbourne (MP/Box/112).
Correspondence of Lord Melbourne (MP/Box/108).
Correspondence of Queen Victoria and Lord Melbourne (VIC/MAIN/A/1 and VIC/
    MAIN/A/3).

National Archives, Kew

(Several of these documents can be accessed online at the Thatcher Foundation Archive – http://www.margaretthatcher.org and I have indicated in the endnotes where this is the case.)

CAB 21/95	CAB 63/57	PREM 11/1152
CAB 21/128	CAB 65/13/24	PREM 11/1457
CAB 21/159	CAB 65/14/3	PREM 11/1578
CAB 21/626	CAB 67/7/47	PREM 11/1734
CAB 21/1281	CAB 104/124	PREM 11/2355
CAB 21/1341	CAB 127/272	PREM 11/3223
CAB 21/2288	CAB 128/30	PREM 13/6
CAB 21/4177	CAB 128/73	PREM 14/2013
CAB 21/4324	CAB 128/83	PREM 14/20
CAB 21/4768	CAB 130/3	PREM 15/81
CAB 21/4959	CAB 150/3	PREM 15/2015
CAB 23/14/46	CAB 150/4	PREM 16/804
CAB 23/47/1	CAB 163/8	PREM 19/27
CAB 23/52/24	CAB 163/9	PREM 19/179
CAB 23/52/25	CAB 195/1	PREM 19/191
CAB 23/86/12	CAB 195/3	PREM 19/282
CAB 23/86/15	CAB 195/9	PREM 19/669
CAB 23/95/11	CAB 195/12	PREM 19/1332
CAB 23/94	CAB 195/15	PREM 19/1335
CAB 24/87	CAB 301/106	PREM 19/3124
CAB 24/92	CAB 301/141	State Papers (SP) 36/83
CAB 24/210/17	CAB 301/163	State Papers (SP) 36/89
CAB 41/6	CAB 301/166	State Papers (SP) 36/95
CAB 41/25	DO 1/9/1046	T162/589
CAB 41/35	LCO 2/3215	T 172/1112
CAB 63/19	PREM 8/1486	T 199/65
CAB 63/33	PREM 11/268	Work 12/682

Bank of England Archives

J. C. R. Dow, 'Short term economic policy group (STEP)', 15 January 1981, BOE, 7A173/8, MTFW 128043.

Imperial War Museum Archive

Alfred John Digby Winnifrith, Interview, 1982 <http://www.iwm.org.uk/collections/item/object/80006177> [accessed 1 September 2016].
Edward Ian Claude Jacob, Interview, 26 September 1979 <http://www.iwm.org.uk/collections/item/object/80004439> [accessed 1 September 2016].
Margaret Walker, Interview, 2012 <http://www.iwm.org.uk/collections/item/object/80033495> [accessed 1 September 2016].

George Bush Presidential Library, Texas

PP005-01 #220897, WHORM Subject Files.

Harry S. Truman Library, Missouri

Secretary of State File, Acheson Papers.

Jimmy Carter Presidential Library, Georgia

NLC-31-145-7-2-8.

John F. Kennedy Library, Massachusetts

Country Files, President's Office Files.

Margaret Thatcher Foundation

'Speech to the College of Europe', 20 September 1988 <http://www.margaretthatcher. org/document/107332> [accessed, 3 October 2016].

National Archives and Records Administration, Washington DC

US Department of State, Central Foreign Policy Files, 1973–79.

National Security Archive, George Washington University, Washington DC

DNSA Collection: Kissinger Telephone Conversations, 1969–77.

Ronald Reagan Presidential Library, California

London – United Kingdom (1), Box 15, Douglas McMinn Papers.
Box 91331, Exec Sec, NSC: Country File, United Kingdom.
Box 91154, Stephen Danzansky (NSC) Files.
Nelson Ledsky Papers.

Newspapers

'The War Cabinet Report: The Work of 1917', *The Times*, 19 March 1918.
'The Secretariat', *The Times*, 30 March 1921.
'The Cabinet Secretariat', *The Times*, 13 June 1922.
'Reception for Lord Normanbrook', *The Times*, 13 February 1963.
'Cable Vetting Sensation', *Daily Express*, 29 February 1967.
'"Sensationalized" Story on State Secrets', *The Times*, 22 February 1967.
'Lord Normanbrook', *The Times*, 16 June 1967.
'Sir Jeremy Heywood: the civil servant propping up the government', *The Guardian*, 6 December 2012.

Marquand, David, 'Labour's Own Captain Mainwaring', *New Statesman*, 2–8 September 2016.

British Oral Archive of Political and Administrative History

Interview with Baron Croham, 1980.

Interview with Lord Home of the Hirsel, 1980.

Interview with Lord Muirshiel, 1980.

Interview with Lord Roberthall, 1980.

Interview with Sir Antony Part, 1980.

Interview with Lord Shackleton, 1980.

Interview with Lord Sherfield, 1980.

Witness Seminar: Britain and Brussels, Britain and Strasbourg, 23 February 1995.

Witness Seminar: 1975 EU Referendum, 5 June 1995.

Printed Primary Sources

Asquith, Margot, *Margot Asquith's Great War Diary 1914–1916: The View from Downing Street* (Oxford, 2014).

Blair, Tony, *A Journey* (London, 2011).

Blunkett, David, *The Blunkett Tapes: My Life in the Bear Pit* (London, 2006).

Brock, Michael and Eleanor (eds), *H. H. Asquith, Letters to Venetia Stanley* (Oxford, 1985).

Brown, Sarah, *Behind the Black Door* (London, 2002).

Bulmer, Simon, and Burch, Martin, 'Adaptation of UK central government 1951–99' (University of Manchester, 2000), Queen's Papers on Europeanisation, No. 9/2000.

Butler et al., *Review of Intelligence on Weapons of Mass Destruction*, House of Commons, 14 July 2004.

Campbell, Alastair, *Diaries, Vol. 2: Power and the People, 1997–1999* (London, 2011).

Campbell, Alastair, *Diaries, Vol. 3: Power and Responsibility, 1999–2001* (London, 2012).

Campbell, Alastair, *Diaries, Vol. 4: The Burden of Power: Countdown to Iraq* (London, 2012).

Castle, Barbara, *The Castle Diaries, 1964–70* (London, 1984).

Catterall, Peter (ed.), *The Macmillan Diaries, Vol. 2: Prime Minister and After, 1957–1966* (London, 2011).

Chilcot, John, et al., *The Report of the Iraq Inquiry*, Section 4.1 (London, 2016).

Churchill, Winston, *The World Crisis, 1911–1918* (New York, 1931).

Churchill, Winston, *The Second World War, Vol. 2: Their Finest Hour* (London, 1939).

Colville, John, *Footprints in Time: Memories* (London, 1976).

Danchev, Alex and Todman, Daniel (eds), *War Diaries 1939–1945: Field Marshal Lord Alanbrooke* (London, 2001).

Donoughue, Bernard, *Prime Minister: The Conduct of Policy under Harold Wilson and James Callaghan* (London, 1987).

Donoughue, Bernard, *Downing Street Diary: With Harold Wilson in Number 10* (London, 2005).

Donoughue, Bernard, *Downing Street Diary: With James Callaghan at No. 10* (London, 2009).

Eden, Anthony, *The Memoirs of Sir Anthony Eden: Full Circle* (London, 1960).

Evans, Harold, *Downing Street Diary: The Macmillan Years, 1957–1963* (London, 1981).

Guedalla, P. (ed.), *Gladstone and Palmerston: Being the Correspondence of Lord Palmerston with Mr Gladstone, 1851–1865* (London, 1928).

Hankey, Maurice, *Government Control in War* (Cambridge, 1945).

Hankey, Maurice, *The Supreme Command, 1914–1918* (London, 1961).

Hankey, Maurice, *Politics, Trials and Errors* (Oxford, 1950).

Hansard, HC Debs, 5 Series, Vol. 155.

Hansard, HC Debs, Vol. 295.

Hansard, HC Debs, 5 Series, Vol. 378.

Hansard, HC Debs, Vol. 558.

Hansard, HL Debs, Vol. 30.

Heath, Edward, *The Course of My Life* (London, 1998).

Heath, Edward, 'Burke Trend', *Dictionary of National Biography* (rev. first published 2004) <http://dx.doi.org/10.1093/ref:odnb/39887> [accessed 13 September 2016].

Heseltine, Michael, *Life in the Jungle: My Autobiography* (London, 2000).

Holt, Andrew, and Dockter, Warren (eds), *Foreign Affairs Private Secretaries* (London, 2017).

Home, Lord, *The Way the Wind Blows* (London, 1976).

Howard, A. (ed.), *The Crossman Diaries: Selections from the Diaries of a Cabinet Minister* (London, 1979).

Ismay, Lord, *The Memoirs of General The Lord Ismay* (London, 1960).

Laws, David, *22 Days in May: The Birth of the Lib Dem–Conservative Coalition* (London, 2010).

Lawson, Nigel, *The View from No. 11: Memoirs of a Tory Radical* (London, 1992).

Lowe, Rodney, *The Official History of the British Civil Service: Reforming the Civil Service, Vol. 1: The Fulton Years, 1966–81* (London, 2011).

Macmillan, Harold, *Riding the Storm: 1956–1959* (London, 1971).

Mallaby, George, *From My Level: Unwritten Minutes* (London, 1965).

Mallaby, George, *Each in his Office* (London, 1972).

Mandelson, Peter, and Liddle, Roger, *The Blair Revolution: Can New Labour Deliver?* (London, 1996).

Mandelson, Peter, *The Third Man: Life at the Heart of New Labour* (London, 2010).

The Manuscripts of the Earl of Dartmouth (London, 1887).

Middlemas, Keith (ed.), *Thomas Jones Whitehall Diary, Vol. 1: 1916–1925* (London, 1969).

Middlemas, Keith (ed.), *Thomas Jones Whitehall Diary, Vol. 2: 1926–1930* (London, 1969).

Moran, Lord, *Churchill: The Struggle for Survival, 1945–60* (London, 2006).

Parker, Charles Stuart (ed.), *Sir Robert Peel: From his Private Papers, Vol. 3* (London, 1899).

Pimlott, Ben, *Harold Wilson* (London, 1992).

Plowden, William, *Inside the Think-Tank: Advising the Cabinet, 1971–1983* (London, 1990).

Powell, Jonathan, *The New Machiavelli: How to Wield Power in the Modern World* (London, 2010).

Purcell, Hugh, *Lloyd George* (London, 2006).

Rothchild, Victor, *Meditations of a Broomstick* (London, 1977).

Thatcher, Margaret, *The Downing Street Years* (London, 1993).

Warrington, Earl of, *The Works of the Right Honourable Henry Late L. Delamar, and Earl of Warrington* (1694) <https://books.google.co.uk/books?id=_MIIuvu8vAMC&pg> [accessed 21 August 2016].

Wheeler-Bennett, John (ed.), *Action this Day* (London, 1968).

Secondary Sources

Aldrich, Richard I., and Cormac, Rory, *The Black Door* (London, 2016).

Bagehot, Walter, *The English Constitution: New and Revised Edition* (Boston, 1873).

Ball, Stuart, and Seldon, Anthony, *The Heath Government, 1970–74: A Reappraisal* (London, 1996).

Ballinger, Chris, and Seldon, Anthony, 'Prime Ministers and Cabinet', in Seldon, Anthony, and Hickson, Kevin (eds), *New Labour, Old Labour: The Wilson and Callaghan Governments, 1974–79* (London, 2004).

Bastion, Frederick, *The Battle of London: Trudeau and Thatcher and the Fight for Canada's Constitution* (Toronto, 2014).

Baston Lewis, and Seldon, Anthony, 'Number 10 Under Edward Heath', in Ball, Stuart, and Seldon, Anthony (eds), *The Heath Government 1970–74* (London, 1996), pp. 47–74.

Baugh, Daniel, *The Global Seven Years War* (London, 2011).

Blake, Robert, *Disraeli* (London, 1969).

Blake, Robert, *The Office of Prime Minister* (London, 1975).

Blick, Andrew, and Jones, George, *Premiership: The Development, Nature and Power of the Office of the British Prime Minister* (Exeter, 2010).

Blick, Andrew and Jones, George, *At Power's Elbow* (London, 2013).

Bower, Tom, *Broken Vows: Tony Blair, the Tragedy of Power* (London, 2016).

Burch, Martin, and Holliday, Ian, *The British Cabinet System* (London, 1995).

Campbell, John, *Edward Heath: A Biography* (London, 1994).

Campbell, John, *Margaret Thatcher: The Iron Lady* (London, 2003).

Cassar, George, *Asquith as War Leader* (London, 1994).

Chapman, Richard A., *Ethics in the British Civil Service* (London, 1988).

Campbell, John, *Margaret Thatcher, Vol. 2: The Iron Lady* (London, 2003).

Crosby, Travis L., *The Unknown Lloyd George* (New York, 2014).

Dalyell, Rom, *Dick Crossman: A Portrait* (London, 1989).

Davis, Jon, *Prime Ministers and Whitehall 1960–74* (London, 2007).

Devanny, Joe, and Harris, Josh, 'The National Security Council', in *Contemporary History of Whitehall* (Institute for Government, 2014).

Edwards, Giles (ed.), *The Gresham Reader on Cabinet Government* (London, 2004).

Fanning, Ronan, *Fatal Path: British Government and Irish Revolution 1910–1922* (London, 2013).

Green, Andrew, *Writing the Great War: Sir James Edmonds and the Official Histories: 1915–1948* (London, 2003).

Greenleaf, W. H., *Much Governed Nation: The British Political Tradition, Part 2, Vol. 3* (London, 2003).

Grigg, John, 'Churchill, the Crippled Giant: His Last Two Years of Power', in *Encounter* (April 1977), pp. 9–15.

Halpern, David, *Inside the Nudge Unit: How Small Changes can Make a Big Difference* (London, 2015).

Haupt, Paul, 'The Etymology of Cabinet', *Journal of the American Oriental Society* 28 (1907), pp. 108–11.

Hennessy, Peter, *The Prime Minister: The Office and its Holders Since 1945* (London, 2000).

Hennessy, Peter, *Having it So Good: Britain in the Fifties* (London, 2007).

Hennessy, Peter, *The Secret State: Whitehall and the Cold War* (London, 2003).

Hennessy, Peter, *The Secret State: Preparing for the Worst, 1945–50* (London, 2010).

Hennessy, Peter, *Cabinet* (London, 1986).

Hennessy, Peter, 'Cabinet Government: A Commentary' in *Contemporary Record*, Vol. 8, Issue 3 (1994), pp. 484–94.

Hogg, Sarah, and Hill, Jonathan, *Too Close to Call: Power and Politics – John Major in No. 10* (London, 1995).

Holt, Andrew, and Dockter, Warren (eds), *Foreign Affairs Private Secretaries* (London, 2017).

Horne, Alistair, *Macmillan: The Official Biography, Vol. 2* (London, 2008).

Hoskyns, John, *Just in Time: Inside the Thatcher Revolution* (London, 2000).

Jenkins, Terence Andrew, *Parliament, Party and Politics in Victorian Britain* (London, 1996).

Kavanagh, Dennis, and Seldon, Anthony (eds) *The Major Effect* (London, 1994).

Kavanagh, Dennis, and Seldon, Anthony, *The Powers Behind the Prime Minister: The Hidden Influence of Number 10* (London, 1999).

Leonard, Dick, *A History of British Prime Ministers: Walpole to Cameron* (London, 2015).

Macintyre, Ben, *A Spy Amongst Friends: Kim Philby and the Great Betrayal* (London, 2014).

Mackesy, Piers, *The War for America, 1775–1783* (Harvard, 1993).

Massie, Robert K., *Castles of Steel: Britain, Germany and the Winning of the Great War at Sea* (London, 2005).

Matthew, H. C. G., *Gladstone, 1809–1898* (Oxford, 1997).

Moggridge, Donald Edward, *Maynard Keynes: An Economists Biography* (London, 1992).

Moore, Charles, *Margaret Thatcher: The Authorized Biography, Vol. 1: Not for Turning* (London, 2013).

Mosley, R. K., *The Story of the Cabinet Office* (London, 1969).

Naylor, John, *A Man and an Institution: Sir Maurice Hankey, the Cabinet Secretariat and the Custody of the Cabinet Secretary* (Cambridge, 1984).

Overy, Robert, *Why the Allies Won* (London, 2006).

Pearce, Robert, *Attlee's Labour Governments 1945–51* (London, 1993).

Pimlott, Ben, *Harold Wilson* (London, 1992).

Purcell, Hugh, *Lloyd George* (London, 2006).

Rawnsley, Andrew, *The End of the Party* (London, 2010).

Rawnsley, Andrew, *The End of the Party*, Second Edition (London, 2010).

Richards, Julian, *A Guide to National Security: Threats, Responses and Strategies* (Oxford, 2012).

Roberts, Andrew, *Masters and Commanders: How Roosevelt, Churchill, Marshall and Alanbrooke Won the War in the West* (London, 2008).

Ronaldshay, Earl of, *The Life of Lord Curzon, Vol. 3* (London, 1928).

Roskill, Stephen, *Hankey: Man of Secrets, Vol. 1, 1877–1918* (Annapolis, 1970).

Roskill, Stephen, *Hankey: Man of Secrets, Vol. 2, 1919–1931* (Annapolis, 1972).

Roskill, Stephen, *Hankey: Man of Secrets, Vol. 3, 1931–1963* (Annapolis, 1974).

Sandbrook, Dominic, *State of Emergency: The Way We Were: Britain 1970–74* (London, 2010).

Seldon, Anthony, *Churchill's Indian Summer: The Conservative Government, 1951–1955* (London, 1981).

Seldon, Anthony, 'The Cabinet Office and Coordination, 1979–87', *Public Administration*, Vol. 68, Issue 1 (March 1990).

Seldon, Anthony, 'Ideas Are Not Enough', in Marquand, David and Seldon, Anthony (eds), *The Ideas that Shaped Post-War Britain* (London, 1996), pp. 257–89.

Seldon, Anthony, *Major: A Political Life* (London, 1998).

Seldon, Anthony, *10 Downing Street: The Illustrated History* (London, 1999).

Seldon, Anthony, 'The Cabinet System', Bogdanor, Vernon (ed.), *The British Constitution in the Twentieth Century* (London, 2003), pp. 97–137.

Seldon, Anthony, *Blair* (London, 2005).

Seldon, Anthony, *Blair Unbound* (London, 2007).

Seldon, Anthony, and Lodge, Guy, *Brown at 10* (London, 2010).

Seldon, Anthony, and Lodge, Guy, *Brown at 10*, Second Edition (London, 2010).

Seldon, Anthony (ed.), *The Coalition Effect, 2010–2015* (London, 2015).

Seldon, Anthony, *Cameron at 10* (London, 2015).

Shepherd, John, and Laybourn, Keith, *Britain's First Labour Government* (London, 2013).

Taylor, A. J. P., *English History, 1914–1945* (Oxford, 1965).

Travers, Tim, *Gallipoli* (Stroud, 2003).

Theakston, Kevin, *The Civil Service Since 1945* (London, 2009).

Theakston, Kevin, *Leadership in Whitehall* (London, 1999).

Thomas-Symonds, Nicklaus, *Attlee: A Life in Politics* (London, 2010).

Thorpe, D. R., *Eden: The Life and Times of Anthony Eden First Earl of Avon, 1897–1977* (London, 2004).

Thorpe, D. R., *Alec Douglas-Home* (London, 2007).

Thorpe, D. R., *Supermac: The Life of Harold Macmillan* (London, 2010).

Tombs, Robert, *The English and their History* (London, 2014).

Thomas, Peter, *Tea Party to Independence: The Third Phase of the American Revolution, 1773–1776* (Oxford, 1991).

Williams, Trevor, 'The Cabinet in the Eighteenth Century', *History* 22 (1937), pp. 240–52.

Williamson, Philips, *Stanley Baldwin: Conservative Leadership and National Values* (Cambridge, 1999).

Wilson, Harold, *The Labour Government 1964–70: A Personal Record* (London, 1971).

Wilson, Harold, *The Governance of Britain* (London, 1976).

Wilson, Stephen Shipley, *The Cabinet Office to 1945* (London, 1975).

Winnifrith, John, 'Edward Ettingdean Bridges – Baron Bridges, 1892–1969', *Biographical Memoirs of Fellows of the Royal Society*, Vol. 16 (1970), pp. 38–56.

Television

'The Secret World of Whitehall: The Real Sir Humphrey', BBC Television, 16 March 2011.

'Five Days that Changed Britain', BBC Parliament, 29 July 2010.

Internet

Beesley, Ian, 'Hunt, John Joseph Benedict, Baron Hunt of Tanworth (1919–2008)', *Oxford Dictionary of National Biography*, Oxford University Press, Jan 2012; online edn, Sept 2012 <http://www.oxforddnb.com/view/article/99950> [accessed 29 August 2016].

Bowie, Jess, 'Jeremy Heywood Interview', *Civil Service World*, 19 October 2015 <http://www.civilserviceworld.com/articles/interview/jeremy-heywood-interview-cabinet-secretary-and-head-civil-service-life-top> [accessed 28 September 2016].

Clegg, Nick, 'No wonder there was a Nick Clegg Looking Sad website', *The Guardian*, 5 September 2016 <https://www.theguardian.com/politics/2016/sep/05/

nick-clegg-book-extract-no-wonder-there-was-a-nick-clegg-looking-sad-website>
[accessed 28 September 2016].

Cox, Montagu H., and Norman, Philip (eds), *Survey of London, Vol. 13, St Margaret, Westminster, Part II: Whitehall I* (London, 1930). Available from *British History Online* <http://www.british-history.ac.uk/survey-london/vol13/pt2/pp180-192> [accessed 17 August 2016].

'Government Expenditure', 2016 <http://www.ukpublicspending.co.uk/past_spending> [accessed 21 August 2016].

Harper, Douglas, 'Cabinet', 2016 <http://www.etymonline.com/index.php?term=cabinet> [accessed 21 August 2016].

Hibben, Ashley, 'The role of the modern Cabinet Secretary: a conversation with Sir Jeremy Heywood', *Institute for Government*, 23 September 2015 <http://www.instituteforgovernment.org.uk/blog/12459/the-role-of-the-modern-cabinet-secretary-a-conversation-with-sir-jeremy-heywood/> [accessed 27 September 2016].

History of Government, '1 Horse Guards Road' <https://www.gov.uk/government/history/1-horse-guards-road> [accessed 21 September 2016].

Iraq Inquiry <http://www.iraqinquiry.org.uk/>.

'Lord Turnbull evidence to the Iraq Inquiry', 13 January 2010 < http://www.iraqinquiry.org.uk/the-evidence/witnesses/t/the-lord-turnbull/> [accessed 19 September 2016], p. 22.

'Iraq: Conditions for Military Action', 19 July 2002, Cabinet Office <http://www.iraqinquiry.org.uk/media/211007/2002-07-19-note-manning-to-prime-minister-attaching-paper-cabinet-office-iraq-conditions-for-military-action.pdf> [accessed 19 September 2016].

'Letter of Last Resort', ITV Report, 13 July 2016 <http://www.itv.com/news/2016-07-13/letter-of-last-resort-theresa-mays-first-task-as-prime-minister-will-be-to-decide-on-uks-response-to-nuclear-attack/> [accessed 27 September 2016].

Lowe, Rodney, 'Jones, Thomas: Civil Servant and Benefactor', Irish Archives, 2011 <http://treaty.nationalarchives.ie/the-delegates/> [accessed 22 August 2016].

Mason, Chris, 'London 2012: What exactly is a Cobra meeting?' <http://www.bbc.co.uk/news/uk-politics-18958032> [accessed 14 September 2016].

'Men of Secrets: The Cabinet Secretaries' <http://www.cabinetsecretaries.com>.

Interview, Jeremy Heywood, 22 March 2013.

Interview, Lord Armstrong, 6 November 2012.

Interview, Lord Butler, 16 November 2012.

Interview, Lord O'Donnell, February 2013.

Interview, Lord Turnbull, 14 January 2013.

Interview, Lord Wilson, 2 November 2012.

Margaret Thatcher Foundation <http://www.margaretthatcher.org/>.

Margaret Thatcher, Radio Interview, BBC Radio 2 *Jimmy Young Programme,* 27 July 1988, Thatcher Archive: COI transcript <http://www.margaretthatcher.org/document/107075> [accessed 18 September 2016].

Personal letter, Butler to Thatcher, 4 August 1985, Thatcher Archive.

Stephen Wall, Minute, 'Plain and Fundamental Errors', 1 September 1988, FOI 0242-09, FCO release <http://www.margaretthatcher.org/document/111785> [accessed 18 September 2016].

Margaret Thatcher, 'The Bruges Speech', 20 September 1988, Thatcher Archive: COI transcript <http://www.margaretthatcher.org/document/107332> [accessed 18 September 2016].

Oxford Dictionary of National Biography <http://www.oxforddnb.com>.

Theakston, Kevin, 'Brook, Norman Craven, Baron Normanbrook (1902–1967)', *Oxford Dictionary of National Biography*, Oxford University Press, 2004; online edn, January 2011 <http://www.oxforddnb.com/view/article/32089> [accessed 29 August 2016].

Panchamia, Nehal, and Thomas, Peter, 'The Next Steps Initiative' <http://www.instituteforgovernment.org.uk/sites/default/files/case%20study%20next%20steps.pdf> [accessed 18 September 2016].

PICTURE CREDITS

INDEX